Greene and Fletcher

# The Law and Practice of Receivership in Scotland

# Greene and Fletcher
# The Law and Practice of Receivership in Scotland

**Third Edition**

by

I M Fletcher
LLB LTCL LRAM ARCO WS

*Solicitor in Scotland*
*Solicitor of the Supreme Court in England*
*Licensed Insolvency Practitioner*

and

Roy Roxburgh

*Solicitor in Scotland*
*Licensed Insolvency Practitioner*

Tottel
publishing

Tottel Publishing, Maxwelton House, 41–43 Boltro Road, Haywards Heath, West Sussex RH16 1BJ



A CIP Catalogue record for this book is available from the British Library.

ISBN 1 84592 199 2

Printed and bound in Great Britain by Athenæum Press Limited, Gateshead, Tyne & Wear

**Title management by Etica Press Ltd – www.eticapress.com**

# Foreword

## The Right Honourable Lord Hope of Craighead

The hallmark of a really useful legal textbook is its ability to be kept up to date. This does not happen automatically, nor do new editions come easily. The publishers have to be persuaded that there is a market for a new edition, and the authors or their successors as editors have to be persuaded that all the effort that is needed to produce it will be worthwhile.

There was a gap of five years between the first and second editions of this book. This time the gap has been extended to more than ten. Many changes occurred during this further interval, and it had been clear for some time that, if it was to continue to be useful, this book would have to take account of them. There were, of course, changes in legislation and in practice that would have to be dealt with. But there were important developments too in the relevant case law. It might have been thought that the law on the effect of a floating charge in Scots law was settled when the House of Lords gave its decision in *Sharp v Thomson* 1997 SC (HL) 66, 1997 SLT 636. The case of *Burnett's Trustee v Grainger*, which had begun as long ago as 1995 when the sheriff sisted the *Grainger* case to await the outcome in *Sharp v Thomson*, then intervened. That, as its name indicates, was not a case about receivership. It was a case about personal bankruptcy. But it raised some of the fundamental issues about Scots property and bankruptcy law which had been dealt with by the House of Lords in *Sharp v Thomson*. So the law on these issues was for a time once again in a state of uncertainty. Wisely, before completing their work the editors decided to await the outcome of that litigation. In the event the House of Lords was able to hold in *Burnett's Trustee v Grainger* 2004 SC (HL) 19, 2004 SLT 513, that *Sharp v Thomson* was distinguishable. So the need to amend the draft text was not as fundamental as had been feared. It was possible to make rapid progress in finalising the text for submission to the publishers.

This is not an academic treatise, nor was it ever meant to be. It is a practical work, written by practitioners for practitioners. That is its great strength. The simplicity and accessibility of the original text have been preserved in this new edition. This has been achieved by carefully pruning out redundant material and by making full use of footnotes and of the many helpful appendices when introducing into the text what is new.

Receivership faces an uncertain future following the changes which were made by section 250 of the Enterprise Act 2002 to support the new administration order procedure, as the editors point out in their preface. The holder of a floating charge which has been created after 15 September 2003 will have certain rights under the amended administration procedure, but he will no longer able to appoint a receiver at his own hand. It will be open to him to apply to the court for a receiver to be appointed in certain circumstances, but this will no longer be the usual remedy. Nevertheless it is too early to say farewell to this branch of jurisprudence. It is as important as it ever has been that receiverships are conducted in a fair and diligent manner according to law. The assistance which this new edition will provide to the maintenance of these standards is very welcome, and the editors are to be congratulated for what they have done to make this possible.

David Hope

*Edinburgh*
*March 2005*

# Preface

It is nearly 20 years since the Insolvency Act 1986 was enacted and it is some 13 years since the second edition appeared in print. Throughout this period, there have been enormous developments both nationally and internationally in the field of insolvency culminating within the United Kingdom in the enactment of the Enterprise Act 2002. The 'rescue culture' is firmly established within the United Kingdom and there is a clear shift in political philosophy from the old mantra that the interests of creditors are at all costs of paramount importance, to a recognition that there are many stakeholders involved and having an interest in the affairs of a company. The interests of creditors are not necessarily of paramount importance!

Such a change in political philosophy has resulted in the abolition of government preferential status and the inability of the holders of floating charges to appoint receivers in respect of charges created on or after 15 September 2003. In future, the Government anticipates that a much greater use will be made of the administration procedure first introduced into the law of the United Kingdom in 1986 but so far, perhaps disappointingly, not much employed in Scotland.

Given the legal and structural changes which have taken place in recent years, it might well be queried why a third edition is now necessary. It has certainly been suggested to us that, notwithstanding such various changes, the holders of floating charges, while it is still open to them to do so, may well prefer to control the destiny of an insolvent company by appointing a receiver in respect of floating charges created before 15 September 2003. It is for that reason that the authors have decided to seek to update this book, acknowledging fully that as the years pass, the importance of receivership jurisprudence will become less and less relevant in the development of insolvency law in Scotland in this whole area.

The Right Honourable Lord Hope of Craighead, one of the Scottish law lords, has always been extremely encouraging of our efforts in relation to this publication. We are very honoured and delighted that he has once again agreed to consent to write a foreword to the third edition.

Once again, we are greatly indebted to our professional colleagues and clients, many of whom have provided much constructive criticism and assistance in the years since the first two editions were published. We also wish to thank Peter Macari and Gordon Hobkirk of Iain Smith & Co, Aberdeen who have read the final text as well as making constructive comments on its terms. Due acknowledgement should also be given to Philip Goodchild and Jennifer Watson of Stephenson Harwood, London who provided valuable commentary and additional material in respect of the pensions sections. Thanks should also be recorded to the Council of R3 (and its predecessor the Society of Practitioners of Insolvency) for their authority and approval in making the various Statements of Practice of Insolvency available to us as set out in Appendix 15. We would also like to mention our former co-author, John Greene, now a retired solicitor, who has encouraged us to write a third edition.

Finally, we wish to thank our partners at Stephenson Harwood and Iain Smith & Co for their patience and encouragement, to our secretaries Janice Richardson and Joyce Gauld, who have made the amendments to the existing manuscript, and also to the directors and staff of Tottel Publishing who have provided us with much professional assistance in connection with the printing and publishing of this edition.

We have sought to state the law as at 30 November 2004.

I M Fletcher
Roy Roxburgh

*21 February 2005*

# Contents

Foreword – The Rt Hon Lord Hope of Craighead .......... v
Preface .......... vii
References .......... xix
Table of statutes .......... xxi
Table of cases .......... xxv

CHAPTER 1

**Appointment of receiver** .......... 1

General introduction .......... 1
Authorisation of members of recognised professional bodies .......... 5
Application for authorisation .......... 6
Grant, refusal and withdrawal of authorisation .......... 7
Reference to tribunal .......... 8
Power of holder of floating charge to appoint receiver .......... 10
Power of court to appoint receiver .......... 10
Form of wording .......... 11
Circumstances justifying appointment by holder of charge .......... 12
Circumstances justifying appointment by the court .......... 14
Mode of appointment by holder of charge .......... 15
Execution of instrument of appointment .......... 15
Effective date of appointment and notification to the Registrar .......... 17
Receipt of the instrument of appointment .......... 18
Acceptance of appointment .......... 18
Notification to the Registrar of Companies and the Accountant in Bankruptcy .......... 18
Attachment to property covered by floating charge .......... 19
Failure to register floating charge .......... 19
Rectification of register .......... 20
Avoidance of certain floating charges .......... 22

Checking the validity of the appointment ........ 24
Mode of appointment by court ........ 26
Precedence among receivers ........ 26
Validity of assignation of floating charges ........ 27
Competition between receiver and liquidator ........ 27

CHAPTER 2

**Effect of appointment of receiver ........ 29**

Attachment of floating charge ........ 29
General ........ 29
Effect of attachment or crystallisation ........ 30
The property and undertaking of the company ........ 30
Effect of attachment or crystallisation in relation to specific property and assets ........ 33
Security for principal and interest ........ 37
Effect of attachment or crystallisation in relation to diligence ........ 38
Other effects of appointment of receiver ........ 41
Powers of directors ........ 41
Responsibilities of directors ........ 45
Remuneration of directors ........ 46
Effect of fixed charges ........ 46
Effect of other floating charges ........ 46
Extent of security ........ 47
Ranking of the floating charge creditor in respect of assets acquired after attachment of the floating charge ........ 48
The proceeds of actions under section 213 or 214 IA 1986 ........ 51
Extortionate credit transactions in terms of section 244 of IA 1986 ........ 52
A Burnett's Trustee v Grainger sale of a property ........ 53
The proceeds of a misfeasance action ........ 53
Trust assets ........ 53
Ranking of charges ........ 54

CHAPTER 3

**Powers, liabilities and agency of receiver ........ 55**

Powers contained in charge ........ 55
Statutory powers ........ 55
General ........ 55
To take possession of property ........ 55
To sell property ........ 58
To borrow ........ 58
Appointment of solicitor and other advisers ........ 59
Power to seek directions ........ 60
Legal proceedings ........ 60
Arbitration ........ 61

Insurances ... 61
Use of company seal ... 61
Execution of deeds ... 62
Negotiable instruments ... 62
Agents and employees ... 62
Work on property ... 62
Incidental payments ... 62
Carrying on of business ... 62
Leases and tenancies ... 63
Arrangements or compromises ... 63
Uncalled capital ... 63
Establishment of subsidiaries ... 63
Ranking in debtors' estates ... 64
Change of registered office ... 64
Winding-up petitions ... 64
Incidental powers ... 65
Powers subject to rights of certain persons ... 65
Disposal of interest in property ... 66
Persons dealing with receiver ... 67
Exercise of powers outwith jurisdiction ... 67
Duties of receiver ... 68
General ... 68
Duty to company ... 68
Duty to guarantor ... 70
Duty to creditor other than holder of floating charge ... 71
Duty to employees ... 72
Duty in relation to pension schemes ... 72
Agency and liability of receiver ... 74
Agent of company ... 74
Termination of agency on winding up ... 76
Pre-receivership contracts ... 78
General ... 78
Leases ... 80
Effect of suspension of receiver's powers ... 81
Receiver's liability if appointment invalid ... 81

CHAPTER 4

**Typical legal problems arising on receivership ... 83**

Contracts ... 83
General position ... 83
Building contracts ... 84
Continuing essential contracts ... 86
Essential licences and permits ... 87
Leases – company in receivership as landlord ... 88
Right to receive rent ... 88

Leases – company in receivership as tenant ..... 89
Receiver as custodian of goods ..... 96
Bills of lading ..... 98
Intellectual property ..... 99
Hire-purchase and leasing contracts ..... 100
Right of third parties against insurers ..... 101
Liens and hypothecs ..... 102
Liens ..... 102
Special lien and general lien ..... 102
Maritime lien ..... 105
Copyright on drawings and engineering certifications ..... 106
Hypothec and sequestration for rent ..... 106
Threatened winding-up petition ..... 107
General ..... 107
Prevention of liquidator's appointment ..... 109
Ownership of documents created by receivers ..... 109
Set-off ..... 110
General ..... 110
Crown set-off ..... 116
Data protection ..... 117

CHAPTER 5

**Retention of title ..... 119**

Background ..... 119
Practical application ..... 121
Incorporation in contract ..... 121
Course of dealing ..... 122
Resolution of dispute ..... 125
Validity of retention of title conditions and trusts over funds ..... 126
Accession and specification ..... 135
Confusion ..... 136

CHAPTER 6

**Receivership as it affects officers of company and its employees ..... 139**

Effect on officers of company and their powers ..... 139
Position of directors ..... 140
Position of employees ..... 141
Rights of employees on receivership ..... 143
Preference for wages ..... 143
Entitlements under employment protection legislation ..... 145
Redundancy payments ..... 145
Notice ..... 145
Protective award ..... 146
Maternity pay ..... 146

Unfair dismissal ..... 147
(a) Basic award ..... 147
(b) Compensatory award ..... 147
(c) Enhancement on failure to obey a tribunal order to reinstate or re-engage ..... 147
Guarantee payment ..... 147
Suspension on medical grounds ..... 148
Time off for trade union or employee representative activities ..... 148
Time off to look for employment or arrange training ..... 148
Time off to act as a pension trustee ..... 148
Treatment of employees' claims including statutory preferential rights and employment protection entitlements on receivership ..... 149
Occupational pension schemes ..... 149
Sale of the business ..... 150
Liabilities that transfer or do not transfer on a relevant transfer ..... 153

CHAPTER 7

**Sale of receivership assets ..... 157**

Introductory considerations ..... 157
Duties of receiver ..... 158
Form of agreements ..... 159
Status of finished goods ..... 160
Assignation of rights and obligations under contracts ..... 160
Supplies on or about the Transfer Date ..... 161
Books and records of the company ..... 162
Patents and trade marks ..... 162
Premises ..... 162
Book debts ..... 163
Liabilities prior to the Transfer Date ..... 163
Goodwill ..... 163
Early transfer of the Business ..... 164
Mechanics of sale of the Business-form of sale ..... 164
Missives ..... 164
Designation of vendor and liability of receiver ..... 165
Terms of agreement for sale of business ..... 165
Recital ..... 166
Interpretation ..... 166
Consideration ..... 166
Exclusion of warranty ..... 167
Good title ..... 167
Miscellaneous provisions ..... 168
VAT ..... 168
Stamp duty ..... 168
Section 61 petition ..... 169
Hive down agreements ..... 170

Nature of hive down agreements .... 170
Reasons for hive down agreement .... 170
Management buy-outs .... 170
Preparation of financial package .... 171
Finalising documentation .... 171
Employees .... 172
Property matters .... 172
Power of execution by receiver after appointment of liquidator .... 173
Letters of obligation .... 173
Personal obligation .... 174
Property, Personal and Charges Registers .... 174
Our client's title or our clients' title .... 175
Proposals .... 175
Property Register .... 175
Personal Register .... 175
Companies Charges Register .... 177
Pension matters .... 177
Change of name .... 179

CHAPTER 8

**Extent and ranking of securities, guarantees and related matters ... 181**

General position .... 181
Ranking agreements and related problems .... 182
Running account .... 182
Interest and additional interest .... 183
Wages preference .... 184
Option in loan documentation to heritable creditor .... 185
General duty to guarantors .... 186
Position of inhibitions in ranking .... 186
Position of arrestors in ranking .... 187
Fixed charge by an English registered company over book debts .... 188
Directors' borrowing limits exceeded .... 189
Unlimited guarantees and letters of set-off .... 190
Suggested approach of receiver .... 190
Proper division of guarantee liability .... 195
Avoidance of certain floating charges .... 196

CHAPTER 9

**Payments and distributions .... 203**

Provisions of section 60 .... 203
Liabilities, expenses and remuneration of receiver .... 206
Priority of debts .... 207

Amounts payable by way of remuneration ........ 209
Orders ........ 210
Money advanced for the purpose of remuneration or accrued holiday remuneration ........ 210
Right to combine accounts ........ 213
'Gross' or 'net' ........ 215

CHAPTER 10

**Notification and information where receiver appointed ........ 217**

Registration and notification of appointment ........ 217
Appointment by holder of floating charge ........ 217
Appointment by the court ........ 219
Receiver should seek confirmation of registration ........ 219
Non-registration of appointment ........ 219
Other publication of receiver's appointment ........ 220
Notification of appointment on invoices ........ 220
Statement to be made to and report to be made by a receiver ........ 221
Statement to be made by officers to receiver ........ 221
Report by receiver ........ 223
Abstract of receipts and payments ........ 225
Committee of creditors ........ 225
Enforcement provisions ........ 227
Reports on conduct of directors of insolvent companies ........ 228
Provisions of Rules of general application ........ 229
Forms ........ 231

CHAPTER 11

**Vacation of appointment of receiver ........ 233**

General ........ 233
Remuneration and indemnity ........ 234
Notification of cessation of appointment ........ 234
Ownership of documents ........ 235
Re-floating of charge ........ 236
Single receiver ........ 236
Joint receivers ........ 236
Effect of re-floating of charge ........ 236

APPENDIX 1

**Floating Charge ........ 239**

APPENDIX 2

**Extract minute of meeting of directors ........ 243**

Appendix 3

**Letter of request to appoint receiver** .............................245

Appendix 4

**Deed of appointment** .............................247

Appendix 5

**Style of letter to debtor** .............................249

Appendix 6

**Style of letter to creditor** .............................251

Appendix 7

**Style of letter to landlord** .............................253

Appendix 8

**Caveat** .............................255

Appendix 9

**Hive down agreement** .............................257

Appendix 10

**Agreement for the sale of the business** .............................277

Appendix 11

**Form of letter for collection of book debts** .............................299

Appendix 12

**Form of letter of indemnity to receiver in the case of early delivery of the business** .............................301

Appendix 13

**Share purchase agreement** .............................303

Appendix 14

**Exceptions to Restrictions on Appointment of Receivers** .............................309

APPENDIX 15

**Statements of Insolvency Practice** .............................. **313**

Statement of Insolvency Practice 1 (Scotland)
A Receiver's Responsibility for the Company's Records (Scotland) ... 313
Society of Practitioners of Insolvency Technical Release 5
Non-preferential claims by employees dismissed without proper notice by insolvent employers .............................. 319
Society of Practitioners of Insolvency Technical Release 6
Treatment of Directors' Claims as 'Employees' in Insolvencies ...... 329
Statement of Insolvency Practice 13 (Scotland)
Acquisition of Assets of Insolvent Companies by Directors ......... 334
Statement of Insolvency Practice 7 (Scotland)
Preparation of Insolvency Office Holders' Receipts and Payments Accounts (Scotland) .............................. 341
Statement of Insolvency Practice 9 (Scotland)
Remuneration of Insolvency Office Holders ...................... 348
Statement of Insolvency Practice 15 (Scotland)
Reporting and providing information on their functions to committees (and commissioners in sequestrations) in formal insolvencies ... 353

APPENDIX 16

**Unlimited guarantee** .............................. **363**

APPENDIX 17

**Letter of set-off** .............................. **367**

APPENDIX 18

**Assignation** .............................. **371**

**Index** .............................. **373**

# References

Throughout this book unless the context otherwise requires the references shall have the meanings ascribed as follows:

| | |
|---|---|
| the 1948 Act | Companies Act 1948 |
| the 1981 Regulations | Transfer of Undertakings (Protection of Employment) Regulations 1981 (SI 1981 No 1794) |
| the 1985 Act | Companies Act 1985 |
| the CA 1985 | Companies Act 1985 |
| the IA 1985 | Insolvency Act 1985 |
| the IA 1986 | Insolvency Act 1986 |
| the 1989 Act | Companies Act 1989 |
| the TULRCA 1992 | Trade Union and Labour Relations (Consolidation) Act 1992 |
| the 1996 Act | Employment Rights Act 1996 |
| the 2002 Act | Enterprise Act 2002 |
| the Scottish Rules | The Receivers (Scotland) Regulations 1986 (SI 1986/1917)S 141<br>The Insolvency (Scotland) Rules 1986 (SI 1986/1915) S 139 |

# Table of statutes

References at the right-hand side of the column are to paragraph numbers.


PARA

Administration of Justice Act 1956
Pt V (ss 45-50) .................. 4.57
Administration of Justice Act 1977
s 7 .............................. 3.41
Bankruptcy Act 1914
s 31 ............................ 9.30
Bankruptcy (Scotland) Act 1985
s 31(1), (b) ..................... 2.05
56a, 56g ................. 1.04, 1.06
Sch 7
para 21 ..................... 2.16
24(3) ..................... 2.16
Civil Jurisdiction and Judgments Act
1982 .......................... 8.20
Companies Act 1929 ........... 8.52; 9.21
Companies Act 1948
s 101 ........................... 1.48
317 ........................... 9.30
327(1)(a) ..................... 3.06
Companies Act 1985 ................ 1.56
s 35 ............................ 8.21
59 ........................... 10.42
132 .................... 10.48, 10.49
139 .......................... 11.07
140 .......................... 10.42
141 .......................... 11.02
154 . 10.42, 10.43, 10.44, 10.45, 10.46
320 ........................... 7.39
288, 353, 383 ............... App 15
Pt XII (ss 395-424) ..... 8.02, 8.04, 8.44
s 404 ...................... 1.48, 1.49
407 ......................... App 15
410(2), (3) .................... 1.43
420 ...................... 1.45, 1.46
462(5) ........................ 2.07
463(1) ............... 2.01, 2.37, 2.38
(4) ........................ 2.15
464 ........................... 2.43
(1) ........................ 8.01
(2) .................. 8.01, 8.02
(3) ........................ 1.23
(4) ........................ 1.23
(a) ..................... 8.02
(5) ........................ 8.04

PARA

Companies Act 1985—*contd*
s 471(1)(a) ....................... 1.68
724 ........................... 3.41
736 .......................... App 1
744 ...................... 1.61; 3.11
Companies Act 1989 ...... 1.45, 1.48, 1.56
s 107, 122 ............... 10.11; 11.06
130 ......................... App 15
Sch 15
para 3 ...................... 11.06
Sch 16 ......................... 10.11
Sch 24 ................. 10.11; 11.06
Companies (Floating Charges and
Receivers) (Scotland) Act
1972 .......... 1.01, 1.20, 1.22, 1.23;
2.11, 2.15, 2.22, 2.26,
3.01, 3.61; 4.77,
4.78, 4.81, 4.82
s 15 ............................ 2.25
(1)(a) ...1.68; 2.12, 2.13, 2.14; 3.06
(f) .................. 2.12, 2.13
(4) ......................... 3.41
21 .................... 7.34, 7.35
Companies (Floating Charges) (Scotland)
Act 1961 ...................... 2.09
Company Directors Disqualification Act
1986 .................... 1.06; 3.30
s 6 ............................ 10.41
(2) ........................ 10.43
7 ............................ 10.41
Compenstion Act 1592 ............. 4.73
Conveyancing and Feudal Reform
(Scotland) Act 1970 ....... 4.54; 7.54
s 9(8) .......................... 2.07
19 ............................ 4.13
25, 35 ........................ 3.44
Sch 3
para 9(2)(c) ................. 4.14
Crown Proceedings Act 1947
s 50 ............................ 4.87
(2)(d) ....................... 4.89
Data Protection Act 1998 ........... 4.90
Disability Discrimination Act 1995 ... 6.19
Employment Relations Act 2004 ..... 3.30

PARA

Employment Rights Act 1996
Pt III (ss 28-35) . . . . . . . . . . . . . 6.13; 9.18
s 28-35 . . . . . . . . . . . . . . . . . . . . . . . 6.28
52 . . . . . . . . . . . . . . . . . . . . 6.23; 9.18
56 . . . . . . . . . . . . . . . . . . . . . . . . . 9.18
59 . . . . . . . . . . . . . . . . . . . . . . . . . 6.24
62 . . . . . . . . . . . . . . . . . . . . 6.22; 9.18
Pt VII (ss 64-70) . . . . . . . . . . . . 6.13; 9.18
s 64 . . . . . . . . . . . . . . . . . . . . . . . . . 6.21
86 . . . . . . . . . . . . . . . . . . . . . . . . . 6.16
118-121 . . . . . . . . . . . . . . . . . . . . . 6.19
122 . . . . . . . . . . . . . . . . . . . . . . . . 6.19
(3), (d) . . . . . . . . . . . . . . . . . . . 6.13
123, 123a, 126 . . . . . . . . . . . . . . . 6.19
183, 185 . . . . . . . . . . . . . . . . . . . . 6.26
220-229 . . . . . . . . . . . . . . . . . . . . . 6.25
230(1), (2) . . . . . . . . . . . . . . . . . . 6.04
240 . . . . . . . . . . . . . . . . . . . . . . . . 6.13
Sch 1
para 29 . . . . . . . . . . . . . . . . . . . . . 6.13
Explosives Act 1875 . . . . . . . . . . . . . . . 3.20
Enterprise Act 2002 . . . . . . . . . . . . . App 16
Sch 16 . . . . . . . . . . . . . . . . . . . . . . App 1
Factors Act 1889 . . . . . . . . . . . . . . . . . 5.34
Family Law (Scotland) Act 1985
s 4 . . . . . . . . . . . . . . . . . . . . . . . . . . 4.23
(1)(a) . . . . . . . . . . . . . . . . . . . . . . 4.22
5 . . . . . . . . . . . . . . . . . . . 4.23, 4.25, 4.26
(3) . . . . . . . . . . . . . . . . . . . . . . . . . 4.22
6 . . . . . . . . . . . . . . . . . . . . . . . . . . . 4.23
Finance Act 1986
42 . . . . . . . . . . . . . . . . . . . . . . . . 7.37A
Sch 10 . . . . . . . . . . . . . . . . . . . . . . 7.37A
Finance Act 1989 . . . . . . . . . . . . . . . . . 4.62
Finance Act 2000
s 129 . . . . . . . . . . . . . . . . . . . . . . . . 7.33
Sch 24 . . . . . . . . . . . . . . . . . . . . . . . 7.33
Finance Act 2002
s 116 . . . . . . . . . . . . . . . . . . . . 7.21, 7.33
Sch 37 . . . . . . . . . . . . . . . . . . . 7.21, 7.33
Finance Act 2004
s 296-305 . . . . . . . . . . . . . . . . . . . . . 7.33
Sch 39-41 . . . . . . . . . . . . . . . . . . . . . 7.33
Finance Act 2003
s 42-124 . . . . . . . . . . . . . . . . . . . . . . 7.33
Sch 3-19 . . . . . . . . . . . . . . . . . . . . . . 7.33
Financial Services and Markets Act
2000 . . . . . . . . . . . . . . . . . . . . . . . . 7.04
Health and Safety at Work etc Act
1974 . . . . . . . . . . . . . . . . . . . . . . . . 6.21
s 6 . . . . . . . . . . . . . . . . . . . . . . . . . . 7.30
Income and Corporation Taxes Act 1988
s 393 . . . . . . . . . . . . . . . . . . . . . . . 7.37A
Industrial and Provident Societies Act 1965
s 59(a)(ii) . . . . . . . . . . . . . . . . . . . . . 1.21
Insolvency Act 1985 . . . . . 1.01, 1.20; 10.39
s 58 . . . . . . . . . . . . . . . . . . . . . . . . . 6.09
Insolvency Act 1986
1986 . . . 4.80; App 4; App 9; App 10
s 14(4) . . . . . . . . . . . . . . . . . . . . . . . 2.19
15(1)(a) . . . . . . . . . . . . . . . . . . . . . . 8.17
29 . . . . . . . . . . . . . . . . . . . . . . . . . . 3.58

PARA

Insolvency Act 1986—*contd*
s 31(1) . . . . . . . . . . . . . . . . . . . . . . . . 1.04
(3) . . . . . . . . . . . . . . . . . . . . . . . . . . 1.04
42(1) . . . . . . . . . . . . . . . . . . . . 3.59; 7.45
44 . . . . . . . . . . . . . . . . . . . . . . . 3.59, 3.60
(1)(a) . . . . . . . . . . . . . . . . . . . 3.58, 3.62
(b), (c) . . . . . . . . . . . . . . . . . . . . . 3.59
Pt III (ss 50-71) . . . . . . . . . . . . . . . . . 3.43
s 51 . . . . . . . . . . . . . . . . . . . . . . 1.20, 1.21
(1) . . . . 1.23, 1.27, 1.33, 1.64; 11.11
(2) . . . . . . . . . . . . . . . 1.22, 1.32; 11.11
(6) . . . . . . . . . . . . . . . . . . . . . . . . . 11.11
52 . . . . . . . . . . . . . . . . . . . . . . . . . . 1.27
(1)(c) . . . . . . . . . . . . . . . . . . . . . . . 1.67
(d) . . . . . . . . . . . . . . . . . . . . 2.02; 7.55
(2) . . . . . . . . . . . . . . . . . . . . . . . . . . 1.32
(a) . . . . . . . . . . . . . . . . . . . . . . . . . 1.22
53 . . . . . . . . . . . . . . . . . . . . . 1.56; 10.11
(1) . . . . . . . . . . . 1.33, 1.34, 1.41, 1.57
(2) . . . . . . . . . . . . . . . 1.61, 1.64; 10.11
(3)(a) . . . . . . . . . . . . . . . . . . . . . . . 2.16
(5) . . . . . . . . . . . . . . . . . . . . . . . . . . 1.41
(6) . . . . . . . . . . . . . . . . . 2.37; 9.16, 9.18
(a) . . . . . . . . . . . . . . . . . . . . . . . . . 1.39
(7) . . . . . . . . . . 1.42; 2.01, 2.04, 2.14,
2.37; 4.01, 4.75, 4.81
54(2) . . . . . . . . . . . . . . . . . . . . . . . . . 1.61
(3) . . . . . . . . 1.61, 1.62; 10.08, 10.11
(4) . . . . . . . . . . . . . . . . . . . . 1.62; 10.08
(5) . . . . . . . . . . . . . . . . 1.62; 9.16, 9.18
(6) . . . . . . . . . . . . . . . . 1.62; 4.01, 4.81
55 . . . . . . . . . . . . . . . . . 1.26; 2.25; 8.39
(3) . . . . . . . . . . . . . . . . . . . . . . . . . . 3.33
(a) . . . . . . . . . . . . . . . . . . . . . 2.16, 2.17
(b) . . . . . . . . . . . . . . . . . . . . . . . . . 2.19
(4) . . . . . . . . . . . . . . . . . . . 3.40; 7.27A
56 . . . . . . . . . . . . . . . . . . . . . . 2.32, 2.33
(1) . . . . . . . . . . . . . . . . 1.63; 2.02, 2.31
(2) . . . . . . . . . . . . . . . . . . . . . . . . . . 2.02
(3) . . . . . . . . . . . . . . . . . . . . . 1.64; 7.44
57 . . . . . . . . . . . . . . . . . . . . . . 3.47; 4.42
(1) . . . . . . 3.54, 3.56; 4.03; 6.10; 7.25
(1A) . . . . . . . . . . . . . . . . . . . 4.01, 4.03
(2) . . . . . . . . . . 3.08, 3.54, 3.55, 3.56,
3.61, 3.63; 4.01, 4.03, 4.04,
4.06; 6.09, 6.10; 7.26
(2A)-(2D) . . . . . . . . . 4.01, 4.03; 6.09
(3) . 3.08, 3.45; 4.04, 4.09; 7.26; 9.11
(4) . . . . . . 3.55, 3.63; 4.01, 4.02, 4.32
(5) . . . . . . . . . . . 3.55, 3.57; 4.03; 6.09
(7) . . . . . . . . . . . . . . . . . . . . . . . . . . 6.08
58(1), (2) . . . . . . . . . . . . . . . . . . . . . 9.12
(3) . . . . . . . . . . . . . . . . . . . . . . . . . . 9.13
59 . . . . . . . . . . . . . . . . . . . . . . 8.09; 9.01
(1) . . . . . . . . . . . . . . . . . . . . . 9.14, 9.15
(2) . . . . . . . . . . . . . . 9.14, 9.15; 10.12
(3) . . . . . . . . . . . . . . . . . . . . . . . . . . 9.16
60 . . . . . . . . . . . . . . . . 3.06, 3.43; 11.02
(1) . . . . . . . . 9.01, 9.02; 11.04, 11.05
(a) . . . . . . . . . . . . . . . . . . . . . . . . . 3.54
(b) . . . . . . . . . . . . . . . . . . . . . . . . . 9.08
(c) . . . . . . . . . . . . . . . . . . . . . . . . . 9.10

PARA

Insolvency Act 1986—*contd*
s 60(1)(d) 3.08; 7.26; 9.11
(2) 9.02
(c) 3.28
(3) 9.03
61 2.18; 3.35; 7.34, 7.35, 7.53; 8.12; 9.02, 9.07, 9.01
(1) 3.36
(2) 3.36, 3.39
(3)-(5) 3.37
(6), (7) 3.39
(8) 3.38
(9) 3.39
62(1), (2) 11.01
(3) 3.47; 11.01
(5) 11.08
(6) 11.10
63 3.11
(2) 1.44
64(1) 10.13
65 10.09
(1) 10.03
(a) 10.06
(2) 10.03
(3) 10.04
(4) 10.05; 10.11
66 6.01; 10.15, 10.25
(1) 10.16, 10.50
(2) 10.16, 10.18
(3) 10.16, 10.17
(4) 10.20, 10.50
(5) 10.20
(a), (b) 10.21
(6) 10.22
67 10.15, 10.23
(1) 10.24
(2) 10.27, 10.28, 10.34
(4) 10.29
(5) 10.25
(6) 10.30
(7) 10.31
(8) 10.32
68 10.15, 10.23, 10.34; 11.02
(2) 10.35
69 10.40
70 2.11; 3.44; 4.75, 4.82, 4.84; 7.52, 7.54; 8.15; App 1
(1) 2.03, 2.07, 2.14, 2.19
72 3.41
72a 1.20
(1), (2) 1.20; App 14
(4) 1.20
72b, 72c-72ga, 72h App 14
98 4.57
103 2.21
120 1.21
122 4.69
(1)(e), (f) 3.28
123 1.51; 4.69; 8.46, 8.47
127 3.62; 7.46
129(2) 1.67
145 1.51; 2.05

PARA

Insolvency Act 1986—*contd*
s 175 6.11; 9.17
(2) 9.34
185 7.53; 8.15
(1)(a) 3.06
213, 214 2.37, 2.38
225 1.21
233 3.05; 4.10
234 App 15
(1)-(4) 3.04
235 4.52; App 15
(2), (3) 3.05
236 4.52; 7.51A; App 15
(2) 3.05
242 1.55; 2.39; 8.58
243 3.29; 8.58
244 2.37, 2.39
245 1.50, 1.51, 1.54, 1.66; 2.39; 8.45, 8.46, 8.49, 8.50, 8.51, 8.52, 8.55, 8.56, 8.58
(2) 1.52
(a) 8.51
(3) 1.51
246 4.52
249 8.59
251 1.01, 1.40, 1.61
386 6.11; 9.17
(1) 9.06
387(4)(b) 6.11; 9.16
Pt XIII (ss 388-398) 1.15
s 388(1)(a) 1.02
390 1.02
(1) 1.04
(2) 1.04, 1.10
(4), (5) 1.06
391(1), (2) 1.10, 1.11, 1.14
(2) 1.10
(3) 1.12, 1.14
(4) 1.10
392(2), (4), (6)-(8) 1.13
393 1.04
394(1) 1.15
(2) 1.15, 1.16, 1.17
(3), (4) 1.15
395 1.16
396(1) 1.19
(2), (3) 1.17, 1.19
397(2), (3) 1.18
398 1.04
Pt XV (ss 411-422) 1.15
s 430 1.04
435 8.49
Sch 1 3.59
Sch 2 1.24; 2.25; 3.01, 3.02; 4.65; 8.39
para 1 1.68; 2.12, 2.13, 2.14; 3.06, 4.77, 4.78, 4.89; App 15
5 2.12; 4.78
14 3.67
16 3.23
22 3.27
23 3.67

PARA

Insolvency Act 1986—*contd*
para 55 ... 9.08
Sch 6 ... 6.11; 9.06, 9.15, 9.16, 9.17, 9.17A, 9.35
para 9 ... 9.19
11 ... 9.20, 9.22
12 ... 9.18
13(1) ... 9.18
(a) ... 6.12
(2) ... 6.13; 9.18
14 ... 9.18
(2) ... 6.12
15(a), (b) ... 6.12
Sch 7
para 1(1)(a), (b) ... 1.19
2 ... 1.19
3(1), (2) ... 1.19
4(1)-(3) ... 1.19
Sch 10 ... 1.04
Sch 21
para 8 ... 3.15
Sch B1
para 14 ... App 1
Insolvency Act 1994 ... 3.55, 3.56, 3.61; 4.03; 6.09
Land Registration (Scotland) Act 1979 ... 2.07
s 2(1) ... App 9; App 10
3(3) ... App 9; App 10
12(2) ... App 9; App 10
Leases Act 1449 ... 4.12
Limited Liability Partnerships Act 2000
s 14 ... 1.21
Mental Health Act 1983
Pt VII (ss 93-113) ... 1.06
Mental Health (Scotland) Act 1984
s 125(1) ... 1.06
Pension Schemes Act 1993
s 1 ... 6.27
124 ... 6.27
Sch 4 ... 6.11
Pensions Act 1995 ... 7.59
s 22 ... 3.53
23(4) ... 3.53
24(1) ... 3.53
25 ... 3.53
26(1) ... 3.53
90 ... 6.27
Pensions Act 2004 ... 6.33; 7.59
s 36 ... 3.53
Proceeds of Crime Act 2002 ... 1.04, 1.20, 1.22; 2.08, 2.33; 4.89; 5.01; 9.06
s 251 ... 9.15
Race Relations Act 1976 ... 6.19
Requirements of Writing (Scotland) Act 1995 ... 1.33, 1.34; 3.15; 7.44
s 14(1) ... 1.34

PARA

Requirements of Writing (Scotland) Act 1995—*contd*
Sch 4
para 58(b) ... 1.34
Sch 2
para 3 ... 1.34
Sale of Goods Act 1893 ... 5.03, 5.04, 5.34
Sale of Goods Act 1979 ... 2.09; 5.13
s 17(1) ... 5.04
18 ... 5.04
19(1) ... 5.04
21 ... 5.33
(1) ... 5.19
25 ... 5.34
(1) ... 5.19; 7.31
44 ... 4.36
47(2) ... 4.36
55(4) ... 5.15
61(5) ... 7.10
Sch 1
para 11 ... 5.15
Sale of Goods (Amendment) Act 1995 ... 5.47
Scotland Act 1998 ... 1.33
125(1) ... 11.06
Sch 8
para 23 ... 1.61
(1)-(3) ... 11.06
Sex Discrimination Act 1975 ... 6.19
Social Security Pensions Act 1975
Sch 3 ... 9.15
Social Security Contributions and Benefits Act 1992
s 164-166 ... 6.18
Taxes Management Act 1970 ... 4.62
Third Parties (Rights Against Insurers) Act 1930 ... 4.46
s 1 ... 4.45
2(1) ... 4.47
Titles to Land Consolidation (Scotland) Act 1868 ... 1.47
s 143 ... 1.47
Trade Union and Labour Relations (Consolidation) Act 1992 ... 6.17
s 169 ... 6.22; 9.18
188(7) ... 6.17
193(7) ... 6.17
Trade Union Reform and Employment Rights Act 1993
s 33(5) ... 6.33
Transmission of Moveable Property (Scotland) Act 1862 ... 2.10; 7.11; 8.18
Unfair Contract Terms Act 1977 ... 3.44
s 17 ... 5.13
Value Added Tax Act 1994 ... 4.68; App 9; App 10
s 49 ... App 9; App 10

# Table of cases

**A** PARA


A One Fashions v Customs & Excise Comrs (12 July 2003, unreported) ............ 7.32
Agnew v IRC [2001] UKPC 28, [2001] 2 AC 710, [2001] 3 WLR 454, PC ........... 8.18
Airlines Airspares Ltd v Handley Page Ltd [1970] Ch 193, [1970] 1 All ER 29n, [1970] 2 WLR 163 ........ 3.65, 3.66
Alamo Group (Europe) Ltd v Tucker [2003] ICR 829, [2003] IRLR 266 ............. 6.32
Alloa Brewery Co Ltd v Investors in Industry plc 1992 SLT 121 .................... 8.07
Aluminium Industrie Vaassen BV v Romalpa Aluminium Ltd [1976] 2 All ER 552, [1976] 1 WLR 676, CA ........ 5.01
American Express International Banking Corpn v Hurley [1985] 3 All ER 564, [1985] FLR 350 ........ 3.44, 3 49, 3.50, 3.59
Anderson (Gordon) (Plant) Ltd v Campsie Construction Ltd and Anglo Scottish Plant Ltd 1977 SLT 7 ........ 3.42
Anglo-Austrian Printing and Publishing Union, Re [1895] 2 Ch 891, CA ............ 2.41
Archivent Sales and Developments Ltd v Strathclyde Regional Council 1985 SLT 154, 27 BLR 98 ........ 5.19, 5.34; 7.31
Armagh Shoes Ltd, Re [1982] NI 59 ........ 8.18
Armour v Thyssen Edelstahlwerke AG 1989 SLT 182, 1989 SCLR 26 ............... 5.19
Armour v Thyssen Edelstahlwerke AG [1991] 2 AC 339, [1990] 3 All ER 481, [1990] 3 WLR 810, HL ........ 5.02, 5 19, 5.28, 5.35
Armour and Mycroft, Petitioners 1983 SLT 453 ......... 2.18; 3.35; 7.34, 7.35, 7.52, 7.53; 8.14, 8.15, 8.16; 9.08
Arnold (R M) & Co Ltd, Re [1984] BCLC 535 ........ 1.48
Ash and Newman Ltd v Creative Devices Research Ltd [1991] BCLC 403 ........... 3.66
Asiatic Electric Co Pty Ltd, Re [1970] 2 NSWR 612 ........ 2.41
Atlantic Engine Co (1920) Ltd v Lord Advocate 1955 SLT 17 ..................... 4.89
Aubrey Investments Ltd v DS Crawford Ltd (in receivership) 1998 SLT 628, OH .... 4.25
Aubrey Investments Ltd v DSC (Realisations) Ltd (in receivership) 1999 SC 21, 2000 SLT 183, OH ........ 4.25
Auditglen Ltd v SCOTEC Industries Ltd (in receivership) 1996 SLT 493, OH ....... 4.26
Aveling Barford Ltd, Re [1988] 3 All ER 1019, [1989] 1 WLR 360 .................. 3.05


**B**


Bags More Ltd v Customs & Excise Comrs (22 August 2000, unreported) .......... 7.32
Bank of Baroda v Panessar [1987] Ch 335, [1986] 3 All ER 751, [1987] 2 WLR 208 ........ 1.35, 1.36
Bank of Scotland v T A Nielson & Co 1990 SC 284, 1991 SLT 8 .................. 1.47
Bank of Scotland v Purvis Industries Ltd (unreported) ...................... 9.28, 9.32
Barclays Bank Ltd v Thienel and Thienel (1978) 247 Estates Gazette 385, 122 Sol Jo 472 ........ 3.49
Barclays Bank plc v Stuart Landon Ltd [2001] EWCA Civ 140 , [2001] 2 BCLC 316 . 1.48
Barrows v Chief Land Registrar (1977) Times, 20 October ................... 3.59; 7.46

PARA

Beckmann v Dynamco Whicheloe MacFarlane Ltd: C-164/00 [2002] ECR I-4893, [2002] All ER (EC) 865, [2002] 2 CMLR 1152, [2003] ICR 50, [2002] IRLR 578, ECJ ... 6.33
Bell Bros (HP) Ltd v Aitken 1939 SC 577, 1939 SLT 453 ... 8.06
Bernadone v Pall Mall Services Group [2000] 3 All ER 544, [2000] IRLR 487, CA ... 6.33
Beveridge v Wilson (1829) 1829 7 S 279 ... 3.44
Boston Borough Council v Rees [2002] BCC 495, CA ... 4.14
Brechin Auction Co Ltd (Liquidator of) v Reid (1895) 22 R 711, 1895 32 SLR 539 ... 5.19, 5.33
British Bank of the Middle East v Sun Life Assurance Co of Canada (UK) Ltd [1983] 2 Lloyd's Rep 9, HL ... 5.16
British Crane Hire Corpn Ltd v Ipswich Plant Hire Ltd [1975] QB 303, [1974] 1 All ER 1059, [1974] 2 WLR 856, CA ... 5.11, 5.12
Buchler v Talbot [2004] UKHL 9, [2004] 2 AC 298, [2004] 1 All ER 1289, [2004] 2 WLR 582 ... 1.68; 2.26; 3.06, 3.54
Burnett's Trustee v Grainger [2004] UKHL 8, 2004 SC (HL) 19, 2004 SLT 513 ... 2.05, 2.37, 2.40
Burston Finance Ltd v Speirway Ltd [1974] 3 All ER 735, [1974] 1 WLR 1648 ... 1.44

C

Callaghan (Myles J) Ltd (in receivership) v Glasgow District Council 1987 SC 171, 1988 SLT 227, 3 BCC 337 ... 2.13, 2.14; 4.74, 4.85
Caparo Industries plc v Dickman [1990] 2 AC 605, [1990] 1 All ER 568, [1990] 2 WLR 358, HL ... 3.46, 3.50
Chaigley Farms Ltd v Crawford, Kaye & Grayshire Ltd [1996] BCC 957 ... 5.42
Chantry House Developments plc, Re [1990] BCC 646, [1990] BCLC 813 ... 1.49
CIN Properties Ltd v Dollar Land (Cumbernauld) Ltd 1992 SC (HL) 104, 1992 SLT 669 ... 4.22
Clark Taylor & Co Ltd v Quality Site Development (Edinburgh) Ltd 1981 SC 111, 1981 SLT 308 ... 5.19, 5.22, 5.24, 5.26; 7.19
Clydebank Engineering and Shipbuilding Co Ltd v Don Jose Ramos Yzquierdo y Castaneda [1905] AC 6, 74 LJPC 1, [1904-7] All ER Rep 251, HL ... 8.06
Cripps (R A) & Son Ltd v Wickenden [1973] 2 All ER 606, [1973] 1 WLR 944 ... 1.36
Cuckmere Brick Co Ltd v Mutual Finance Ltd [1971] Ch 949, [1971] 2 All ER 633, [1971] 2 WLR 1207, CA ... 3.44
Cumbernauld Development Corpn v Mustone Ltd 1983 SLT (Sh Ct) 55 ... 2.19; 8.02
Customs and Excise Comrs v Dearwood Ltd [1986] STC 327 ... 7.35
Customs and Excise Comrs v Padglade Ltd [1995] STC 602 ... 7.32

D

Demite Ltd v Protec Health Ltd [1998] BCC 638 ... 7.39
Destone Fabrics Ltd, Re [1941] Ch 319, [1941] 1 All ER 545, 111 LJ Ch 38, CA ... 8.52
Devaynes v Noble, Clayton's Case 8 LJ Ch 256, 1 Mer 572 ... 8.57; 9.24
Deutz Engines Ltd v Terex Ltd 1984 SLT 273 ... 5.19, 5.20
Dollar Land (Cumbernauld) Ltd v CIN Properties Ltd 1998 SC (HL) 90, [1998] SLT 992, [1998] 51 EG 83 ... 4.22
Dorchester Studios (Glasgow) v Stone 1975 SC (HL) 56, 1975 SLT 153 ... 4.19
Dryburgh v Gordon 24 R 1, 34 SLR 19, 1896 4 SLT 113 ... 7.52; 8.16
Durant v Financial Services Authority [2003] EWCA Civ 1746, Times, 2 January ... 4.90

E

Elwick Bay Shipping Co Ltd v Royal Bank of Scotland Ltd 1982 SLT 62 ... 1.37, 1.56
Emerald Stainless Steel Ltd v South Side Distribution Ltd 1982 SC 61, 1983 SLT 162 ... 5.19, 5.20
Export Credits Guarantee Department v Turner 1981 SLT 286 ... 5.19, 5.22, 5.23
Export Credits Guarantee Department v Universal Oil Products Co [1983] 2 All ER 205, [1983] 1 WLR 399, HL ... 8.06

F

Fairway Magazines Ltd, Re [1992] BCC 924 ... 8.52

PARA

Fields (HMV) Properties Ltd v Skirt 'n' Slack Centre of London Ltd 1982 SLT 477 .......... 4.16, 4.22
First National Tricity Finance Ltd v OT Computers Ltd (in administration) [2004] EWCA Civ 653, [2004] Ch 317, [2004] 3 WLR 886 .......... 4.47
Fleming v Secretary of State for Trade and Industry [1997] IRLR 682 .......... 6.04
Forth & Clyde Construction Co Ltd v Trinity Timber & Plywood Co Ltd 1984 SLT 94 .......... 2.11, 2.14, 2.16; 3.03, 3.07, 3.12, 3.44, 3.51; 4.74, 4.75, 4.82, 4.83, 4.84; 7.04; 8.15, 8.17
Foster Clark Ltd's Indenture Trusts, Re, Loveland v Horscroft [1966] 1 All ER 43, [1966] 1 WLR 125 .......... 6.06
Foxhall & Gyle (Nurseries) Ltd, Petitioners 1978 SLT (Notes) 29 .......... 3.31; 4.69, 4.70
Freeman and Lockyer (a firm) v Buckhurst Park Properties (Mangal) Ltd [1964] 2 QB 480, [1964] 1 All ER 630, [1964] 2 WLR 618, CA .......... 5.16
Freevale Ltd v Metrostore (Holdings) Ltd [1984] Ch 199, [1984] 1 All ER 495, [1984] 2 WLR 496 .......... 3.66, 3.67; 4.31, 4.40; 8.11

G

Garnett v McKewan (1872) LR 8 Exch 10, 42 LJ Ex 1, 21 WR 57 .......... 9.28
Gomba Holdings UK Ltd v Homan [1986] 3 All ER 94, [1986] 1 WLR 1301 .......... 2.21, 2.26; 3.45; 6.03
Gomba Holdings UK Ltd v Minories Finance Ltd [1989] 1 All ER 261, [1988] 1 WLR 1231, 5 BCC 27, CA .......... 4.71, 4.72; 11.09
Gosling v Gaskell [1897] AC 575, HL .......... 3.59
Graham (Thomas) & Sons Ltd v Glenrothes Development Corpn 1967 SC 284, 1968 SLT 2 .......... 5.19, 5.34; 7.31
Granor Finance Ltd v Liquidator of Eastore Ltd 1974 SLT 296 .......... 8.06
Grayston Plant Ltd v Plean Precast Ltd 1976 SC 206, 1976 SLT 74 .......... 5.10, 5.12, 5.14
Griffiths v Secretary of State for Social Services [1974] QB 468, [1973] 3 All ER 1184, [1973] 3 WLR 831 .......... 6.06, 6.07
Group 4 Total Security Ltd v Ferrier 1985 SLT 287 .......... 1.29
Grove v Advantage Healthcare (T10) Ltd [2000] 1 BCLC 661 .......... 1.43, 1.56

H

Hamlyn & Co v Talisker Distillery [1894] AC 202, 58 JP 540, 21 R 21, HL .......... 5.37, 5.39
Hammer and Sohne v HWT Realisations Ltd 1985 SLT (Sh Ct) 21 .......... 5.19, 5.35, 5.36, 5.39
Hardwick Game Farm v Suffolk Agricultural and Poultry Producers' Association Ltd [1966] 1 All ER 309, [1966] 1 WLR 287, CA .......... 5.11
Hastings Black Construction Ltd v AIR (Air Conditioning and Refrigeration) Ltd (1984) (4 October, unreported), Glasgow Sheriff Court .......... 2.24, 2.25
Hawking v Hafton House Ltd 1990 SC 198, 1990 SLT 496 .......... 2.36; 8.15, 8.17; 9.08
Hill Samuel & Co Ltd v Laing 1989 SC 301, 1989 SLT 760 .......... 3.08, 3.54
Hollier v Rambler Motors (AMC) Ltd [1972] 2 QB 71, [1972] 1 All ER 399, [1972] 2 WLR 401, CA .......... 5.11, 5.12

I

Imperial Hotel (Aberdeen) Ltd v Vaux Breweries Ltd 1978 SC 86, 1978 SLT 113 .......... 2.22, 2.24, 2.25, 2.30; 6.02
Independent Automatic Sales Ltd v Knowles and Foster [1962] 3 All ER 27, [1962] 1 WLR 974 .......... 1.43
Independent Pension Trustee Ltd v L A W Construction Co Ltd 1997 SLT 1105, OH .......... 2.21, 2.26; 6.02, 6.03
International Banking Corpn v Ferguson Shaw & Sons 1910 SC 182, 2 SLT 377 .......... 5.19, 5.27, 5.30, 5.41
Inverness District Council v Highland Universal Fabrications Ltd 1986 SLT 556n .......... 3.56
Iona Hotels Ltd (in receivership) v Craig 1990 SC 330, 1991 SLT 11 .......... 2.16; 8.17; 9.09

PARA

**J**

Johnson (B) & Co (Builders) Ltd, Re [1955] Ch 634, [1955] 2 All ER 775, [1955] 3 WLR 269, CA ........ 3.44
Junior Books Ltd v Veitchi Co Ltd [1983] 1 AC 520, [1982] 3 All ER 201, [1982] 3 WLR 477, 1982 SLT 492, HL ........ 3.46

**K**

Karl Construction Ltd v Palisade Properties plc 2002 SC 270, 2002 SLT 312 ........ 2.18
Keenan Bros Ltd, Re [1985] IR 401 ........ 8.18
Kendall (Henry) & Sons (a firm) v William Lillico & Sons Ltd [1969] 2 AC 31, [1968] 2 All ER 444, [1968] 3 WLR 110, HL ........ 5.11
Kerr v McArthur's Trustees (1848) 11 D 301 ........ 3.44
Knight v Lawrence [1991] BCC 411, [1993] BCLC 215 ........ 3.44

**L**

Laing (Liquidator of Inverdale Construction Co Ltd) v Lord Advocate 1973 SLT (Notes) 81 ........ 4.89
Larsen's Executrix v Henderson 1990 SLT 498, [1990] IRLR 512 ........ 3.14, 3.52
Latchford v Beirne [1981] 3 All ER 705 ........ 3.49
Lewis v IRC [2001] 3 All ER 499, [2001] 2 BCLC 392, CA ........ 2.38
Leyland DAF Ltd v Automotive Products plc [1994] 1 BCLC 245, CA ........ 5.18
Libertas-Kommerz GmbH v Johnson 1977 SC 191, 1978 SLT 222 ........ 1.65; 8.52, 8.53
Lindop v Stuart Noble & Sons Ltd [1999] BCC 616, 1998 SCLR 648 ........ 6.09
Lipe Ltd v Leyland DAF Ltd [1993] BCC 385, [1994] 1 BCLC 84, CA ........ 4.09
Litster v Forth Dry Dock and Engineering Co Ltd [1990] 1 AC 546, [1989] 1 All ER 1134, [1989] 2 WLR 634, HL ........ 6.29; 7.42
London Iron and Steel Co Ltd, Re [1990] BCC 159, [1990] BCLC 372 ........ 3.04
Longden and Paisley v Ferrari Ltd and Kennedy International Ltd [1994] ICR 443, [1994] IRLR 157 ........ 6.31
Lord Advocate v Aero Technologies Ltd (in receivership) 1991 SLT 134 ........ 3.22
Lord Advocate v Royal Bank of Scotland Ltd 1977 SC 155, 1978 SLT 38 ........ 2.04, 2.11, 2.16; 8.17; 9.08

**M**

Mace Builders (Glasgow) Ltd v Lunn [1987] Ch 191, [1986] 3 WLR 921, 2 BCC 99, CA ........ 1.54
Mack Trucks (Britain) Ltd, Re [1967] 1 All ER 977, [1967] 1 WLR 780 ........ 6.06
Macleod v Alexander Sutherland Ltd 1977 SLT (Notes) 44 ........ 2.27; 3.64; 4.31, 4.39, 4.40; 8.11
Manley, Petitioner 1985 SLT 42 ........ 1.68; 3.61; 4.65; 6.10; 9.06, 9.14
Martin v South Bank University: C-4/01 [2004] 1 CMLR 472, [2004] ICR 1234, [2004] IRLR 74, ECJ ........ 6.33
Mawcon Ltd, Re [1969] 1 All ER 188, [1969] 1 WLR 78 ........ 2.21
McCrone v Boots Farm Sales Ltd 1981 SLT 103 ........ 5.14
McCutcheon v David MacBrayne Ltd 1964 SC (HL) 28, [1964] 1 All ER 430, [1964] 1 WLR 125 ........ 5.12
McDonald v Provan of Scotland Street Ltd 1960 SLT 231 ........ 5.19, 5.30, 5.31
McPhail v Cunninghame District Council 1985 SLT 149 ........ 4.86
McPhail v Lothian Regional Council 1981 SLT 173 ........ 2.12, 2.13; 3.03; 4.74, 4.76, 4.79, 4.81
Michelin Tyre Co Ltd v Macfarlane (Glasgow) Ltd 1917 2 SLT 205, 55 SLR 35, HL ........ 5.19, 5.32
Miller v Mitchell (1860) 22 D 833 ........ 7.48
Mitchell v Burnett & Mouat (1746) 1746 Mor 4468 ........ 5.39
Mitchell (George) (Chesterhall) Ltd v Finney Lock Seeds Ltd [1983] QB 284, [1983] 1 All ER 108, [1982] 3 WLR 1036, CA ........ 5.15
Morel (EJ) (1934) Ltd, Re [1962] Ch 21, [1961] 1 All ER 796, [1961] 3 WLR 57 ........ 9.26, 9.28, 9.29
Mortimer (Thomas) Ltd, Re (1925) [1965] Ch 186n, [1964] 3 WLR 427n ........ 8.53

PARA

## N

National Commercial Bank of Scotland Ltd v Liquidators of Telford Grier Mackay & Co 1969 SC 181 .......... 2.15
National Westminster Bank Ltd v Halesowen Presswork and Assemblies Ltd [1972] AC 785, [1972] 1 All ER 641, [1972] 2 WLR 455, HL .......... 9.28, 9.30, 9.31
Newhart Developments Ltd v Co-operative Commercial Bank Ltd [1978] QB 814, [1978] 2 All ER 896, [1978] 2 WLR 636, CA ... 2.21, 2.22, 2.23, 2.24, 2.26; 3.48; 6.02
Nicoll v Cutts [1985] BCLC 322, 1 BCC 99, 427, CA .......... 6.06, 6.09
Norfolk House plc (in receivership) v Repsol Petroleum Ltd 1992 SLT 235n .... 2.35; 3.41
NRG Vision Ltd v Churchfield Leasing [1988] 4 BCC 56, [1988] BCLC 624 .......... 1.60
NWL Ltd v Woods, The Nawala [1979] 3 All ER 614, [1979] 1 WLR 1294, [1979] ICR 867, HL .......... 1.29

## O

Oasis Merchandising Services, Re [1995] BCC 911, [1995] 2 BCLC 493 .......... 2.38
On Demand Information plc (in administrative receivership) v Michael Gerson (Finance) plc [2002] UKHL 13, [2003] 1 AC 368, [2002] 2 All ER 949, [2002] 2 WLR 919 . 4.42
Orleans Motor Co Ltd, Re [1911] 2 Ch 41 .......... 8.52

## P

Park Ward & Co Ltd, Re [1926] Ch 828 .......... 3.62
Parkes Garage (Swadlincote) Ltd, Re [1929] 1 Ch 139, 98 LJ Ch 9 .......... 1.54
Potters Oils Ltd, Re [1986] 1 All ER 890, [1986] 1 WLR 201 .......... 1.69
Powdrill v Watson; Talbot v Cadge; Talbot v Grundy [1995] 2 AC 394, [1995] 2 All ER 65, [1995] 2 WLR 312, HL .......... 3.55; 4.03; 6.09; 9.01, 9.11
Powdrill v Watson [1994] 2 All ER 513, [1994] ICR 395, [1994] IRLR 295, CA .......... 6.09
Power v Sharp Investments Ltd [1993] BCC 609, [1994] 1 BCLC 111, CA .......... 1.52

## R

R v Registrar of Companies, ex p Central Bank of India [1986] QB 1114, [1986] 1 All ER 105, [1986] 2 WLR 177, CA .......... 1.49
R v Registrar of Companies, ex p Esal (Commodities) Ltd [1986] QB 1114, [1985] 2 All ER 79, [1985] 2 WLR 447 .......... 1.56
Reed Stenhouse (UK) Ltd v Brodie 1986 SLT 354 .......... 1.29, 1.30
Renfrew District Council v AB Leisure (Renfrew) Ltd 1988 SLT 635n .......... 4.26
Retail Equity Pty Ltd v Custom Credit Corpn Ltd (1991) 9 ACLC 404 .......... 1.60
Rimmer v Thomas Usher & Son Ltd 1967 SLT 7 .......... 3.44
Ritchie v EFT Industrial Ltd 1998 SLT 11 .......... 3.03
Ross v Taylor 1985 SLT 387 .......... 2.01, 2.37, 2.38

## S

Scottish & Newcastle plc v Ascot Inns Ltd (in receivership) 1994 SLT 1140 .......... 1.01
Scottish Exhibition Centre Ltd v Mirestrop (in administration) No 2) 1996 SLT 8, OH .......... 4.25
Scottish Tourist Board v Deanpark Ltd 1998 SLT 1121, OH .......... 4.26
Secretary of State for Trade and Industry v Bottrill [1998] ICR 564, [1998] IRLR 120 . 6.04
Secretary of State for Trade and Industry v Bottrill [2000] 1 All ER 915, [1999] ICR 592, [1999] IRLR 326, CA .......... 6.04
Shanks v Central Regional Council 1988 SC 14, 1988 SLT 212 .. 2.21, 2.22, 2.26; 6.02, 6.03
Sharp v Thomson 1997 SC (HL) 66, 1997 SLT 636 .......... 2.04, 2.05, 2.40
Shiells v Ferguson, Davidson & Co 1876 4 R 250, 14 SLR 172 .......... 4.75
Shoe Lace Ltd, Re [1994] 1 BCLC 111, [1993] BCC 609 .......... 8.55
Siebe Gorman & Co Ltd v Barclays Bank Ltd [1979] 2 Lloyd's Rep 142 .......... 8.18
Silven Properties Ltd v Royal Bank of Scotland plc [2003] EWCA Civ 1409, [2004] 4 All ER 484, [2004] 1 WLR 997 .......... 3.44; 8.13
Slavenburg's Bank NV v Intercontinental Natural Resources Ltd [1980] 1 All ER 955, [1980] 1 WLR 1076 .......... 1.43
Smith v Liquidator of James Birrell Ltd 1968 SLT 174 .......... 5.19, 5.21, 5.22

PARA

Smith v Lord Advocate (No 2) 1980 SC 227, 1981 SLT 19 .................... 4.88, 4.89
Smiths Ltd v Middleton [1979] 3 All ER 842 ................................ 2.28; 10.39
Snow (John) & Co Ltd v D B G Woodcroft & Co Ltd [1985] BCLC 54 .............. 5.08
South Western of Venezuela (Barquisimeto) Rly Co, Re [1902] 1 Ch 701, 71 LJ Ch 407 .................................................................... 2.29
Special Mouldings Ltd, Re (1987) (13 February, unreported) ...................... 3.55
Standard Chartered Bank Ltd v Walker [1982] 3 All ER 938, [1982] 1 WLR 1410, CA ............................................... 3.49, 3.50, 3.51; 7.04; 8.13

## T

Taylor, Petitioner 1981 SC 408, 1982 SLT 172 ................2.04, 2.13; 3.03, 3.12; 4.74, 4.78, 4.80, 4.81, 4.84, 4.85
Taymech Ltd v Rush & Tompkins Ltd 1990 SLT 681 .............. 2.17; 7.53; 8.15, 8.16
Telemetrix plc v Modern Engineers of Bristol (Holdings) plc [1985] BCLC 213, [1985] LS Gaz R 1561 ........................................... 3.66; 4.31, 4.40; 8.11
Telomatic Ltd, Re [1993] BCC 404, [1994] 1 BCLC 90 ............................ 1.46
Thomas v Todd [1926] 2 KB 511 ................................................ 3.59
Thompson v SCS Consulting Ltd [2001] IRLR 801 ................................. 6.30
Toynar Ltd v Whitbread & Co plc 1988 SLT 433 ........................... 1.28; 11.03
Trade Development Bank v Crittall Windows Ltd 1983 SLT 510 ..................... 4.12
Trade Development Bank v David W Haig (Bellshill) Ltd 1983 SLT 510 ............ 4.12
Trade Development Bank v Warriner & Mason (Scotland) Ltd 1980 SC 74, 1980 SLT 223 ........................................................................ 4.12
Transport and General Workers' Union v James McKinnon [2001] ICR 1281, [2001] IRLR 597 ............................................................. 6.33
Tudor Grange Holdings Ltd v Citibank NA [1992] Ch 53, [1991] 4 All ER 1, [1991] 3 WLR 750 .................................... 2.21, 2.23, 2.26; 6.02, 6.03
Turner v IRC 1994 SLT 811 ..................................................... 4.89

## U

United Railways of Havana and Regla Warehouses Ltd, Re [1960] Ch 52, [1959] 1 All ER 214, [1959] 2 WLR 251, CA ........................................ 5.36
University of Oxford (Chancellor, Master and Scholars) v Humphreys [2000] 1 All ER 996, [2000] 1 CMLR 647, [2000] IRLR 183, CA ..................... 6.33

## V

Victoria Housing Estates Ltd v Ashpurton Estates Ltd [1983] Ch 110, [1982] 3 All ER 665, [1982] 3 WLR 964, CA ......................................... 1.48

## W

Watts v Midland Bank plc [1986] BCLC 15, 2 BCC 98, 961 ................... 3.44, 3.48
Wheeler v Patel [1987] ICR 631, [1987] IRLR 211 ................................ 6.30
Woolwich Building Society v Taylor [1995] 1 BCLC 132 .......................... 4.47
Wylie and Lochhead v Mitchell (1870) 7 SLR 310, 42 J 258, 8 M 552 ........... 5.30, 5.46

## Y

Yagerphone Ltd, Re [1935] Ch 392, 104 LJ Ch 156 ................................ 2.37
Yeovil Glove Co Ltd, Re [1965] Ch 148, [1964] 2 All ER 849, [1964] 3 WLR 406, CA ...................................................... 8.53, 8.56, 8.57

## Z

Zahnrad Fabrik Passau GmbH v Terex Ltd 1986 SLT 84 ............... 5.19, 5.37, 5.38s

CHAPTER 1

# Appointment of receiver

## General introduction

**1.01** The Companies (Floating Charges and Receivers) (Scotland) Act 1972 ('the 1972 Act') introduced for the first time in Scotland the office of receiver thus enabling the holder of a floating charge (which form of security is available only to certain entities[1] and was itself first introduced into the law of Scotland in 1961) to appoint or seek the appointment by the court of a receiver over the property subject to the charge. Between 1961 and 1972 the only remedy available to the holder of a floating charge wishing to realise his security was to have the company placed in liquidation. Whether the whole or only part of the company's property was subject to the floating charge, the person so appointed after 1972 was known simply as a receiver. However, the IA 1985 introduced a distinction in such an appointment depending on the extent of the company's property covered by the floating charge. Where a receiver is now appointed by the holder of a floating charge in a case where the whole (or substantially the whole) of the company's property is attached by the floating charge then he is known as an administrative receiver.[2] The UK Government, after extensive consultation, has been anxious to promote entrepreneurial activity and perhaps to loosen the traditional protection of creditors' rights as part of the rescue culture. To that end the 2002 Act places restrictions on the holder of a floating charge to appoint an administrative receiver: still the distinction between a receiver and an administrative receiver is important under the 2002 Act. This distinction is also of importance in relation to administration orders, some new general insolvency provisions, and to the necessity to report to the Secretary of State on the conduct of directors of insolvent companies, but otherwise within the general context of receivership law is not of importance. Accordingly, all references in this book to a receiver or receivers include an administrative receiver or receivers and only where the latter are specifically referred to does it include such administrative receiver or receivers alone.[3] It should be remembered that the holder of a floating charge over the whole of the property of the company is entitled to restrict the property covered by the floating charge.[4] This could be a restriction to cover all the property other than a piece of land or building (which could be the subject of a standard security). With effect from 1 July 1999, the Scottish Parliament rather than the UK Parliament has the power to legislate in respect of receivers in most respects. From that date the Accountant in Bankruptcy is also given functions to administer. Interestingly, to maintain consistency across the UK, the Scottish Parliament passed over such power to the UK Parliament in connection with the enactment of the 2002 Act. Whom can the holder of the floating charge appoint as receiver?

1 See para 1.21 below.
2 IA 1986, s 251.
3 But see David A.Bennett's article in issue 67 (January 2004) of Business Law wherein he suggests that, due to drafting errors in the 2002 Act, it may still be possible if the post 2002 Act floating charge is worded appropriately to have a receiver appointed.
4 *Scottish & Newcastle Breweries plc v Ascot Inns Ltd (in receivership)* 1994 SLT 1140.

**1.02** Until the passing of the IA 1985, although there was previously no statutory requirement to do so, the person normally appointed in Scotland to be a receiver of a company was a chartered accountant experienced in insolvency matters. It should be emphasised that the appointment was and still is a personal one. A person who is not an individual is not qualified to act as an insolvency practitioner[1] and a person acts as an insolvency practitioner in relation to a company if he acts as its administrative receiver.[2]

1 IA 1986, s 390(1).
2 Ibid, s 388(1)(a).

**1.03** The Cork Report[1] stated at paragraph 735 that:

> 'One subject of much criticism is the absence of any requirement that insolvency practitioners should possess some minimum professional qualification. We have received a number of suggestions for remedying this deficiency, in an endeavour to ensure that insolvent estates are administered only by competent practitioners. It is significant that many of these proposals have been put forward by insolvency practitioners themselves.'

The Report[1] recommended at paragraph 756 that:

> '... some minimum professional qualification and control is necessary. It is essential that measures are introduced to ensure a high standard of competence as well as integrity in the persons who are eligible for appointment as insolvency practitioners.'

1 Report of the Review Committee on Insolvency Law and Practice (Cmnd 8558).

**1.04** The IA 1986[1] now provides that a person who is not an individual is not qualified to act as an insolvency practitioner nor is a person qualified to act as an insolvency practitioner at any time unless, at that time, he is authorised to act as an insolvency practitioner by virtue of being so authorised by a recognised professional body or holds an authorisation granted under section 393. Any person who acts as an insolvency practitioner in relation to a company at a time when he is not qualified to do so is liable:[2]

(a) on summary conviction, to imprisonment for a term not exceeding six months or to a fine not exceeding the statutory maximum or to both;
(b) on conviction on indictment, to imprisonment for a term not exceeding two years or to a fine or to both.

A person also commits an offence if he acts as a receiver while he is either an undischarged bankrupt or a bankruptcy restrictions order is in force in respect of him[3] (unless acting under an appointment made by the court).[4]

1 Section 390(1), (2).
2 Ibid, ss 398, 430 and Sch 10.
3 Section 31(1) as amended by the 2002 Act or s 56A or 56G of the Bankruptcy (Scotland) Act 1985, both to be further extended by paras 1 and 7 of Sch 4A of the Bankruptcy and Diligence etc (Scotland) Bill 2005.
4 Ibid, s 31(3).

**1.05** Section 390(3)[1] provides that a person is not qualified to act as an insolvency practitioner in relation to another person at any time unless:[2]

(a) there is in force at that time security or, in Scotland, caution for the proper performance of his functions; and
(b) that security or caution meets the prescribed requirements with respect to his acting in relation to that other person.

1 IA 1986.
2 the Scottish Rules.

**1.06** In terms of section 390(4),[1] a person is not qualified to act as an insolvency practitioner at any time if, at that time:

(a) he has been adjudged bankrupt or sequestration of his estate has been awarded and (in either case) he has not been discharged;
(b) he is subject to a disqualification order made under the Company Directors Disqualification Act 1986; or
(c) a bankruptcy restrictions order is in force in respect to him[2] ; or he is a patient within the meaning of Part VII of the Mental Health Act 1983 or section 125(1) of the Mental Health (Scotland) Act 1984; or he has had a guardian appointed to him in terms of the Adults with Incapacity (Scotland) Act 2000.

1 IA 1986.
2 Section 390(5) of the IA 1986 as inserted by the 2002 Act or s 56A or 56G of the Bankruptcy (Scotland) Act 1985, both to be further extended by paras 1 and 7 of Sch 4A of the Bankruptcy and Diligence etc (Scotland) Bill 2005.

**1.07** Under the professional rules of The Institute of Chartered Accountants of Scotland[1] where there has been a continuing professional relationship with a company, no principal or employee of the practice should accept appointment as receiver in relation to that company. A continuing professional relationship arises where a practice, or, subject to the following provisions, the principal or a current employee of a practice, is carrying out, or has during the three previous years carried out, professional work for a client.[2] Such a relationship commences at the date of appointment of a practice by a client, at the date of issue of letters of engagement or at the commencement of work, whichever is the earliest. The ethical rules also provide that although an isolated appointment for a particular assignment at some time during the three year period may not appear to constitute a continuing professional relationship, careful consideration should be given to the question of whether such an appointment could, or could be seen to, prejudice objectivity. A continual professional relationship would not normally arise where the relationship is one which springs from the appointment of the practice by, or at the instigation of, a creditor or other party having an actual or potential financial interest in a company or business to investigate, monitor or advise on its affairs, unless there has been a direct involvement in the management of the company or business.[3] Such a relationship may, however, arise where a practice has been appointed to carry out professional work for any director or shadow director of the company, and a member should take reasonable steps to ascertain whether such work has been performed prior to his or her acceptance of any insolvency appointment.[3]

1 *The Ethics of Insolvency Practice* issued by The Institute of Chartered Accountants of Scotland (May 1987; revised February 1989), para (9).
2 Op cit, para (12).
3 Op cit, para (13).

**1.08** When two practices merge, principals of the merged practice become subject to common ethical constraints in relation to accepting new insolvency appointments to clients of either of the former practices. However, existing appointments which are rendered in apparent breach of the guidance by such merger, need not be determined automatically, provided that a considered review of the situation by the practice discloses no obvious and immediate conflict, such as the need to sue a new colleague.[1] Where a principal or an employee of a practice has, in any former practice, undertaken work upon the affairs of a company in a capacity which is incompatible with an insolvency assignment of his or her new practice, he or she should not personally work or be employed on that assignment, save in the case of an employee of such junior status that his or her duties in the former practice did not involve the exercise of any professional judgment or discretion.[2] In practice, this means that if a firm of chartered accountants acts as auditors of a company, none of the partners or employees of that firm is eligible to accept appointment as the receiver of the company or if any of the partners or employees of the firm have been the receiver of a company, none of the partners or employees of the firm is eligible to accept appointment as liquidator of the company.

1 *The Ethics of Insolvency Practice* issued by the Institute of Chartered Accountants of Scotland (May 1987; revised February 1989), para (26).
2 Op cit, para (27).

**1.09** As there is a general trend for the governing bodies of insolvency practitioners to adopt common standards, it is not surprising to note the position under the professional rules of the Insolvency Practitioners Association. Under those rules, no partner or employee of a practice should accept appointment as administrative receiver in relation to a company where the practice or a partner in or a person at that time in the employment of the practice has, or during the previous three years has had, a continuing professional relationship with the company.[1] Continuing professional relationship commences at the date of appointment of a practice by a client, at the date of issue of letters of engagement or at the commencement of work, whichever is the earliest.[2] A continuing professional relationship would not normally arise where the relationship is one which springs from the appointment of a practice by, or at the instigation of, a creditor or other party having an actual or potential financial interest in a company or business to investigate, monitor or advise on its affairs, unless there has been a direct involvement in the management of the company or business.[3] Such a relationship may, however, arise where a practice has been appointed to carry out work for any director or shadow director of the company and a member should take reasonable steps to ascertain whether such work has been performed prior to his acceptance of any insolvency appointment.[3] Where a partner or an employee of a practice has, in any former practice, undertaken work upon the affairs of a company in a capacity which is incompatible with an insolvency assignment of his new practice, he should not personally work or be employed in that assignment, save in the case of an employee of such junior status that his duties in the former practice did not involve the exercise of any professional judgment or discretion.[4] The wording of the relevant provisions of the ethical code of the Insolvency Practitioners Association is almost exactly similar to the equivalent provisions applicable to members of The Institute of Chartered Accountants of Scotland and has also been adopted in similar form by the English and Irish Institutes of Chartered Accountants. For an interesting discussion on insolvency regulation, see Insolvency Regulation Working Party – A Review of Insolvency Practitioner Regulations (February 1999) and its principal recommendation, subsequently implemented, of the establishment of the Insolvency Practices Council.

1 *Guide to Professional Conduct and Ethics of the Insolvency Practitioners Association* (8 June 1987 edition), para (4).
2 Op cit, para (7).
3 Op cit, para (8).
4 Op cit, para (19).

## Authorisation of members of recognised professional bodies

**1.10** Section 390(2)[1] states that a member of a recognised professional body is authorised to act as an insolvency practitioner if he is permitted so to act by or under the rules of that body. The Secretary of State may by order declare a body which appears to him to fall within section 391(2)[1] to be a recognised professional body for the purposes of section 391 and any such order may be revoked by a further order if it appears to the Secretary of State that the body no longer falls within section 391(2).[2]

1 See IA 1986, s 391(1).
2 See ibid, s 391(4).

**1.11** A body may be recognised under section 391(1)[1] if it regulates the practice of a profession and maintains and enforces rules for securing that such of its members as are permitted by or under the rules to act as insolvency practitioners:

(a) are fit and proper persons so to act;
(b) meet acceptable requirements as to education and practical training and experience.

1 See IA 1986, s 391(2).

**1.12** An order under section 391[1] has effect from such date as is specified in the order and any such order revoking a previous order may make provision whereby members of the body in question continue to be treated as authorised to act as insolvency practitioners for a specified period after the revocation takes effect. Reference to members of a recognised professional body are references to persons who, whether members of that body or not, are subject to its rules in the practice of the profession in question.[2] The Secretary of State has determined that The Chartered Association of Certified Accountants, The Insolvency Practitioners Association, The Institute of Chartered Accountants in England and Wales, The Institute of Chartered Accountants in Ireland, The Institute of Chartered Accountants of Scotland, The Law Society and The Law Society of Scotland are recognised professional bodies for the purposes of section 391.[3] R3 is not a recognized professional body.

1 IA 1986.
2 Ibid, s 391(3).
3 Insolvency Practitioners (Recognised Professional Bodies) Order 1986, SI 1986/1764.

## Application for authorisation

**1.13** An application for authorisation under section 392[1] should contain or be accompanied by such information as the competent authority may reasonably require for the purposes of determining the application and should be accompanied by the prescribed fee. The competent authority is defined by section 392(2)[1] as (a) in relation to a case of any description specified in directions given by the Secretary of State, the body or person so specified in relation to cases of that description and (b) in relation to a case not falling within paragraph (a), the Secretary of State. There are provisions in section 392(4), (6), (7)[1] requiring the applicant to furnish additional information, making clear that directions and requirements given or imposed may differ as between different applications, requiring any information to be furnished to the competent authority, if it so requires, to be in such form or verified in such manner as it may specify and stating that an application for authorisation may be withdrawn before it is granted or refused. Any sums received by a competent authority under section 392(8)[1]other than the Secretary of State may be retained by that authority and any sums received under the same section by the Secretary of State must be paid into the Consolidated Fund.

1 IA 1986.

## Grant, refusal and withdrawal of authorisation

**1.14** In terms of section 393(1)[1] the authority may, on an application duly made in accordance with section 392[1] and after being furnished with all such information as it may require under that section, grant or refuse the application. An authorisation, in terms of section 393(3),[1] unless previously withdrawn, continues in force for such period not exceeding the prescribed maximum as may be specified in the authorisation. This is currently three years. [2] The competent authority is empowered to grant the application in terms of section 393(2)[1] if it appears to it from the information furnished by the applicant and having regard to such other information, if any, as it may have:

(a) that the applicant is a fit and proper person to act as an insolvency practitioner; and
(b) that the applicant meets the prescribed requirements with respect to education and practical training and experience.

Matters for determining whether an applicant is fit and proper and the education and training and experience requirements are set out in the Insolvency Practitioners Regulations 1990, SI 1990/439 regulations 4 to 8. The DTI also provides Guidance Notes that may be obtained from the web at www.insolvency.gov.uk. New regulations for determining whether an applicant is fit and proper and providing requirements relating to education and training are likely to be introduced with effect from around 1 April 2005 when the Insolvency Practitioners Regulations 2005 come into effect.

It is understood that there are presently 18 Scottish solicitors who are authorised by the Law Society of Scotland to hold insolvency licences, 120 Scottish chartered accountants who are authorized by The Institute of Chartered Accountants of Scotland and 4 by the DTI.

1 IA1986.
2 Insolvency Practitioners Regulations 1990, SI 1990/439, reg 11.

**1.15** The competent authority is empowered in terms of section 393(4)[1] to withdraw an authorisation issued pursuant to section 393(1)[1] if the holder of the authorisation is no longer a fit and proper person to act as an insolvency practitioner or without prejudice thereto, the holder of the authorisation has failed to comply with any provision of Part XIII of the IA 1986 or of any regulations made under that Part or Part XV or, in purported compliance with any such provision, has furnished the competent authority with false, inaccurate or misleading information. Where the competent authority grants an authorisation it must give notice of that fact to the applicant specifying the date on which the authorisation takes effect. When the competent authority proposes to refuse an application or to withdraw an authorisation under section 393(4),[1] it must give the applicant or holder of the authorisation written notice of its intention to do so, (usually referred to as 'a minded to' notice) setting out particulars of the grounds on which it proposes to act.[2] In the case of a proposed withdrawal the notice must state the date on which it is proposed that the withdrawal should take effect[3] and where an application is to be refused or an authorisation to be withdrawn, any such notice must give particulars of the rights exercisable under sections 395 and 396[4] by a person on whom the notice is served.

1 IA 1986.
2 Ibid, s 394(2).
3 Ibid, s 394(3).
4 Ibid, s 394(4).

**1.16** A person on whom a notice is served under section 394(2)[1] may within fourteen days after the date of service make written representations to the competent authority who must have regard to any representations made in determining whether to refuse the application or withdraw the authorisation, as the case may be.[2]

1 IA 1986.
2 Ibid, s 395.

## Reference to tribunal

**1.17** Section 396(2)[1] provides that a person on whom a notice is served under section 394(2)[1] may within twenty-eight days after the date of service give written notice to the competent authority requiring the case to be referred to the Insolvency Practitioners Tribunal in relation to which the provisions of Schedule 7[1] apply and the Insolvency Practitioners Tribunal (Conduct of Investigations) Rules 1986 SI 1986/952 apply. Where a requirement is made in accordance with section 396(2)[1] then, unless the relevant authority within the twenty-eight day period mentioned in section 396(2)[1] decides to grant the application or, as the case may be, decides not to withdraw the authorisation and gives written notice of that fact within seven days to the person by whom the requirement was made, it shall refer the case to the tribunal.[2]

1 IA 1986.
2 Ibid, s 396(3).

**1.18** On a reference pursuant to section 396,[1] the tribunal must investigate the case and make a report to the competent authority stating what would in their opinion be the appropriate decision in the matter and the reasons for that opinion and it is the duty of the competent authority to decide the matter accordingly.

The tribunal must send a copy of the report to the applicant or, as the case may be, the holder of the authorisation and the competent authority must serve him with a written notice of the decision made by it in accordance with the report.[2] The competent authority may, if it thinks fit, publish the report of the tribunal.[3]

1 IA 1986.
2 Ibid, s 397(2).
3 Ibid, s 397(3).

**1.19** Section 396(1)[1] provides for the continuation of the tribunal established by the IA 1985 for the purposes of section 396(2)[1] and the provisions of Schedule 7[1] apply to the operation of such a tribunal. Schedule 7[2] provides for the Secretary of State to draw up and from time to time to revise, firstly, (under para 1(1)(a)) a panel of persons who are barristers, advocates or solicitors in each case of not less than seven years' standing and are nominated for the purpose by the Lord Chancellor or by the Lord President of the Court of Session and, secondly, (under para 1(1)(b)) a panel of persons who are experienced in insolvency matters. The Secretary of State is entitled out of money provided by Parliament to pay to members of the tribunal such remuneration as may be approved by the Treasury and such expenses as may be approved by the Secretary of State and the Treasury.[3] The tribunal may sit either as a single tribunal or in two or more divisions[4] and their functions require to be exercised in relation to any case referred to them by three members consisting of a legal chairman (from the panel set up under para 1(1)(a)) and two other members (from the panel set up under para 1(1)(b)).[5] Any investigation by the tribunal requires to be so conducted as to afford a reasonable opportunity for representations to be made to the tribunal by or on behalf of the person whose case is the subject of the investigation.[6] For the purposes of any such investigation, the tribunal may require any person to attend by notice in writing, to give evidence or produce any books, papers and other records in his possession or under his control which the tribunal considers it necessary to examine for the purpose of its investigation and may take evidence on oath and for that purpose administer oaths. No person is required to go more than ten miles from his place of residence unless the necessary expenses of his attendance are paid or tendered to him.[7] Every person who fails to attend a tribunal without reasonable excuse or who suppresses or refuses to produce any document which the tribunal may require shall be liable to a fine on summary conviction.[8] While not having a concern about the appeal procedure from a decision of a recognized professional body, there could be a potential problem under Article 6(1) of the Convention on Human Rights where the appeal is from a decision by the Secretary of State and it is a tribunal chosen by the Secretary of State from panels drawn up by the Secretary of State and paid for by the Secretary of State.[9]

1 IA 1986.
2 Ibid, Sch 7, para 1(1).
3 Ibid, para 2.
4 Ibid, para 3(1).
5 Ibid, para 3(2).
6 Ibid, para 4(1).

7 Ibid, para 4(2).
8 Ibid, para 4(3).
9 *Cable v United Kingdom* (18 February 1999, unreported), ECHR.

## Power of holder of floating charge to appoint receiver

**1.20** The 2002 Act[1] has restricted the holder of a floating charge created after the effective date therein, namely 15 September 2003[2], from appointing an administrative receiver, other than in one of the excepted circumstances set out in that Act, and detailed in Appendix 14.[3] The terms of the 2002 Act may not be contracted out of.[4] Where not so restricted, in terms of section 51 of the IA 1986, it is competent under the law of Scotland for the holder of a floating charge (including a floating charge subsisting as such at the commencement of the 1972 Act) over all or any part of the property (including uncalled capital) which may from time to time be comprised in the property and undertaking of an incorporated company (whether a company within the meaning of the 1985 Act or not) which the Court of Session has jurisdiction to wind up, to appoint a receiver of such part of the property of the company as is subject to the charge.

1 By introducing s 72A to the IA 1986.
2 Enterprise Act 2002 (Commencement No 4 and Transitional Provisions and Savings) Order 2003, SI 2003/2093.
3 But see fn 3 to 1.01.
4 Section 72A(4).

**1.21** In most cases the appointment will be as receiver of a company limited by shares incorporated in Scotland under the Companies Acts but section 51 of the IA 1986 does state that a receiver may be appointed over the property of any incorporated company which the Court of Session has jurisdiction to wind up. It is, therefore, possible[1] to appoint a receiver over the property of a company limited by guarantee or an unlimited company or an overseas company[2] or a company incorporated by private act of Parliament or by a Royal Charter or an EEIG[3] or a limited liability partnership[4] or an open-ended investment company[5],but not a company incorporated under the Industrial and Provident Societies Act 1965 (as the sheriff court has exclusive jurisdiction over them under section 59(a)(ii))

1 IA 1986, s 120.
2 Ibid, s 225.
3 European Economic Grouping Regulations 1989 (SI 1989/638).
4 Limited Liability Partnership Act 2000, s 14.
5 Open-Ended Investment Companies (Investment Companies with Variable Capital) Regulations 1996 (SI 1996/2827).

## Power of court to appoint receiver

**1.22** Subject to the terms of the 2002 Act, in terms of section 51(2) of the IA 1986, it is competent under the law of Scotland for the court, on the application of the holder of a floating charge to appoint a receiver of such part of the property of the company as is subject to the charge. It is worth observing that in the years since the 1972 Act came into operation the majority of (if not all) receiverships have resulted from appointments by the holders of floating charges the authors are unaware of any appointments made by the court. The reason is, of course, that it is much simpler, quicker and less expensive for the holder of a floating charge to appoint a receiver by instrument in writing rather than seeking an appointment by a petition to the court. It is possible that an appointment by the court would be authorised if there was doubt as to whether an appointment by the holder of a floating charge had been validly made or, perhaps, where the court is satisfied that the position of the holder of the charge is likely to be prejudiced if no such appointment is made,[1] or where the holder of the floating charge is unable to make a quick appointment under the terms of the floating charge.

1 IA 1986, s 52(2)(a).

**1.23** It should be noted that the holder of a floating charge in terms of section 51(1) of the IA 1986 has power to appoint a receiver in the case of a floating charge created before the 1972 Act (by which receivers were first introduced into the law of Scotland) came into force and good practice in the years since then has normally involved the holder of a floating charge entering into an instrument of alteration (which incidentally does not require to be registered with the Registrar of Companies provided that it does not affect the ranking of securities or otherwise bring it within the ambit of section 466(3) and 466(4) of the 1985 Act) with the charging company whereby it is agreed that in certain specified circumstances additional to those set out in the IA 1986, the holder of the floating charge has power to appoint a receiver. It is unlikely that these provisions will ever be invoked.

## Form of wording

**1.24** The normal form of wording in a typical floating charge giving power to appoint a receiver is as follows:

> 'At any time after any of the sums secured by the floating charge hereby created shall have become due and payable or after the chargee shall have been requested by us in writing so to do, the chargee shall have power by instrument in writing to appoint any person or persons, whether an officer or officers of the chargee or not, to be a receiver or receivers of our property and assets and may in like manner appoint any person or persons to be a receiver or receivers in place of any receiver removed by the court or otherwise who ceases to act.'

**1.25** While every floating charge creditor will wish an unfettered right to appoint a receiver in appropriate circumstances, in the majority of cases the charging company requests the chargee to appoint a receiver either at its own instigation or at the suggestion of the chargee. Often this will follow the directors having been advised that they risk being accused of wrongful trading if they continue to trade. The banks have in recent years been very reluctant to appoint receivers and risk the adverse publicity and have spent more time trying to assist customers to trade out of their problems or find a friendly purchaser for the whole company.

**1.26** The powers of the receiver are those given by the instrument that creates the charge and are supplemented, insofar as not inconsistent with them, by the powers specified in Schedule 2 to the IA 1986.[1]

1 IA 1986, s 55.

## Circumstances justifying appointment by holder of charge

**1.27** The circumstances justifying the appointment of a receiver are set out in section 52 of the IA 1986 where it is provided that a receiver may be appointed by the holder of the floating charge under section 51(1) of that Act on the occurrence of any event which, by the provision of the instrument creating the charge, entitles the holder of the charge to make that appointment and, in so far as not otherwise provided for by the instrument, on the occurrence of any of the following events, namely:

(a) the expiry of a period of twenty-one days after the making of a demand for payment of the whole or any part of the principal sum secured by the charge, without payment having been made;
(b) the expiry of a period of two months during the whole of which interest due and payable under the charge has been in arrears;
(c) the making of an order or the passing of a resolution to wind up the company;
(d) the appointment of a receiver by virtue of any other floating charge created by the company.

The events that would entitle a chargeholder to appoint a receiver could be many and varied. A minor breach such as a failure to provide management information timeously without a threat by the chargeholder to appoint may not be sufficient to justify an appointment whereas a failure to pay on demand would be.[1]

1 See paras 1.35 and 1.36 below.

**1.28** On a demand being served, it is open to the company to apply for an interim interdict against the chargeholder prohibiting it from appointing a receiver, if it is disputed that the charge has been breached. Most banks would have caveats lodged however to avoid being caught unaware by this. In the case of *Toynar Ltd v Whitbread & Co plc*,[1] an interesting discussion took place in the context of an attempt by a company to seek suspension of the appointment of joint receivers and interdict against their continuing to act in that capacity.

The facts were that the joint receivers had been appointed following upon failure of the company to pay interest for a period of two months although this fact was disputed by the company. The company had later paid over a sum in excess of the amounts then outstanding which had been applied by the holder of the floating charge towards the repayment of capital. The Lord Ordinary refused the company's motion for interim suspension and interim interdict and held that the company had a reasonable prospect of establishing that interest had not been in arrears for the two month period. However, he concluded, having regard to the balance of convenience and, in particular (a) that any prejudice caused to the company following upon the advertisement of the appointment of the joint receivers had already occurred, (b) the sole asset of the company was a public house and it appeared to be entirely attached by the interest of the holder of the floating charge and (c) it was undesirable to have further changes in the management of the public house following upon the appointment of joint receivers in all the circumstances, it was appropriate not to grant the interim interdict.

1 1988 SLT 433.

**1.29** However, the company appealed to the Second Division on the grounds that it was not appropriate to consider the balance of convenience when a strong prima facie case was made out. The Second Division held that the Lord Ordinary had only reached the conclusion that the company had reasonable prospects of establishing its case, and that stage having been reached, it was necessary to consider the balance of convenience, the test of which had been correctly applied by the Lord Ordinary. In the course of the opinion of the Second Division, reference was made to *Group 4 Total Security Ltd v Ferrier*,[1] *NWL Ltd v Woods*[2] and *Reed Stenhouse (UK) Ltd v Brodie*.[3] In particular, the speech of Lord Fraser in *NWL Ltd v Woods*, an English case, was carefully considered. At page 1310, Lord Fraser stated:

> 'In Scotland, the practice is otherwise, and the court is in use to have regard to the relative strength of the cases put forward in averment and argument by each party at the interlocutory stage as one of the many factors that may go to make up the balance of convenience. That is certainly in accordance with my own experience as Lord Ordinary, and I believe the practice of other judges in the Court of Session was the same. Whether the likelihood of success should be regarded as one of the elements of the balance of convenience, or as a separate matter, seems to me an academic question of no real importance, but my inclination is in favour of the former alternative. It seems to make good sense; if the pursuer or petitioner appears very likely to succeed at the end of the day, it would tend to be convenient to grant interim interdict and thus prevent the defender or respondent from infringing his rights, but if the defender or respondent appears very likely to succeed at the end of the day, it will tend to be convenient to refuse interim interdict because an interim interdict would probably only delay the exercise of the defender's legal activities.'

1 1985 SLT 287.
2 [1979] 1 WLR 1294, HL.
3 1986 SLT 354.

**1.30** Some debate took place as to whether the Lord Ordinary had reached any conclusions as to the strength of the case. The Lord Ordinary had stated: 'I have therefore come to the conclusion on the limited information before me that the petitioners have reasonable prospects of establishing that interest had not been in arrears for two months at the date of the appointment of the joint receivers.' The Second Division held that what the Lord Ordinary had said regarding the petitioner's prospects was no more than that they had a prima facie case or to quote the words used in *Reed Stenhouse (UK) Ltd v Brodie*[1] 'But manifestly there is a case to argue and a case to answer.'

1 1986 SLT 354 at 358.

**1.31** The Second Division also approved a submission by counsel for the respondents to the effect that if the petitioners were successful at the end of the day, they would have a remedy of damages and that remedy would be against a large public company. On the other hand, if the respondents were to succeed at the end of the day, and were prevented from selling the premises at the present time because of an interim order granted by the court, then the respondents would suffer considerable prejudice, and any action of damages which they might have would be against a company which if not insolvent, would certainly be in financial difficulty. It was clear that there was a dispute between the parties as to the true value of the premises but the Second Division considered it was significant that the premises had apparently been offered for sale for some time and that the only firm offer which had been received was the one which the joint receivers were proposing to accept. The case is important in the sense that it gives guidance to the balance of convenience argument in the context of the circumstances justifying appointment by the holder of a floating charge.

## Circumstances justifying appointment by the court

**1.32** A receiver may, in terms of section 52(2) be appointed by the court under section 51(2) of the IA 1986 on the occurrence of any event which, by the provisions of the instrument creating the floating charge, entitles the holder of the charge to make that appointment and, in so far as not otherwise provided for by the instrument, on the occurrence of any of the following events, namely:

(a) where the court, on the application of the holder of the charge, pronounces itself satisfied that the position of the holder of the charge is likely to be prejudiced if no such appointment is made;
(b) the expiry of a period of 21 days after the making of a demand for payment of the whole or any part of the principal sum secured by the charge, without payment having been made;

(c) the expiry of a period of two months during the whole of which interest due and payable under the charge has been in arrears;
(d) the making of an order or the passing of a resolution to wind up the company.

## Mode of appointment by holder of charge

**1.33** Section 53(1) of the IA 1986 provides that the appointment of a receiver by the holder of the floating charge under section 51(1) of the IA 1986 shall be by means of an instrument subscribed in accordance with the Requirements of Writing (Scotland) Act 1995 ('the instrument of appointment'), a copy (certified in the prescribed manner to be a correct copy) whereof shall be delivered by or on behalf of the person making the appointment to the Registrar of Companies and the Accountant in Bankruptcy[1] for registration within seven days of its execution and shall be accompanied by a notice in the prescribed form[2]. Although section 53(1) makes reference only to the copy being of the instrument of appointment, the prescribed form which must accompany it requires a certified copy of the instrument of appointment, with docquets of receipt and acceptance (see paragraphs 1.39 and 1.40) endorsed on it. If any person without reasonable excuse makes default in complying with the requirements of section 53(1) he is liable to a fine and, for continued contravention, to a daily default fine. It should be noted that failure to lodge the proper particulars with the Registrar of Companies or the Accountant in Bankruptcy does not affect the validity of the appointment but only renders the person who is responsible for lodging the particulars liable to a fine.

1 Scotland Act 1998.
2 The Scottish Rules.

## Execution of instrument of appointment

**1.34** Section 53(1) of the IA 1986 was amended with effect from 1 August 1995 to provide that the instrument of appointment requires to be subscribed in accordance with the Requirements of Writing (Scotland) Act 1995. Schedule 2 paragraph 3 thereof states that unless an enactment provides otherwise (which section 53 does not), where a granter of a document is a company, the document is signed by the company if it is signed on its behalf by a director, or by the secretary of the company, or by a person authorized to sign the document on its behalf. For subscription by others, such as an individual, a partnership or other bodies corporate, reference is made to the Requirements of Writing (Scotland) Act 1995. There is no requirement for the deed to be probative.

If the receiver is to be appointed by the holders of a series of secured debentures, the instrument must be executed on behalf of the holders of the floating charge by any person authorized by resolution of the debentureholders to execute the instrument[1].

1 Requirements of Writing (Scotland) Act 1995, s 14(1), Sch 4, para 58(b) as from 1 August 1995.

**1.35** Without prejudice to the statutory provisions, the instrument creating a floating charge will often provide that at any time the holder of a floating charge may on demand require payment of all sums due and failure by the borrower to do so after the expiry of a period of twenty-four hours will entitle the holder of the floating charge to appoint a receiver. Such entitlement to so appoint a receiver is only appropriate where the holder of the floating charge is able to require payment of the debt on demand and would not be appropriate, for example, in the case of a fixed term loan unless a default provision had been breached, or where the charging company is bound to implement some form of obligation either on its own account or on account of a third party. As to the effect of a demand for payment without specifying a time for payment where the debt is repayable on demand, it has been argued that if a creditor requires payment 'on demand', the debtor, in the absence of a definition of these words in the floating charge, is bound to repay the debt immediately. It is respectfully suggested that a court in construing the meaning of the words 'on demand' would, in all probability, allow the debtor a reasonable opportunity to repay the debt rather than insist on immediate repayment. In the context of a debtor and creditor relationship involving an 'on demand' facility, it is suggested that a period of twenty-four hours from the making of the demand for repayment affords the debtor a reasonable opportunity to repay the debt without serious prejudice to the creditor. While there is contrary authority in England, the authors have certainly experienced in practice a demand for payment and, in the absence of clarification of the word 'demand' in the floating charge, a discretionary period of twenty-four hours was then given to the debtor to make payment. A substantial repayment (approximately 75 per cent of the outstanding debt) was then received within such period of twenty-four hours together with reasonable proposals for discharge of the balance of the outstanding debt within a period of three months thereafter, thereby rendering the proposed appointment of a receiver likely to be inappropriate for a reputable lender. While the authors would respectfully agree with the views[1] expressed in St John Clair and Drummond Young in their book *The Law of Corporate Insolvency in Scotland*, the fact remains that a very practical example experienced by the authors underpins their view that in most cases a period of 24 hours after formal demand will be appropriate in the absence of strong extenuating circumstances such as prejudice to the holder of the floating charge where a shorter period may be justified in line with established English authorities.[2]

1 Third Edition (2004), para 6.28.
2 *Bank of Baroda v Panessar* [1987] Ch 335.

**1.36** In England, there is authority for the view that 'on demand' means that a demand for payment may be requested and a receiver appointed within two hours thereafter. In *Bank of Baroda v Panessar*,[1] the debtor companies reputedly exceeded their overdraft limits and in due course the bank, under powers contained in the debenture in its favour, duly made demands for 'all moneys due to us' but which did not specify the precise amount of the debt. After the demands had been duly served, the bank appointed receivers about one hour later. The court held that there was no need for the bank to specify the precise amount of the debt in making a demand for the moneys due thereunder. It was only necessary to give such time as was necessary for the debtor to implement the mechanics of payment needed to discharge the debt before being in default and that in view of the modern methods of communication and transfer of money available, the time needed was exceptionally short. The court approved the earlier English case of *RA Cripps & Son Ltd v Wickenden*.[2] Most floating charges in favour of banks state that a simple certificate signed by any one of certain senior officials of the holder of the floating charge (eg director, secretary, manager or other authorised signatory) shall determine the amount of indebtedness of a debtor company at any given time. In all cases, it is very important to ensure that, where a demand for payment is made by the holder of the floating charge, the person signing the certificate falls within the category of persons authorised to do so in terms of the floating charge.

1 [1987] Ch 335.
2 [1973] WLR 944.

**1.37** In one case,[1] the bond and floating charge provided that the notice had to be 'in writing signed by a Managing Director, Deputy Managing Director, Regional General Manager, Secretary or Chief Accountant of the Bank'. The notice sent to the company was signed by the bank's law secretary 'P General Manager JSW' and the company sought to reduce the instrument of appointment of the receiver on the ground that the notice was invalid, it not having been signed by one of the five named officials of the bank. The bank contended that the requirement that the notice be 'signed by' one of the named officials was habile to cover signature by another authorised person. Lord Allanbridge held that:

(1) the wording of the bond was clear and precise and required that the notice be signed by one of the five specified officials;
(2) the list was exhaustive and there was no room for any relaxation of the clear words in the bond by allowing someone else to sign either on behalf of the bank or on behalf of one of the five named officials;
(3) the notice, an essential step in the appointment of the receiver, was invalid; and
(4) consequently, the instrument of appointment was invalid as it proceeded upon an invalid notice.

1 *Elwick Bay Shipping Co Ltd v Royal Bank of Scotland Ltd* 1982 SLT 62.

## Effective date of appointment and notification to the Registrar

**1.38** Following the subscription of the instrument of appointment, there are three distinct events that follow. The first is the receipt of the instrument by the proposed receiver or on his behalf. The second is the acceptance by the receiver of the appointment. The third is the notification to the Registrar of Companies and the Accountant in Bankruptcy.

## Receipt of the instrument of appointment

**1.39** The receipt of the instrument of appointment may be by the receiver or on his behalf. There is an obligation to docquet the instrument of appointment to evidence receipt of it in terms of section 53(6)(b) and the actual time of day would be stated. The docquet can be either by the receiver or on his behalf. Subject to the receiver accepting the appointment, this is the point when the receivership commences. The appointment of joint receivers is deemed to be made on the day of and at the time at which the instrument of appointment is received by the last of them as evidenced by the written docquet.

## Acceptance of appointment

**1.40** The receiver, to be validly appointed, requires to accept verbally or in writing the appointment before the end of the business day next following that on which the instrument of appointment is received by him or on his behalf. Section 251 of the IA 1986 defines a business day as meaning any day other than a Saturday, a Sunday, Christmas Day, Good Friday or a day which is a bank holiday in any part of Great Britain. As soon as possible after his acceptance the receiver shall endorse a written docquet to that effect on the instrument of appointment and deliver a copy of the endorsed instrument of appointment to the holder of the floating charge or his agent. If there are joint receivers, it is the joint receiver who last endorses his docquet of acceptance who is required to send a copy of the instrument of appointment to the holder of the floating charge or his agent. Where the instrument provides for joint receivers, the appointment of any of them shall be of no effect unless the appointment is accepted by all of them within the aforementioned timescale.

## Notification to the Registrar of Companies and the Accountant in Bankruptcy

**1.41** The person making the appointment or someone on his behalf requires to deliver within seven days of its execution a copy of the instrument of appointment to the Registrar of Companies and the Accountant in Bankruptcy together with a notice in the prescribed form (see 1.33 above). In terms of section 53(5) of the IA 1986, on receipt of the certified copy of the instrument of appointment in accordance with section 53(1), the Registrar is required on payment of the prescribed fee (currently none is payable) to enter the particulars of the appointment in the register of charges.

## Attachment to property covered by floating charge

**1.42** In terms of section 53(7) of the IA 1986, on the appointment of the receiver under section 53, the floating charge by virtue of which the receiver was appointed attaches to the property then subject to the charge and such attachment has effect as if the charge were a fixed security over the property to which it has attached. In terms of Section 462 of the CA 1985 a floating charge may be created over all or any part of the property (including uncalled capital) which may from time to time be comprised in its property and undertaking. Detailed discussions on attachment to the property on the appointment of a receiver and the importance of the expression 'property and undertaking' are contained in Chapter 2 paragraphs 2.04 to 2.06.

## Failure to register floating charge

**1.43** Section 410(2) of the 1985 Act provides that certain charges, including floating charges, created by a company are, so far as any security is conferred, void against the liquidator or administrator or any creditor of the company unless delivered for registration within twenty-one days of their creation along with the prescribed particulars. If the Registrar refuses to accept the registration in the belief that it does not need to be registered, compliance will have been effected by delivery to the Registrar.[1] If the form submitted with the charge contains errors other than the prescribed particulars the registration and the charge will still be effective, even if by having the wrong company number on the form this has resulted in the Registrar filing the charge in the wrong register[2]. A charge which has not been registered is not by this section made void against the company[3] but only against the liquidator or administrator or any creditor of the company and as long as the company is a going concern it is only void against and so postponed to claims of creditors who have a security on the property subject to the charge. Failure to register does however make the debt instantly repayable[4]. As far as ordinary creditors are concerned their protection is that an unregistered charge is void against the liquidator or administrator and so, in a liquidation or an administration, the holder of such a charge ranks as an ordinary unsecured creditor.

1 *Slavenburg's Bank NV v Intercontinental Natural Resources Ltd* [1980] 1 All ER 955.
2 *Grove v Advantage Healthcare (T10) Ltd* [2000] 1 BCLC 661.
3 *Independent Automatic Sales Ltd v Knowles and Foster* [1962] 3 All ER 27.
4 CA 1985, s 410(3).

**1.44** As an unregistered floating charge is valid as between the holder and the company, the appointment of a receiver is otherwise valid as between them but not against the liquidator or administrator or other creditors of the company although a receiver appointed under such a charge may act until a liquidator or administrator is appointed.[1] He would of course be required to account to a liquidator or administrator for any assets in his hands. While such a receiver in these circumstances might be granted an indemnity under section 63(2) of the

IA 1986, he would almost certainly be reluctant to accept appointment until either the charge is registered after the court had granted an extension of the time for registration or he was granted a satisfactory indemnity from the holder of the floating charge before accepting the appointment.

1 *Burston Finance Ltd v Speirway Ltd* [1974] 1 WLR 1648.

## Rectification of register

**1.45** The court, on being satisfied that the omission to register a charge within the time required by the 1985 Act or that the omission or mis-statement of any particular with respect to any such charge or in a memorandum of satisfaction was accidental, or due to inadvertence or some other sufficient cause, or is not of a nature to prejudice the position of creditors or shareholders of the company, or that it is on other grounds just and equitable to grant relief, may, on the application of the company or any person interested, and on such terms and conditions as seem to the court just and expedient, order that the time for registration shall be extended or (as the case may be) that the omission or mis-statement shall be rectified.[1]

1 CA 1985, s 420 as amended by CA 1989.

**1.46** The effect of such relief will be that the time for registering the charge in question will be extended to allow registration to take place. The Court of Session approved late registration in the unreported case of *Petition of Monklands District Council* (1980). In that case, the district council failed to register a fixed charge and sought relief under the provisions of section 106G of the 1948 Act[1] after the company which had granted the charge went into receivership. It was explained to the court that there would be some prejudice to ordinary creditors if late registration was permitted, but the prejudice for the secured creditor if late registration was not permitted was receiving a very small dividend rather than more or less the full repayment of all sums due by the company which had granted the charge. If late registration was not allowed, the addition of the money purportedly secured by the charge would only increase the dividend to ordinary creditors to a minimal extent bearing in mind the large deficiency to ordinary creditors. Once the failure to register is discovered, it must be dealt with expeditiously.[2]

1 Re-enacted as the CA 1985, s 420.
2 *Re Telomatic Ltd* [1993] BCC 404.

**1.47** An interesting discourse on the interaction of two standard securities is contained in *Bank of Scotland v TA Neilson & Co.*[1] In that case, one standard security was correctly executed, recorded in the Register of Sasines and registered with the Registrar of Companies. Another standard security over the same subjects was also executed at or about the same time, was recorded in the Register of Sasines but was not registered with the Registrar of Companies. There was contained within the competently created security a ranking clause postponing that security to one created in favour of the party whose security had not been registered with the Registrar of Companies. It was thought that a freshly created security to replace the defective one, provided it was properly registered with the Registrar of Companies, would cure the problem but the court held that there was nothing wrong with the first standard security and there was therefore no defect to be cured in terms of section 143 of the Titles to Land Consolidation (Scotland) Act 1868. The error, if there was one, lay in the failure to secure the registration of the charge within twenty-one days of the original recording of the standard security. The court held that, in a competition between the respective charges, the charge which had been competently created at the outset should be ranked and preferred to the unregistered charge albeit that the originally proposed ranking was in the reverse.

1 1990 SC 284.

**1.48** A discussion on failure to register a charge within twenty-one days also took place in *Victoria Housing Estates Ltd v Ashpurton Estates Ltd*[1] where a housing association (Victoria) took a legal charge from a borrowing company (Ashpurton) which was a subsidiary of a group of companies. In November 1980 Victoria demanded payment of all indebtedness and when payment was not forthcoming a receiver was appointed on 6 January 1981. On 27 February 1981 Victoria discovered that the legal charge had never been registered with the Registrar of Companies but nonetheless decided to proceed with the realisations rather than apply to the court for an extension of time under section 101 of the 1948 Act.[2] Section 101[2] only applied where the court was satisfied that the omission to register a charge within the required period was accidental, or due to inadvertence, or to some other sufficient cause, or was not likely to prejudice the position of creditors or shareholders. On 15 May 1981 the board of Ashpurton decided to call an extraordinary general meeting to consider a resolution to wind up and on 12 June Ashpurton went into voluntary liquidation. Realising its position, Victoria issued proceedings on 4 June 1981 under section 101.[2] If it was successful in these proceedings Victoria would have recovered almost all of Ashpurton's indebtedness, but if it ranked as an ordinary creditor it would only have received about 16p in the pound. The court eventually confirmed a decision of the court registrar to the effect that an extension of time should not be granted both on the ground of lack of evidence of inadvertence by Victoria and on the ground of Ashpurton's impending liquidation. Lord Brightman in his judgment concluded as follows:

> '... when an unregistered chargee discovers his mistake, he should apply without delay for an extension of time if he desires to register; and the court, when asked to exercise its discretion, should look askance at a chargee who deliberately defers his application in order to see which way the wind is going to blow.'

It has been held subsequently[3] that, notwithstanding the *Re Ashpurton* decision, the court may make an order pursuant to section 101 to extend the time for registration of a charge in exceptional circumstances even though liquidation proceedings have commenced.

1 [1983] Ch 110, CA; *Barclays Bank plc v Stuart Landon Ltd* [2001] 2 BCLC 316, CA.
2 Re-enacted as the CA 1985, s 404; substituted by CA 1989.
3 *Re RM Arnold & Co Ltd* [1984] BCLC 535.

**1.49** In *Re Chantry House Developments plc*[1] a case relating to a section 404 order, the Halifax Building Society had advanced money to Chantry House in relation to a land development to be secured by mortgage over the land. By an oversight, the charge was not registered with the Companies Registry. One of the points before the court was whether the court should grant an order under section 404. It was established that the failure to register the charge had been due to inadvertence and it would be just and equitable that an order should be granted under section 404 to secure to the Halifax Building Society the security to which it had originally been entitled. However, in view of the company's continuing financial decline, it was thought that the amount payable to unsecured creditors in a winding-up would reduce from approximately 9p in the £1 to 3p in the £1. The court was concerned that the unsecured creditors had not had an opportunity of being heard before the court. In the circumstances, the court agreed to make the order for rectification in favour of the Halifax Building Society on condition that, within a reasonable period, the company would arrange for its substantial unsecured creditors (those creditors having a debt owing in excess of £25,000) to be informed of the section 404 order and of their right to have it discharged. The position was accepted by the Halifax Building Society who also acknowledged the right of the court to vary the terms of the order for rectification. The order may be conditional and is discretionary. However in *Registrar of Companies ex p. Central Bank of India*[2] it was thought that the ordinary creditors did not have sufficient interest to be protected if an extension of time was to be granted unless there was a winding up happening or fraud was involved.

1 [1990] BCC 646.
2 [1986] QB 1114, CA.

## Avoidance of certain floating charges

**1.50** Section 245 of the IA 1986 contains provisions that on the appointment of an administrator, floating charges may in certain circumstances be set aside.

**1.51** Section 245 of the IA 1986 provides that, floating charges created within certain periods[1] are invalid, except to the extent provided, unless in the case of some such charges the company is and remains on the creation of the charge able to pay its debts. These periods are:

(1) In the case of a charge in favour of a person connected with the company, within two years of –
    (a) where an administrator is appointed by an administration order, the date on which the administration application is made;

   (b) where an administrator is appointed following the filing with the court of a copy of notice of intention to appoint, the date on which the copy of the notice is filed; or
   (c) the date of the commencement of the winding up.

   For this purpose a connected person is a director or shadow director (ie a person in accordance with whose directions or instructions the directors are accustomed to act) of the company or an associate of either;

(2) in the case of a charge in favour of any other person, within twelve months of any of the events mentioned in (1) above except that in such a case the charge will not be invalid unless at the date of the creation of the charge the company either –
   (a) is unable to pay its debts within the meaning of section 123 of the IA 1986; or
   (b) becomes unable to so pay its debts in consequence of the transaction under which the charge is created; and

(3) in the case of a charge in favour of a person whether connected or not, at a time between the making of an administration application in respect of the company and the making of an administration order on that application; or at a time between the filing with the court of a copy of notice of intention to appoint an administrator and the making of such appointment.

1 IA 1986, s 245(3).

**1.52** Floating charges created within these periods are invalid (with the exception in the circumstances mentioned of charges in favour of unconnected persons) except to the extent of the aggregate of:

(a) the value of so much of the consideration for the creation of the charge as consists of money paid, or goods or services supplied, to the company at the same time as, or after, the creation of the charge;
(b) the value of so much of that consideration as consists of the discharge or reduction, at the same time as, or after, the creation of the charge[1], of any debt of the company; and
(c) the amount of such interest (if any) as is payable on the foregoing amount in pursuance of any agreement under which the money was paid or the goods or services supplied.[2]

1 *Power v Sharp Investments Ltd* [1993] 1 BCC 609.
2 IA 1986, s 245(2).

**1.53** For these purposes, the value of any goods or services supplied by way of consideration for a floating charge is the amount in money which at the time of their supply could reasonably have been expected to be obtained for supplying them in the ordinary course of business and on the same terms (apart from the consideration) as those on which they were supplied to the company.

**1.54** While a floating charge may be completely invalidated under the provisions of section 245 of the IA 1986, the charge only is invalidated and not the validity or enforceability of the debt (except on the grounds of fraudulent preference),[1] the repayment of which prior to liquidation by a receiver cannot except on such grounds be attacked.[2]

1 *Re Parkes Garage (Swadlincote) Ltd* [1929] 1 Ch 139.
2 *Mace Builders (Glasgow) Ltd v Lunn* [1987] Ch 191, CA.

**1.55** The consequences of these various statutory provisions relating to the validity of certain floating charges are that any receiver appointed under a charge created within the periods specified, or referred to by reference in sections 242, 243 or 245 of the IA 1986, should only act before the expiry of the relative period or periods if satisfied after full enquiry that the charge is valid in whole or in part, or, alternatively, after obtaining a satisfactory indemnity from the holder of the charge. In the case of a floating charge not open to challenge under these statutory provisions, a receiver will also require to satisfy himself that such charge is not open to challenge at common law as a fraudulent preference or by statute as an unfair preference.[1]

1 IA 1986, s 244.

## Checking the validity of the appointment

**1.56** Over the years the points that need to be checked to confirm the validity of the appointment by the holder of the floating charge have changed. The position since the 4 February 1991 when the changes introduced by the 1989 Act to the 1985 Act were introduced has been more straightforward. Currently, as well as considering the validity or otherwise of the charge in light of the matters discussed in paragraphs 1.45 to 1.55 inclusive, the following documents should be examined:

(a) a copy of the floating charge (a style of which is given in Appendix 1) to ascertain the property subject to the charge, that the charge has been properly constituted and executed and that the holder had power to appoint a receiver in the particular circumstances;
(b) a copy of the certificate of registration of the charge to ensure that the charge has been registered with the Registrar of Companies within twenty-one days of its date of creation, bearing in mind that in terms of section 418 of the 1985 Act the certificate of the Registrar is conclusive evidence that the requirements as to registration have been complied with.[1] A mistake in the company's registered number on registration of a charge does not invalidate the charge on the basis that it is not 'a particular of the charge' that requires registration;[2]
(c) evidence of the circumstances justifying appointment: for example, where the receiver has been appointed on the written request of the company, a copy of the board minute of the company resolving to request the appointment of a receiver (a style of which is given in Appendix 2) and a copy of the letter from the company to the floating charge holder requesting such appointment (a style of which is given in Appendix 3) or, where the

appointment followed a demand for payment, a copy of the letter of demand from the holder of the floating charge together with evidence that such letter of demand was properly made in terms of the floating charge;[3] and

(d) a copy of the instrument of appointment (a style of which is given in Appendix 4) to check that it has been properly executed and accepted in terms of section 53 of the IA 1986.[4]

1 *R v Registrar of Companies, ex p Esal (Commodities) Ltd* [1986] QB 1114, CA.
2 *Grove v Advantage Healthcare (T1O) Ltd* [2000] 1 BCLC 661.
3 See *Elwick Bay Shipping Co Ltd v Royal Bank of Scotland Ltd* 1982 SLT 62.
4 See 1.38 to 1.40 above.

**1.57** Although it is the duty in terms of section 53(1) of the IA 1986 of the holder of the floating charge or a person on his behalf to deal with the completion of the notice in the prescribed form and to file such notice with the Registrar of Companies, it is prudent for the receiver to check, from the point of view of general publicity, that the correct particulars have been filed with the Registrar of Companies and the Accountant in Bankruptcy.

**1.58** On a matter of practice, it is usually the case that a solicitor acting for a receiver will be invited to examine photocopies of original documents rather than the originals. This really does not matter in the case of some documents such as the memorandum and articles or the certificate of registration but it is clearly important in the case of documents such as the floating charge or the instrument of appointment to examine originals to be certain that such documents have been validly executed.

**1.59** In most cases, sight of the instrument of appointment can be arranged easily but in the case of the floating charge itself many holders of floating charges may be reluctant to allow the original document to pass out of their hands. It is for this reason that many solicitors acting for receivers will qualify their confirmation of validity of appointment by the words 'the photocopy documents in my possession bearing to have been validly executed'. No stamp duty has been payable on a deed of appointment of a receiver since 19 March 1985.

**1.60** A defect in the procedural steps to appoint a receiver may render the appointment invalid but it is a question of degree or of materiality in each case as to whether any such defect may prove fatal to the appointment. It is clear that many of the requirements specified above are subject to the provisions of the general law of Scotland with which it is not proposed to deal in this book and, in the vast majority of cases (particularly, where the lender uses a standard form) a holder of a floating charge will have ensured that requirements of execution and procedure will have been followed at the time of creation of the floating charge. The courts have been prepared to accept that where there were defaults other than those in contemplation when the initial appointment was made that an appointment would remain effective.[1]

1 *NRG Vision Ltd v Churchfield Leasing* [1988] 4 BCC 56 and *Retail Equity Pty Ltd v Custom Credit Corpn Ltd* (1991) 9 ACLC 404.

## Mode of appointment by court

**1.61** Section 54 of the IA 1986 provides that the appointment of a receiver by the court under section 51(2) of that Act shall be by petition to the court which shall be served on the company and in terms of section 54(2) on such application the court shall, if it thinks fit, issue an interlocutor making the appointment of a receiver in such terms as to caution as the court may think fit. The reference to the court in this connection means the court having jurisdiction to wind up the company,[1] which depending on the issued share capital could be either the sheriff court or the Outer House of the Court of Session.[2] Section 54(3) provides that a copy (certified by the clerk of the court to be a correct copy) of the court interlocutor making the appointment shall be delivered by or on behalf of the petitioner to the Registrar of Companies and the Accountant in Bankruptcy t:[3] for registration, accompanied by a notice in the prescribed form[4] within seven days of the date of the interlocutor or such longer period as the court may allow. If any person without reasonable excuse makes default in complying with the requirements of s 54(3) of the IA 1986 he is liable to a fine and, for continued contravention, to a daily default fine.

1 Section 744 of the 1985 Act through Section 251 of the IA 1986.
2 Rule 14.2 of the Act of Sederunt (Rules of the Court of Session 1994), SI 1994/1443.
3 Scotland Act 1998, Sch 8, para 23 jurisdiction for companies with an issued share capital in excess of £120,000 will always be with the Court of Session – see ibid 2.
4 Form 2 (Scot) per the Schedule to the Scottish Rules.

**1.62** Section 54(4) of the IA 1986 provides that on receipt of the certified copy of the interlocutor in accordance with section 54(3) and on receipt of a certificate by the appropriate officer of the court that caution as ordered by the court has been found, the Registrar shall on the payment of the appropriate fee (none prescribed at this time), enter up particulars of the appointment in the Register of Charges and in terms of section 54(5) the receiver shall be regarded as having been appointed on the date of his being appointed by the court. In terms of section 54(6), on the appointment of the receiver under this section, the floating charge by virtue of which he was appointed shall attach to the property then subject to the charge and such attachment shall have effect as if the charge were a fixed security over the property to which it has attached.

## Precedence among receivers

**1.63** Section 56(1) of the IA 1986 provides that where there are two or more floating charges existing over all or any part of the property of the company, a receiver may be appointed by virtue of each such charge but a receiver appointed by, or on application of, the holder of a floating charge having priority of ranking over any other floating charge by virtue of which a receiver is appointed shall have the powers given to a receiver to the exclusion of any other receiver. Where two or more floating charges rank equally with one another and two or more receivers have been appointed by virtue of such charges, the receivers so appointed shall be deemed to have been appointed as joint receivers.

**1.64** The power to the holder of a floating charge and to the court to appoint a receiver under sections 51(1) and (2) of the IA 1986 includes the power to appoint joint receivers and in terms of section 56(3) receivers appointed or deemed to have been appointed as joint receivers shall act jointly unless the instrument of appointment or respective instruments of appointment otherwise provide. In receiverships of any size where joint receivers are to be appointed it is normal practice that provision is made in the instrument of appointment for each receiver to act individually thereby avoiding the necessity of requiring all documents to be signed by both receivers as otherwise administrative and logistical problems tend to arise.

**1.65** If joint receivers have been appointed to a group of companies the holding company and some subsidiaries of which are Scottish, but which also has English subsidiaries, care should be taken to ensure that it is competent to appoint joint receivers of the English subsidiaries with power to act individually. The critical test will be the terms of the English debenture and floating charge giving rise to the appointment: unless power has been specifically taken in the debenture, the appointment of joint receivers with power to act individually may be invalid.

## Validity of assignation of floating charges

**1.66** From time to time questions have arisen as to the effectiveness or validity of assignation of floating charges. The principal advantage of assigning a floating charge rather than creating a new one is that it may avoid potential challenge under the provisions of the IA 1986[1] in the event of the winding up of or the making of an administration order affecting the charging company within certain periods of the constitution of such new floating charge. In the leading case on this subject *Libertas–Kommerz GmbH v Johnson*[2] a Scottish company granted a bond and floating charge over its property in favour of an individual who purported to assign his interest to company A who in turn purported to assign its interest to company B. Company B lodged a claim in the liquidation of the original Scottish company. Lord Kincraig held that the floating charge was assignable.[3] A guarantor who makes a payment to a chargeholder has been held in an unreported case to be entitled to subrogate into the place of the chargeholder.[4]

1 IA 1986, s 245.
2 1977 SC 91.
3 But for a criticism of this decision see W. Lucas 'The Assignation of Floating Charge' 1996 SLT 203.
4 JLSS February 1996 p 59.

## Competition between receiver and liquidator

**1.67** Questions sometimes arise as to priority when a liquidator is either appointed before or after a receiver is appointed. In terms of section 52(1)(c) of the IA 1986, the winding up of the company entitles the holder of a floating charge to appoint a receiver and in terms of section 129(2) of the IA 1986, a winding up by the court is deemed to have commenced at the date of presentation of the petition to the court. What happens if the liquidator is appointed either prior to or after the receiver?

**1.68** The answer is that the receiver acts in the first instance to discharge his statutory duties, prior and preferably to the liquidator.[1] The underlying reason for such an approach is simply that the holder of the floating charge, even in liquidation, should be entitled to exercise his security over the assets of a company. In *Manley, Petitioner*, the liquidator's appointment preceded the receiver's appointment. In his judgment, Lord Kincraig rebutted the argument that the liquidator had effectually executed diligence and gave effect to the receiver's contention that in terms of section 15(1)(a) of the 1972 Act[2] he was entitled to take precedence over the rights of the liquidator in order to satisfy the debt of the holder of the floating charge. Lord Kincraig also concluded that the receiver was liable for the payment of the secured and preferential creditors of the company but not the costs of the liquidator. In the course of his judgment, Lord Kincraig stated:

> 'The whole scheme of the 1972 Act is to give the receiver precedence over the liquidator in the administration of the whole property of the company, even if appointed after the commencement of the liquidation.'

More recently the House of Lords[3] have considered the extent to which a liquidator's expenses are payable from the proceeds of the sale of assets covered by a floating charge in priority to the sums due to the holder of the floating charge. They held that they would not be payable from the proceeds of the sale of the assets covered by a floating charge ahead of the principal and interest due to the chargeholder, save only to the extent that they relate to the preservation or realization of those assets.

1 *Manley, Petitioner* 1985 SLT 42.
2 Re-enacted as the CA 1985, s 471(1)(a); see now IA 1986, Sch 2, para 1.
3 *Buchler v Talbot (The Leyland Daf Case)* [2004] 2 AC 298, HL.

**1.69** It has been held[1] in England that a debenture holder who was contractually entitled to appoint a receiver was free to do so in order to protect his own interests and was under no duty to refrain from exercising his rights on the grounds that to do so might cause loss to the company or its unsecured creditors, or because the appointment of a receiver might be unnecessary in that it merely duplicated the efforts of the liquidator.

1 *Re Potters Oils Ltd* [1986] 1 All ER 890.

CHAPTER 2

# Effect of appointment of receiver

## Attachment of floating charge

### *General*

**2.01** As noted in Chapter 1, a floating charge may be created by a company over all or any part of the property (including uncalled capital) comprised from time to time in its property and undertaking for the purpose of securing any debt or other obligation (including a cautionary obligation or an obligation ad factum praestandum) of the company or any other party. Unlike a fixed charge which from the outset attaches to the property subject to it, a floating charge as its name suggests only floats without attachment over the property of the description or class specified in such charge which from time to time forms part of the property and undertaking of the company. For the importance of the expression 'forms part of the property and undertaking' see paras 2.04 to 2.06 below. However, on the appointment of a receiver the floating charge by virtue of which he was appointed 'attaches'[1] to the property then subject to the charge. It is normal to word the floating charge widely and if the wording permits the charge will cover acquirenda of the company as well.[2] A slightly different effect occurs on the crystallization taking place on the commencement of the winding up of the company which created it.[3] In these circumstances, the floating charge ceases to float and instead attaches to the property *then* comprised in the property and undertaking. For a more detailed discussion of this apparently slight difference between the effect of crystallisation on the appointment of a receiver and on a winding up see paras 2.37 to 2.42 below.

1 IA 1986, s 53(7).
2 *Ross v Taylor* 1985 SLT 387.
3 CA 1985, s 463(1).

**2.02** Attachment or crystallisation of a floating charge only occurs on the appointment of a receiver under that charge or on winding up: it does not, for example, occur on the appointment of a receiver by the holder of another floating charge, such other charge alone attaching in these circumstances to the property then subject to it. The appointment of a receiver by the holder of a floating charge created by the company, however, entitles the holder of any other floating charge created by the company to appoint a receiver[1] and so effect the attachment or crystallisation of that charge. Where a company has granted more than one floating charge, there is nothing to prevent each holder appointing his own receiver[2] but the usual practice in these circumstances, for obvious practical reasons, is for each holder to appoint the same person.[3] In the event of a different receiver being appointed, the 1985 Act contains provisions regulating precedence amongst such receivers.[4]

1 IA 1986, s 52(1)(d).
2 Ibid, s 56(1).
3 Ibid, s 56(7).
4 See paras 1.63-1.65.

### *Effect of attachment or crystallisation*

**2.03** On the appointment of a receiver, the floating charge by virtue of which he was appointed attaches to the property and assets of the description or class specified in the floating charge as being subject to it and which form part of the property and undertaking of the company, either at the time of appointment or subsequently, as if such charge were a fixed security over such property and assets. A fixed security is defined[1] as, in relation to any property of a company, any security, other than a floating charge or a charge having the nature of a floating charge, which on the winding up of the company in Scotland would be treated as an effective security over that property.

1 IA 1986, s 70(1).

## The property and undertaking of the company

**2.04** The most widely debated case on receivership law in the 1990s was undoubtedly *Sharp v Thomson*.[1] It even resulted in the Scottish Law Commission producing a 'Discussion Paper on Sharp v Thomson' (Discussion Paper 114) to which reference is made for the significant number of articles written on this subject. The facts of the case are worth setting out in full.

A company which had granted a floating charge to its bank sold a property to a brother and sister. The company received payment in full and the money was credited to the company's bank account. For a reason which does not impact on the facts, there was a delay in the delivery and recording of the disposition. After the delivery of the disposition, but before it was recorded, the bank appointed a receiver. The disposition was then recorded. Section 53(7) of the IA 1986 narrates that on the appointment of a receiver the floating charge attaches to the property then subject to the charge and such attachment has effect as if the charge was a fixed security over the property to which it has attached. As the company was still infeft in the property on the date the receiver was appointed, the receiver argued that the floating charge had immediately upon the appointment of the receiver crystallised and become the equivalent of a standard security (being the only type of security which could be granted over heritable property). Consequently, the crystallised charge gave a better right to the property than the delivered, but unrecorded, disposition. In effect this would result in the bank receiving the proceeds of the property twice.

In the Outer House[2] and the Inner House[3] their lordships favoured the position of the receiver and expounded in detail the conveyancing law of Scotland, the sanctity of the registers and the problems that would be caused for the conveyancing law of Scotland if what was considered to be a possible new right between a personal right and a real right was to be created to defeat the right of the receiver. The result however was different in the House of Lords[4]. In the House of Lords detailed speeches were delivered by Lord Clyde and Lord Jauncey, with the other two judges concurring with them. Regrettably the detailed explanations expounded by Lord Clyde and Lord Jauncey differed, albeit that the other two concurred, which has resulted in some suggestions that there will continue to be some uncertainty in the future. The fundamental reasoning behind the House of Lords' decision was that the seller's right in the property after it had been sold no longer formed part of the 'property and undertaking' of the company to which the charge subsequently attached and had ceased to be beneficially owned by the company. Property and undertaking did not necessarily include everything to which the company had a real right. In effect their lordships dealt with it as a matter of statutory interpretation rather than as an interpretation of the conveyancing law of Scotland. The lower courts had concentrated on the meaning of 'property' in conveyancing law down the ages. The House of Lords accepted that the correct approach to the construction of any provision of companies' legislation is to construe it according to its context and in line with the manifest purpose of the Act and how a business person rather than an academic conveyancer would interpret it. The words of Lord Ross in *Taylor Petitioner* [5]at pages 176 and 177 are worth remembering in the consideration of any receivership case, when he explained: 'It does not appear to me … that receivership is so similar to bankruptcy or liquidation that the principles of law applicable to insolvency should be applied.' He then made reference to *Lord Advocate v Royal Bank of Scotland*[6] where both the Lord President and Lord Cameron stress that receivership was quite different from liquidation. Lord Ross further states

> 'In bankruptcy there is a trustee concerned with the interests of the general body of creditors, whereas in receivership the primary duty of the receiver is to the security holder in whose interests he has been appointed. Sequestration or liquidation is a more drastic remedy than receivership; a receiver may be appointed although there is no insolvency.'

Normal practice on the settlement of the purchase of a property from a company has for some time been to seek from the holder of any floating charge a certificate of non-crystallisation and to incorporate therein a statement that on the property being acquired it will cease to form part of the assets subject to the floating charge.[7] Notification of this to the Registrar of Companies is not required. The Registers of Scotland in their *Registration of Title Practice* (2nd edn) 5.37 have set out their attitude to the registration of deeds granted by a receiver to reflect what is perceived to be the risk of the title being defeated by a person holding a previously delivered but unregistered conveyance. They consider the risk of a latent unregistered disposition surfacing once registration has been completed is too small to justify a policy of blanket indemnity exclusion for all sales by receivers, but consider appropriate enquiries should be made of the receiver and advice sought from the Keeper's Pre-Registration Enquiries Section if there are doubts.

1 1997 SLT 636.
2 1994 SLT 1068.
3 1995 SLT 837.
4 1997 SLT 636.
5 1982 SLT 172.
6 1978 SLT 38.
7 *Scottish & Newcastle plc v Ascot Inns Ltd* 1993 GWD 27-1666.

**2.05** Although bankruptcy and liquidation are outwith the scope of this book, a bankruptcy case in this area of law has also now been decided by the House of Lords[1] and it is worth noting the reasons why a different decision appears to have been reached. In *Burnett's Trustee v Grainger* a property was sold and a disposition delivered to the purchaser in exchange for the price. Some time thereafter a trustee in bankruptcy was appointed and the trustee on becoming aware that the purchaser had not recorded the disposition, recorded a notice of title to the property in the Register of Sasines. At first instance the sheriff (pre *Sharp v Thomson*) had no hesitation in finding for the trustee on the basis that he had won what is normally referred to as 'the Race to the Register'. The sheriff principal[2], on appeal felt that he was bound by the House of Lords decision in *Sharp v Thompson*[3] which had by then been delivered. The Inner House[4] and the House of Lords[5] did not however feel so constrained. Bankruptcy was considered different from receivership in that, on a receivership, the receiver could only acquire rights from the company (the debtor) whereas on a sequestration the trustee acquires not only all the rights that the debtor would have, but also all the rights that the creditors would have (per Lord Hope in *Burnett's Trustee v Grainger*[5] p 524). It would be open to a creditor to have adjudged against the property of the debtor (adjudication having been part of the law of Scotland since the beginning of the 13th century) and the rights of an adjudging creditor who records a title would beat those of an uninfeft proprietor (such as the purchaser who had not recorded his title) even where the adjudging creditor was aware of the existence of the uninfeft purchaser, because the adjudging creditor takes the debtor's heritable property free of the debtor's personal obligations. Section 31(1)(b) of the Bankruptcy (Scotland) Act 1985 specifically states that the act and warrant shall have the same effect as if a decree of adjudication ... had been pronounced in favour of the permanent trustee. It is a statutory adjudication. Liquidations are different from sequestrations in that, unlike s 31 of the Bankruptcy (Scotland) Act 1985 which vests the assets of the debtor in the trustee, the appointment of a liquidator does not vest the property of the company in the liquidator. The liquidator does however have power to apply to the court in terms of section 145 of IA 1986 for a vesting order. In terms thereof the court may direct that all or any part of the property of whatsoever description belonging to the company or held by trustees on its behalf shall vest in the liquidator. Whether a liquidator could seek an order to have all the property of the company of whatsoever description vested in him and then record a notice of title to defeat a purchaser who has not recorded his disposition is an interesting question. Writers over the years have taken different views on this with only one having committed her view to writing post *Burnett's Trustee v Grainger*[6]. The writers can see cogent arguments for both sides, but are inclined to the view that the words 'of whatever description' are as widely drawn as they can be and that since a liquidation is a collective procedure, like a sequestration, with the liquidator representing all the creditors, the liquidator ought not to have less powers than the individual creditors and ought to be able to follow the adjudication process, albeit starting further back when doing so than a trustee in sequestration. If the liquidator still manages to win the race to the Register, starting later and further back in the process, then so be it. The logical follow on question would be 'to whom should the proceeds of the subsequent sale of the property be paid?' and the answer to that would be to follow the thought process in para 2.40 below.

1 *Burnett's Trustee v Grainger* 2004 SLT 513.
2 2000 SLT (ShCt)116.
3 1997 SLT 636.
4 2002 SLT.
5 2004 SLT.
6 Donna McKenzie Skene being the most recent and coming down in favour of the view that the liquidator would not find it easy to succeed. 2004 SLT 71.

**2.06** Whereas the above deals with heritable property, the same principles would apply for moveable property. Accordingly, a patent which was being transferred and had not yet been registered or share transfers whether before or after approval of a transfer by the directors but before the writing up of the share register or an unintimated assignation of a book debt would come into this category and be dealt with in the same way.

## Effect of attachment or crystallisation in relation to specific property and assets

**2.07** To cover the case of heritable property subject to a floating charge the definition of a fixed security[1] includes a heritable security within the meaning of section 9(8) of the Conveyancing and Feudal Reform (Scotland) Act 1970. Since a security over heritable property in Scotland to be effective must be constituted a real right by recording or registration in the appropriate land register, it is specifically provided[2] that a floating charge shall have effect in relation to any heritable property to which it relates notwithstanding that the instrument creating it is not recorded in the Register of Sasines or registered in accordance with the Land Registration (Scotland) Act 1979.

1 IA 1986, s 70(1).
2 CA 1985, s 462(5).

**2.08** A floating charge by its nature does not attach to heritable property any more so than it does to any other kind of property from the time of its creation which means the company granting it is, subject to any contractual restrictions undertaken by it to the floating charge creditor, free to deal with such property until the floating charge attaches and in the event of receivership or liquidation the claims of preferred creditors take priority over the claim of the floating charge creditor. The effect of this has been significantly reduced by the abolition of crown preference in the 2002 Act. Where possible, therefore, a creditor of a company owning heritable property should seek a fixed charge over such property as, unlike a floating charge, such fixed charge will attach from the outset thus restricting the company's ability to deal with the property, the creditor's rights will be capable of exercise without the necessity of appointing a receiver and his claim will not be postponed to those of preferred creditors or subject to the prescribed part.

**2.09** Corporeal moveable property in the form of plant, equipment and stock often form a substantial part of a trading company's assets and it is over such assets (with or without book debts or other incorporeal moveable property) a creditor more often than not wishes to obtain security. A floating charge affords security over corporeal moveable property contrary to the basic principle of the law of Scotland that security over such property cannot be created without actual or constructive delivery. Prior to 1961 Scottish companies were at a disadvantage compared to their English counterparts in that floating charges were not known to the law of Scotland and consequently, for most practical purposes, it was impossible for a trading company to effectively create a security over corporeal moveables with one notable exception peculiar to Scotland. It was and still is possible to create a fixed security over stocks of Scotch whisky by effecting constructive delivery to the creditor provided they are held in an independent warehouse. The Companies (Floating Charges) (Scotland) Act 1961 however introduced floating charges into the law of Scotland for the first time thus removing the impediment to the creation of charges over corporeal moveable property by Scottish companies. On attachment or crystallisation a floating charge attaches to all the property (which as noted in para 2.01 can include future assets) then subject to the charge and which forms part of the property and undertaking of the company as if it were an effective fixed security created by delivery. Care needs to be taken to ensure that goods in the possession of the company have not had title passed under a contract of sale to a customer before the appointment of a receiver. This could happen on the unconditional appropriation of the goods under the Sale of Goods Act 1979.

**2.10** The incorporeal moveable property of a trading company with most value is usually its book debts and a creditor seeking a floating charge will more often than not wish such book debts included. It is of course legally possible in Scotland to create a fixed charge over a book debt by assignation to the creditor followed by intimation to the party owing the debt[1] but the requirement of intimation to the party owing the debt has practical problems against a trading background where both the identity and amount of book debts are constantly changing. There is less of a problem on the assignation of rent under a lease or a master agreement to supply goods where the goods are called off over a period, and the use of assignations to create fixed charges in such situations will become more common in the future. It is also possible to create a trust over book debts as, for example under an invoice discounting arrangement[2] so divesting the company of their beneficial ownership with the result that a floating charge does not attach to them. On attachment or crystallisation a floating charge accordingly attaches to incorporeal moveable property beneficially owned by the company such as book debts, as if it were an effective security created by assignation and intimation. The creation of a fixed charge over book debts in England does not have the same practical problems although this has recently been called into question.[3]

1 Transmission of Moveable Property (Scotland) Act 1862.
2 *Tay Valley Joinery Ltd v CF Financial Services Ltd* 1987 SLT 207.
3 See Chap 8 paras 8.18 to 8.20.

**2.11** On attachment or crystallisation a floating charge is accordingly, in effect, converted into a fixed security over the property subject to it. Lord Cameron in one of the first cases[1] to come before the Court of Session on the interpretation of the 1972 Act[2] said:

> 'I think ... that when the definition of a "fixed security" in s 312 is examined it becomes clear that the intention of the legislature was to provide, in the shape of a floating charge, a form of security over the property of a debtor company which, at the discretion of the security holder, or on application to the court and on the appointment of a receiver, should operate as a fixed security, and that this should be so when the circumstances were appropriate for the secured creditor to be given the right and opportunity to work out his security, without being compelled to proceed into liquidation; the floating charge in these circumstances becomes a valuable and convenient device in the interest both of creditor and company to secure and obtain satisfaction of a debt or claim without recourse to the extreme remedy of liquidation.'

Subsequently[3] Lord President Emslie stated:

> 'The intention [of the Act][4] appears to me to be that the holder of the floating charge shall, on the appointment of a receiver, enjoy all the protection in relation to any item of attached property that the holder of a fixed security over that item thereof would enjoy under the general law.'

1 *Lord Advocate v Royal Bank of Scotland Ltd* 1978 SLT 38 at 47 per Lord Cameron.

2 See now the IA 1986, s 70.
3 *Forth & Clyde Construction Co Ltd v Trinity Timber & Plywood Co Ltd* 1984 SLT 94.
4 Now consolidated in the IA 1986.

**2.12** The concept of a floating charge being converted into a fixed charge on crystallisation as a result of the appointment of a receiver has given rise to difficulties in relation to book debts of the company attached by the floating charge.[1] Paragraph 1 of Schedule 2 to the IA 1986 bestows on a receiver power to take possession of, collect and get in the property subject to the floating charge from the company or a liquidator thereof or any other person and for that purpose to take such proceedings as may seem to him expedient. In the *McPhail* case,[1] Lord Grieve held in relation to proceedings for recovery of a debt due to the company that as a receiver had power by virtue of the equivalent section of the 1972 Act to raise a claim in his own name to so recover property for behoof of the security holder there were no grounds for holding that the receiver was precluded from recovering property from another person in his own name and that while section 15(1)(f) of the 1972 Act[2] gave him power to bring or defend any action or other legal proceedings in the name and on behalf of the company this was not to be construed as limiting the powers of the receiver in connection with the raising of legal proceedings. Section 15(1)(a) of the 1972 Act[3] accordingly gave the receiver a discretion as to whether to seek to recover such property in his own name or in that of the company.

1 *McPhail v Lothian Regional Council* 1981 SLT 173.
2 See now the IA 1986, Sch 2, para 5.
3 Ibid, para 1.

**2.13** In the *Taylor* case[1] however Lord Ross did not follow the *McPhail* decision[2] and held that as under section 15(1)(a) of the 1972 Act[3] the receiver's power was limited to taking possession from the company of a right to debts due to it by others, namely a *jus crediti*, the provisions of that section would enable the receiver to obtain from the company an assignation of those debts but not to sue the debtors for payment of the debts because, at the date of his appointment, what the company owned was not the sums of money due by the debtors but a mere *jus crediti*. Accordingly, the receiver's power under section 15(1)(f) of the 1972 Act[4] was limited to taking proceedings in the name of the company for recovery of debts due to it. This decision has been followed in a subsequent case[5] in which Lord Prosser stated:

> 'When a *jus crediti* of the company is being vindicated against a third party debtor, it appears to me that the appropriate action would require to be raised in the name and on behalf of the company.'

1 *Taylor, Petitioner* 1982 SLT 172; see also 'The Receiver and Book Debts' 1982 SLT (News) 129.
2 *McPhail v Lothian Regional Council* 1981 SLT 173.
3 See now the IA 1986, Sch 2, para 1.
4 Ibid, para 5.
5 *Myles J Callaghan Ltd v City of Glasgow District Council* 1988 SLT 227.

**2.14** In a later case[1] the concept was considered on appeal by the Inner House. The facts of that case were that, on the day after joint receivers had been validly appointed by the holders of a floating charge over the whole property of a company, a creditor upon the faith of a warrant to arrest on the dependence of an action against the company arrested in the hands of Strathclyde Regional Council a sum due by the council to the company under certain building contracts. The company's receivers in the exercise of their powers under section 15(1)(a) of the 1972 Act[2] sought to collect the debt due to the company by the regional council but the creditor, a company which was in liquidation, would not agree to the regional council releasing the sum in question. The receivers accordingly presented a petition for recall of the purported arrestment and were successful both at first instance and on appeal by the respondent creditor. In his judgment, Lord President Emslie (section references being to the 1972 Act) stated:

> 'Upon a proper construction of the words of section 13(7)3 ... read together with the definition of the words "fixed security" in section 31(1),4 in the context of an Act which repeatedly draws a distinction between a fixed security and any diligence, one has to ask, in order to give effect to section 13(7)5 in the case of a book debt, what kind of security over it (other than a diligence) would be treated by the law of Scotland as an "effective security" over it in the winding up of a company in Scotland. There is only one such security and that is an assignation in security of the right to receive payment of the debt, duly intimated to the debtor.'

On that basis the court held that the regional council's liability to pay the debt to the company for its own behoof had disappeared and so on the date of the purported arrestment the debt was no longer susceptible to arrestment at the instance of a creditor of the company. This decision, approved by the court in the *Myles J Callaghan* case,[6] looking both to the provisions of what is now section 53(7) of the IA 1986 and the other sections of the 1972 Act to which the court referred, gives effect to the overall objective of the legislation. On the appointment of a receiver, while the company remains entitled to recover its book debts, it no longer does so on its own behalf, but on behalf of the holder of the floating charge and the receiver in exercise of his powers will seek to recover these debts in the company's name with a view to satisfying the debt due by the company to the holder of the floating charge within the framework laid down in the legislation.

1 *Forth & Clyde Construction Ltd v Trinity Timber & Plywood Ltd* 1984 SLT 94.
2 See now the IA 1986, Sch 2, para 1.
3 Ibid, s 53(7).
4 Ibid, s 70(1).
5 Ibid, s 53(7).
6 *Myles J Callaghan Ltd v City of Glasgow District Council* 1988 SLT 227.

## Security for principal and interest

**2.15** The attachment or crystallisation of a floating charge on the appointment of a receiver affords security not only for the principal of the debt or obligation in question but also for both pre- and post-receivership interest until payment of the sum due under the charge.[1] A provision in similar terms was first introduced in the 1972 Act to remove any doubt on the matter following a decision[2] to the effect that the holder of a floating charge was entitled to interest from the date of liquidation until payment.

1 CA 1985, s 463(4).
2 *National Commercial Bank of Scotland Ltd v Liquidators of Telford Grier Mackay & Co* 1969 SC 181.

## *Effect of attachment or crystallisation in relation to diligence*

**2.16** Powers given to a receiver are made subject to the rights of any person who has effectually executed diligence on property of the company prior to the appointment of the receiver.[1] It has been held[2] that an arrestment which postdates the creation of the floating charge under which the receiver is appointed and which, prior to the receiver's appointment, has not been followed by a decree of furthcoming is not 'effectually executed diligence' within the meaning of section 55(3)(a) of the IA 1986. The provisions of that section are not thought to be exhaustive and if the arrestment predates the creation of the floating charge this has the effect of rendering the sum arrested litigious with the result that the debtor cannot defeat it by any posterior voluntary deed.[3] In these circumstances the property to which the floating charge attaches is subject to the rights of the arresting creditor. This result has been the subject of some academic criticism and could lead to anomalous situations. A poinding executed after the creation of a floating charge and which has not been succeeded by a sale prior to a receiver's appointment likewise cannot be effectually executed diligence. This is to be contrasted with the position arising on liquidation where an arrestment or poinding executed more than sixty days prior to the commencement of liquidation is effectual as against the liquidator[4] although, if there exists a floating charge over the assets affected by such diligence, such floating charge crystallises subject to the rights of any person who has effectually executed diligence.[5] Where there is a floating charge and a liquidation rather than a receivership ensues, if the arrestment is more than sixty days before the liquidation it will rank ahead of the floating charge in the liquidation whereas it would not on a receivership.[6] An arresting or poinding creditor, who has not proceeded to furthcoming or sale prior to a receiver's appointment, does not have any preference for the expenses of such ineffectually executed diligence which again is to be contrasted with the position on liquidation where a creditor who has arrested or poinded within 60 days of liquidation does have such a preference.[7] An arrestment executed after the appointment of a receiver is also ineffectual.[8]

1 IA 1986, s 55(3)(a).
2 *Lord Advocate v Royal Bank of Scotland Ltd* 1978 SLT 38.
3 *Iona Hotels Ltd (in receivership) v Craig* 1991 SLT 11.
4 Bankruptcy (Scotland) Act 1985, Sch 7, para 24(3).
5 IA 1986, s 55(3).
6 *Commissioners of Customs and Excise v John D Reid Joinery Ltd* 2001 SLT 588.

7 Bankruptcy (Scotland) Act 1985, Sch 7, para 21.
8 *Forth & Clyde Construction Co Ltd v Trinity Timber & Plywood Co Ltd* 1984 SLT 94; see also 'Receivers and Arrestors' 1984 SLT (News) 177.

**2.17** An inhibition registered before the appointment of a receiver is not 'effectually executed diligence' within the meaning of section 55(3)(a) of the IA 1986[1].

1 *Taymech Ltd v Rush & Tompkins Ltd* 1990 SLT 681.

**2.18** The effect of an inhibition in relation to receivership depends also on the date of the inhibition. As an inhibition prohibits inter alia the granting of a voluntary deed such as the subsequent granting by the debtor of any security over his heritable property, an inhibition granted before a floating charge will prevail in so far as such charge extends over a debtor company's heritable property.[1] Where, however, a floating charge predates an inhibition it is unaffected by it and this remains the position when such charge attaches or crystallises on the appointment of a receiver. This was the position in the *Armour and Mycroft* case[2] but, the joint receivers having contracted to sell part of the company's heritable property, the inhibiting creditor refused to discharge its inhibition or to consent to the sale except upon the joint receivers presenting an application to the court under what is now section 61 of the IA 1986 seeking power to sell the property in question free of any security, interest, burden or encumbrance. The court rejected the claim of the inhibiting creditor that its debt should be satisfied before those of the floating charge holders but held that the former's debt should be satisfied from the sale proceeds before satisfaction of any of the claims of ordinary creditors. Without a section 61 order, the purchaser will find that the Keeper will not grant a Land Certificate without an exclusion of indemnity, the Keeper in such situations referring to Gretton on Inhibitions for his authority for so doing. The writers consider that he is misinterpreting Gretton, and only if a good and marketable title is one where there is no inhibition, even if the inhibition is ineffective, would that be the case. In a later case[3] the court recalled inhibitions clearly ineffective against the receivers subject only to the imposition of a condition preserving any priority that the inhibiting creditors might have created against the company. Following this case the practitioner may find an application to recall the ineffective inhibition a faster route to achieving the desired objective of being able to sell the heritable property. As there is already a court process appearing in that ought to be faster than applying to court under section 61. The traditional use of diligence on the dependence of an action, with no requirement to show that there were good grounds for doing so, to put pressure on a debtor, particularly one vergens ad inopiam, which might have a receiver appointed to it, was always likely to come into conflict with the European Convention on Human Rights. The first case to consider this was *Karl Construction Ltd v Palisade Properties plc*[4], which considered whether the automatic grant of warrant for inhibition, without any justification having been stated was an infringement of Article 1 of the First Protocol to the Convention, which provides for the right to peaceful enjoyment of possessions. The purpose of diligence on the dependence to ensure that there are assets to satisfy the claim of a successful pursuer is also a legitimate objective and the question is accordingly whether the law provides a proportionate balance between the objective and the right, being not significantly greater than is required.

In the Outer House, Lord Drummond Young considered that the common law on diligence on the dependence did not provide the required proportionality. He considered that four requirements were the minimum to achieve that. They were:

(i) the pursuer must establish a prima facie case on the merits;
(ii) the pursuer must establish that there is a specific need for an interim remedy;
(iii) a hearing before a judge to consider (i) and (ii) is required; and
(iv) if there is no objective justification and the pursuer is unsuccessful, the defender should be entitled to damages.

This decision came up for consideration by the Inner House in *Advocate General for Scotland v Taylor*[5]. They reduced the requirements set out in *Karl Construction Ltd* deciding that no actual hearing before a judge was required as long as there was a judicial act which could be the consideration by a judge of material placed before him. Furthermore there only requires to be established a prima facie case on the merits of the action. The necessity for diligence does not need to be established although it will assist the grant if it is. For a more detailed consideration of the position, reference is made to Professor Gerry Maher QC's article 'Diligence on the dependence : reform needed' 2004 SLT 167.

1 Unless the granting of the floating charge is in terms of a prior contractual obligation.
2 *Armour and Mycroft, Petitioners* 1983 SLT 453.
3 *Taymech Ltd v Rush & Tompkins Ltd* 1990 SLT 681.
4 2002 SLT 312.
5 2003 SLT 1340.

**2.19** Sequestration for rent is the process of diligence available to a landlord for enforcing his hypothec for unpaid rent or obtaining security for future rent. There have been conflicting sheriff court decisions on whether a receiver's powers prevail over a landlord's right to sequestrate for rent after the receiver's appointment.[1] The earlier decision of *Cumbernauld Development Corpn v Mustone Ltd*, which was in favour of the receiver, was universally critised and the decision in *Grampian Regional Council v Drill Stem (Inspection Services) Limited (in Receivership)*, which was against the receiver, is accepted as being the better view. Section 55(3)(b) of the IA 1986 provides that where all or any part of the property of a company is subject both to a floating charge and to a fixed security arising by operation of law, the fixed security shall have priority over the floating charge. A landlord's hypothec is under the law of Scotland a real right in security which arises by operation of law and section 70(1) of the IA 1986 provides that for the purposes of that part of the Act any security that is not a floating charge or of the nature of a floating charge is a fixed security. The Scottish Executive have indicated that they are minded to abolish sequestration for rent in 'Enforcement of Civil Obligations in Scotland: A Consultative Document' (April 2002).

1 *Cumbernauld Development Corpn v Mustone Ltd* 1983 SLT (Sh Ct) 55 and *Grampian Regional Council v Drill Stem (Inspection Services) Ltd (in receivership)* 1994 SCLR 36.

**2.20** Where a receiver sells or wishes to sell property covered by the floating charge under which he has been appointed and is unable to obtain the consent of a creditor who has effectually executed diligence he may apply to the court for the appropriate authority.[1]

1 See para 2.18 and 7.34-7.36.

## Other effects of appointment of receiver

### *Powers of directors*

**2.21** There are no express statutory provisions as to the effect on the powers of the directors of the company on the appointment of a receiver which is to be contrasted with the position in a creditor's voluntary winding-up.[1] In a court winding-up the directors' powers cease on the making of the winding-up order,[2] but only to the extent that these powers have passed to the liquidator. Section 14(4) of the IA 1986 covers the position in an administration. As however a receiver's powers include power to take possession of the property of the company subject to the floating charge under which he was appointed, the powers of the directors to deal with such property are suspended. In the majority of cases the floating charge extends over the company's whole undertaking and assets and as the receiver's powers include power to carry on the company's business the directors in these circumstances are effectively relieved of all powers of management of the company, its business and assets. This does not necessarily mean that the directors have no powers in any circumstances to deal in any way (including the raising of proceedings) with assets of a company in receivership which are attached by the floating charge where so doing does not in any way impinge prejudicially upon the position of the floating charge creditor by threatening or imperilling the assets which are covered by the charge.[3]

1 IA 1986, s 103.
2 *Re Mawcon Ltd* [1969] 1 All ER 188.
3 *Newhart Developments Ltd v Co-operative Commercial Bank Ltd* [1978] QB 814, CA; *Gomba Holdings UK Ltd v Holman* [1986] 1 WLR 1301; *Shanks v Central Regional Council* 1987 SLT 410; *Tudor Grange Holdings Ltd v Citibank NA* [1991] BCLC 1009; *Independent Pension Trustee Ltd v L A W Construction Co Ltd* 1997 SLT 1105, OH.

**2.22** On the first occasion on which the question of the powers of directors of a company in receivership came before the court in Scotland it ruled that the directors had no power whatsoever to deal with property subject to the charge[1] but a later decision ruled otherwise.[2] In the *Imperial Hotel* case[1] a hotel company had granted a brewery company both a floating charge and a fixed charge in the form of a standard security over the hotel. It had also granted to its bank a floating charge over all its assets. The bank appointed a receiver and at a later date the brewery company called up its standard security and in exercise of its power of sale sold the hotel to another brewery company. The directors of the company in receivership raised an action in the name of the company seeking reduction of the contract for the sale of the hotel on the grounds that the security holder in exercising its power of sale had failed to take all reasonable steps to ensure that the hotel was sold for the best price that could reasonably have been obtained. The court held that where a receiver had been appointed over the whole of the assets of a company, the directors of the company were not entitled to deal in any way with the property of the company during the currency of the receivership. In the course of his judgment (section references being to the 1972 Act) Lord Grieve (at 116) said:

> 'It would be quite contrary to the object of the Act if a company, all of whose assets were attached to the receiver because all were covered by a floating charge or floating charges could interfere, through its directors, with the exercise by the receiver of his discretion by, for instance, raising actions which the receiver did not consider should be raised. In my opinion it is quite apparent from the terms of the 1972 Act and the nature of the duties which a receiver appointed under it is empowered to perform, that the receiver's primary duty is to the security holder, and that, in order to perform it properly, his discretion is not to be subject to interference by the directors of the company concerned.'

Again (at 117):

> 'I am quite satisfied that the terms of the Act of 1972 do not empower the directors of a company, whose assets are the subject of a floating charge in connection with which a receiver has been appointed, to deal in any way with assets of theirs which are the subject of such a charge during the currency of the receivership.'

Shortly after the *Imperial Hotel* decision the English Court of Appeal ruled[3] that if directors remain in office after the appointment of a receiver they can continue to exercise their powers in spite of the fact that the receiver has equivalent powers under his instrument of appointment, provided that the directors in exercise of such powers do not thereby impede the proper conduct of the receivership. In that case[3] the directors had raised an action in the name of the company and in the course of its judgment the court said (per Shaw LJ at 819):

> 'There is not a total extinction of the function of the directors. It is only within the scope of its assets which are covered by the debenture, and only in so far as it is necessary to apply those assets in the best possible way in the interests of the debenture holders, that the receiver has a real function. If in the exercise of his discretion he chooses to ignore some asset such as a right of action, or decides that it would be unprofitable from the point of view of the debenture holders to pursue it, there is nothing in any authority which has been cited to us which suggests that it is not then open to the directors of the company to pursue that right of action if they

think it would be in the interests of the company. Indeed, in my view, it would be incumbent on them to do so.'

1 *Imperial Hotel (Aberdeen) Ltd v Vaux Breweries Ltd* 1978 SLT 113.
2 *Shanks v Central Regional Council* 1987 SLT 410
3 *Newhart Developments Ltd v Co-operative Commercial Bank Ltd* [1978] QB 814, CA.

**2.23** The court went on to hold in the *Newhart* case[1] that the appointment of a receiver accordingly did not divest the directors of the company of their power, as the governing body of the company, of instituting proceedings in a situation where so doing did not in any way impinge prejudicially upon the position of the debenture-holders by threatening or imperilling the assets which were subject to the charge. In particular, the directors were entitled to pursue a right of action in the name of the company, provided however that the company was indemnified against liability for costs. This decision has been confirmed in a subsequent case.[2]

1 *Newhart Developments Ltd v Co-operative Commercial Bank Ltd* [1978] QB 814, CA.
2 *Tudor Grange Holdings Ltd v Citibank NA* [1991] BCLC 1009.

**2.24** The question was next considered in an unreported sheriff court case.[1] In that case the pursuers, a company, itself both in receivership and liquidation, were suing for loss arising from breach of contract. In the course of the proceedings the defenders had a receiver appointed over their whole property and assets. The pursuers sought to have the receiver of the defenders sisted as a party to the action but the receiver was unwilling to be so sisted, the pursuers being unable to compel him to do so. However, the directors of the defenders decided to continue the defence of the action at their own expense. The pursuers maintained that the effect of the appointment of a receiver over the whole property and assets was to deprive the defenders' directors of any power to continue the defence of the action. The defenders on the other hand argued that they should be allowed to continue the defence as in so doing the defenders' directors were not in any way interfering with the receiver in the exercise of his functions nor eroding the funds available to him since he would incur no liability in respect of any obligations which he had not authorised. The sheriff in reaching his decision had the benefit of considering both the *Imperial Hotel* and *Newhart* decisions[2] and was able to draw a distinction between the facts in the *Imperial Hotel* case and the facts in the case before him.

1 *Hastings Black Construction Ltd v AIR (Air Conditioning and Refrigeration) Ltd* (4 October 1984, unreported) Glasgow Sheriff Court.
2 *Imperial Hotel (Aberdeen) Ltd v Vaux Breweries Ltd* 1978 SLT 113; *Newhart Developments Ltd v Co-operative Commercial Bank Ltd* [1978] QB 814.

**2.25** The attempt by the directors of Imperial Hotel (Aberdeen) Limited to prevent the sale of property comprised in the receivership was in the sheriff's view[1] a very obvious interference with the receiver in the execution of his functions whereas in the case before him the continuation of the defence to the action did not interfere in any way with the performance by the receiver of his functions. While the sheriff in drawing this distinction overlooks the fact that in the *Imperial Hotel* case[2] the sale was effected not by the receiver but by a heritable creditor in exercise of such creditor's right of sale, the property did form part of the receivership assets over which the receiver's powers extended subject always to the prior rights of the heritable creditor. As section 15 of the 1972 Act[3] contained no prohibition on the directors of a company in receivership from taking any of the actions which a receiver is entitled to take and as the continuation of the defence of the proceedings did not interfere with the exercise by the receiver of his functions, the sheriff found in favour of the defenders. In his judgment while the sheriff states that the major premise of Lord Grieve's reasoning in the *Imperial Hotel* case would appear to be that any actings by the board of directors which could interfere with the exercise by the receiver of his discretion would be illegal, he does express the view that in more borderline cases wherein actings of the directors might or might not be said to so interfere, it might be necessary to consider carefully the meaning and effect of Lord Grieve's statement at 117 of his judgment[2] to the effect that the directors of a company in receivership have no power to deal in any way with assets subject to the floating charge.

1 *Hastings Black Construction Ltd v AIR (Air Conditioning and Refrigeration) Ltd* (4 October 1984, unreported), Glasgow Sheriff Court.
2 *Imperial Hotel (Aberdeen) Ltd v Vaux Breweries Ltd* 1978 SLT 113.
3 See now the IA 1986, s 55 and Sch 2.

**2.26** This in effect the court did in a subsequent Court of Session case[1] in which the *Newhart* decision was approved: a case which again involved an action raised by the directors of a company in receivership, the action being in both their own names and that of the company. In his decision Lord Weir differed from the view expressed in the *Imperial Hotel* case that the directors of a company have no power to deal in any way with the property subject to the charge, stating instead that the views expressed by Shaw LJ were capable of general application and that he did not consider that in principle these views were in conflict with the provisions of the 1972 Act. He accordingly decided that an action brought by a company where a receiver has been appointed is not inherently incompetent or necessarily a fundamental nullity. The benefit from any successful litigation, even where the receiver refused to become involved would still be an asset of the company and likely therefore to be covered by the floating charge. The costs of unsuccessful litigation would be an ordinary debt of the company (and indeed if caution was sought, perhaps of the directors pursuing the claim) and the costs of successful litigation would be against the defenders with any unawarded costs being able to be claimed from the funds received under the *Leyland Daf*[2] principle of being able to deduct expenses of protecting those assets. In the most recently reported case in this area[3], Lord Hamilton doubted both *Newhart*[4] and *Shanks*[1], the former having been narrowly construed in *Gomba*[5] and seriously doubted in *Tudor Grange*[6] and said:

> 'In Scotland, in my view, the board has during the currency of the receivership no power over assets in the possession or control of the

receiver. While the directors do not lose office on the appointment of a receiver, they cannot thereafter act at their own hand in respect of assets falling and remaining under the charge.'

Again,

'Assets of the company include not only its property in the narrow sense but its rights and powers, in so far at least as these have commercial value or significance. It may be in some circumstances, such as where there is a conflict of interest, a receiver may in practical terms be disabled from exercising a right or power of the company. In such circumstances the board may be entitled to exercise that right or power. It may be that the decision in *Newhart* can be justified on that basis or on the alternative basis that the right of action in that case had in effect been renounced by the receiver (*Gomba Holdings*), though I share the substantial doubts expressed by the Vice Chancellor in *Tudor Grange* as to the correctness of the decision in *Newhart*. It follows that I also have substantial doubts about the correctness of the decision in *Shanks*.'

1 *Shanks v Central Regional Council* 1987 SLT 410
2 [2004] UKHL 9, [2004] 2 AC 298.
3 *Independent Pension Trustee Ltd v L A W Construction Co Ltd* 1997 SLT 1105, OH.
4 *Newhart Developments Ltd v Co-operative Commercial Bank Ltd* [1978] QB 814, CA.
5 *Gomba Holdings UK Ltd v Homan* [1986] 1 WLR 1301.
6 *Tudor Grange Holdings Ltd v Citibank NA* [1991] BCLC 1009.

**2.27** In one other reported Scottish case[1] touching on the effect of the appointment of a receiver on the powers of the directors, a case where the court was asked to order a company in receivership to obtemper a decree of specific implement, the Lord Ordinary (Lord Stott) in deciding that a company in receivership could only act through the agency of its receiver said:

'It is plain that the defenders are not in a position to obtemper decree of specific implement through their directors as would normally be the position if the company was not in receivership.'

1 *Macleod v Alexander Sutherland Ltd* 1977 SLT (Notes) 44; but see paras 4.39-4.41.

## *Responsibilities of directors*

**2.28** While, except to the limited extent described, the directors' powers of management over the assets covered by the floating charge cease to have effect, the appointment of the directors as such does not cease nor are they relieved of their statutory obligations. Likewise, the appointment of the secretary of the company does not cease. The directors remain, for example, under obligation to maintain accounting records.[1]

1 *Smiths Ltd v Middleton* [1979] 3 All ER 842.

## *Remuneration of directors*

**2.29** It has been held in England[1] that while directors cannot claim remuneration from a receiver unless he employs them, they can nevertheless claim from the company any remuneration to which they are entitled.

1 *Re South Western of Venezuela (Barquisimeto) Rly Co* [1902] 1 Ch 701.

## *Effect of fixed charges*

**2.30** The exercise by a receiver in Scotland of his powers are subject inter alia to the rights of the holder of a charge ranking prior to or pari passu with the floating charge by virtue of which he was appointed.[1] The rights, however, of the holder of a fixed charge over heritable property in the form of a standard security remain intact on the appointment of a receiver provided that such charge has been validly registered as a charge. The creditor in such a standard security may accordingly, as was done in the *Imperial Hotel* case,[2] exercise all the powers competent to him as heritable creditor including the power of sale. The position is the same in relation to any other validly created form of fixed security over the company's assets.

1 IA 1986, s 55(3)(b).
2 *Imperial Hotel (Aberdeen) Ltd v Vaux Breweries Ltd* 1978 SLT 113.

## *Effect of other floating charges*

**2.31** If a floating charge covers a company's whole property comprised in its property and undertaking then, on the appointment of a receiver under it, it attaches to or crystallises on all such property. Any other floating charge granted by the company, whatever its ranking in relation to the floating charge under which the receiver has been appointed, does not automatically attach or crystallise on the appointment of such receiver. Any other floating charge only attaches or crystallises on either the appointment of a receiver by its holder or on the winding-up of the company although, of course, the appointment of a receiver by the holder of a floating charge entitles the holder of any other floating charge granted by the company to appoint a receiver.[1]

1 IA 1986, s 56(1); see paras 1.63-1.65.

**2.32** So on the appointment of a receiver by the holder of a floating charge, the holder of any other floating charge in order to crystallise his charge, and generally in his own interests particularly to preserve any priority ranking, should likewise appoint a receiver who, unless there is some compelling reason why he should not be so appointed, will normally be the person or persons already appointed by the holder of the first floating charge. As has already been seen,[1] section 56 of the IA 1986 contains provisions governing precedence among receivers, the effect of which on the appointment of a different person would be that depending on the ranking of the floating charges in question either only one of the receivers would be entitled to exercise the powers given to a receiver under the IA 1986 or, unless the respective instruments of appointment otherwise provided, the receivers so appointed would act jointly in the exercise of such powers. If, on the other hand, a floating charge covers part but not all of a company's assets then, on the appointment of a receiver under it, it attaches or crystallises on these assets alone and the effect on the attachment or crystallisation, or rather non-attachment or non-crystallisation, of any other floating charge over assets other than those covered by the first charge is as described earlier. Accordingly, the holder of any other such floating charge must make his own decision as to whether it is appropriate at that time in his own interests to appoint a receiver under that charge and whether it should be the same receiver as already appointed under the first charge. In these circumstances where the charges cover different assets the provisions as to precedence among receivers do not apply.

1 Paragraphs 1.63 to 1.65.

## Extent of security

**2.33** On appointment, a receiver, on being satisfied that his appointment has been validly made, requires to investigate immediately the assets covered by the charge under which he has been appointed and, if there are other charges, to investigate at an early date the ranking of the floating charge with any other such charges. He should also ascertain if an enforcement administrator has been appointed in respect of the company in terms of the Proceeds of Crime Act 2002 as a receiver appointed in such a situation cannot exercise his functions in relation to the property covered by the charge, the chargeholder's interest being protected by that Act. Circumstances in which immediate consideration of the ranking position is necessary are where a different person is appointed receiver by the holder of another floating charge, because of the provisions relating to precedence among receivers[1] or where the holder of another floating charge ranking in priority or pari passu over certain assets has not appointed a receiver. The question of the assets covered by the floating charge raises no particular problem in the normal course when the charge extends over the company's whole property and assets. It can raise problems, however, where the assets covered are restricted.

1 IA 1986, s 56.

**2.34** In the receivership of an English manufacturing company whose premises were situated in Scotland the receiver on examination of the floating charge under which he was appointed found that it was granted over the company's property and undertaking with the exception of 'heritable, real and leasehold' property and certain other specified current assets. The intention had been that the floating charge should extend over the company's plant and machinery but as the majority of such plant and machinery was beyond dispute heritable in nature the charge failed to achieve this object because of the exception.

**2.35** In another case in practice, involving the receivership of a Scottish company, the floating charge contained in a debenture in favour of an English institution contained general words of charge over its property and undertaking and then proceeded to state that the 'charge hereby created shall be a first fixed charge on the heritable freehold and leasehold property of the company wheresoever situate and the fixed plant fixtures and machinery therein and thereon and a first floating charge as to all other property and assets'. In the absence of a heritable security in statutory form no fixed security existed over the company's heritable property and because of the particular wording of the charge document the floating charge, contrary to the intention, did not extend over such property. Similarly a clause in a floating charge granted by an English company which purported to convert a floating charge into a fixed charge on the occurrence of certain events as well as being inept to create an heritable security over heritable property in Scotland was also held to be inept in Scots law to attach the charged property in Scotland on the occurrence of such an event as a floating charge can crystallise only on the winding up of the company or on the appointment of a receiver.[1] With respect to St Clair and Drummond Young[2], the writers do not agree that there is a crystallisation of the floating charge on administration.

1 *Norfolk House plc (in receivership) v Repsol Petroleum Ltd* 1992 SLT 235n.
2 *The Law of Corporate Insolvency in Scotland* (3rd edn, 2004) 173.

**2.36** It has been held that the consignation of funds in court by a company effectively removes such funds from the property of the company so that they are not attached by a floating charge.[1] The right in the reversion would however remain secured. Accordingly it would be good practice when litigating against a company and arresting funds to try to have the funds consigned rather than left as arrestments which would be defeated by a receiver. The converse would be, when acting where personal guarantees had been granted by directors to the bank and the company is vergens ad inopiam, to resist any such move.

1 *Hawking v Hafton House Ltd* 1990 SLT 496.

## Ranking of the floating charge creditor in respect of assets acquired after attachment of the floating charge

**2.37** There are various situations where it is not obvious whether or not the floating charge will rank the holder ahead of ordinary creditors. The following six will be considered.

1. The proceeds of successful reductions of unfair preferences and gratuitous alienations (para 2.37).

2. The proceeds of actions under sections 213 or 214 IA1986 (para 2.38).
3. Extortionate Credit Transactions in terms of section 244 IA1986 (para 2.39).
4. A *Burnett's Trustee v Grainger* sale of a property (para 2.40).
5. The proceeds of a misfeasance action (para 2.41).
6. Trust assets (para 2.42).

The question of whether or not a floating charge attaches to the assets resulting from the reduction of an unfair preference (or fraudulent preference as it was formerly described) has never been decided in Scotland. An unfair preference in the case of a company can only be reduced on the company's winding-up and so if a floating charge exists it will have crystallised either on such winding-up or on the earlier appointment of a receiver by the holder of the charge (and again on the appointment of a liquidator if such appointment follows a receivership). In an English case[1] the joint liquidators of a company recovered moneys from a creditor who had been fraudulently preferred. The company had granted a floating charge in favour of one of its creditors who claimed unsuccessfully, that such charge attached to the moneys so recovered. The court's decision was that:

(1) at the date of the crystallisation of the charge, the moneys which had been paid to the preferred creditor no longer formed part of the assets and undertaking of the company; and
(2) such moneys recovered by the liquidators were impressed in their hands with a trust for the creditors. In the absence of any judicial authority in Scotland, the *Yagerphone* decision[1] is considered by some to be authority for the proposition that in Scotland also the proceeds of assets coming to a company from the reduction of a fraudulent preference or unfair preference are not attached by a floating charge and so become available for the other creditors. This view has been questioned however.[2] There has also been a decision[3] which, while not dealing with the precise point, at least affords guidance.

The facts in the *Ross v Taylor* case[3] were that shortly before the appointment by the holder of a floating charge of a receiver over a company's whole property and assets, certain goods were sold to a loan creditor and the invoiced value of such goods was applied in reduction of the company's indebtedness to such creditor. After the receiver was appointed, he persuaded the creditor (under threat of challenge as a fraudulent preference on winding-up) to return the goods to the company and the question was whether the goods (or the proceeds of their sale by the receiver) fell to be attached by the floating charge or were available for the general body of creditors. The argument for the liquidator was that on the appointment of a receiver the floating charge, in terms of what is now section 53(7) of the IA 1986, attached to the property then subject to the charge. In the case of new assets coming to the company after the date of appointment of the receiver, as these did not form part of the company's property at the time the floating charge attached to such property, they were not attached by the floating charge. The case of *Re Yagerphone Ltd*[1] was quoted as authority for this proposition.

The opinion of the court was delivered by the Lord President, who stated that the court had found that the case of *Re Yagerphone Ltd*[1] did not afford any reliable assistance in the solution of the problem which was before the court, in that it turned upon its own facts and the particular terms of the debenture in question. In the court's opinion the problem before it fell to be resolved upon a proper construction of what is now section 53(7) of the IA1986 read together with the scope of the charge as defined in the instrument creating it. The floating charge was expressed to relate to the whole assets of the company, present and future, while the instrument was in force. Accordingly, the true question was not 'what was the property comprised in the company's property and undertaking on the date of the receiver's appointment?' but 'what was the property subject to the charge on the date of the receiver's appointment?' The answer to that question was to be found in the instrument creating the charge. Upon a proper construction of that instrument, the charge was over the whole of the property existing and from time to time emerging and it followed that under the particular provisions of the floating charge, the goods which were re-acquired after the receiver's appointment fell under the attachment of the charge. Any property which came into the company's hands after the appointment of the receiver would be attached and available, if need be, for realisation by the receiver.

The Lord President in his judgment went on to say that even if the court was wrong in so saying, there was a further reason for holding that the goods re-acquired by the company after the receiver's appointment should fall under the attachment of the charge. Counsel for the liquidator had correctly accepted that under what is now section 53(7) of the IA1986 the charge did not attach only to the particular items of property held by the company on that date and that goods acquired by the company by purchase or conversion of other goods, while the receiver carried on its business, would fall under the attachment. In the circumstances, the simple position was that items of stock and trade were re-acquired by the company on credit terms, in effect by means of an additional loan from the creditor. The powers of a receiver included the power to borrow and, in the court's opinion, no material distinction was to be found between the acquisition of stock in trade by immediate payment and the acquisition of stock in trade on credit terms.

The second question put to the court in *Ross v Taylor*[3] was, if the goods or the proceeds thereof did not form part of the company's assets at the date of appointment of the receiver, on the liquidation of the company would the floating charge recrystallise to the effect that any acquirenda since the date of the receiver's appointment would fall within the assets covered by the floating charge for distribution purposes in such liquidation? The court answered the question in the affirmative on the grounds that the floating charge, on the commencement of a winding up, attached to the property then comprised in the company's property and undertaking and had effect as if it were a fixed security over such property.

The wording of what are now section 463(1) of the 1985 Act and sections 53(7) and 54(6) of the IA 1986 should be contrasted. The first of these sections provides in effect that on winding up, a floating charge created by the company attaches to the property then comprised in its property and undertaking, or any part of the same, whereas the other two sections provide that on the appointment of a receiver, the floating charge attaches to the property then subject to the charge. There is an argument, however, that a company's undertaking includes the right to acquired property. As DP Sellar QC pointed out[2] in the article referred to above, Bell, Comm.,II, 217 expressly notes on the effect of the reduction of a preference that 'the answer seems to be, that a restitutio in integrum is no part of the reduction on the Act 1696, nor necessarily implied as a condition of it; but that as the creditors are entitled to reduce only in so far as the deed is prejudicial to them, their success will be limited to the effect of restoring them to the full benefit of the rights they would have enjoyed had the deed never been granted'. In effect the writers view is that the property so recovered should be treated as if it had never left the estate of the insolvent and would accordingly be covered by the floating charge.

1 *Re Yagerphone Ltd* [1935] Ch 392.
2 D P Sellar 'Floating Charges and Fraudulent Preferences' 1983 SLT 253.
3 *Ross v Taylor* 1985 SLT 387.

## *The proceeds of actions under section 213 or 214 IA 1986*

**2.38** Fraudulent trading actions in terms of section 213 of IA 1986 and wrongful trading actions in terms of section 214 of IA 1986 can only be progressed on the application of the liquidator and accordingly have no direct relevance in a receivership. The question does however need to be considered of whether a floating charge would attach to any sums received by a liquidator under these sections. In particular it should be noted that the sections refer to the court declaring that certain persons would be liable to make such contribution (if any) to the company's assets as the court things proper. In *Re Oasis Merchandising Services Ltd*[1] the court considered that the proceeds of a successful section 214 action would not be property of the company and any contribution to the company's assets was not to be deemed to have been an asset of the company immediately before the commencement of the winding up. Accordingly it would appear to be accepted in England that a floating charge would not attach to the proceeds of a successful section 214 claim. On the basis however that this claim related to champerty, which is a concept unknown in Scots Law, the comments in the case that the proceeds of a section 214 action would not be attached by a floating charge could be described as obiter comments in a case outwith Scotland relating to a concept unknown to Scots Law. Accordingly this must be considered to be a point undecided in Scots Law. Since, in *Ross v Taylor*[2], the court accepted where the floating charge related to the whole assets of the company, present and future, it would appear logical that contributions received by the company from the directors in terms of section 213 of the IA 1986 or section 214 of the IA 1986 would form part of the future property and undertaking of the company. It must be remembered however that on a winding up the crystallisation attaches the floating charge to the property then (ie at the date of the winding up) comprised in the company's property and undertaking[3].

There is accordingly a statable view that if the security has crystallised in terms of a winding up then it would not cover section 213 or section 214 proceeds as they were not property of the company on the date of the commencement of the winding up, but if there has been a crystallisation on the appointment of a receiver (since there cannot be a receivership without a liquidation as only a liquidator can raise section 213 or section 214 actions), then that crystallization permits the floating charge to attach to the future property of the company (per *Ross v Taylor*[2]). These sections have not been designed to benefit creditors who have specifically lost out as a result of credit being taken by the directors after they ought to have commenced an insolvency procedure. The Court of Appeal in England in *Lewis v IRC, sub nom Floor Fourteen Limited*[4] which related to the question of whether the costs of a section 214 action could be recovered from the company's assets by a liquidator held that they could not on the basis that the English rule 4.218(a) and (m) referred to expenses properly chargeable or incurred by the liquidator in preserving, realising or getting in any assets of the company and potential claims under section 214 were not assets of the company. The Scottish equivalent rule (rule 4.67(1)) refers only to outlays incurred by the liquidator in carrying out his functions rather than referring to assets of the company. However, in ranking such a claim, there might be a strong desire by the courts to have the same decision north and south of the border. And, possibly also the same result where the proceeds flow from an action which can only be raised by a liquidator, where there is a receiver and a liquidator or just a liquidator.

1 [1995] BCC 911.
2 1985 SLT 387.
3 CA 1985, s 463(1).
4 [2001] 3 All ER 499n.

## *Extortionate credit transactions in terms of section 244 of IA 1986*

**2.39** This section allows the court to make an order if the transaction is or was extortionate and was entered into in the period of three years ending with the date on which an administration order was made or (as the case may be) the company went into liquidation. A transaction is extortionate if, having regard to the risk accepted by the person providing the credit – (a) the terms of it are or were such as to require grossly exorbitant payments to be made (whether unconditionally or in certain contingencies) in respect of the provision of the credit; or (b) it otherwise grossly contravened ordinary principles of fair dealing. The whole section would appear to be drafted as a reduction and indeed sub-section (5) notes that the powers conferred by this section are exercisable in relation to any transaction concurrently with any powers exercisable in relation to that transaction as a transaction at an undervalue or under section 242 of the IA 1986 (gratuitous alienations in Scotland). Accordingly the writers consider that the effect of reducing such a transaction would be the same as the successful reduction of an unfair preference or a gratuitous alienation as referred to in paragraph 2.37 above.

## *A Burnett's Trustee v Grainger sale of a property*

**2.40** It is to be hoped that this is an academic point only in that any diligent solicitor on purchasing a property would have obtained a certificate of non–crystallisation of the floating charge incorporating a statement that the property conveyed would cease to form part of the property covered by a floating charge. If that however had not been done and a liquidator was subsequently appointed who became vested in a property and then won a race to the register in competition against the holder of a delivered disposition, would the proceeds of any subsequent sale of the property be covered by the floating charge or not? As was decided in *Sharp v Thomson*[1] the right to the property would not form part of the property comprised in the property and undertaking of the company at the date of appointment of a receiver but if property became an asset of the company by the *Burnett's Trustee v Grainger*[2] route then would it be covered by a floating charge which covered the present and future assets of the company? It would be possible to construct arguments that it either did form part of the future assets of the company and thus was covered by the floating charge crystallized on a receivership, but not on a winding up or that the sums recovered through this route were for the benefit of the creditors generally, particularly as the holder of the floating charge would not be entitled through a receivership to gain control of such property. The writers would be inclined to prefer the view that the proceeds of the sale of such a property by a liquidator would be covered by the floating charge crystallized on a receivership, but not on a liquidation only, although acknowledge that this would not be a popular view in the presently constituted House of Lords.

1 1997 SLT 636.
2 2004 SLT 513.

## *The proceeds of a misfeasance action*

**2.41** The position in England is settled[1] in that the proceeds of a misfeasance action are covered by the floating charge and there is no reason to believe that the Scottish Courts would find differently.

1 *Re Anglo-Austrian Printing & Publishing Union* [1895] 2 Ch 891 and *Re Asiatic Electric Co Pty Ltd* (1970) WN (NSW) 361.

## *Trust assets*

**2.42** Any property held in trust is not affected by the floating charge in that the property held in trust does not form part of the property and undertaking of the company.[1]

1 *Tay Valley Joinery Ltd v CF Financial Services Ltd* 1987 SLT 207.

## Ranking of charges

**2.43** The ranking of floating charges both amongst themselves and in relation to fixed charges is governed by the provisions of section 464 of the 1985 Act and this topic is dealt with in Chapter 8.

CHAPTER 3

# Powers, liabilities and agency of receiver

## Powers contained in charge

**3.01** A receiver has, in relation to the property attached by the floating charge under which he is appointed, the powers (if any) contained in the instrument creating the charge in addition to the statutory powers referred to in paragraph 3.02. If a creditor taking a floating charge considers that these statutory powers are likely to be deficient to any extent, then such deficiencies can be remedied by incorporating further powers in the instrument creating the charge. However, since the enactment of the IA 1986 when many areas of doubt arising out of the 1972 Act were clarified, most floating charge creditors have been prepared to accept the powers (if any) contained in the instrument creating the charge together with the statutory powers.[1]

1 IA 1986, Sch 2.

## Statutory powers

### *General*

**3.02** As noted in paragraph 3.01, a receiver has certain statutory powers[1] in relation to the property attached by the charge under which he is appointed provided that these statutory powers are not inconsistent with any provision contained in such instrument. These statutory powers are summarised in the succeeding paragraphs.

1 IA 1986, Sch 2.

### *To take possession of property*

**3.03** Power to take possession of, collect and get in the property from the company or liquidator of the company or any other person and to take such proceedings as may seem to him expedient for that purpose.

This power lies at the root of the receiver's functions, the primary purpose of which is to realise on behalf of his appointer the assets subject to the floating charge with a view to satisfying the claim of the holder. It enables a receiver to take control and possession of property of the company to which the charge has attached to enable him to satisfy the debt of the floating charge creditor after satisfaction of prior claims in accordance with the statutory scheme of distribution contained in section 60 of the IA 1986. It enables him,[1] for example, to collect book debts due to the company by taking proceedings in the name of the company.

1 *McPhail v Lothian Regional Council* 1981 SLT 173: *Taylor, Petitioner,* 1982 SLT 172; *Forth & Clyde Construction Co Ltd v Trinity Timber & Plywood Co Ltd* 1984 SLT 94; *Ritchie v EFT Industrial Ltd* 1998 SLT 11; and see 'The Receiver and Book Debts 1982 SLT (News) 129, and paras 2.12 to 2.14.

**3.04** Where any person has in his possession or control any property, books, papers or records to which the company appears to be entitled, the court may require that person forthwith (or within such period as the court may direct) to pay, deliver, convey, surrender or transfer the property etc to the receiver.[1] It has been held that the court has jurisdiction under section 234(2) to order property to be handed over to the office holders designated in section 234(1) (which includes receivers) even though there is a dispute as to its ownership.[2] Except in so far as negligent, a receiver is given statutory protection if he seizes or disposes of property not belonging to the company.[3] Attention is also drawn to the discussion on liens at paragraph 4.48 et seq.

1 IA 1986, s 234(2).
2 *Re London Iron and Steel Co Ltd* [1990] BCLC 372.
3 IA 1986, s 234(3) and (4).

**3.05** Various designated persons[1] are required to co-operate with a receiver in supplying information to him in relation to the company and its business, property etc.[2] In addition, on the application of a receiver, the court may summon any officer of the company and certain other persons to appear before it with a view to the recovery of company property or debts due to it or generally obtaining information on its business, property etc;[3] these provisions being supported by enforcement powers.[4] It has been held in a case[5] where the receivers of a group of companies sought an order under section 236 of the IA 1986 for the production by a company's solicitors of documents relating to the company that the receivers were not acting on behalf of the company alone but were in the same position as a third party who was entitled to production of the documents as against the client. Accordingly, since the solicitors could not assert a lien as against a third party they could not refuse to produce the documents to the receivers on the ground that they had a lien over the documents for the companies' unpaid costs. It is suggested that, from a Scottish legal standpoint, the *Aveling Barford* case[5] may be suspect in that an artificial distinction appears to have been drawn between the company and the receiver when, in fact, the receiver is the agent of the company. Certainly, from a practical Scottish perspective, Scottish solicitors holding documents of title and owed fees on the date of receivership are in a powerful position to reach a satisfactory settlement with a receiver without prejudicing their obligations under section 236.[6] Attention is also drawn to the discussion in *McBryde*.[7]

1 IA 1986, s 235(3).
2 Ibid, s 235(2).
3 Ibid, s 236(2).
4 Ibid, s 237.
5 *Re Aveling Barford Ltd* [1988] 3 All ER 1019.
6 IA 1986.
7 McBryde *Bankruptcy* (2nd edn) 10-46 to 54.

**3.06** In the event of a liquidator having been appointed on the winding-up of the company whether before or after the receiver's appointment, the liquidator is required to deliver to the receiver the property covered by the charge by virtue of this statutory power conferred on the receiver.[1] In *Manley, Petitioner* the company in question was ordered to be wound-up by the court (the date of commencement of the winding-up being 15 November 1982) and following his appointment as provisional liquidator Mr Manley was appointed liquidator on 6 December 1982. On the same date the Bank of Scotland, in whose favour the company had granted a floating charge over its whole property and undertaking, appointed a receiver. Following upon a demand by the receiver on the liquidator in terms of section 15(1)(a) of the 1972 Act[2] to deliver up the property of the company to the receiver, the liquidator presented a petition for directions (1) as to whether the liquidator was obliged to comply with the demand and (2) as to whether the liquidator or the receiver was primarily liable for the payment of the secured and preferential creditors of the company. On the first question, Lord Grieve decided that whether the receiver is appointed before or after the commencement of the winding-up his rights take precedence over the rights of the liquidator and he is entitled to take control of the property of the company in order to satisfy the debt of the holder of the floating charge. The argument put forward by the liquidator was that as the receiver's power to take possession of the company's property was subject to the rights of any person who had effectually executed diligence, this power was subject to the rights of the liquidator being a person who had effectually executed diligence by virtue of the terms of section 327(1)(a) of the CA 1948[3] which rendered the winding-up equivalent to complete and effectual diligences of the forms mentioned in that section. Lord Grieve, however, having taken the view that the purpose of section 327[3] was to cut down and equalise diligences and that the liquidator was not a person who had effectually executed diligence on the property of the company, then went on to state – 'The whole scheme of the 1972 Act is to give him (the receiver) precedence over the liquidator in the administration of the whole property of the company, even if appointed after the commencement of the liquidation'. On the second matter on which directions were sought, namely whether the liquidator or the receiver was primarily liable for the payment of the secured and preferential creditors, Lord Grieve decided the receiver was so liable. The payment of such debts is considered later in this book.[4] There has been considerable interest in England following the *Leyland Daf* decision[5] which held that liquidation expenses are not payable out of the proceeds of floating charge assets in priority to the secured creditor's debt. The House of Lords has drawn a distinction between two distinct funds: namely, the assets subject to the floating charge available to the secured creditor and the company's free assets available to the general body of creditors. While the *Leyland Daf* decision[5] is likely to be persuasive in Scotland, it should be noted that the development of Scottish jurisprudence in this area has taken place on a basis quite different to England. It has always been accepted practice in Scotland where there were concurrent appointments of a receiver and a liquidator that, after categories of persons identified in section 60[6] have been satisfied, only then were funds available to pay the liquidator's expenses.

1 *Manley, Petitioner* 1985 SLT 42.
2 See now the IA 1986, Sch 2, para 1.
3 Ibid, s 185(1)(a).
4 See para 9.14 et seq.
5 [2004] UKHL 9, [2004] 2 AC 298.
6 IA 1986.

## To sell property

**3.07** Power to sell, feu, hire out or otherwise dispose of the property by public roup or private bargain, with or without advertisement.

This power gives a receiver a wide discretion as to the method of disposal of the property covered by the charge but in exercising this power the receiver has a duty to take reasonable care.[1] It has been stated obiter[2] that 'in exercising his powers [the receiver] must no doubt, for example, exercise care to see that he does not realise company assets for less than the value which might reasonably be expected to be obtained'. Subject to this duty, a receiver exercises his commercial judgment backed up by whatever professional or other advice he may consider it prudent to obtain in deciding what method to employ in disposing of the company's business and assets either as a going concern or otherwise.

1 See para 3.44 and sequentia.
2 *Forth & Clyde Construction Co Ltd v Trinity Timber & Plywood Co Ltd* 1984 SLT 94, per the Lord President at 97.

## To borrow

**3.08** Power to raise or borrow money and grant security therefore over the property.

A receiver if he wishes to carry on the companyss:'s business almost invariably requires to obtain temporary facilities from a bank, normally the one appointing him and this power enables him to do so. As a receiver is personally liable on any contract entered into by him, except in so far as the contract otherwise provides,[1] unless expressly agreed with the bank to the contrary, such borrowing becomes the personal liability of the receiver. A receiver cannot exclude such liability by relying on provisions in some other contract to which he is not a party such as the floating charge under which he was appointed.[2] Should a receiver incur personal liability there is a right of indemnity out of the property attached by the charge.[3] The power to borrow is accordingly one which requires to be exercised with caution as the property could prove to be insufficient to satisfy such right of indemnity. If a receiver wishes to arrange a bank facility in circumstances where he is unwilling to accept personal liability he should make the position clear to the bank and obtain, if the bank is agreeable, the express written confirmation of or an indemnity from the bank that he will be relieved of personal liability. In view of the provisions of section 57(2) of the IA 1986 only with such confirmation or such an indemnity will the receiver be relieved of personal liability should the proceeds of sale of the company's property prove insufficient to meet the indebtedness so incurred to the bank. While in practice it is unusual for a receiver to create a security over the property (save for the case where the receiver procures the creation by a subsidiary of a charge, usually a floating charge, over its property following the hive-down to such subsidiary of part or all of the business of the company in receivership), the existence of this power should not be overlooked when acquiring property from a receiver.

1 IA 1986, s 57(2).
2 *Hill Samuel & Co Ltd v Laing* 1989 SLT 760.
3 Ibid, ss 57(3) and 60(1)(d).

## *Appointment of solicitor and other advisers*

**3.09** Power to appoint a solicitor or accountant or other professionally qualified person to assist the receiver in the performance of his functions.

Most receivers in Scotland are accountants and so are concerned with the appointment of a solicitor to assist in the receivership. As legal problems can arise in the early days of a receivership, particularly in relation to retention of title claims by suppliers and to employee redundancies, it is always advisable and particularly so in major receiverships that in his own interests the receiver should appoint a solicitor as soon as possible after his own appointment. Experienced receivers often ascertain in advance of appointment that a solicitor or one of his partners will be available to assist. An early task for such a solicitor is checking the title of the company to its various properties and also considering the likely impact of relevant irritancy clauses in any leases. As well as being in a position to seek immediate legal advice when confronted by a problem, the receiver is then able to instruct the solicitor so appointed to confirm without delay the validity of his appointment. As in the case of voluntary liquidations, the accounts of solicitors do not normally require to be submitted for taxation.

**3.10** In major receiverships, particularly where a group of companies is involved, the sale of the business or businesses is a major undertaking requiring skill and expertise on the receiver's part but which can often only be carried through with the help of adequate back-up staff with insolvency experience and various professional and other advisers. In these circumstances the gathering together at an early date of a team of such persons will hopefully result in a successful outcome to the receivership from the point of view of both the receiver's appointer and also other creditors and employees.

## *Power to seek directions*

**3.11** Power to apply to the court for directions.

This could be a very useful power available to a receiver where in the course of carrying out his function he is uncertain as to the validity of any procedural or other step which he is proposing to take. As far as is known however the power has so far rarely been used by receivers. The court means the court having jurisdiction to wind up the company.[1] The power to seek directions is now covered by the provisions of section 63 of the IA 1986 which provides that the court, on the application of either the holder of a floating charge by virtue of which a receiver has been appointed or a receiver, may give directions to the receiver in respect of any matter arising in connection with the performance of his duties.

1 CA 1985, s 744 and also the IA 1986, s 120.

## *Legal proceedings*

**3.12** Power to bring or defend any action or other legal proceedings in the name and on behalf of the company.[1]

A receiver in so doing is acting as agent for the company without incurring any personal liability, other than to agents whom he may instruct in this connection without excluding such liability, although, in that event he is entitled to be indemnified out of the property subject to the floating charge. A receiver is not infrequently faced with the problem as to whether or not to continue to defend an action raised against the company prior to his appointment. This is particularly so if, for example, the claim is for substantial damages against which the company may either not be insured at all or only partially insured and on the information then available to the receiver there may be surplus funds after satisfaction of the floating charge creditor's claim. In that event while the claimant in the damages action if successful would only be entitled to an ordinary ranking in the liquidation, the effect of such a claim succeeding might be to substantially reduce the dividend to other ordinary creditors. As, in these circumstances, it is the ordinary creditors who are likely to be affected and not the receiver's appointer, one course open to the receiver is to petition for the company's winding up and to leave the liquidator to take a decision on whether or not the action should continue to be defended. If there are no prospects of surplus funds after satisfaction of the floating charge creditor, the receiver has no interest to see any such action defended unless there are consigned funds that might be returned to the company. Should, however, the outcome of any such action against the company have a potentially adverse effect on any guarantee obligations of directors, the receiver should take no steps prejudicial to the interests of such persons without their authority and should afford them the opportunity of continuing the defence of the action. The same considerations apply in the case of proceedings raised against the company after the receiver's appointment.

1 Eg to collect a debt due to the company (*Taylor, Petitioner* 1982 SLT 172) and to recall an arrestment (*Forth & Clyde Construction Co Ltd v Trinity Timber & Plywood Co Ltd* 1984 SLT 94).

## *Arbitration*

**3.13** Power to refer questions affecting the company to arbitration.

This is presumably as an alternative to legal proceedings, subject to the agreement of the other party or parties. If the company is party to an agreement which specifically restricts the resolution of disputes to arbitration then in the event of such a dispute arising before or after the appointment of a receiver there is no alternative to arbitration in these circumstances.

## *Insurances*

**3.14** Power to effect and maintain insurances in respect of the company's business and property.

It would of course only be prudent for the receiver to ensure that the property subject to the floating charge is adequately insured. In practice, most receivers have special arrangements with insurance companies for block cover immediately upon intimation to the insurance company concerned of the receiver's appointment. Prior to cancelling any form of insurance taken out for the benefit of employees, the duty of care owed to those employees should be considered.[1]

1 *Larsen's Executrix v Henderson* 1990 SLT 498.

## *Use of company seal*

**3.15** Power to use the company's seal.

In earlier days prior to the IA 1986, problems arose particularly in England over the use of the company's seal but the relevant power is now contained in the IA

1986.[1] Execution requirements in Scotland are now contained in the Requirements of Writing (Scotland) Act 1995.

1 See IA 1986, s 42 and Sch 21, para 8.

### *Execution of deeds*

**3.16** Power to do all acts and to execute in the name and on behalf of the company any deed, receipt or other document.

### *Negotiable instruments*

**3.17** Power to draw, accept, make and endorse any bill of exchange or promissory note in the name and on behalf of the company.

### *Agents and employees*

**3.18** Power to appoint agents where appropriate and to employ and dismiss employees.[1]

1 For employees generally see Chap 6.

### *Work on property*

**3.19** Power to do everything necessary (including the carrying out of works) for the realisation of the property covered by the charge.

### *Incidental payments*

**3.20** Power to make any payment necessary or incidental to the performance of his functions.

### *Carrying on of business*

**3.21** Power to carry on the company's business (or any part of it).

Whether or not to exercise this power is a decision with which a receiver of a trading company is faced immediately on his appointment and one which he takes after careful consideration of all relevant factors, bearing in mind his potential personal liability if he trades at a loss.

## *Leases and tenancies*

**3.22** Power to grant or accept a surrender of a lease or tenancy of any property covered by the charge and also to take a lease or tenancy of any property required or convenient for the company's business.

In exercising any of these powers a receiver will of course require to consider carefully his own position in relation to personal liability. A receiver may also require to consider any statutory obligations imposed upon occupiers of premises. In one case[1] a company and its receivers were held to be joint occupiers of the company's factory for the purposes of the Explosives Act 1875 and the court granted an interim interdict against the receivers in order to prevent explosive materials being left in an insecure position. While the scope of this book does not include other similar issues, serious consideration in relevant circumstances should certainly be given to environmental matters and matters arising under the Mines and Quarries legislation.

1 *Lord Advocate v Aero Technologies Ltd (in receivership)* 1991 SLT 134.

## *Arrangements or compromises*

**3.23** Power to make any arrangement or compromise on behalf of the company.

This power is now contained in the IA 1986[1] along with the following powers: to call up uncalled capital, form subsidiaries and transfer to them the business of the company or any part of it and any of the property covered by the charge. The power to make an arrangement or compromise could be useful in that it confers on a receiver a degree of flexibility in dealing with creditors.

1 Sch 2, para 16.

## *Uncalled capital*

**3.24** A receiver now has statutory power to call up any uncalled capital of the company.

## *Establishment of subsidiaries*

**3.25** A receiver has statutory power to establish subsidiaries and to transfer to such subsidiaries the whole or any part of the company's business or the property covered by the charge. This power used to be of importance in the days when receivers often hived the business or businesses of a company into a subsidiary company or companies. However, as noted in Chapter 7[1], for tax reasons, hiving down of businesses is much less used today.

1 Paras 7.37 and 7.38.

## *Ranking in debtors' estates*

**3.26** Power to rank and claim in the bankruptcy, insolvency, sequestration or liquidation of debtors of the company, to receive dividends and to accede to trust deeds for creditors of any such debtors.

## Change of registered office

**3.27** Power to change the situation of the company's registered office.[1]

This is often necessary in that the receiver frequently sells or vacates the company's premises and this power enables him to alter the company's registered office without reference to its directors.

1 IA 1986, Sch 2, para 22.

## *Winding-up petitions*

**3.28** Power to present or defend a petition for the winding up of the company.

The most normal circumstances in which a receiver will wish to petition for the company's winding up are where there is a surplus remaining after satisfaction of the floating charge creditor's debt but which is clearly insufficient to meet in full the claims of ordinary creditors. In that event the receiver will present such a petition to the court on the grounds that the company is unable to pay its debts[1] whereupon the court on being satisfied that such is the case[2] will duly make a winding-up order and appoint a liquidator to whom the receiver may then deliver the surplus.[3] The court will normally be satisfied as to the company's inability to pay its debts on the production with the winding-up petition of a statement of assets and liabilities prepared by the receiver revealing such position. If, due perhaps to lengthy litigation where the outcome remains uncertain, a receivership runs on for a lengthy period, the receiver should remember that liquidation stops prescription, but receivership does not. Accordingly, ordinary creditors who have not commenced litigation before the expiry of the relevant prescriptive period will be prejudiced by a lengthy receivership without a liquidation being commenced.

1 IA 1986, s 122(1)(f).
2 Ibid, s 123(1)(e).
3 Ibid, s 60(2)(c).

**3.29** A receiver may also wish to petition for winding up, having obtained the prior approval of the floating charge creditor if there is unlikely to be sufficient to meet such creditor's debt in full, where it appears that the company has granted an unfair preference or gratuitous alienation. Such approval is not strictly necessary, but it may be prudent for the receiver to obtain it. In that event the statutory period or periods within which unfair preferences are rendered invalid should be kept in mind[1] although a common law challenge is possible. The question of whether the assets recovered by such proceedings are attached by the floating charge or become available for the ordinary creditors is dealt with elsewhere.[2]

1 IA 1986, s 243.
2 See Chap 2 para 2.37.

**3.30** There may also come to the notice of a receiver circumstances which justify the winding up of the company in order to bring into play those sections of the IA 1986 which provide remedies or create offences only in the event of the company's winding up.[1]

1 eg wrongful trading, fraudulent trading or misfeasance: see also the Company Directors Disqualification Act 1986. But note that the EA 2002 provides that the liquidator will need the sanction of the court or the liquidation committee to commence a wrongful trading action.

**3.31** In one case[1] a receiver of a company's whole assets opposed the grant of the first order for intimation, advertisement and service of a petition presented by an ordinary creditor on the grounds that both this and any subsequent winding-up order would be detrimental to the interests of the secured creditors and sought the summary dismissal of the petition. It was held, however, that where a creditor seeks a winding-up order on the ground that a company is unable to pay its debts, the petition should not be summarily dismissed unless there are compelling reasons for so doing.

1 *Foxhall & Gyle (Nurseries) Ltd, Petitioners* 1978 SLT (Notes) 29; see also paras 4.64 to 4.70.

### *Incidental powers*

**3.32** Power to do all other things incidental to the exercise of his powers. This gives to a receiver general ancillary powers necessary for the exercise of the specific powers referred to in the foregoing paragraphs.

## Powers subject to rights of certain persons

**3.33** The powers of a receiver are subject to the rights of certain persons, namely:

(a) any person who has effectually executed diligence on all or any part of the property of the company prior to the receiver's appointment; and
(b) any person holding a fixed security or floating charge over all or any part of the property of the company ranking prior to or *pari passu* with the floating charge under which the receiver was appointed.[1]

1 IA 1986, s 55(3).

**3.34** The effect in relation to diligence of attachment or crystallisation of the floating charge on a receiver's appointment has already been discussed.[1] The powers of a receiver are also subject to the rights of any person holding a charge over property of the company ranking prior to or *pari passu* with the floating charge under which the receiver was appointed. The rights of heritable creditors are unaffected by the appointment of a receiver and while another floating charge does not automatically attach or crystallise on the appointment of a receiver other than under it, the holder has then grounds for himself appointing a receiver to enable his charge to attach or crystallise.

1 Paragraphs 2.16 to 2.20.

**3.35** Where a receiver sells or wishes to sell property covered by the floating charge under which he has been appointed and is unable to obtain the consent of either a creditor who has effectually executed diligence or who holds a prior or *pari passu* ranking security he may apply to the court for the appropriate authority.to:[1] Such an application was made by joint receivers where an inhibiting creditor would not consent to the sale of heritable property.[2]

1 IA 1986, s 61; see also paras 7.34 to 7.36.
2 *Armour and Mycroft, Petitioners* 1983 SLT 453.

## Disposal of interest in property

**3.36** Section 61 of the IA 1986 provides[1] that where a receiver sells or disposes or wishes to sell or dispose of property of the company which is subject to the floating charge by virtue of which he was appointed and, which is subject to the security or interest of a prior, *pari passu* or postponed ranking creditor or is property affected by effectual diligence and the receiver cannot obtain the consent of such creditor or the person entitled to such effectual diligence, the receiver may apply to the court for authority to sell or dispose of the property. The court, on such an application may authorise such sale or disposal on such terms or conditions as it thinks fit.[2]

1 IA 1986, s 61(1).
2 Ibid, s 61(2).

**3.37** Section 61(3) of the IA 1986 provides that in the case of an application where a fixed security over the property or interest in question which ranks prior to the floating charge has not been met or provided for in full, the court shall not authorise the sale or disposal of the property or interest in question unless it is satisfied that the sale or disposal would be likely to provide a more advantageous realisation of the company's assets than would otherwise be effected. Section 61(4) further provides that it is a condition of authorisation that (a) the net proceeds of the disposal, and (b) where those proceeds are less than such amount as may be determined by the court to be the net amount which would be realised on a sale of the property or interest in the open market by a willing seller, such sums as may be required to make good the deficiency, are applied towards discharging the sums secured by the fixed security. If there are two or more fixed securities, the above provisions apply in the order of priority of such fixed securities.[1]

1 IA 1986, s 61(5).

**3.38** Section 61(8) of the IA 1986 empowers the receiver to grant to a purchaser an appropriate document of transfer and such document has the effect, or where recording, intimation or registration of such document is a legal requirement for completion of title to the property, then such recording, intimation or registration has the effect, of disencumbering the property of the security and freeing the property from the diligence executed upon it.

**3.39** In terms of section 61(6) of the IA 1986, the receiver is required to send to the Registrar of Companies within 14 days of the granting thereof, a copy of the authorisation certified by the clerk of court obtained pursuant to section 61(2). If the receiver fails to do so without reasonable excuse, he is liable to a fine and, for continued contravention, to a daily default fine.[1] Finally, it is expressly provided in section 61(9) that nothing in the section prejudices the right of any creditor of the company to rank for his debt in the winding up of the company.

1 IA 1986, s 61(7).

## Persons dealing with receiver

**3.40** A person who deals with a receiver in good faith and for value is not concerned to inquire whether the receiver is acting within his powers.[1] This does not however relieve such a person from satisfying himself that a receiver has been validly appointed, whether it is a sole or joint appointment and in the latter case whether the joint receivers can act individually or must act jointly.

1 IA 1986, s 55(4).

## Exercise of powers outwith jurisdiction

**3.41** Section 7 of the Administration of Justice Act 1977 provided that a receiver and/or manager appointed under the law of any part of the United Kingdom under a floating charge may exercise his powers in any other part of the United Kingdom in so far as their exercise is not inconsistent with the law applicable there. The equivalent provisions in the 1985 Act (section 724) were consolidated in section 72 of the IA 1986. In the table of derivations to the 1985 Act, section 724 was stated to be derived from section 7 of the 1977 Act but the provisions are not reproduced precisely in that there are substituted for the references to the United Kingdom narrower references to Great Britain. Section 7 of the 1977

Act was however not repealed by the 1985 Act. Thus, for example, a receiver of a Scottish company may exercise his powers over property in England provided the exercise of any specific power is not inconsistent with the law of England, on which he would be well advised in the appropriate circumstances to take advice. The effect of section 72 of the IA 1986 has been considered by the courts in Scotland in the case of an English company with assets in Scotland.[1] It should be noted that courts in most jurisdictions in Europe are reluctant or indeed will not recognise a UK receiver as he is not a court appointed official.[2]

1 *Norfolk House plc (in receivership) v Repsol Petroleum Ltd* 1992 SLT 235n.
2 Art 2 (definition of 'liquidator') and Annex C of Council Regulation 1346/2000/EC.

**3.42** Prior to the repeal of section 15(4) of the 1972 Act the First Division of the Court of Session had occasion to consider[1] the terms of that section which was restricted to extending the powers of a receiver or manager of an English company to property in Scotland in so far as not inconsistent with the law of Scotland. The facts, put simply, were that following the appointment of a receiver over the whole property of an English company a Scottish creditor having obtained decree in Scotland arrested funds in the hands of a Scottish based debtor of the company and followed this up with an action of furthcoming. In dismissing the action the court held that the appointment of the receiver in England had the effect of attaching or crystallising the floating charge as a fixed security over the company's property both in England and Scotland and that as the creditor had not by the arrestment effectually executed diligence prior to the receiver's appointment, such arrestment was of no effect.

1 *Gordon Anderson (Plant) Ltd v Campsie Construction and Anglo Scottish Plant Ltd* 1977 SLT 7.

## Duties of receiver

### *General*

**3.43** A receiver appointed over the property of a Scottish company operates within the statutory framework of Chapter II (sections 50–71) of Part III of the IA 1986. His powers are defined[1] and he is required to distribute moneys received by him in accordance with mandatory directions.[2] However, nowhere in the IA 1986 are the duties of a receiver laid down. This is not to say, however, that in exercising his powers a receiver has no duties to any particular party.

1 IA 1986, Sch 2.
2 Ibid, s 60.

### *Duty to company*

**3.44** In the first place a receiver is appointed by or at the instigation of the holder of a floating charge, which charge on the appointment of the receiver becomes equivalent to a fixed charge over the property subject to such charge.[1] This is the only method by which the holder of a floating charge can realise his security for the debt owed to him by the company. The receiver then proceeds to exercise his powers on behalf of the holder of the floating charge whose security by then has become in effect a fixed charge.[1] That being the position it must be assumed that a receiver has duties to the company similar to those which the holder of a fixed security exercising a right of sale has towards the debtor. He must exercise his powers without negligence and generally exercise care in disposing of assets for at least the value which they might reasonably be expected to realise.[2] In England, a receiver has a similar duty of care.[3] It is in addition well established under the law of Scotland that the holder of a heritable security is required to have regard for the interests of both the debtor and postponed heritable creditors[4] and that contractual provisions entitling a creditor to sell security subjects at such price as he might think fit cannot relieve him of the obligation to exercise a power of sale bona fide and with regard to the interests of the debtor and to obtain a fair price.[5] This would not, however, require a receiver to make a planning application to try to enhance the value of the property.[6] Such contractual provisions might also be open to challenge as being unreasonable in terms of the Unfair Contract Terms Act 1977. In addition, sections 25 and 35 of the Conveyancing and Feudal Reform (Scotland) Act 1970 impose a duty on certain heritable creditors exercising a power of sale.

1 IA 1986, s 70.
2 *Forth and Clyde Construction Co Ltd v Trinity Timber and Plywood Co Ltd* 1984 SLT 94, Lord President Emslie at 97.
3 *Re B Johnson & Co (Builders) Ltd* [1955] Ch 634; *Cuckmere Brick Co Ltd v Mutual Finance Ltd* [1971] Ch 949; *American Express International Banking Corpn v Hurley* [1985] 3 All ER 564; *Watts v Midland Bank plc* [1986] BCLC 15; *Knight v Lawrence* [1991] BCC 411.
4 *Beveridge v Wilson* (1829) 7 S 279 and *Kerr v McArthur's Trs* (1848) 11 D 301.
5 *Rimmer v Thomas Usher & Sons Ltd* 1967 SLT 7.
6 *Silven Properties Ltd v Royal Bank of Scotland plc* [2003] BCC 1002.

**3.45** It has been held in England[1] that as a receiver's primary responsibility is to the debenture holder, any right which a company has to obtain information from the receiver is qualified by this primary responsibility and entitles the receiver to withhold information where he forms the opinion that disclosure would be contrary to the interests of the debenture holder in realising the security.

1 *Gomba Holdings UK Ltd v Homan* [1986] 3 All ER 94.

**3.46** It has also been suggested,[1] correctly it is thought, that a duty to take reasonable care would be imposed on a receiver in delict on the basis of a decision[2] which established that a prima facie duty of care arises where there is sufficient relationship of proximity between parties such that, in the reasonable contemplation of the one, carelessness on his part may be likely to cause damage to the other. The House of Lords in *Caparo Industries plc v Dickman*[3] set out a tripartite test in an auditor's liability case involving pure economic loss to establish if a duty of care would exist in a novel situation which did not fit within the existing categories of negligence. It is respectfully suggested that a receiver owes a duty to take reasonable care but the extent of such duty is presently unsettled. For a more detailed consideration of this, reference is made to an article by Mark Godfrey 'The Categories of Negligence Revisited.'[4]

1 R J Reed 'Aspects of the Law of Receivers in Scotland – The Receiver's Duty of Care' 1983 SLT 261, p 262.
2 *Junior Books Ltd v Veitchi Co Ltd* 1982 SLT 492.
3 [1990] 1 All ER 568.
4 2005 SLT 9.

**3.47** A receiver in Scotland is, in addition, deemed to be the agent of the company in relation to the property covered by the floating charge under which he is appointed[1] and may only be removed by the court on cause shown and not, where appointed by the holder of a floating charge, by his appointer.[2] These statutory provisions must, it is thought, imply a fiduciary relationship with consequential duties to the company and other parties whose interests are liable to be affected in the exercise by the receiver of his powers.

1 IA 1986, s 57.
2 Ibid, s 62(3).

**3.48** On the basis of an English Court of Appeal decision[1] it is possible that, in the event of a receiver being considered to be in breach of his duty towards the company, proceedings by the company instituted by the directors would be competent. A derivative action by the directors and majority shareholders would, however, not appear to be competent.[2]

1 *Newhart Developments Ltd v Co-operative Commercial Bank Ltd* [1978] QB 814.
2 *Watts v Midland Bank plc* [1986] BCLC 15.

## Duty to guarantor

**3.49** While there is no direct Scottish authority on the subject, the court in England has considered on more than one occasion the question of whether a receiver owes a duty of care towards a guarantor of the company's debt. In two earlier decisions[1] the court held that a receiver did not owe a duty of care to a guarantor but these decisions were not followed in a subsequently reported decision.[2] The Court of Appeal held in that later case that a receiver when realising assets owed a duty both to the company and to a guarantor of its debt to take reasonable care to obtain the best possible price which circumstances permit, a decision which has since been followed.[3]

1 *Barclays Bank Ltd v Thienel and Thienel* (1978) 247 Estates Gazette 385; *Latchford v Beirne* [1981] 3 All ER 705.
2 *Standard Chartered Bank Ltd v Walker* [1982] 1 WLR 1410.
3 *American Express International Banking Corpn v Hurley* [1985] 3 All ER 564.

**3.50** The Court of Appeal decision was referred to in a subsequent Scottish case[1] on consideration by the court of whether a creditor realising a security owes a duty to a guarantor. In his judgment Lord Ross reserved at the procedure roll stage a plea to the relevancy of averments that a creditor had acted in breach of a duty of care owed to a guarantor. In considering this question Lord Ross reached the conclusion that the proposition on which the *Standard Chartered* decision was based was not inconsistent with Scottish authorities and that he could not at that stage hold that a creditor in Scotland owed no duty to act reasonably in a question with a guarantor. If a floating charge creditor in Scotland wishes his security realised, this, in the absence of winding up, can only be effected by the appointment of a receiver. Such receiver operates within a statutory framework and although the agent of the company (as was the receiver in the *Standard Chartered* case) exercises his powers on behalf of the holder of the floating charge which by then has become equivalent to a fixed security. It is, accordingly, reasonable to assume that the receiver owes similar duties to those of the creditor on whose behalf he exercises these powers and, if this assumption is correct, it is suggested that the court in Scotland would be likely to reach the same decision as that in the *Standard Chartered* case. In the *Standard Chartered* case it was also held that the debenture holder might also be attached with responsibility for the receiver's actions if it were shown that such holder had interfered with the conduct of the receivership, a view subsequently approved in another case.[2] It is also suggested that a receiver in Scotland could be liable to a guarantor in delict on the basis that, in the reasonable contemplation of the receiver, negligence on his part in disposing of assets could damage the guarantor.[3]

1 *Lord Advocate v Maritime Fruit Carriers Co Ltd* 1983 SLT 357.
2 *American Express International Banking Corpn v Hurley* [1985] 3 All ER 564.
3 *Caparo Industries plc v Dickman* [1990] 1 All ER 568 (but see discussion in para 3.46).

## *Duty to creditor other than holder of floating charge*

**3.51** If it is accepted that a receiver has a duty to exercise his powers without negligence[1] it is suggested that this duty must extend to any creditors of the company whose interests are liable to be affected by his actings. In the *Standard Chartered* case[2] Lord Denning did say (at 1416) – 'The receiver owes a duty not only to the company, but also to the guarantor, to exercise reasonable care in the disposal of the assets. I say nothing about creditors. We are not concerned with them today'. If a receiver, however, disposes of the assets attached by the floating charge in a way which can clearly be demonstrated resulted in a value being realised which was less than could reasonably be expected, he has acted negligently and the relationship of the other creditors of the company, is, it is suggested, in such proximity to him that it must have been in his reasonable contemplation that lack of care on his part was likely to cause damage to them. R3 (formerly SPI) produced in January 2000 a Statement of Insolvency Practice 14 (for Scotland) on 'a receiver's responsibility to preferential creditors' and reference is made to this for a detailed analysis of this situation.[3]

1 *Forth & Clyde Construction Co Ltd v Trinity Timber & Plywood Co Ltd* 1984 SLT 94.
2 *Standard Chartered Bank Ltd v Walker* [1982] 1 WLR 1410.
3 Appendix 15.

## *Duty to employees*

**3.52** In *Larsen's Executrix v Henderson*[1] where a receiver terminated a retirement benefits scheme which provided for a death benefit it was held that while a receiver owes a duty of care to the employees of the company and must act reasonably in the discharge of such duty, he was not in breach of duty to the deceased managing director by the way he terminated the scheme in question.

1 1990 SLT 498.

## *Duty in relation to pension schemes*

**3.53** On being appointed, a receiver needs to give consideration to any pension schemes that the company may have and members thereof as he has a number of duties to perform. These include:

(i) He should notify the trustees of every scheme that he has been appointed. Once section 36 of the Pensions Act 2004 comes into force, there will be a statutory duty to give written notice to the trustees, the Pensions Regulator and the Board of the Pension Protection Fund as soon as reasonably practicable after he has begun to act as an insolvency practitioner in relation to certain schemes.

(ii) Persons competent to act in respect of an occupational pension scheme can apply to the Secretary of State requiring the Secretary of State to pay certain unpaid employers' and employees' contributions to the scheme. The Secretary of State would then have a claim in the receivership.

(iii) As the law currently stands (see (iv) below), one of the most important duties relates to the appointment of independent trustees in accordance with sections 22-26 of the Pensions Act 1995 ('PA1995') as modified by the Occupational Pension Schemes (Independent Trustee) Regulations 1997 (SI 1997/252) (as amended by SI 1997/3038).

The obligations under PA 1995, sections 22-26 do not apply:

(a) if the scheme is not established under trust;
(b) where each member is a trustee;
(c) where all the benefits are money purchase ones or payable only on death so that no member has any accrued rights, or where the scheme would be a money purchase scheme but for the fact that it provides guaranteed minimum pensions;
(d) where all the benefits are secured by insurance policies specifically allocated to members;
(e) where the scheme is not Inland Revenue approved;
(f) where the scheme was established only for members outwith the UK; or
(g) to certain other schemes.

On the company going into receivership, the insolvency practitioner is under an obligation to satisfy himself that, in relation to certain types of scheme, at all times (during the appointment) at least one of the trustees is an independent person. If the insolvency practitioner is not so satisfied he must appoint, or secure the appointment of, an independent person as a trustee. Accordingly even once such a person is appointed, if that person ceases to be independent, resigns or dies, the obligation needs to be fulfilled again. The PA 1995 gives the power to appoint to the insolvency practitioner as an individual and not as receiver, liquidator, etc. The appointment is accordingly not by the receiver acting as agent of the company, as the writers have sometimes seen it, and in the view of the writers such an appointment would not be valid. The independent person should be appointed within three months of the date on which the insolvency practitioner forms the opinion that there was no independent trustee. This time limit was inserted with effect from 1 April 2002 by the Occupational Pension Schemes (Winding-Up Notices & Reports, etc) Regulations 2002. If two or more insolvency practitioners are acting in different capacities, the duty falls on the liquidator, provisional liquidator or administrator (Pensions Act 1995, s 23(4)). If the insolvency practitioner neglects or refuses to discharge his duty, a member of the scheme may apply to the court for an order requiring him to do so (PA 1995, s 24(1)).

An obligation is placed on the insolvency practitioner to provide information to the scheme trustees (PA 1995, s 26(1)), the expenses so incurred being recoverable as being in discharge of his duties. The insolvency practitioner need do nothing where the expenses cannot be so recovered unless the trustees of the scheme undertake to meet them (PA 1995, s 26(3)).

(iv) The position will change once section 36 of the Pensions Act 2004 ('PA 2004') comes into force, at a date yet to be determined. PA 2004, section 36 provides for the amendment of PA 1995, sections 22-26. Under the new provisions, when a person begins to act (or when he ceases to act) as insolvency practitioner in relation to a company, he must, as soon as reasonably practicable, give written notice to the Pensions Regulator, the Board of the Pensions Protection Fund and the trustees of the scheme. Subsequent regulations will set out the information to be provided in the notice. The requirement for the practitioner to appoint, or secure the appointment of, an independent trustee will be repealed. Instead, the Pensions Regulator will have the power to appoint an independent trustee, who is an 'independent person', as defined in PA 1995, section 23 (as amended by PA 2004) and is on the register which will be maintained by the Pensions Regulator, in accordance with regulations.

The receiver may wish to consider if any sums paid into a scheme are recoverable as either ultra vires payments or gratuitous alienations. He may also have a duty to his appointed to find out if there is likely to be a surplus in the scheme.

Reference is made to the duty to employees who are members of a scheme in paragraph 3.52 above.

A receiver may be able to exercise beneficial powers of the company under a pension scheme but not fiduciary powers. Further discussion of this strays into trust law and outwith the scope of this book although it is worth pointing out that conflicts of interest are highly likely to arise.

## Agency and liability of receiver

### *Agent of company*

**3.54** A receiver is deemed to be the agent of the company in relation to the property of the company attached by the charge under which he is appointed.[1] Accordingly, the receiver in exercising his powers in relation to such property, providing he makes clear that he does so as receiver of the company, is acting as an agent for a disclosed principal and both his liability and that of the company are, subject to the provisions of the IA 1986, governed by the principles and rules of the law of agency. However, a receiver (including one whose powers are suspended on the appointment of another receiver under a prior ranking floating charge) is personally liable on any contract entered into by him in the performance of his functions, except in so far as the contract otherwise provides.[2] Such liability cannot be excluded by reliance on a contract to which the receiver is not a party such as the floating charge under which he was appointed.[3] In the event of personal liability not being excluded in terms of the contract, the receiver has a right of indemnity against the property covered by the charge.[4] This right of indemnity is postponed to the rights of fixed charge creditors ranking in priority to or *pari passu* with the floating charge and creditors who have effectually executed diligence.[5] The provisions of section 57(1) of the IA 1986[6] do not limit any right to indemnity which the receiver would have apart from them, nor limit his liability on contracts entered into or adopted without authority nor confer any right to indemnity in respect of that liability. A contract entered into without authority is presumably one outwith the receiver's powers, statutory or otherwise.

1 IA 1986, s 57(1).
2 Ibid, s 57(2).
3 *Hill Samuel & Co Ltd v Laing* 1989 SLT 760.
4 Ibid, s 57(3).
5 Ibid, s 60(1)(a) and (b) – see also the *Leyland Daf* decision [2004] 1 All ER 1289.

**3.55** As a result of the provisions of the IA 1986,[1] a receiver is also now personally liable (without the right to exclude such liability) on any contract of employment adopted by him in the carrying out of his functions while at the same time a receiver is not to be taken to have adopted such a contract by reason of any act or omission within 14 days of his appointment.[2] During such period only a positive act of adoption will, it is assumed, make a receiver personally liable on such a contract but on the expiry of the period if a receiver continues any contract of employment there will, presumably, be an assumption that he has adopted such contract and thus accepted personal liability notwithstanding the provisions of section 57(4) to the effect that a receiver is not by virtue of his appointment alone personally liable on a pre-receivership contract to which the company is a party. This amendment effectively reversed an English Court of Appeal decision.[3] However, it is very important to appreciate fully the developments in England in the last 10 years or so in employment matters. In view of all of the difficulties caused by the *Specialised Mouldings* case[4] and the decision in the subsequent *Paramount* cases[5] the Government, following pressure from insolvency practitioners deeply concerned about the commercial consequences after the Court of Appeal decision in *Paramount* and prior to the hearing of the House of Lords Appeal, enacted the IA 1994 amending the IA 1986 which provides that the only liabilities secured are limited to amounts payable by way of wages or salary. Such amounts would also include holiday pay, absence from work through sickness and contributions to an occupational pension scheme. For further discussion on the above matters, attention is drawn to Chapter 6 [6].

1 IA 1986, s 57(2).
2 Ibid, s 57(5).
3 *Nicoll v Cutts* (1985) BCLC 322.
4 *Re Specialised Mouldings Ltd* (13 February 1987, unreported), per Harman J.
5 [1995] 2 AC 394 per Lord Browne-Wilkinson at 448G et seq.
6 Para 6.09.

**3.56** The statutory framework of section 57(1) and (2) of the IA 1986 appears to be that, in the first place, in relation to the property covered by the charge, the receiver is agent of the company. However, should he enter into any contract in the exercise of his powers, not directly in relation to such property, he is personally liable under such contract unless it provides otherwise and remains so even if his powers are suspended on the appointment of a receiver by the holder of a prior ranking floating charge. He is also personally liable in respect of qualifying liabilities as defined by section 57(2) of the IA 1986 as amended by the IA 1994 on any employment contract adopted by him. For practical reasons, this is the only way in which a receiver could effectively exercise his powers as third parties and employees would be reluctant to enter into or continue contracts with the receiver (eg for the supply of goods or services) unless there was a reasonable guarantee of payment in full by the receiver undertaking personal liability. Put another way, entering into or continuing a contract with the agent of a disclosed but apparently insolvent principal without such agent accepting personal liability does not make commercial sense. It is arguable that, by virtue of the provisions of section 57(1) of the IA 1986, the receiver's personal liability is excluded in respect of the exercise of his powers as receiver directly in relation to the property covered by the charge (eg in selling such property) but it is prudent of a receiver who wishes to exclude such personal liability to expressly so contract to the effect that he does so as receiver and without any personal liability. The presumption of agency is rebuttable.[1] A receiver incurring personal liability must bear in mind the limitations on his indemnity: namely his right of relief extends to the property covered by the charge alone and then only after satisfaction of the rights of certain other creditors. The maximum value of his indemnity is, therefore, the net value of such property after deducting the claims of such creditors. This point assumes greater importance where the receiver carries on the company's business after his appointment, particularly if this involves carrying on or entering into substantial contracts in, for example, the construction or engineering industries.

1 *Inverness District Council v Highland Universal Fabrications Ltd* [1986] SLT 556n.

**3.57** A receiver whose powers are suspended as a result of the subsequent appointment of another receiver by the holder of a prior ranking floating charge is entitled to retain property (including letters or documents) and not to release them to the other receiver until given by him a valid indemnity in respect of any expenses, charges and liabilities he may have incurred in the performance of his functions as receiver.[1] This indemnity is similarly limited and the first receiver should in obtaining such an indemnity take into account the fact that the property in question will cease to be under his control and that its value may decrease under the control of the other receiver.

1 IA 1986, s 56(5).

## Termination of agency on winding up

**3.58** Whereas the office of receiver was only introduced into the law of Scotland in 1972, it has existed in England for over a century with the appointment being capable of being made both by the court and also out of court, the framework of the law being a mixture of common law and statute law. A receiver appointed by the court in England being an officer of the court is neither an agent for the company nor the debenture holder whereas a receiver appointed out of court is usually, in terms of the debenture by virtue of which he is appointed, agent for the company. This agency, in the case of an administrative receiver appointed out of court, is now given statutory authority[1] and is a general agency not restricted to the assets covered by the charge although of course an administrative receiver is defined as a receiver or manager of the whole or substantially the whole of a company's property.[2]

1 IA 1986, s 44(1)(a).
2 Ibid, s 29.

**3.59** In England, it has been judicially established that the liquidation of the company, voluntary or compulsory, terminates the agency of a receiver appointed out of court[1] but not the receivership powers which the receiver remains entitled to exercise in the name of the company,[2] albeit subject to personal liability in that he is then acting as a principal. Statutory authority for the termination of such agency has also now been introduced[3] but at the same time provisions governing a receiver's liability on contracts similar to the equivalent Scottish provisions have also been introduced[4] as have statutory powers which include power to carry on the business of the company.[5] It has also been held in England[6] that on the termination of such agency a receiver who continues to act may in certain circumstances become the agent of his appointer, for example, if his appointer treats him as such. As a result, it was held, in the absence of an express exclusion in the agency contract, that the appointer was entitled to an indemnity from the receiver in respect of negligence on his part.

1 *Gosling v Gaskell* [1897] AC 575; *Thomas v Todd* [1926] 2 KB 511.
2 *Barrows v Chief Land Registrar* (1977) Times, 20 October.
3 IA 1986, s 44.
4 Ibid, s 44(1)(b) and (c).
5 Ibid, s 42(1) and Sch 1.
6 *American Express International Banking Corpn v Hurley* [1985] 3 All ER 564 (but see discussion in para 3.46).

**3.60** The Cork Committee noted[1] that there had been much criticism of the rule that the receiver's agency came to an end on liquidation which they stated caused particular difficulty in the case of a compulsory liquidation since its effect was in general to terminate all contracts of employment with the result that if the receiver decided to retain employees, he became personally liable for their wages and for any redundancy pay if they were later made redundant. As a result some receivers, rather than face the prospect of such personal liability, considered it prudent to close down the business. While an administrative receiver's agency will in England still terminate on winding-up the receiver will be entitled to an indemnity out of the assets of the company in respect of any personal liability incurred on any contract entered into by him in performance of his functions[2] prior to the effective date of the winding up.

1 Report of the Review Committee on Insolvency Law and Practice (Cmnd 8558) para 453 et seq.
2 IA 1986, s 44.

**3.61** Receivership was introduced in Scotland by the 1972 Act (which was consolidated in the 1985 Act and again in the IA 1986) and from the outset all receivers in Scotland, whether appointed by the holder of a floating charge or by the court, have operated within a statutory framework. A receiver in Scotland is agent of the company in relation to the property attached by the charge under which he is appointed and, subject thereto, is, except where otherwise provided, personally liable on contracts which he enters into and is also personally liable without exception (but subject to the qualifying liabilities as defined in section 57(2) of IA 1986 as amended by IA 1994) on contracts of employment adopted by him. One of the receiver's powers is to carry on the company's business or any part of it. The exercise of this power remains unaffected by the liquidation of the company, his rights whether appointed before or after liquidation taking precedence over the rights of the liquidator.[1]

1 *Manley, Petitioner* 1985 SLT 42. See also para 3 06 above and Ch 6.

**3.62** The IA 1986 does not in Chapter II of Part III (which deals with Receivers in Scotland) include a provision equivalent to that contained in section 44(1)(a) terminating the agency of an administrative receiver in England on the liquidation of the company. That being the case and in the absence of any judicial authority it is not clear whether the statutory agency of a receiver in Scotland is terminated by liquidation. What is clear, however, is that notwithstanding the liquidation of the company he is still entitled to exercise all the powers conferred on him which includes the power to carry on all or part of the company's business and dispose of property subject to the charge. In this connection the provisions of section 127 of the IA 1986, which avoid any disposition of the company's property after the commencement of the winding-up, do not apply as the 'disposition' is the charge under which the receiver was appointed.[1] In exercising such powers, however, a receiver must accept personal liability on all contracts entered into by him after liquidation whether or not they relate to the property covered by the charge, unless of course the contract expressly provides otherwise. Against that background he should bear in mind the extent of his indemnity against the property subject to the charge and that his actings will be liable to scrutiny by the liquidator.

1 *Re Park Ward & Co Ltd* [1926] Ch 828.

## Pre-receivership contracts

### *General*

**3.63** Any contract entered into by the company prior to the appointment of a receiver continues in force in spite of such appointment, unless the contract specifically provides for termination on receivership [1]. Such provision may render a contract voidable only, entitling the other party to terminate should he so wish. In the event of a contract so continuing, the receiver does not automatically by his appointment alone incur personal liability[2] although it will be a question of fact in each case whether the receiver has by his actings adopted any particular contract so as to incur personal liability unless specifically excluded. As a result of an amendment introduced by the IA 1986[3] it is now provided that a receiver is personally liable (in respect of qualifying liabilities as defined in section 57(2) of IA 1986 as amended by IA 1994) on any contract of employment adopted by him in the carrying out of his functions.

1 Eg. irritancy provisions in a lease.
2 IA 1986, s 57(4).
3 IA 1986, s 57(2).

**3.64** This provision that a pre-receivership contract remains in force does not mean that a receiver must implement the contract as agent of the company and the court will not necessarily force him to do so.[1] In *Macleod v Alexander Sutherland Ltd* the pursuer had sold ground to a company under and in terms of missives, one of the terms of which was that the purchasing company should perform certain specified building and construction work on the ground. The purchasing company had a receiver appointed over its whole assets before any of this work was carried out and ceased trading. The pursuer raised an action of specific implement against the company and, failing implement, damages. As a matter of fact, implement of the contract was impossible in that having ceased trading the company had no materials or employees. The court refused to grant decree of specific implement, stating that it would be inequitable to grant such a decree against a company which could act only through the agency of a receiver and which, if the receiver should decline to act, would inevitably be in contempt of court in respect of an omission which it would be powerless to remedy.

1 *Macleod v Alexander Sutherland Ltd* 1977 SLT (Notes) 44.

**3.65** Similarly in England the court has refused to grant decree of specific implement.[1] In *Airline Airspares Ltd v Handley Page Ltd* it was held that a receiver appointed out of court was in a better position than the company in relation to current contracts and, having decided not to implement a pre-receivership contract, could not be prevented from following a course of action which would effectively repudiate or frustrate a pre-receivership contract provided this would not adversely affect the company's goodwill or the realisation of its assets.

1 [1970] Ch 193.

**3.66** The contract in *Airline Airspares Ltd v Handley Page Ltd*[1] obliged the company to pay commission on the sale of a certain aircraft which it manufactured, the action being raised by the plaintiff on learning of the proposed sale by the receiver of such aircraft manufacturing business. These decisions should be contrasted with two subsequent English decisions[2] where the court did make orders for specific performance. However, in the earlier of these cases the contract in question was for the sale of land, the vendor company having been placed in receivership before completion had taken place and in the later the contract involved options over land. These decisions can be distinguished in that the contracts were ones which could have been subject to an order for specific implement whether or not receivership had intervened and in addition there was no question of the receiver having to incur any personal liability as the only alternative to being in contempt of court. The decision in another case in England should be noted.[3] In that case where a third party holding a pre-emption right from a company in receivership over certain of its machinery obtained an order from the court restraining the company from selling the machinery without allowing the third party to exercise such pre-emption right, the court on an application to discharge the order refused to do so. The court held that since the party holding the right of pre-emption had a good arguable case and damages would not be an adequate remedy, the court had to consider the balance of convenience in deciding whether or not to discharge its order. Since the administrative receiver would not suffer any harm from the continuation of the order, it was appropriate that it should be continued but should be varied to provide that (a) the third party would not reveal the right of pre-emption to alternative possible purchasers and (b) the third party must accept or refuse promptly any offer of sale at the price matching any other offer and must offer terms which match those of any other offer.

1 [1970] Ch 193.
2 *Freevale Ltd v Metrostore (Holdings) Ltd* [1984] 1 All ER 495 and *Telemetrix plc v Modern Engineers of Bristol (Holdings) Ltd* [1985] LS Gaz R 1561.
3 *Ash & Newman Ltd v Creative Devices Research Ltd* [1991] BCLC 403.

**3.67** A receiver in Scotland is empowered to carry on the company's business or any part of it[1] and is given wide powers of sale and power to 'do all other things incidental to the exercise' of his powers.[2] It, accordingly, is thought that only in limited circumstances (such as in the *Freevale* case)[3] would the court prevent a receiver in Scotland from taking action which would effectively frustrate a pre-receivership contract.

1 IA 1986, Sch 2, para 14.
2 Ibid, para 23.
3 *Freevale Ltd v Metrostore (Holdings) Ltd* [1984] 1 All ER 495.

**3.68** Failure by a receiver to implement a contract entered into by a company prior to his appointment renders the company liable to damages for breach of contract but any such claim is entitled to an ordinary ranking only. In these circumstances the receiver in the exercise of his powers, in declining as agent for the company to implement a pre-receivership contract, should not have any liability to the other party to the contract for inducing its breach. In considering whether or not to implement a pre-receivership contract a receiver must, nevertheless, exercise reasonable care in reaching his decision to avoid a possible claim on the grounds of breach of duty in that his action had a detrimental effect on the realisation of the company's assets which could have been avoided had he exercised such care. Having decided to implement a pre-receivership contract the receiver in adopting it and carrying it through becomes effectively personally liable although with a right of relief against the assets covered by the charge.

## Leases

**3.69** One of the commonest pre-receivership contracts encountered is a lease of the company's premises. A receiver of a company occupying premises under a lease is under no obligation to implement the lease and, unless specifically agreeing to do so, he incurs no personal liability for the tenant's obligations.[1] Should the receiver wish to continue the company's occupation for a limited period, for example, until he removes the company's property, he should endeavour to reach agreement with the landlord that he is responsible for rent alone for that limited period from the date of his appointment on the clear understanding that he accepts no personal liability whatsoever for any other of the company's obligations as tenant. More detailed reference to this subject is contained in paragraphs 4.15 and 4.27.

1 *Inverness District Council v Highland Universal Fabrications Ltd* 1986 SLT (Notes) 556.

## Effect of suspension of receiver's powers

**3.70** As has been seen a receiver who accepts personal liability under a contract entered into by him[1] remains so liable even though his powers are suspended.[2] In addition, any contract entered into by a receiver (whether or not he accepted personal liability), subject always to its terms, continues in force notwithstanding the suspension of the receiver's powers.[3]

1 Paragraph 3.8.
2 IA 1986, s 57(2).
3 Ibid, s 57(7).

## Receiver's liability if appointment invalid

**3.71** If a person appointed by the holder of a floating charge to act as a receiver takes possession of and deals with assets of a company and subsequently his appointment is discovered to be invalid, he will incur personal liability. This could arise if the floating charge by virtue of which he was appointed turned out for one reason or another to be invalid because in these circumstances it would not attach to the assets, thereby depriving the person appointed of any right to exercise the powers of a receiver. Some essential step in the appointment might be invalid thus rendering the appointment itself invalid[1] or the instrument of appointment might have been invalidly executed. Of critical importance in any receivership appointment is to check the registration number of the company. It is a truism in the experiences of receivers that changing the names of all the companies in a group can be a precursor to the appointment of a receiver some six months or so later.

1 *Elwick Bay Shipping Co Ltd v Royal Bank of Scotland Ltd* 1982 SLT 62.

**3.72** Should however the appointment of a person as receiver by the holder of a floating charge be discovered to be invalid whether as a result of the invalidity of the instrument of appointment or otherwise, the court may order such holder to indemnify the person so appointed against any liability arising solely by reason of the invalidity of the appointment.[1] These provisions only apply in the case of a receiver appointed by the holder of a floating charge and not in the case of a receiver appointed by the court.

1 IA 1986, s 63(2).

**3.73** Notwithstanding such a provision for indemnity, it is in the interests of every person appointed as a receiver to satisfy himself that the appointment is valid. It is also in the interests of the appointer to ensure the appointment is valid. One basis for challenging the validity of a floating charge is under section 245 of the IA 1986[1]. The provisions of section 245 render invalid in certain circumstances floating charges created within specified periods prior to the making of an administration order, an administrator being appointed following the filing with the court of a copy of notice of intention to appoint or the company going into liquidation. Should a person appointed receiver be in any doubt as to the validity of his appointment, whether by reference to these provisions or otherwise, he should consider his position carefully before dealing with the company's assets and whether it might be appropriate to seek an indemnity from his appointer before acting.

1 See para 8.45 et seq.

CHAPTER 4

# Typical legal problems arising on receivership

## Contracts

### *General position*

**4.01** Although in terms of sections 53(7) and 54(6) of the IA 1986 on the appointment of a receiver the floating charge by virtue of which he was appointed attaches to the property then subject to the charge, the appointment per se does not necessarily affect any contract in existence on the date of his appointment. As has been stated in Chapter 3 paragraph 3.63, section 57(4) of the IA 1986 goes further by making it clear that any contract entered into by or on behalf of the company prior to the appointment of a receiver continues in force (subject to its terms) notwithstanding that appointment but the receiver does not by virtue only of his appointment incur any personal liability on any such contract. The result is that the receiver has to decide in any circumstances where a contract continues in force whether or not to proceed with the particular contract and, if he decides to do so, he must exclude his personal liability.[1] The rules in relation to contracts of employment are different and are set out in the IA 1986 as amended by the IA 1994 in relation to contracts of employment adopted on or after 15 March 1994.[2]

1 IA 1986, s 57(2).
2 Ibid, s 57(1A), (2A)-(2D).

**4.02** Some contracts, particularly those which have been formally constituted, will usually provide a catalogue of events of default (which may or may not include receivership) entitling the innocent party on the occurrence of any one of such events of default to invoke certain remedies. If nothing is said in the contract, the presumption will be that section 57(4) of the IA 1986 will apply. An event entitling one party to invoke certain remedies, such as the right to terminate the contract, is to be distinguished from rights arising from a breach of contract which may give rise to a claim for damages or specific implement or rescission of the contract.

**4.03** In terms of section 57(1) of the IA 1986, a receiver is deemed to be the agent of the company in relation to such property of the company as is attached by the floating charge by virtue of which he was appointed. In terms of section 57(2), a receiver (including a receiver whose powers are subsequently suspended under section 56) is personally liable on any contract entered into by him in the performance of his functions, except in so far as the contract otherwise provides, and to the extent of any qualifying liability, on any contract of employment adopted by him in the carrying out of those functions. Section 57(5) provides that for the purposes of section 57(2) a receiver is not to be taken to have adopted a contract of employment by reason of anything done or omitted to be done within fourteen days after his appointment. If a receiver continues to employ any employee after the expiry of the fourteen day period the relative contract of employment will be taken to have been adopted. The concept of qualifying liabilities was introduced by the 1994 Act to resolve the problems which arose from the decision in *Re Paramount Airways td (No 3)*[1]. What is a qualifying liability is set out in section 57(2A) to 57(2D). It is a liability to pay a sum by way of wages or salary or contribution to an occupational pension scheme, if it is incurred while the receiver is in office, and it is in respect of services rendered wholly or partly after the adoption of the contract. Where the services are rendered partly before and partly after the adoption of the contract liability only extends to so much of the sum as is payable in respect of services rendered after the adoption of the contract. Payments for periods of holiday or absence from work through sickness or other good cause are dealt with under subsection (2C) and (2D).

1 [1995] BCC 319.

**4.04** Hence, it is vitally important in contracts made by the receiver and also in relation to those contracts in existence on the date of appointment which are adopted or ratified by the receiver that the personal liability of the receiver should, where possible, be expressly excluded. Section 57(3) of the IA 1986 does provide some relief in that a receiver who is personally liable by virtue of section 57(2) of that Act is entitled to be indemnified out of the property in respect of which he was appointed. However, that Act states that section 57 does not limit any right to indemnity which the receiver would have apart from it, nor limit his liability on contracts entered into or adopted without authority, nor confer any right to indemnity in respect of that liability. A discussion on the receiver's position in relation to personal liability and to contracts in existence on the date of his appointment is contained in Chapter 3 paragraphs 3.63 to 3.69.

## *Building contracts*

**4.05** Insolvency (which may or may not be involved on the appointment of a receiver) is not a ground of determination of a building contract unless the contract so provides. Determination is a remedy which is normally only available to an innocent party faced with a material breach of contract on the part of the other party but the parties can previously agree that certain breaches shall be deemed sufficiently material to justify determination. In practice, insolvency of the contractor usually results in a failure on the part of the contractor to perform, ultimately leading to determination on some ground but delay and expense will be incurred by the employer. The Standard Form of Building Contract issued by the Joint Contracts Tribunal as amended by the Scottish Supplement incorporated in the Scottish Building Contract provides inter alia that, on the appointment of a receiver to the assets and undertaking of a contractor, the employment of the contractor, *not the contract* will be automatically determined forthwith subject always to the possibility of reinstatement on terms to be agreed. The interest of the employer is to get a completed building on time at no extra cost. The interest of the contractor and its receiver is to earn more upon the contract. The employer, failing agreement on reinstatement, has to find another contractor or enter into a new contract with the company and its receiver.

**4.06** There have been instances where a receiver of a contracting company has negotiated a new contract on terms that the company accepts no liability for latent defects and the employer keeps the retention moneys but otherwise the company will complete on the same terms and conditions as previously save for an express exclusion of the employer's right of set-off in respect of claims arising from work carried out on the pre-receivership contract. In these circumstances, the company acting by its receiver will be unwilling to agree to complete by a specific date, if at all possible, and, in view of the terms of section 57(2) of the IA 1986, an express exclusion of the receiver's personal liability must be provided in the new contract. The employer may well accept such terms and conditions because in this way he should minimise his loss in that the contract should be completed reasonably quickly at no additional cost and, as the employer would rank as an unsecured creditor against the company if it goes into liquidation, his position is not further weakened even if latent defects do appear and there may be no funds for unsecured creditors. As part of such arrangements, the employer would normally be entitled to keep the retention money which is reasonable in the circumstances. The benefit to the receiver is additional earnings for the company thus increasing the aggregate realisations. Such additional earnings will arise from work done under the new contract to which can be added earnings due under the old contract, together with sums certified under further certificates for work done under the old contract but not valued as at the date of its determination. The Scottish Building Contracts Committee, 7 Manor Place, Edinburgh, EH3 7DN has produced an excellent 'Insolvency Practice Guide' (current edition January 2001) which draws from, and in certain cases, paraphrases the 'Practical Guide for Use by Employers in the Event of the Insolvency of the Main Contractor' published by the Joint Contracts Tribunal and the Insolvency Practitioners Association. Reference should be made to this for a more detailed analysis of the law and practice for insolvency generally in this specific area.

**4.07** A deed of novation is the deed under which a contracting company in receivership, subject always to the consent of the employer as *delectus persona* is involved in such contracts, assigns its rights and obligations under a building contract to another contractor who takes over the role of contractor and completes the work. There may also be a side agreement between the contractor acting by its receiver and the substitute contractor as to the terms upon which the contractor in receivership 'sells' the contract and the new contractor 'buys it'. Obviously, if there is no advantage to the receivership in completing or if no one will buy the contract, the receiver simply allows the determination machinery to operate or positively intimates as agent of the company in receivership and without incurring any personal liability that the company will not fulfil the contract. In due course (if appropriate) the employer and also any sub-contractors will be left to make claims in the liquidation (if any) of the company. A style of Conditional Novation Agreement is annexed to the Insolvency Practice Guide referred to in 4.06 above.

## *Continuing essential contracts*

**4.08** On his appointment a receiver is immediately faced with normal commercial contracts (principally supply contracts both for goods and for services) which require to be continued, even if only on a short-term basis until the receiver decides whether to carry on the business with a view to its sale. Most receivers within a day or two of their appointment despatch letters (a style of which is given in Appendices 5 and 6) to all known debtors and creditors advising them of the appointment of a receiver. Such a letter to creditors should make it clear that the receiver is acting as agent of the company without personal liability and that debts due by the company in receivership before the appointment of the receiver cannot be set off against debts to become due to the company after such appointment. If the creditor is prepared to continue to deal with the company on such a basis, no difficulty arises.

**4.09** However, commercial realities do assume importance in such circumstances and it would be naive to assume that in such situations all creditors will necessarily agree to continue on such a basis. Many creditors will insist on a personal undertaking from the receiver that payment will be forthcoming in respect of goods and services provided to the receiver and if the receiver is prepared to give such an undertaking he is entitled to be indemnified out of the property in respect of which he was appointed in terms of section 57(3) of the IA 1986. In these circumstances, most receivers will be prepared to undertake personal liability for goods and services ordered by the receiver or an authorised member of his staff. Care needs to be taken to ensure that all such obligations are closed out when the business is sold, particularly if the authorised person is not a member of the receiver's staff and might indeed become an employee of the entity that acquires the business. In *Lipe Ltd v Leyland DAF Ltd*[1] a creditor claiming a retention of title sought to preclude a receiver from using the parts supplied. The receiver, who was disputing the retention of title undertook to pay the cost of the parts if he was wrong and the Court of Appeal considered that the supplier was adequately protected by this and the balance of convenience was strongly in favour of allowing the receiver to use the parts in carrying on the business.

1 [1994] 1 BCLC 84.

**4.10** Some creditors, although not statutorily preferential creditors, used to be placed in a very privileged position:[1] monopoly suppliers such as the power companies and British Telecom were, notwithstanding their unsecured status, in a position to force a receiver to settle all pre-receivership arrears otherwise the service would be forthwith discontinued. If the receiver had any hope whatsoever of selling the business as a going concern or even conducting an orderly run-down, circumstances dictated that such creditors were settled at least in some degree. While most receivers were extremely reluctant to be pressurised in such a way, any such action taken in these circumstances required to be capable of being justified to the holder of the floating charge or indeed any other creditor on the grounds that such action was likely to maximise the realisation of the company's assets. Some receivers were sometimes disposed in such circumstances to threaten to publicise the attitude of the particular monopoly supplier in question and link its attitude with a possible loss of jobs or failure to conclude an agreement for the sale of the business to a purchaser. Obviously, such a possible course of action was not a legal matter and was a decision for each individual receiver to consider in the particular circumstances. The government decided that such monopoly suppliers should not be entitled to enjoy such a privileged position and section 233 of the IA 1986 gave statutory effect to that principle.[2]

1 A very helpful section on this subject appears in the Report of the Review Committee on Insolvency Law and Practice (Cmnd 8558) Ch 33 para 1451-1462 inclusive.
2 See para 7.39.

## *Essential licences and permits*

**4.11** On appointment the receiver will set about immediately ascertaining if any licences or permits are required to operate the business and if he has rights to operate under them. An example of this would be a Heavy Goods Vehicle Operator's Licence, a standard condition of which is to inform the local Traffic Commissioners of any changes that might affect the business and it is likely that receivership will mean that the company no longer meets the requirement to be of the appropriate standing. The Traffic Commissioner, on being notified, is empowered to authorise the receiver for up to 18 months to continue to trade. Some licences, such as those under the Welfare of Animals (Slaughter or Killing) Regulations 1995, are personal to employees of the business rather than the company itself. The redundancy of all such licenceholders would preclude a slaughterhouse, for example, from continuing to trade. Similarly with a liquor licence there will be an individual natural person, the nominated person, who is responsible for the day-to-day running of the premises, and that person's employment is essential or an alternative needs to be installed following an application to substitute.

## Leases – company in receivership as landlord

**4.12** In cases where the company in receivership is the landlord under a valid lease, there is, save as follows, little change occasioned by the appointment of a receiver. If the lease is for a period of up to 20 years, the tenant is entitled to rely on his real right under and in terms of the Leases Act 1449 (whether or not receivership has occurred) and provided the four essentials of a valid lease are present (viz (1) the lease (if for more than one year) is in writing (2) there is a rent (3) there is an ish or term of expiry and (4) the tenant has entered into possession), the tenant has nothing to fear from the receiver. If the lease exceeds 20 years in length registration in the Land Register is also required. This can prove problematic if the landlord˜'s title has not previously been registered in the Land Register. The only qualification in relation to the tenant's position would be if in granting the lease the landlord had breached an obligation not to grant a lease, referred to in the standard conditions contained in a standard security, in favour of a heritable creditor who had either called up that security or, pursuant to the provisions of a floating charge in his favour, had appointed a receiver with a view to realisation of the property subject to the heritable security whereupon the lease would be regarded as of no effect.[1] Although the point does not appear to have been judicially considered in Scotland, it is arguable that the grant of a lease by a landlord who has created, prior in date to such lease, a floating charge over the whole property and undertaking which contains a prohibition upon such landlord from granting such a lease, would fall to be determined in a manner similar to a breach of the equivalent provision in the standard conditions contained in a standard security. Against that however, it may not be evident from the Register of Charges that the floating charge had such a restriction and the holder of the floating charge may be personally barred if it knew that money was coming into a bank account from a tenant. Because the holder of the floating charge is not a party to the lease, and there is no way of the tenant being aware of the restriction, unless told by the landlord, an argument could be constructed under Protocol 1, Article 1 of the European Convention of Human Rights. The position will change if the recommendations of the Scottish Law Commission in the 'Report on Registration of Rights in Security by Companies' (No 197 September 2004) are adopted since they recommend that there be created a Register of Floating Charges and the full text of the charge is shown therein. The above assumes that the landlord is the owner of the property and not itself a tenant under a headlease.

1 *Trade Development Bank v Warriner & Mason (Scotland) Ltd* 1980 SLT 49, 223; *Trade Development Bank v David W Haig (Bellshill) Ltd* 1983 SLT 510; and *Trade Development Bank v Crittall Windows Ltd* 1983 SLT 540.

## Right to receive rent

**4.13** Questions sometimes arise as to whether the holder of a standard security or the receiver is entitled to the benefit of rent received from the tenant in the period from the appointment of the receiver until the property in question is finally sold either by the holder of the standard security exercising his power of sale or by the receiver. It is thought that any such rent is properly due for the receivership account unless (a) the holder of the standard security has called up his standard security in terms of section 19 of the Conveyancing and Feudal Reform (Scotland) Act 1970 (the 1970 Act) and in these circumstances any such rent in the period after such holder has taken possession of the subjects will be due to the holder of the standard security; (b) the holder of the standard security has exercised his rights under the 1970 Act on insolvency of the debtor and obtained an order from the court that such rent is due to him as such holder; or (c) the holder of the standard security has taken an assignation of the rental, which has been registered as a charge and become a real right.

**4.14** For the purpose of paragraph 9(2)(c) of Schedule 3 to the 1970 Act insolvency includes the appointment of a receiver. In practice, a receiver, in these circumstances, will usually recognise the rights of a heritable creditor without involving the creditor in the expense of court proceedings. This can be a helpful position for the heritable creditor due to the receiver having been held not to be in rateable occupation of the premises[1], whereas a heritable creditor who had called up his security may not have such a beneficial position.

1 *McKillop v Tayside Regional Council* 1995 SLT 216; *Boston Borough Council v Rees* [2002] BCC 495.

## Leases – company in receivership as tenant

**4.15** As previously mentioned in paragraph 4.01, the appointment of a receiver does not per se involve any personal liability on the receiver under any pre-existing contract. For liability to fall on the receiver for the tenant's obligations under a lease, some positive act or acts on the part of the receiver would be required eg the payment of rent or continuance of trading from the premises (as a principal as opposed to an agent for the company).

**4.16** On the other hand, the landlord may be entitled to irritate the lease either because of the appointment of the receiver (if there is provision to that effect in the lease) or for non-payment of rent. For this reason, most receivers who wish to continue in occupation of the company's premises even for a relatively short time (often only for the purpose of realising assets) will open negotiations with the landlord and perhaps write to the landlord (a style of which appears in Appendix 7) whereby the receiver undertakes without adopting the lease to pay rent for the period of his occupation but accepts liability for none of the tenant's other obligations. Such an arrangement is normally acceptable to a landlord as at least it guarantees some rental payments thereby minimising his loss pending a new tenant being found and on irritating the lease the landlord would become the rateable occupier. It should also be remembered that an irritancy can only be enforced by the landlord once he has obtained a decree of removing. That will not happen overnight and may allow a receiver sufficient time to achieve his objective by trading out the business to a sale. The landlord is entitled to be paid a reasonable sum for the period of occupancy[1]. Although irritancy in the context of the European Convention of Human Rights has not been considered by the Scottish courts, the English equivalent of forfeiture has been found not to be a violation of Protocol 1, Article 2.[2]

1 *HMV Fields Properties Ltd v Skirt 'n' Slack Centre of London Ltd* 1987 SLT 2.
2 *Di Palma v United Kingdom* (1988) 10 EHRR 123.

**4.17** It has sometimes been questioned whether a receiver is obliged to enter such arrangements with a landlord in relation to the payment of rent. On a strict legal basis, the receiver is not obliged to pay rent provided he has not taken positive action, by, for example, continuing to trade from the premises or actually paying rent in either case as a principal as opposed to as an agent of the company, thereby rendering himself personally liable. However, against the background of the irritancy rights of landlords as a matter both of goodwill and commercial sense, most receivers will be prepared to pay rent on the basis set out above in the hope of securing the co-operation of the landlord while attempts are made to try to find a purchaser for the business.

**4.18** To obtain a proper understanding of the relevant law it is essential to understand the background and how the present position has been reached. Older leases (ie pre-1972) of property in Scotland are often defective from the landlord's point of view in that the appointment of a receiver is not usually included as a ground for termination of the lease. In these circumstances, provided the receiver reaches agreement with the landlord along the lines previously described and no other breach of the lease has taken place, the landlord cannot normally terminate the lease on receivership.

**4.19** The decision in a leading case,[1] which highlighted the principle that a conventional irritancy cannot be purged, was one of the factors which led to less severe irritancy provisions being introduced into leases particularly in relation to the liquidation or receivership of the tenant. In the case in question, the House of Lords refused to allow an irritancy, incurred by the tenant's failure to pay an instalment of rent on the due date required under the lease, to be purged by an offer of payment of the arrears in full made shortly after that date and before the action was raised to irritate the lease.

1 *Dorchester Studios (Glasgow) v Stone* 1975 SC (HL) 56.

**4.20** As a result, many commercial leases thereafter contained wording qualifying irritancy rights along the following lines:

> 'in the case of the Tenants (or the Guarantors, if any) going into liquidation (other than for the purposes of reconstruction or amalgamation) or in the case of a receiver being appointed over the whole assets and undertaking of the Tenants the Landlords shall not exercise such option of forfeiture

on the grounds of appointment of a liquidator or of a receiver unless and until they shall have allowed the liquidator or receiver (as the case may be) a period of six months from the date of such appointment in which to dispose of the Tenants' interest in this lease [and only then if the liquidator or receiver (as the case may be) shall personally accept full responsibility for payment of rent (whether due in respect of a period occurring before or after the date of liquidation or receivership) and for performance of all the obligations on the part of the Tenants under this lease for a maximum period of six months from the date of such appointment (as the case may be) to the expiry of such period, or, if earlier, the date of entry under such disposal.]'.

Failure to agree to such a restriction could lead to rent being increased by less than the amount by which it otherwise might have increased by if this point were taken by a tenant's surveyor at a rent review.

**4.21** While the inclusion in leases of such provisions restricting the exercise of irritancy rights has helped in receivership situations, few receivers have been enthusiastic about accepting, even for a limited period, personal liability for payment of rent and performance of the other obligations of the tenant. Depending upon the circumstances it has sometimes been impossible for the receiver to re-negotiate the irritancy provisions with the landlord on the basis of a personal obligation by him to pay rent without accepting liability for any other obligations. However, the decision varies according to the circumstances and may be affected by, for example, the receiver's desire to dispose of the leasehold property which is secured by way of a standard security to the holder of the floating charge under which he was appointed. Unless he accepts some risk (and, probably, a full indemnity or at least a firm written undertaking from the holder of the floating charge) such standard security may prove to be totally worthless in the event of the landlord if so entitled irritating the lease. The Scottish Law Commission in their report dated 19 November 1982 on Irritancies in Leases[1] formed the view that if the relation of the irritancy to receivership was to be considered it would be more appropriately considered in connection with the law relating to receivers and not as a special case in the law of irritancy as such. Such view follows a suggestion to the Commission from the Institute of Bankers in Scotland to the effect that the particular considerations applicable to receivership might be regarded as justifying special provisions, to prevent an irritancy operating to the disadvantage of a receiver in cases where the company had been a tenant under a lease. The Report stated that it was not really very beneficial in the present economic climate to any of the parties involved if the lease automatically terminated on the appointment of a receiver when one of the objectives of receivership was to ensure the continuance of a business enterprise. It should be emphasised here that a lease does not automatically terminate on receivership and only if the lease entitles the landlord to do so, may he irritate the lease.

1 Scot Law Com No 75.

**4.22** There followed statutory restrictions on the exercise of a landlords' right of irritancy. Under the provisions of the Family Law (Scotland) Act 1985,[1] a landlord cannot irritate a lease if the tenant has failed to pay rent or make any other payment on or before the due date or such later date or within such period as may be provided for in the lease or if such failure is or is deemed by a provision of the lease to be, a material breach of contract unless, after the rent or other payment has become due, he has given the tenant not less than fourteen days' notice or such longer period as may be provided for in the lease requiring the tenant to pay and has stated that the lease will be irritated if he does not do so. The landlord is only entitled to irritate the lease if the tenant has not complied with the requirement specified in any such notice. In the case therefore of a tenant company in receivership the landlord will be unable to irritate the lease on the grounds of failure to pay rent or to realise some other payment alone without giving the requisite notice and then only if the receiver fails to pay within the requisite period. The terms of the notice will however be strictly adhered to, even if it appears to unjustifiably enrich the landlord[2]. In relation to non-pecuniary obligations,[3] section 5 provides that a landlord is not entitled to rely on a provision in a lease which purports to terminate it, or to enable the landlord to terminate it, in the event of an act or omission by the tenant (other than such a failure as is mentioned in section 4(1)(a)) or of a change in the tenant's circumstances or on the fact that such act or omission or change is, or is deemed by a provision of the lease to be, a material breach of contract, if in all the circumstances of the case a fair and reasonable landlord would not seek so to rely. In the consideration of the circumstances of a case where an act, omission or change is alleged to constitute a breach of provision of the lease or a breach of contract and the breach is capable of being remedied in reasonable time, regard shall be had to whether a reasonable opportunity has been afforded to the tenant to enable the breach to be remedied.[4]

1 Section 4 which came into force on 1 January 1986.
2 See the two cases involving the same property, *CIN Properties Ltd v Dollar Land (Cumbernauld) Ltd* 1992 SLT 669 and *Dollar Land (Cumbernauld) Ltd v CIN Properties Ltd* 1998 SLT 992.
3 Section 5 which came into force on 1 January 1986.
4 LR MPS Act 1985, s 5(3).

**4.23** The parties to a lease are not entitled to disapply from the lease any provision of sections 4 or 5[1] and it is not possible to contract out of these statutory provisions. If a lease entitled the landlord to irritate on the appointment of a receiver over any of the property and assets of a company tenant, this is a provision entitling the landlord to irritate on a change in the tenant's circumstances and so cannot be relied on by the landlord if in all the circumstances a fair and reasonable landlord would not seek so to rely. Case law is now starting to build up around the interpretation of what is meant by the expressions 'all the circumstances of the case' and 'the fair and reasonable landlord' and the Scottish Law Commission are again looking at the position [2].

1 LR MPS Act 1985, s 6.
2 Scot Law Com Discussion Paper No 117, 2001.

**4.24** The interpretation of 'all the circumstances of the case' was considered in *Blythswood Investments (Scotland) Ltd v Clydesdale Electrical Stores Ltd (in receivership)*[1] and caused the judge to observe that the result was possibly not in the contemplation of the Scottish Law Commission whose recommendations resulted in the provisions contained in the Law Reform (Miscellaneous Provisions) (Scotland) Act 1985. He held that section 5 involved the consideration of fair and reasonable in the position of the actual landlord and not just a hypothetical fair and reasonable landlord. Accordingly advantages which would accrue to the actual landlord in being able to irritate the lease and reorganise the way in which the industrial estate was laid out were relevant.

1 1995 SLT 150.

**4.25** In *Aubrey Investments Ltd v DS Crawford Ltd (in receivership)*[1],having given initially the receivers time to find an assignee, the landlords commenced irritancy proceedings. The receivers contended that a fair and reasonable landlord would not have done so. At debate the arguments were considered by Lord Penrose who agreed that a proof be fixed. The proof is reported as *Aubrey Investments Ltd v DSC (Realisations) Ltd (in receivership)*[2]. In his judgement, Lord MacFadyen noted that the most difficult part of applying the fair and reasonable landlord test is to judge what weight should be attached to each of the multifarious considerations which such a landlord would take into account from all the circumstances of the case. There should be an overall view. He did not consider that the fair and reasonable landlord was a wholly altruistic landlord who subordinated his own interests to those of the tenant. He was the landlord who was prepared to exercise his right to irritate the lease, unless it would be unfair or unreasonable of him to do so. During his judgement he set out the various considerations in what is the most detailed case yet on the interpretation of the 'fair and reasonable landlord'. The key ones in this particular case, which will not necessarily be the same in other cases, were as follows:

(a) The remedy in section 5 of the Law Reform (Miscellaneous Provisions) (Scotland) Act, 1985 was not expressed in terms of penal effect, but in terms of what would have been done in all the circumstances of the case by a fair and reasonable landlord. That sets an objective standard and does not confer on the court a general discretion to do as it thinks fair and reasonable. While the question for the court must be whether in all the circumstances of the case a fair and reasonable landlord would not have enforced the irritancy, it is legitimate to bear in mind in interpreting and implying the 'fair and reasonable landlord' test the fact that it was adopted as a means of avoiding the mischief of penal enforcement.

(b) In general the hypothetical fair and reasonable landlord must be taken to have been in the same state of knowledge as the actual landlord was in from time to time. The actual state of knowledge of the landlord may affect what circumstances fall to be taken into account in applying the fair and reasonable landlord test but the generality of that proposition would be qualified to the extent that if it is shown that a fair and reasonable landlord would have made enquiries which the actual landlord did not make, the fair and reasonable landlord may be taken to have had any additional knowledge that the evidence shows would have been obtained by making those enquiries.

(c) The words 'all the circumstances of the case' are wide. They are unlimited except in respect that they connote that circumstances extraneous to 'the case' are irrelevant. Lord MacFadyen did not consider that it was possible to rule out of consideration any circumstances relating to the receivership, on the ground either that the receiver who had not adopted the lease was not the tenant or that the circumstances which were relevant were only those directly arising out of the tenancy of the particular property. He thought it unrealistic to regard the circumstances of the receivership, the conduct of the receiver and his interests and objectives, as not being part of the circumstances of the case.

(d) Counsel had accepted that the onus was on the receivers of establishing that in all the circumstances of the case a fair and reasonable landlord would not seek to rely on the appointment of the receivers as a ground for irritating the lease and Lord MacFadyen agreed with that. It is suggested[3] that this is inconsistent with the earlier decision in *Scottish Exhibition Centre Ltd v Mirestop (in administration)*[4], but the writers would respectfully agree with Lord MacFadyen and note that the other case relates to an administration which is an inclusive procedure and not a receivership.

(e) The relevant time at which the test falls to be applied is the time at which the landlord seeks to rely on the irritancy by serving a notice of irritancy.

(f) The fair and reasonable landlord test does not involve two separate criteria, 'fairness' and 'reasonableness', but rather used the two overlapping expressions to define a single concept.

(g) The tests set by section 5 were avowedly derived from the legislation controlling the operation of notices to quit agricultural holdings and accordingly it was legitimate to look to the cases under the agricultural holdings legislation to see if they cast light on the proper interpretation or application of the fair and reasonable landlord test.

(h) The fair and reasonable landlord test cannot be reduced to a balance of hardship and a fair and reasonable landlord would not look exclusively to his own interests but would also take into account the impact which enforcement of the irritancy would have on the interests of the tenant.

(i) The interests which the landlord would have in mind as potentially requiring to be protected by the enforcement of the irritancy were (i) the income stream produced by the let property, and (ii) the investment value of that property. (Although not referred to in the case in such a situation the fact that the landlord would become the rateable occupier on the irritancy would be a point worth making.)

(j) Time is a matter of very great importance in the proper application of the fair and reasonable landlord test in the circumstances of certain cases. There would inevitably come a time when even a fair and reasonable landlord would decide that enough time had been allowed.

(k) The reasonable landlord does not ignore his own commercial interests. He may find that he has to moderate the extent to which he pursues them but the mere fact that a particular course of action brings with it a collateral benefit to the landlord does not taint it with unfairness or unreasonableness.

1 1998 SLT 628.
2 2000 SLT 183.
3 Angus McAllister *Scottish Law of Leases* (3rd edn) 109.
4 1994 GWD 15-917.

**4.26** The most recent case on section 5 is one that could prove a significant tool to any tenant, including in certain circumstances a receiver, being threatened with irritancy.[1] The property let was a listed building and a listed building repair notice was received by the landlords who requested the tenants to carry out the works. Discussions took place without any work being carried out by the tenants which resulted in the landlords serving a notice that they intended to irritate unless the work was commenced by a certain date and completed by another specified date. When the work was not carried out the landlords sought to irritate and the tenants defended the action. Evidence was led that the tenants had not been given a reasonable opportunity to remedy the breach, in that the time periods were too short, but more importantly Lord MacFadyen considered that it was not fair and reasonable for the landlords to irritate the lease when the lease provided that the landlords could carry out the repairs themselves in terms of the lease and charge the tenants. This case seems to have moved the law back slightly in favour of the tenant. A claim by a landlord for violent profits does not arise while the tenant is contesting (provided he has a *probabilis causa*) the validity of the landlord's entitlement to terminate the lease.[2] There are other points that a receiver as tenant of a property may wish to consider prior to negotiating with the landlord. The specific wording of the lease is important.[3] Ascertaining as early as possible what a landlord will wish prior to considering an assignation will also assist in being able to show whether the landlord is acting as a fair and reasonable landlord would. Not only will it assist in speeding up an application for assignation but the landlord will be exposed if he is trying to be unreasonable by for example seeking to impose new conditions or that a premium be paid for consenting to an assignation. In such circumstances reference should be made to the cases of *Renfrew District Council v AB Leisure (Renfrew) Ltd*[4] and *Scottish Tourist Board v Deanpark Ltd*[5].

1 *Euro Properties (Scotland) Ltd v Alam* 2000 GWD 23-896 fully reported on www.scotcourts.co.uk.
2 *Perth City Wall Ltd v Smart Events Ltd* GWD 23-866 and *HMV Fields Properties Ltd v Skirt 'n' Slack Centre of London Ltd* 1996 SLT 493.
3 *Auditglen Ltd v SCOTEC Industries Ltd (in receivership)* 1996 SLT 493.
4 1988 SLT 536.
5 1998 SLT 1121.

**4.27** The Scottish Law Commission Discussion Paper No 117, 2001 has proposed that there should be a revised pre-irritancy notice procedure for both monetary and non monetary breaches. They have also set out proposals which involve changes in the status of a tenant which would cover a liquidator or a receiver. They consider that there should be a mandatory statutory scheme providing insolvency practitioners with an opportunity to dispose of the tenant's interest within a minimum period during which the landlord's contractual right of irritancy should be put 'on hold'.

The proposal is as follows:

(a) A landlord would require to serve a pre-irritancy notice on the tenant and the insolvency practitioner indicating the landlord's intention to irritate the lease upon expiry of the notice. The requirements for service of the notice would be similar to notices in relation to monetary and non-monetary breaches.
(b) The minimum notice period should be six months.
(c) The insolvency practitioner would require to intimate his adoption of the statutory scheme within 28 days of the service of the pre-irritancy notice.
(d) Upon adoption of the statutory scheme, the insolvency practitioner would be deemed to have undertaken to perform all of the tenant's obligations under the lease (including any outstanding obligations) other than any obligation to trade or to occupy the subjects of let for the period from the date of the notice until the disposal of the tenant's interest or, if earlier, the expiry of the notice period.
(e) During the notice period the landlord would be entitled to irritate the lease for non-performance of any obligations of the insolvency practitioner.
(f) Upon completion of an assignation of the tenant's interest, the pre-irritancy notice would fall.
(g) Upon expiry of the pre-irritancy notice without the completion of an assignation, the landlord would be entitled to irritate the lease by service of a notice of irritancy.

## Receiver as custodian of goods

**4.28** From time to time situations can arise where the receiver not only takes possession of the property and undertaking of a company but also acquires possession of goods belonging to third parties which are stored in a building or a factory occupied by the company in receivership. Questions may arise in the context of the exercise of the receiver's power of disposal of the building and assets of the company as to what provision should be made for those goods belonging to third parties.

**4.29** One receiver in the authors' experience faced exactly this problem when he was appointed receiver in November of a boat repairing company whose main asset was a boatyard which contained several yachts being stored for the winter. Some, but not all, of the yacht owners had, before the appointment of the receiver, paid storage accommodation charges for the period to the spring of the following year. The receiver had various meetings with the yacht owners to ascertain whether they would be prepared to pay an extra amount over and above the storage charges to defray the costs of running the boatyard over the winter. No agreement could be reached and the receiver indicated to the yacht owners that he intended to write to them, stating that, with a view to the sale of the boatyard, he would be relinquishing responsibility for the yachts. The yachts were insured by the yacht owners and the receiver had no responsibility in that matter.

**4.30** It is thought that, in such circumstances, the receiver could effectively exclude any liability for possible damage by writing a letter to the yacht owners (preferably despatched by recorded delivery) indicating that he would no longer be responsible for the safety of the yachts in the boatyard. The receiver would, in these circumstances, however, be well-advised to intimate to the yacht owners that supervision of the yachts would continue for a further reasonable period and would only become unavailable after a certain date (eg say, thirty days from the date of despatch of the letter). What is reasonable notice will obviously vary according to the particular circumstances but it is thought that a period of thirty days for making alternative arrangements to store a yacht is reasonable. On general principles of the law of negligence, the receiver, it is thought, would be obliged to show some degree of care for the yachts in the boatyard, foreseeability being now the general criterion for liability in negligence.[1]

1 *Caparo Industries plc v Dickman* [1990] 1 All ER 568 (but see discussion in para 3.46).

**4.31** The contract of storage described above would continue notwithstanding the appointment of the receiver[1] so that the receiver would not render himself liable under the contract unless he took positive steps to personally fulfil the terms of the contract. Specific implement would not necessarily be enforced against a receiver where he would be involved in accepting onerous obligations[2] and the yacht owner's claim if he were to suffer loss would rank as an ordinary claim against the company.

1 See para 4.01.
2 *Macleod v Alexander Sutherland Ltd* 1977 SLT (Notes) 44; but see *Freevale Ltd v Metrostore (Holdings) Ltd* [1984] 1 All ER 495 and *Telemetrix plc v Modern Engineers of Bristol (Holdings) Ltd* [1985] LS Gaz R 1561.

**4.32** The receiver in the circumstances mentioned above considered as an additional remedy taking an action for removal of the yachts, such removal to be effected by the yacht owners themselves or, alternatively, in the event of the failure to do so, by the receiver or his agents. As mentioned above, section 57(4) of the IA 1986 protects the receiver provided he does not by some positive act undertake personal liability: however, raising an action for removal would have been a very positive act and the receiver could have been rendered personally liable if any damage to any of the yachts were to result from their removal by him or his agents. An additional problem was that the yachts were stored under and in terms of pre-receivership contracts and at least in some of the cases the yacht owners had paid the full storage charges and so had fulfilled all their obligations under their contracts with the company in receivership. An action against such yacht owners could well have been regarded by the court as being effectively an attempt to ratify a breach of contract on the company's part induced by the receiver and accordingly, any such action, it is thought, would have been unsuccessful.

## Bills of lading

**4.33** From time to time problems can arise in receivership situations in relation to title to goods delivered from foreign countries in which bills of lading are involved. Suppose, for example, that jute is supplied from India and the company in receivership normally obtained its supplies of jute from the suppliers' agent in Scotland. While a particular consignment of jute is on the high seas, the bill of lading is endorsed by the suppliers' agent in favour of the company prior to its receivership against payment by bank draft of ninety days sight. The receiver is appointed to the company a few days after endorsation of the bill of lading.

**4.34** *Bell's Principles* state[1] that 'bills of lading are, by the law and usage of merchants, negotiable instruments passing to onerous bona fide endorsees and other holders untrammeled by any latent claim or exception.' Later on in the same paragraph he states that 'the endorsation and delivery of the bill of lading by custom of merchants passes the property of the goods which it represents'. In the supposed circumstances, title to the jute would pass when the bill of lading was endorsed by the suppliers' agent in favour of and delivered to the company in receivership provided the bill of lading was not marked 'not negotiable' or 'not transferable' and further provided that the contract between the supplier or his agent and the company in receivership did not provide otherwise.

1 Paragraph 417.

**4.35** If payment was effected by the company in receivership accepting a bill of exchange when the bill of lading was delivered, then non-payment on maturity date of the bill of exchange by the company would merely give the suppliers' agent the right to sue the company in receivership, a claim which would only be entitled to an ordinary ranking. If payment was effected by bank draft, then the bank in question would be required to meet the obligation.

**4.36** A further point should be noted in relation to the position where a consignment of goods is in course of transit and the bill of lading has already been endorsed in favour of and delivered to the company in receivership, thereby transferring the title to the goods. In these circumstances, the receiver could demand delivery from the carrier on presentation of the bill of lading.[1] Therefore, no question of retention would arise in relation to any claims which the suppliers' agent might wish to make but if the original supplier was unpaid, he would have a right of stoppage of goods in *transitu* by virtue of the terms of section 44 of the Sale of Goods Act 1979. Such right would, however, be defeated by a bona fide transfer of the bill of lading for value by endorsement in favour of the company in receivership.[2]

1 *Bell's Principles* para 417.
2 Sale of Goods Act 1979, s 47(2).

**4.37** The position arising under the supposed circumstances mentioned above would of course be quite different if the bill of lading was endorsed with the instruction to deliver to the order of the sellers' agent's bank. Even if the company in receivership subsequently acquired possession of the goods, title would still vest in the seller or sellers' agents unless the bank of the sellers' agents authorised unconditional delivery of the goods to the company in receivership.

## Intellectual property

**4.38** It is not unusual for an inventor whose invention has been patented to enter into an agreement with a company for the future exploitation of that patent. Such an agreement might, in appropriate cases, provide for a lump sum payment to be made to the inventor on execution of the agreement and for royalties on an agreed basis to be remitted to the inventor for a period of time, all in consideration of the beneficial ownership of the patent being immediately transferred to the company subject to the company being obliged, on the happening of the usual events of default occurring (including the appointment of a receiver), to immediately re-transfer such beneficial ownership to the inventor.

**4.39** On the appointment of a receiver the floating charge under which he was appointed, if over the whole assets of the company, would attach to the patent in the beneficial ownership of the company and at one time, on the basis of the only Scottish decision in point[1] the court might not in these circumstances have ordered specific implement of the provision for re-transfer of the patent, leaving the inventor with a claim for damages entitled only to an ordinary ranking.

1 *Macleod v Alexander Sutherland Ltd* 1977 SLT (Notes) 44.

**4.40** However, it is by no means certain, as a result of two subsequent English decisions,[1] that a Scottish court would necessarily decide a receiver's responsibility for contracts in existence on the date of his appointment on the basis of the decision in *MacLeod v Alexander Sutherland Ltd*.[2] In the *Freevale* case,[1] a limited company had entered into a contract to sell land but the transaction was not completed before a receiver was appointed over the property and undertaking of the vendor company. The judge held (at 503) that the mere fact of receivership of the defendants afforded no defence to a claim for specific performance. On the basis of these two decisions the inventor, in the example above, might well be protected by his agreement with the company prior to the appointment of the receiver.

1 *Freevale Ltd v Metrostore (Holdings) Ltd* [1984] 1 All ER 495; and *Telemextrix plc v Modern Engineers of Bristol (Holdings) Ltd* [1985] LS Gaz R 1561.
2 1977 SLT (Notes) 44.

**4.41** It is thought that the decisive factor in assessing a receiver's position in such circumstances will be the nature of the contract in question. If the receiver is required to implement a contract which will involve him in no costs or personal liability of any materiality, it is suggested that the receiver will require to implement such a contract. If, on the other hand, the receiver is, for example, required to implement a major building or engineering project, it is thought that the court would not order specific implement on the receiver. The subject is, however, considered in more detail in paragraphs 3.64-3.68.

## Hire-purchase and leasing contracts

**4.42** In almost every case, a receiver finds that the company has entered into hire-purchase and leasing contracts relating in some instances to some of the most valuable items of plant and machinery used by the company. In all of such contracts, title will remain (in the case of leasing contracts at all times) with the finance house until all payments due under the contract have been made. The floating charge does not accordingly attach to such items but the continued use of such terms by the receiver may be vital if he is to continue the business and sell it as a going concern. The receiver, bearing in mind the provisions of section 57 of the IA 1986, will, therefore, require to make early arrangements to continue the payments under such contracts pending the sale of the business unless, of course, the contracts specifically entitle the owner to terminate them on the appointment of a receiver and such right is exercised.[1] If no sale of the business is envisaged, the receiver, acting as agent of the company in receivership and without incurring personal liability will usually request the owner of such plant and machinery to remove it.

1 In certain circumstances, if the agreement grants the company a right to terminate the lease and sell the equipment with the proceeds being shared, the courts might preclude such forfeiture: *On Demand Information plc v Michael Gerson (Finance) plc* [2002] BCC 122.

**4.43** It is not unusual to find where there are a number of hire-purchase contracts with a particular hire-purchase company, that under one of such contracts almost all the payments have been made to the hire-purchase company leaving a substantial equity value available to the company on payment of the outstanding balance. However, the hire-purchase company will often have included provisions in all such contracts with the company to the effect that if there is a substantial debit balance on one account, such debit balance may be offset against an account on which there is an equity value. It is important to check in every case the precise terms of each such hire-purchase contract.

**4.44** If the receiver is successful in finding a potential purchaser for the company's business, he will in all probability, as agent of the company endeavour to reach some form of settlement with the finance houses involved so that the company will be in a position to sell as beneficial owner or assign to the purchaser its interests under hire-purchase or leasing contracts relating to its plant and machinery. A more advantageous settlement is often achieved if negotiated directly by the potential purchaser. The receiver is not in a good negotiating position in that his only interest is to dispose of the business and assets whereas a purchaser is in a better position in that he will be a potential source of ongoing business and will relieve the hire-purchase or leasing company from the necessity to make arrangements for the removal of the plant and machinery in question.

## Right of third parties against insurers

**4.45** A creditor of a company in receivership may find himself in a more favourable position than normally would be the case where a liability to such creditor is established, being a liability which has been insured against by the company. The Third Parties (Rights against Insurers) Act 1930 (the 1930 Act) provides that where, under any contract of insurance, a company is insured against liabilities to third parties which it may incur, then in the event inter alia of a receiver being appointed if any such liability is incurred by the insured, the rights of the insured against the insurer under the contract in respect of the liability shall, notwithstanding anything in any Act or rule of law to the contrary, be transferred to and vest in the third party to whom the liability was so incurred.[1] While there have been a number of cases over the years, largely in the English courts, involving companies in liquidation, the authors are not aware of any recent cases involving receivership where the 1930 Act has been invoked.

1 Third Parties (Rights against Insurers) Act 1930, s 1.

**4.46** The 1930 Act applies to Scotland and the word 'receiver' is also used in the English law sense of 'receiver or manager of a company's business or undertaking' although, when the 1930 Act was enacted, the appointment of a receiver was not, of course, competent under the law of Scotland. The 1930 Act covers the situation where, for example, a few days before the appointment of a receiver, the driver of one of the company's lorries negligently collides with a stationary private motor car belonging to a third party. If the company was adequately insured for such an eventuality, then the company's rights against the insurer would be automatically transferred to the owner of the private motor car.

**4.47** One aspect of the 1930 Act is that an obligation is placed on a receiver by the terms of section 2(1) of the 1930 Act to give, at the request of any person claiming that the company in receivership is under a liability to him, such information as may reasonably be required by him for the purpose of ascertaining whether any rights have been transferred to and vested in him by the 1930 Act and for the purpose of enforcing such rights and any contract of insurance under the 1930 Act. Such information needs to be provided on being requested and the liability of the insured to the third party does not need to be established before the obligation arises.[1] If such information is given in terms of section 2(1) of the 1930 Act and discloses grounds for supposing that there may have been transferred to him rights against any particular insurer, that insurer is subject to the same duty as is imposed on a receiver. There is also a duty in terms of section 2(3) of the 1930 Act to allow all contracts of insurance to be inspected and copies thereof to be taken.

1 *First National Tricity Finance Ltd v OT Computers (in administration)* [2004] EWCA Civ 563, [2004] Ch 317, overturning *Woolwich Building Society v Taylor* [1995] 1 BCLC 132.

## Liens and hypothecs

### *Liens*

**4.48** In many receiverships the exercise of a lien is claimed by some person or other: it can range from a carrier of goods for his charges to a solicitor in respect of unpaid fees. In every case, it is essential to establish clearly the circumstances under which the alleged right of lien came into being. A right of lien exists where one person has goods in his possession for some purpose at the instance of another person and the first person declines to part with possession of such goods until his charges for work transacted or services rendered have been fully satisfied. Absolutely central to the existence of a valid lien is actual or constructive possession legally obtained and if such possession is lost, the lien ceases to exist.

### *Special lien and general lien*

**4.49** A distinction should be drawn between a special lien and a general lien. A special lien exists where the goods are in the possession of one party who is entitled to withhold delivery of such goods until satisfaction of his charges in respect of the particular contract relating to work done on the goods. An example of a special lien is where garage owners repair a vehicle belonging to a company over whose assets a receiver is subsequently appointed. The garage owners would be entitled to exercise a valid special lien over the vehicle for settlement of the costs of the particular repair. In the absence of contractual provisions to the contrary, it would not be competent for the garage owners to seek settlement of a whole series of accounts relating to other vehicles or, indeed, to earlier repairs to the particular vehicle.

**4.50** On the other hand, a general lien exists where the person in possession of the goods can competently seek satisfaction of all outstanding claims arising out of a contractual arrangement or course of dealing and not simply be restricted to claims under the particular contract in question. Examples of general liens almost always arise from custom of certain trades and professions or from contract express or implied: viz the standard terms and conditions of the Road Haulage Association provide that a general lien will exist over goods in the possession of the carrier in respect of all outstanding claims against the party despatching such goods. On being met by a claim to such a lien, a receiver if he is satisfied that such a term has been incorporated into the contract of carriage and that a general lien can validly be claimed, will require to settle the outstanding claims to effect release of the goods. By so doing, he should be able to ensure that the carrier will complete the particular delivery or deliveries, the customers should be satisfied and also the receiver will have retained a great deal of goodwill which will be important if the receiver has any reasonable expectations of selling the business as a going concern.

**4.51** What happens if the person claiming the lien factored his own debts? Can the lien be validly exercised? It is thought that a lien cannot in such circumstances be validly exercised because the sums due by the company in receivership are not actually owed to the person exercising the lien, provided the assignation of the debt to the factoring company has been duly intimated to the company in receivership. It is possible, but doubtful, that the benefit of the lien could be assigned to the factoring company by delivery of the goods held by the person claiming the lien but it is suggested that in these circumstances, as the exercise of the lien by the factoring company would take place after the appointment of the receiver, the company in receivership could not possibly be held to have consented to the assignation of the lien. On the other hand, as the right of lien arises by operation of law, it should not be necessary for the company to consent to the assignation of the lien. If the factoring company took possession of the goods before the appointment of the receiver, the factoring company would be able to argue with some prospects that a valid lien had been established. If possession is transferred to the factoring company after the appointment of the receiver, it must be considered doubtful whether a valid lien can be established by the factoring company. The rights of the various parties must be established as at the date of appointment of the receiver and the factoring company would, in addition, find it difficult to rebuff the argument of bad faith. It is understood that the position in England in such circumstances is that the lien is certainly capable of being assigned but there is considerable doubt as to whether a subrogated right in equity to the lien can be maintained unless with the consent of the company in receivership. However, for commercial reasons, it may be more advantageous for the receiver in the long term to recognise the lien to protect the business rather than rest on the legal position and risk expensive and lengthy delay to the detriment of the receivership.

**4.52** It is instructive to compare the provisions of sections 236 and 246 of the IA 1986. Section 236 applies where an administrative receiver has been appointed and provides that, on the application of the administrative receiver to the court, any person known or suspected to have in his possession any property of the company or who may be capable of giving information concerning the promotion, formation, business, dealings, affairs or property of the company may be summoned before the court. It is clear, failing an intention to co-operate with an administrative receiver pursuant to section 235 of the IA 1986, such a person could be a solicitor who is owed fees for outstanding services rendered to the company before it went into receivership. The proper thing for the solicitor to do is clearly to co-operate with the administrative receiver and avoid the requirement on the administrative receiver to invoke the provisions of sections 236. On the other hand, section 246 does not apply to administrative receivership but applies to administration or liquidation. A lien or other right to retain possession of any books, papers or other records of the company is unenforceable to the extent that its enforcement would deny possession of any books, papers or other records to the administrator or liquidator but the lien does not apply on documents which give a title to property and are held as such.

**4.53** The case of *In re Aveling Barford Ltd*[1], while it is an English case, is important in the context of solicitors' liens. The administrative receivers obtained an order under section 236 against solicitors in respect of the production of documents of which the solicitors were held not entitled to refuse production on the grounds that they had a lien over them for unpaid costs. Hoffman J stated:

> 'In my judgment s 236 and s 246 are dealing with different concepts and the one throws no light on the continuation of the other. Section 236 is concerned with obtaining information while section 246 deals with rights of property to documents. An office-holder who is able to assert the company's proprietary right to a document under section 246 will have no need to obtain an order for its production under section 236. But that circumstance does not mean that when resort is had to section 236, it should be construed more narrowly than its ordinary meaning would require. For example, section 246 does not apply to "documents which give a title to a property and are held as such." A solicitor who has a lien over such a document cannot be required to deliver it up to a liquidator. If the solicitor will not disclose the document and the liquidator wants to know what it says, he will have to seek an order for production under section 236.'

It would therefore appear that, applying the principles of *Re Aveling Barford Ltd*[1], to Scotland, unless a solicitor holds a document of title to property (other than heritable property, bearing in mind also the provisions of paragraph 4.54 below), the solicitor's lien is of highly doubtful value. If the receiver wishes to know the contents of a document of title, he need only invoke the provisions of section 236, thereby destroying any potential value to the solicitor in withholding such contents. There are however no reported cases in Scotland approving *Re Aveling Barford Ltd*[1], and the receiver does not have an automatic right to recover documents without good cause being shown. In that case the receivers presented a confidential memorandum in support of their application to produce documents. There is also authority in Scotland that a solicitor's lien cannot be evaded by raising an action and obtaining a diligence for recovery of the documents.[2] Section 236 is not restricted to use against 'any person' within the jurisdiction of the court.[3]

1 [1988] 3 All ER 1019.

2 See *Train & McIntyre v Forbes* 1925 SLT 286 and *Garden Haig Scott & Wallace v Stevenson's Trustees* 1962 SC 51.
3 McIsaac and Wilson Petitioners 1995 SLT 498.

**4.54** From time to time, the solicitor who acted for the company prior to the appointment of the receiver seeks to enforce a lien over the miscellaneous documents, title deeds and other papers which he holds against settlement of his fees and outlays. The solicitors's lien is based on professional usage and is not enjoyed, for example, by accountants who are entitled only to exercise a right of lien for work transacted by them on a particular matter for which the papers were specifically given. Since the introduction under the Conveyancing and Feudal Reform (Scotland) Act 1970 of extracts as acceptable alternatives to original titles, the value of a solicitor's lien over title deeds in his possession is negligible and extends to the cost of obtaining appropriate extracts. However, there can be occasions when speedy delivery and examination of title deeds is vital to a successful quick sale of the business: and the receiver requires again to carefully consider his priorities. The importance or otherwise of any other papers will depend largely on the circumstances of the particular case. It should also be remembered that urgent and detailed assistance can often be obtained from the solicitor claiming the lien if some form of speedy settlement of his claim is agreed.

## *Maritime lien*

**4.55** Three types of lien may be involved where a receiver either finds a vessel in his custody or seeks to recover possession of a vessel from a third party on which work was carried out prior to his appointment. In the normal case, such a lien may be very critical in either recovering amounts due from the owner of the vessel or in ascertaining the net value of the vessel if in either case the vessel is subject to the rights of a mortgagee. In these situations, the types of lien could be (1) maritime lien or (2) statutory lien or (3) a possessory lien.

**4.56** A maritime lien is restricted to claims for salvage, seamen's wages, damage caused by a vessel and the master's wages and disbursements. The right of maritime lien does not extend to repairs to a vessel.

**4.57** A statutory lien arises out of the Administration of Justice Act 1956 which in itself was passed following two Brussels Conventions of 1952. Part V of that Act enumerates nineteen separate claims which may be classified as statutory liens and these categories include maritime liens. A statutory lien like a maritime lien is enforced by way of an action *in rem* but the attachment of the vessel for the purposes of the claim does not arise until either the action *in rem* has formally been raised or the vessel has been arrested. The statutory lien would be defeated in the event of a sale in good faith to a purchaser unless the action *in rem* was served before the date of sale. It is thought that a statutory lien competently secured by an action *in rem* would cover the cost of repairs to a vessel.

**4.58** A possessory lien is available to a custodian of a vessel if repairs have been carried out to the vessel but payment has not been made. In order to enforce the lien, it is necessary that possession of the vessel should be withheld and therefore an action *in rem* as previously described would be the normal route. An action *in personam* is also competent to enforce a possessory lien and has been described in *McMillan's Scottish Maritime Practice* as a 'petitory action with arrestment of the ship [and] with conclusions for judicial sale'.

## Copyright on drawings and engineering certifications

**4.59** A receiver may find a property development included in the assets attached by the floating charge which is perhaps in the early stages of construction or, although all necessary planning and building consents have been obtained, no actual construction has taken place. The receiver will have to decide the most beneficial course of action but bearing in mind his personal liability as receiver and the general potential liabilities hanging over a project of such magnitude, he will probably decide to dispose of the project on the most advantageous terms to the receivership. It is more than likely that architects, in particular, and other advisers will be owed substantial fees for work and services carried out prior to the date of appointment of the receiver. If the receiver decides to dispose of the project in its original form using the plans and documents already prepared, he should carefully consider that if he does so, he may be liable for breach of copyright.

**4.60** It is, therefore, prudent in such circumstances for the receiver to engage independent and skilled project management advisers to assess the viability of the original proposals and comment upon alternative approaches. Obviously, if the project has already commenced, such assessment may not be possible and in these circumstances, if the original professional team is not to be re-engaged by the purchaser, some form of settlement may require to be arranged with them. Similar situations arise with the offshore oil industry where equipment is not permitted offshore unless it has obtained the requisite certification. If a company has received equipment or parts for incorporation into other equipment, but not paid for them, the careful supplier may not have released the certificates prior to payment and be able to negotiate such payment before the documents are released.

## Hypothec and sequestration for rent

**4.61** In many receiverships a receiver will find that the business of the company is conducted from premises on lease from a landlord to whom substantial pre-receivership arrears of rent are due. On the appointment of the receiver, the landlord may wish to secure his position rather than awaiting the disposal of the business to a purchaser who may or may not wish the lease assigned to it, a condition of consent to such assignation being normally payment of rental arrears. The landlord's common law remedy is to claim landlord's hypothec which extends to all corporeal moveable items situated in the premises and used for the purposes of the company's business. Such items as ordinary equipment, furniture, stock and finished goods are covered by a landlord's hypothec, as are in certain cases goods held on hire purchase or finance lease. The action must be raised within three months after the term at which the rental is payable and can be for up to one year's rental (but only for that amount if the rental is payable annually). It can also be in security for the rental due at the next payment date (so that if the rental is payable quarterly, the security is for one quarter's rental).

**4.62** A major qualification on the exercise of hypothec is the requirement under section 64 of the Taxes Management Act 1970 (as now amended by the Finance Act 1989) to pay off certain outstanding taxes as a preferential claim before enforcing the hypothec. These are now restricted to one year's PAYE and deductions under the construction industry deduction scheme.

**4.63** In many cases, the landlord takes the matter no further on learning of the extent of one year's preferred tax outstanding. An astute landlord might threaten the procedure and ask the receiver to rank him according to his rights thus avoiding additional costs and waiting to see the level of outstanding tax. The ranking of the right of hypothec, following upon the appointment of a receiver, has been analysed in paragraph 2.19 above.

## Threatened winding-up petition

### *General*

**4.64** A receiver who wishes to sell a business as a going concern must do so in the expectation that a liquidator is not appointed on or prior to the date of sale. The appointment of a liquidator may, subject to certain exceptions relating to employees in some forms of liquidations, terminate all contracts and such an appointment is clearly unhelpful from the point of view of the sale of business, particularly in relation to taxation.[1]

1 See Chapter 7.

**4.65** However, it has long been accepted in practice that if a receiver has been appointed and is still acting as such, the appointment of a liquidator does not preclude the receiver from continuing to realise assets of the company with a view to satisfaction of the floating charge. To support this proposition, reliance is placed on the terms of Schedule 2 to the IA 1986 which makes it clear that the receiver enjoys not only a power of sale but also the power to take possession of, collect and get in the property from the company or a liquidator thereof. The courts have also approved such proposition.[1] The practical and legal position is, therefore, that although a liquidator may have been appointed and the agency of the receiver may technically have been terminated, the receiver will continue to realise assets of the company in satisfaction of the charge while the liquidator will only be entitled to take possession of any assets remaining after the floating charge has been fully satisfied or any assets which fall outwith the scope of the floating charge[2].

1 *Manley, Petitioner* 1985 SLT 42; and see para 3.61.
2 See also para 1.68 above.

**4.66** Most receivers, certainly in the early stages of a receivership will wish to avoid the appointment of a liquidator on the grounds that such an appointment would: (a) be prejudicial in the context of a sale of the business as a going concern when such a sale might be more advantageous to the creditors as a whole; (b) cause unnecessary confusion and anxiety in the minds of employees of the company and unhelpful publicity when attempts are being made to sell the business; and (c) cause adverse taxation problems when, for example, large parcels of land still remain unsold involving substantial capital gains tax.[1] However, as will be noted in paragraph 4.69 the receiver cannot prevent the appointment of a liquidator if valid grounds to do so exist.

1 See Chapter 7.

**4.67** In this context the form of liquidation envisaged is liquidation by the court. Members' voluntary liquidation will usually be quite inappropriate as the company is almost certainly, but not necessarily, insolvent and a creditors' voluntary liquidation requires action by the company to convene meetings under section 98 of the IA 1986. It is thought that any actions by the directors which might interfere with the conduct of the receivership will not find favour with the courts in Scotland and in the particular circumstances, it is thought that action by directors to cause the appointment of a liquidator may be deemed to be prejudicial. i:[1]

1 Paragraphs 2.21-2.26.

**4.68** Value added tax and bad debt relief is covered by section 36 of the Value Added Tax Act 1994 and the Value Added Tax Regulations 1995 as amended. From 1 January 2003, a creditor is entitled to a repayment of input tax where the consideration for the supply is not paid within six months following the date of supply or, if later, the date on which the consideration for the supply or (as the case may be) the unpaid part of it became payable. Insolvency or receivership is not a relevant factor. Problems can arise where book debts have been assigned as the Customs & Excise take the view that the original creditor ceases to be entitled to bad debt relief. This is however a very technical area outwith the scope of this book.

**4.69** The effect of lodging caveats is no guarantee of protection to the receiver but at least the receiver is entitled to be heard in any court proceedings before an order is made by the court. This is of particular benefit in resolving retention of title disputes. It should be borne in mind that, however convincing the arguments of the receiver may seem, the court will normally take the view that if sections 122 and 123 of the IA 1986 apply and the debt is not disputed, the granting of the first order in the liquidation process is the proper course of action.[1] Indeed the receiver should remember that the bar on prescription applying does not apply on the receiver being appointed whereas it does on a liquidator being appointed. Accordingly precluding the appointment of a liquidator could be detrimental to ordinary creditors in some cases.

1 *Foxhall & Gyle (Nurseries) Ltd, Petitioners* 1978 SLT (Notes) 29.

### *Prevention of liquidator's appointment*

**4.70** In the *Foxhall & Gyle (Nurseries)* case,[1] Lord Kincraig allowed a petition for liquidation to proceed to the first order and dismissed the submissions of the receiver regarding the adverse consequences of the granting of such first order. Lord Kincraig stated that where a creditor seeks a winding-up order on the ground that a company is unable to pay its debts, the petition for winding-up should not be dismissed unless there are compelling reasons for it. It would therefore seem that it will only be in exceptional circumstances that the court will decline to grant the first order in a winding-up process.

1 *Foxhall & Gyle (Nurseries) Ltd, Petitioners* 1978 SLT (Notes) 29.

## Ownership of documents created by receivers

**4.71** The case of *Gomba Holdings UK Ltd v Minories Finance Ltd*[1] has clarified to a large extent an area of law which had concerned insolvency practitioners for some time. The questions raised in the case were whether documents created by the receivers during the course of the receivership belonged to the company or to the receivers. At first instance, Hoffmann J held that the ownership of documents arising out of or connected with the receivership depended on whether they were created to enable a receiver to discharge his duties to the company or the debenture holder or neither. If the documents were created pursuant to the duties of the receiver to manage the company's business or sell its assets, then any such documentation belonged to the company. On the other hand, the receiver was required from time to time to deliver reports to the debenture holder and such documentation belonged to the debenture holder. Similarly, the receiver created documents to better discharge his professional duties and in that case such documentation belonged to the receiver himself. The question of ownership of the documents did not depend upon whether the information related to the company or any of its assets, the issue was a proprietary claim depending on in which capacity the receiver was acting when the document was brought into existence. In relation to documents in which matters therein contained could not be so simply categorised, it was arranged between the plaintiffs and the receivers that a photocopy of such documents could be produced by the receivers to the plaintiffs with the section not relevant to the plaintiffs being crossed out.

1 [1989] 5 BCC 27, CA.

**4.72** The implications of the case, thought to be equally applicable to Scottish receiverships, are potentially very significant as it now appears that any documents which could be regarded as documents belonging to the company will have to be passed to a future liquidator. It has always been the practice in the past of receivers to keep company documents segregated from documents created during the receivership. It remains to be seen how the practice will be changed in the future (if at all) following upon the *Gomba* decision[1]. It is thought that there will be much greater and more rigorous control by receivers over the capacity in which any particular document is created during the receivership along the lines identified by the judge in the *Gomba* case.[1]

1 [1989] 5 BCC 27, CA.

## Set-off

### *General*

**4.73** Set-off or compensation of one debt against another with the result that each such debt is *pro tanto* extinguished was originally introduced by statute.[1] Its elements are principally that there must be *concursus debiti et crediti*: namely that the parties must be in the same capacity and at the same time debtor and creditor. Set-off must be pleaded and it is only competent in general as between liquid debts save for cases of insolvency where the debtor may defend himself against a present demand by setting off a debt that is future or contingent although the time of payment is after insolvency.[2] No guidance from the courts is available as to whether the right of set-off opens up upon the appointment of a receiver as it does upon insolvency but it is submitted that while the appointment of a receiver need not coincide with insolvency, in most instances it does so.

1 The Compensation Act 1592, c 143.
2 Bell's Commentaries 122.

**4.74** Set-off in the context of receivership has been the subject of judicial consideration. This has arisen principally from two cases namely *McPhail v Lothian Regional Council*[1] and *Taylor Petitioner*,[2] the conflicting decisions in which have caused uncertainty as to the correct legal position. The subsequent case of *Forth & Clyde Construction Co Ltd v Trinity Timber & Plywood Co Ltd*,[3] although not concerned with set-off, has to some extent clarified the position in its application to book debts. Subsequently, the question of receivership set-off was considered in *Myles J Callaghan Ltd v City of Glasgow District Council*[4].

1 1981 SLT 173.
2 1982 SLT 172.
3 1984 SLT 94.
4 1987 SCLR 627.

**4.75** Section 53(7) of the IA 1986 states that on the appointment of a receiver, the floating charge by virtue of which he was appointed attaches to the property then subject to the charge; and such attachment has effect as if the charge was a fixed security over the property to which it has attached. Fixed security is defined by section 70 of that Act in relation to any property of a company as security, other than a floating charge or a charge having the nature of such, which on the winding-up of the company in Scotland would be treated as an effective security over that property. Thus, in the case of a book debt due to a company it would include a security created by an assignation of such debt duly intimated to the debtor.[1] Set-off is subject to the legal principle *assignatus utitur jure auctoris*, the effect of which is that a debtor on receiving a claim for payment of the debt can competently plead against an assignee of the debt any defences which would have been competent against the cedent. Such defences would include the right of set-off[2] but they would require to have been competent before the assignation was intimated. If it is accepted that on the appointment of a receiver the attachment of the floating charge to the company's book debts is equivalent to a completed assignation in security in favour of the holder it follows that a debtor wishing to plead set-off would require to have been in a position to counter claim prior to the receiver's appointment. If the counter claim is only competent in respect of a debt arising after the receiver's appointment, the principles of *assignatus utitur jure auctoris* and *concursus debiti et crediti* will not apply. According to Bell,[3]

> 'the right to compensate passes against assignees, if once vested against the cedent by a proper concourse before assignation. But if a debt be assigned, and the assignation intimated before the counter-debt arises, the concourse is prevented, and there is no compensation.'

Bell[4] also states that, in cases of insolvency, a future or contingent debt, even although the time of payment is after insolvency, may be set-off against a due debt. Receivership does not necesssarily involve insolvency although frequently the company is in fact insolvent.

1 *Forth & Clyde Construction Co Ltd v Trinity Timber & Plywood Co Ltd* 1984 SLT 94.
2 *Shiells v Ferguson, Davidson & Co* 1876 4 R 250.
3 II Bell's Commentaries 138.
4 Bell's Commentaries 122.

**4.76** The facts in the *McPhail* case[1] were that the receiver of a company appointed under a floating charge over the whole property of the company raised an action in his own name in his capacity as receiver to recover from the statutory successors of a local authority a sum admittedly due to the company under a contract between it and the authority's predecessors. The defenders argued that the receiver had no title to sue in his name and contended, furthermore, that they were entitled to apply set-off in respect of a debt due by the company before the appointment of the receiver to the predecessors of the defenders. The receiver rejected the set-off argument on the ground that there was no *concursus debiti et crediti* although as a result the defenders maintained that if that was so the receiver should have raised a plea as to the competency of the counter claim.

1 *McPhail v Lothian Regional Council* 1981 SLT 173.

**4.77** Lord Grieve held in the Outer House that the receiver, in terms of the equivalent provisions in the 1972 Act to those contained in paragraph 1 of Schedule 2 to the IA 1986, had power to recover property of the company in his own name and his powers were not to be limited by such provisions to raising proceedings in the name of the company. His Lordship also accepted the argument that as the counter claim did not justify a decree because the averments were based on a claim to set-off which was unsound in law a plea to the relevancy of the counter claim had been legitimately taken. As the action had been raised by the receiver in his own name, there was no *concursus debiti et crediti* and the counter claim was dismissed.

**4.78** The facts in *Taylor, Petitioner*[1] were that a receiver who was appointed over the whole property and undertaking of a company sought to recover sums due from debtors who, subsequently to his appointment, had assigned to them by a creditor debts due to such creditor by the company, in one case for full value and in the other case for certain good and onerous causes. Both assignations had been properly intimated to the company. The receiver sought a declaration from the court that he was entitled to recover the debts in terms of the equivalent provisions in the 1972 Act to those contained in paragraphs 1 and 5 of Schedule 2 to the IA 1986 and secondly that set-off by the debtors was inappropriate. The receiver argued in relation to set-off that as he was entitled to recover the debts under the relevant statutory provisions, the debtors were not entitled to set-off since this would be contrary, amongst other things, to insolvency law and that similar rules applied to receivership as to bankruptcy. Once the floating charge had crystallised, a fixed security was thereby created. Accordingly, *concursus debiti et crediti* would require to have existed prior to his appointment and as the assignations of the debts post-dated his appointment, the plea of compensation would be repelled.

1 1982 SLT 172.

**4.79** Lord Ross held that the receiver's rights under the equivalent provisions in the 1972 Act to those contained in paragraph 1 of Schedule 2 to the IA 1986 were limited to taking possession of a right to debts, a mere *jus crediti*, as on the appointment of the receiver the company owned not the sums of money due by debtors but only the right to recover the debts. Secondly, his Lordship held that the receiver, unlike *McPhail's* case[1] only had the power to take proceedings in the name of the company for payment of the debts and consequently the creditors to whom the debts had been assigned were entitled to set-off against the company's claim against them the debts due by the company which had been assigned to them. It was considered such action would not be prejudicial to the security holder's security over the *jus crediti* of the company, the principles of law relative to insolvency having no application to cases of receivership and there being no justification upon grounds of equity or public policy for introducing any such exception into the law.

1 *McPhail v Lothian Regional Council* 1981 SLT 173.

**4.80** Following upon the decision in *Taylor, Petitioner*[1] it was considered necessary by some receivers and their advisers for the company immediately upon the appointment of a receiver to assign all of its book debts to the receiver thereby, hopefully, overcoming the difficulty posed by the decision in *Taylor, Petitioner*.[1] On further consideration, some of those receivers and their advisers abandoned the idea of such an assignation. Quite apart from the burden of *ad valorem* stamp duty on the aggregate value of the book debts which in most cases would be very substantial, it was considered that a *jus crediti* was effectively assigned by the terms of the 1972 Act[2] and the receiver had, in terms of the *Taylor, Petitioner* decision, the right to take proceedings in the name of the company. An assignation of the book debts would not really achieve any particular purpose. In view of the implications of the decision in the case in so far as it related to set-off the advice given to receivers faced with similar circumstances was that no intimation of assignation of a debt due by the company in receivership should be accepted.

1 1982 SLT 172.
2 Now re-enacted as part of the IA 1986.

**4.81** While many receivers were unhappy with the *McPhail* decision, the *Taylor, Petitioner* decision[1] offered no real comfort. It is suggested that the principal defect of the decision in *Taylor, Petitioner*[1] was that neither the effect of the equivalent provisions of the 1972 Act to those contained in sections 53(7) and 54(6) of the IA 1986 (crystallisation of a floating charge) nor the question of possible bad faith in assigning post receivership were properly argued in court.

1 1982 SLT 172.

**4.82** The question of whether the attachment of a floating charge to a book debt, upon the appointment of a receiver could be regarded as a fixed security (as defined in the equivalent provisions in the 1972 Act to those contained in section 70 of the IA 1986), notwithstanding that the only way to so constitute an effective fixed security was to assign in security the right to receive payment of the debt and to intimate such assignation to the debtor, was considered by the First Division in *Forth & Clyde Construction Co Ltd v Trinity Timber & Plywood Co Ltd*.[1] In that case, an arrestment was served on Strathclyde Regional Council the day after the appointment of joint receivers in respect of a debt due by the petitioners to the company. The court held that the attachment of the book debt in question by the floating charge must have had effect as if on the date of appointment of the joint receivers there had been duly intimated to the third party debtor by the petitioners an assignation thereof in security in favour of the holder of the floating charge.

1 1984 SLT 94.

**4.83** In his judgment in the case[1] the Lord President stated, in relation to the attachment of the debt:

> 'the intention appears to me to be that the holder of the floating charge shall, on the appointment of a receiver, enjoy all the protection in relation to any item of attached property that the holder of a fixed security over that item thereof would enjoy under the general law.'

and later in his judgment:

> 'It follows, accordingly, that in the case of an attached book debt one can only reasonably discover the effect of the attachment by treating it as if there had been granted in relation to it the only relevant "effective security" known to the law, namely an assignation in security, duly intimated. To adopt any other approach would in my opinion deprive the holder of the charge of the advantages which he was intended to enjoy, namely the advantages which would be enjoyed by the holder of an "effective security" recognised by the law, over each and every form of property attached by the charge. It could also result in frustrating a receiver in the exercise of his powers in the interests of the holder of the floating charge who has appointed him. It is, of course, the case that the 1972 Act has not expressly provided that the book debts shall be regarded as having been assigned in security to the holder of the floating charge on the date upon which it attaches to them but the language of section 13(7)2 makes it quite clear that the attachment is to have effect "as if" such an assignation in security had been granted and intimated by the company. From the date of appointment of a receiver the company, no doubt, retains the title to demand payment of the debt but no longer for its own behoof. The interest in the recovery of the debt is that of the holder of the floating charge, and a receiver who seeks recovery in the name of the company does so in order to secure the application of the recovered sum towards the satisfaction of the company's debt due to the creditor in the floating charge.'

1 *Forth & Clyde Construction Co Ltd v Trinity Timber & Plywood Co Ltd* 1984 SLT 94.
2 See now the IA 1986, s 53(7).

**4.84** The effects of the *Forth & Clyde* decision[1] may be summarised as follows:

(a) on the appointment of a receiver, a book debt is deemed to be assigned in security to the holder of a floating charge and duly intimated to the debtor as if it were a fixed security (as defined in section 70 of the IA 1986);

(b) the receiver only is capable on behalf of the company in receivership of recovering the debt even though the beneficiary of the proceeds of the debt is the holder of the floating charge;
(c) the debtor may not be able to set-off debts due by the company in receivership which he acquired by assignation duly intimated to the company in receivership after the appointment of the receiver. This would be contrary to the decision in *Taylor, Petitioner*[2] which with its concept of *jus crediti* is at variance with the fixed security concept of the *Forth & Clyde* decision.[3]

1 *Forth & Clyde Construction Co Ltd v Trinity Timber & Plywood Co Ltd* 1984 SLT 94.
2 1982 SLT 172.
3 See n 1 above.

**4.85** The facts in *Myles J Callaghan Ltd v City of Glasgow District Council*[1] were that the pursuers entered into a contract with the defenders for the renovation of certain buildings. During the course of the works, the pursuers went into receivership and subsequently into liquidation and it was necessary for the defenders to retain the services of a third party to complete the works. In terms of the original contract, it was competent for the defenders to retain plant and equipment on the site which belonged to the pursuers. The work was eventually completed by the third party and the pursuers sued the defenders for the return of the plant and equipment. The defenders counter-claimed for the extra costs which they had incurred by reason of the receivership of the pursuers. It was argued on behalf of the pursuers that set-off was incompetent as being directed against both the company and the receiver. In any event, set-off could not be pleaded to defeat the security which the holder of a floating charge obtains through the appointment of a receiver. There was also a further argument that the defenders' claim only arose post the appointment of the liquidator and therefore could not be set-off against a claim from the pursuers which arose at the time of the termination of the contract, ie pre-liquidation. The court held that, in effect, the pursuers were one and the same person and the defenders were accordingly entitled to claim against them. Lord Prosser stated that he concurred with the approach of Lord Ross in the *Taylor* case[2] that the company and only the company is the proper person to seek payment of any debts in terms of a pre-existing contract. Any action raised should be in the name and on behalf of the company. The court reiterated that the receiver through his power to litigate in the name of the company could vindicate on crystallisation of the floating charge the right to sue for outstanding debts: he did not acquire a right to the property in question and the receiver could only acquire what was available on his appointment to the company. Finally, the court took the view that the pursuers' claim to return the property for payment arose prior to liquidation and a proof before answer was allowed.

1 1987 SCLR 627.
2 1982 SLT 172.

**4.86** The question of set-off in receivership can by no means be regarded as settled. The courts will, however, it appears, be prepared to accept that set-off is competent after a company becomes insolvent in the circumstances set out in *Gloag on Contract* (2nd edn) at 626. Gloag states that the rule that a demand for a liquid debt is not relevantly met by a defence founded on an illiquid or unascertained claim does not hold where the pursuer is bankrupt or where it is averred that he is insolvent. He continues that on the principle of retention or, in Bell's words, of balancing accounts in bankruptcy, the party who is sued on a claim which he admits to be payable may put forward in defence claims which are not yet due, which involve only a contingent liability or which are disputed and require to be established by proof.[1]

1 *McPhail v Cunningham District Council* 1985 SLT 149.

## Crown set-off

**4.87** From time to time, the right of the Crown or some other person to claim set-off against the other has arisen judicially. The statutory provisions relating to Scotland governing such right are contained in section 50 of the Crown Proceedings Act 1947 and state:

> '(2) The following provisions shall apply as regards proceedings in the Court of Session or the sheriff court:
> (a) where decree in absence has been granted against the Crown the decree shall not be operative without the leave of the court obtained on an application of which notice has been given to the Crown;
> (b) a person shall not be entitled to avail himself of any set-off or counter claim in any proceedings by the Crown for the recovery of taxes, duties or penalties, or to avail himself in proceedings of any other nature by the Crown of any set-off or counter claim arising out of a right or claim to repayment in respect of any taxes, duties or penalties;
> (c) a person shall not be entitled without the leave of the court to avail himself of any set-off or counter claim in any proceedings by the Crown if the subject matter of the set-off or counter claim does not relate to the Government department on whose behalf the proceedings are brought;
> (d) the Crown, in any proceedings against a Government department, or against the Lord Advocate on behalf of a Government department, shall not, without the leave of the Court, be entitled to avail itself of any set-off or counter claim if the subject matter thereof does not relate to that department.'

**4.88** The leading Scottish case on the matter is *Smith v Lord Advocate (No 2)*[1] where the pursuer, as liquidator of Upper Clyde Shipbuilders (UCS), sued the Lord Advocate as representing the Ministry of Defence in Scotland. The liquidator of UCS sought payment of a substantial sum in respect of the construction and repair to certain naval vessels. The liability to pay was not disputed by the Lord Advocate but he claimed the right to set-off this liability against (a) the amount of a loan due by UCS to be paid to the Secretary of State for Trade and Industry (b) an amount of unsecured loan stock due for repayment to the Secretary of State for Trade and Industry (c) an amount in respect of national insurance contributions due to the Secretary of State for Health and Social Security and (d) an amount due by UCS to the Department of Inland Revenue.

1 1980 SLT 105.

**4.89** As noted in paragraph 4.87, section 50(2)(d) only allows set-off with the leave of the court, if the subject matter does not relate to that department.[1] The court held that by virtue of section 50, government departments were to be regarded as separate legal entities from the Crown so far as set-off and counter claim were concerned and that sub-section (d) of section 50 applied to the circumstances of the case.[2] Lord Kincraig considered at page 109 that the court should be furnished with facts and circumstances to enable it to come to a decision as to whether, viewing the issue judicially, leave should be granted or not. His Lordship, having accepted the pursuer's submission that set-off should not be allowed unless circumstances are put before it to enable it to exercise its discretion in favour of set-off by the Crown, made reference to two earlier Scottish cases[3] in which in neither case was evidence heard, the parties evidently wishing the court to decide the issue on the averments in the pleadings. Lord Kincraig considered that, in the present case, the defenders' averments of the circumstances which should be regarded as relevant to the granting of leave were not significant and he, accordingly, refused leave. Although the point may now be an academic one, following the abolition of crown preference by the 2002 Act, the question of whether set off could be against the non-preferential debt or ought to be pro-rated has been considered and found in favour of the Crown[4].

1 Crown Proceedings Act 1947.
2 *Smith v Lord Advocate (No 2)* 1980 SLT 105.
3 *Atlantic Engine Co (1920) Ltd v Lord Advocate* 1955 SLT 17; *Laing (Liquidator of Inverdale Construction Co Ltd) v Lord Advocate* 1973 SLT (Notes) 81.
4 *Turner v IRC* 1994 SLT 811.

## Data protection

**4.90** If a company which is registered as a data controller under the Data Protection Act 1998 (DPA 1998) goes into receivership, the receiver as agent of the company would be entitled to continue processing data. Where no such registration has taken place, and accordingly it would be an offence for the company to process data, the receiver would not be entitled to do so either. Although the DPA 1998 does not specifically provide this, it is evident that this would be the case and the receiver would need to seek such registration for the company before processing data. Where a party seeks information or documents from case files on the ground that they are entitled to such material under the DPA 1998, consideration should be given by the receiver to the Court of Appeal decision in *Durant v Financial Services Authority*[1] which set out guidelines on what constitutes 'personal data' and a 'relevant filing system' for the purposes of the DPA 1998.

1 [2003] EWCA Civ 1746 Court of Appeal (Civil Division).

Chapter 5

# Retention of title

## Background

**5.01** The seller of goods on credit, where possession and ownership has passed to a customer who goes into liquidation (other than a members' voluntary winding up) or has a receiver appointed over its property and undertaking before payment, ranks as an ordinary creditor for the price. The credit made available in this way by suppliers may well have enabled the customer to continue trading when practically insolvent and when bankruptcy intervenes the claims of the preferential and secured creditors will often swallow up most, if not all, the available assets resulting in such suppliers receiving little, if anything, by way of dividend on their claims. The position of such suppliers in the 1970s and the 1980s was aggravated by the increasing range of preferential debts, a trend now quite reversed by the enactment of the 2002 Act abolishing government preferential debt. Suppliers still have to contend, in Scotland, with the ability since 1961 of incorporated companies to create floating charges over all or any of their assets. It is hardly surprising, therefore, that suppliers of goods have looked for ways of protecting their interests in the event of a customer's insolvency and one method of doing so, namely by retaining title to goods sold on credit until payment of the price, was highlighted by a celebrated English case[1] which has become so well known that contracts of sale containing retention of title provisions are now commonly known as 'Romalpa Clauses'. The normal practice of most major suppliers to now include such provisions in their Standard Conditions of Sale stems to a large extent from the wide publicity given to the decision in that case. While such provisions apply whether or not insolvency occurs, the event against which they are primarily intended to protect the supplier is the insolvency of the customer. As a result, the supply of goods subject to such conditions to a company which goes into receivership often presents the receiver, at least in the early stages, with significant practical and legal problems. For this reason, the topic deserves special attention.

1 *Aluminium Industrie Vaassen BV v Romalpa Aluminium Ltd* [1976] 2 All ER 552.

**5.02** It should be made clear at the outset that, because of differences between the legal systems of Scotland and England, the treatment of such conditions by the Scottish and English courts has not always been the same but the decision in *Armour v Thyssen Edelstahlwerke AG*[1] has brought the two legal systems much closer than previously. A receiver of a Scottish company is more likely to be concerned with the position under the law of Scotland in relation to goods in the company's possession situated in premises in Scotland at the time of his appointment but, if the company has premises in England, could also be concerned with the position under the law of England.

1 [1990] 3 WLR 810.

**5.03** Before discussing retention of title in a receivership context, it is necessary to understand what it is. Put simply, it is when possession but not title passes. In the case of the sale of goods, the position under the law of Scotland, prior to the Sale of Goods Act 1893 was that, in the absence of agreement to the contrary, title passed on delivery to the buyer whether or not the price had been paid. The seller and the buyer could, however, agree that while possession would pass, title would not until some condition had been fulfilled, eg payment of the price. Underlying this aspect of the law was the distinction derived from Roman law between a real and a personal right and thus, in this context, the distinction between title and possession.

**5.04** The Sale of Goods Act 1893 introduced a uniform statutory code for both England and Scotland governing the sale of goods. This Act remained in force until re-enacted with some amendments in 1979. Scottish lawyers have experienced difficulty in applying these statutory provisions in so far as they relate to the passing of possession as opposed to title because of the absence in the law of England of a clear distinction between title and possession. Section 17(1) of the Sale of Goods Act 1979 provides that, where there is a contract for the sale of specific or ascertained goods, the property in them is transferred to the buyer at such time as the contracting parties intend it to be transferred. Section 18 then sets out five rules for ascertaining the intention of the contracting parties where the contract is silent on such intention. The 1979 Act does not refer to the transfer of title or ownership but to the transfer of property and with one qualified exception contained in rule 5(2) none of the rules points to property passing at the time of delivery. It is suggested that, for the purposes of the law of Scotland, property must be assumed to mean title or ownership. Section 19(1) of the 1979 Act provides that, where there is a contract for the sale of specific goods, the seller may, by the terms of the contract, reserve the right of disposal of the goods until certain conditions are fulfilled: and, in such a case, notwithstanding delivery to the buyer, the property in the goods does not pass until the conditions imposed by the seller are fulfilled. This statutory provision effectively restates the law of Scotland prior to 1893 in that the seller of goods can impose a condition that title to the goods will not pass until, for example, the price is paid. That is the present basis for the imposition by a seller of goods of a retention of title condition.

## Practical application

**5.05** On appointment, a receiver will almost certainly discover that, included in the company's stock, will be goods in respect of which unpaid suppliers are claiming retention of title and, failing payment in full of the invoice price, are threatening proceedings for re-delivery and perhaps also interdict against the receiver dealing with the goods. The alleged condition may go further than simply retaining title until the price of the goods in question is paid but the efficacy or otherwise of such conditions will be dealt with later. As the receiver will in most cases wish to continue the company's business at least until he has completed a preliminary financial investigation, he will wish to avoid interdict or other proceedings which might prevent his using or disposing of the company's stock-in-trade or finished goods. The receiver must, therefore, as a matter of urgency, discover whether there are goods in the company's possession the price of which is unpaid and which have been obtained from a supplier who is claiming retention of title. If so, the receiver must then ascertain whether a valid retention of title condition does form part of the contract for the sale of these goods. It is advisable for the receivers to consider in any particular case whether caveats should be lodged at the Court of Session and the local Sheriff Court having jurisdiction over the company in receivership in case a supplier seeks to interdict the company in receivership and the receiver from disposing of goods to which such supplier lays claim.

**5.06** It is, therefore, recommended that, at the earliest possible stage and preferably on the first day of the receiver's appointment, a physical stocktaking of goods likely to be the subject of retention of title claims be taken and a careful note of the stock physically located should be made against unpaid invoices of the suppliers maintaining or likely to maintain valid retention of title clauses. It is also worth checking to see if the running account with any supplier has been zero at any date after the date from which stock of that supplied is held. The establishment by the supplier of a valid claim to retention of title is made much more difficult where goods cannot be differentiated by any distinguishing mark and it is reasonable to insist on a supplier matching an unpaid invoice against particular goods located in the company's possession as having been supplied by him since the last time the account was zero, if it is an all sums due retention of title clause. If the goods in question have a serial number or other similar distinguishing mark, the task of the supplier is rendered easier but it clearly depends on the circumstances of the particular case as to whether a supplier can substantiate his claim, the onus being on him to do so.

## Incorporation in contract

**5.07** The receiver must first ascertain whether any retention of title condition has been incorporated into the contract for the sale of the goods. This can be a question of fact or a mixed question of fact and law. The terms of all relevant documentation require to be examined, eg quotations, offers, orders, order acknowledgments or acceptances, delivery notes, catalogues, price lists, invoices etc and any standard or other conditions referred to in any of such documents. Generally speaking, the earlier any such condition is imposed the more likely (in the absence of the attempted imposition by the other party of a contradictory condition) it is to be effective. For example, an attempt to impose such a condition by direct or indirect reference in a delivery note or invoice, particularly if there has been no previous course of dealing between the parties, is unlikely to be successful in that the terms of a contract are established prior to delivery of or payment for the goods.

**5.08** If the supplier appears to have included such a condition in the contract, the receiver should investigate whether the company has effectively rebutted such condition by imposing a contrary condition. In such circumstances, the rules which apply are those generally relating to offers and acceptances and each such case must be examined in light of the facts and the law. It has been held[1] in England that a party wishing to rely on a term incorporated into a standard form contract must show that the term was brought to the notice of the party sought to be bound before or at the time the contract was made. If that party was aware that the contract contained any particular term or if he was unaware that any such term was contained in the contract but the other party had done all that was reasonably sufficient to bring the term to his notice, then he would be bound by such term.

1 *John Snow & Co Ltd v DBG Woodcraft & Co Ltd* [1985] BCLC 54.

## Course of dealing

**5.09** Where a particular condition, such as one of retention of title is not *ex facie* incorporated into the contract documents, it is sometimes possible for a supplier to rely on a regular course of dealing between the parties over a period of time and to maintain that the purchaser knew that the supplier's terms and conditions of business applied to the contract as these had been accepted by the purchaser over a period of time. Reliance on such terms and conditions on the course of dealing argument is not nearly so satisfactory from the supplier's point of view as the specific incorporation in the contract documentation of such terms and conditions. As McBryde[1] points out in his detailed analysis of this area, there is a difference between:

(1) a series of contracts concluded using a form and then a contract without the form; and
(2) contracts consistently followed by the issue of a document with conditions which are not objected to.

The key elements are a course of dealing showing knowledge of and assent to, the terms relied on.

1 *The Law of Contract in Scotland* (2nd en) 170-174.

**5.10** For an interesting consideration of the course of dealing argument, reference is made to *Grayston Plant Ltd v Plean Precast Ltd*[1] where an English company with a place of business in Scotland hired out to manufacturers of prefabricated units a twelve ton telescopic lorry-mounted crane on the basis of a verbal contract with the hirers. The crane overbalanced during the period of the hire and the owners of the crane sued the hirers for the loss. The owners averred that the contract of hire, which inter alia provided that any damage to the crane was the responsibility of the hirer, incorporated the general conditions of hire established by the Contractors' Plant Association of which the hirers were members. After a proof was allowed, it was established that when the contract was made verbally, an acknowledgment of order form, stating that the order was accepted subject to such general conditions of hire, was sent by post to the hirer by way of confirmation. It was further established that in a period of two years, the hirers had hired from the owners plant on some 11 or 12 occasions although proof was not established as to whether the hirers had accepted such general conditions of hire. The court held that the onus of proving that the hirers were aware of such general conditions of hire was upon the owners, that the owners had not discharged such onus and decree of absolvitor was granted.

1 1976 SLT 74.

**5.11** Lord Robertson in the course of his judgment in the *Grayston Plant* case[1] reviewed a number of English cases, namely *Hardwick Game Farm v Suffolk Agricultural and Poultry Producers' Association*,[2] *Hollier v Rambler Motors (AMC) Ltd*[3] and *British Crane Hire Corpn Ltd v Ipswich Plant Hire Ltd*.[4] In the *British Crane* case, both parties were experienced in the hiring of cranes. The owners sent a printed form to the hirers for their signature but before the form was despatched the crane, due to no fault of the hirers, was damaged. Under the conditions which were the same as those used in the plant hire business, the hirers were liable to indemnify the owners for any damage. The owners relied on the course of dealing argument by referring to two previous transactions some months before the present transaction. Lord Denning concluded that the course of dealing argument could not be sustained but he held that since the parties were of similar bargaining strength, the owners were entitled to conclude that the hirers had accepted the conditions because of their wide usage in the plant hire business.

1 *Grayston Plant Ltd v Plean Precast Ltd* 1976 SLT 74.
2 [1966] 1 WLR 287 and [1969] 2 AC 31.
3 [1972] 2 QB 71.
4 [1974] 1 All ER 1059.

**5.12** Lord Robertson in the *Grayston Plant* case[1] then continued:

> 'In my opinion, the mere counting of occasions when a similar transaction has previously been entered into between the parties and thereby obtaining a sufficiently high score, is not all that is required in cases such as this in order to justify the conclusion that a written condition has been

incorporated into a verbal contract. The state of knowledge of the defenders is important (see Salmon LJ in *Hollier*);[2] so, too, is their status and professional experience (*British Crane Hire*).[3] "The judicial task is not to discover the actual intentions of each party; it is to decide what each was reasonably entitled to conclude from the attitude of the other' Lord Reid in *McCutcheon v David MacBrayne Ltd*.[4] It is therefore relevant to consider what steps were taken by the owner to bring to the notice of the hirer the conditions alleged to be incorporated into the contract."

1 *Grayston Plant Ltd v Plean Precast Ltd* 1976 SLT 74.
2 *Hollier v Rambler Motors (AMC) Ltd* [1972] 2 QB 71 at 78.
3 *British Crane Hire Corpn Ltd v Ipswich Plant Hire Ltd* [1974] 1 All ER 1059.
4 1964 SC (HL) 28.

**5.13** Reference is made to two further cases involving incorporation of terms into standard form contracts and the statutory test of 'reasonableness' specified in the Unfair Contract Terms Act 1977 (as amended) (for the purposes of paragraph 5.14 referred to as 'the 1977 Act') and the Sale of Goods Act 1979.

**5.14** In *McCrone v Boots Farm Sales Ltd*,[1] the defenders relied on their general conditions of sale to exclude their liability for an alleged breach that a quantity of weedkiller supplied by the defenders was not fit for the purpose for which it was sold. The defenders also averred that the contract was neither a 'consumer contract' nor a 'standard form contract' within the meaning of section 17 of the 1977 Act. Lord Dunpark held (1) that the defenders' averments were insufficient to establish that the general conditions of sale had been imported into the contract by implication; and (2) in any event, that the term 'standard form contract' within the meaning of section 17 was wide enough to include any contract which included a set of fixed terms applied by their proponer to contracts of the kind in question. His Lordship approved the decision in the *Grayston Plant* case[2] and confirmed the previous tests as to whether general conditions of sale could impliedly be included in a contract. On the question of a standard form contract his Lordship stated:

> 'Counsel for the defenders referred to section 24(1) of the 1977 Act which limits the circumstances relevant to the "reasonableness" test to those which were, or ought reasonably to have been, known to or in contemplation of the parties at the same time when the contract was made. So he argued, ingeniously but fallaciously, this contract was concluded as an oral contract and it could not be transformed into a standard form contract by the addition of the defenders' written general conditions. The fallacy, in my opinion, is that these general conditions were added to the contract after its conclusion. Not so. The basis of the defenders' case that these conditions were incorporated in this particular contract is that the pursuer knew that the defenders always inserted these conditions in their contracts of sale and that the reasonable inference from this knowledge is that the pursuer impliedly accepted them as included in this particular contract at the time it was concluded. The defenders have no averments

which even suggest that their contract was modified after its conclusion by the addition of their general conditions. Accordingly, it follows from the assumption that the general conditions were part of this contract, that it was a standard form contract.'

1 1981 SLT 103.
2 *Grayston Plant Ltd v Plean Precast Ltd* 1976 SLT 74.

**5.15** In *George Mitchell (Chesterhall) Ltd v Finney Lock Seeds Ltd*[1] where the defendants relied on an exclusion clause to avoid liability under a contract, Parker J stated that it was making commercial nonsense of the contract to suggest that either party intended it to operate where what had been delivered was wholly different in kind from what had been ordered and agreed to be supplied. The Court of Appeal held that it would not be 'fair or reasonable' within the meaning of the Sale of Goods Act 1979[2] to permit reliance upon conditions of sale which had not been the subject of prior discussion before the contract was concluded and which in practical terms were not vigorously applied.

1 [1982] 3 WLR 1036.
2 Section 55(4) and Sch 1, para 11.

**5.16** Quite apart from the difficulty of arguing against incorporation where retention of title clauses appear on order forms, catalogues and other pre-documentation, it may also be difficult to argue against incorporation into the contract where some form of contract has been signed on behalf of the company. It is, however, worth checking whether the person who signed the contract had ostensible authority to do so: a person would usually have such authority if the document signed is of a kind which is within the usual authority of a person in such a position with the company.[1]

1 *Freemans and Lockyer (a firm) v Buckhurst Park Properties (Mangal) Ltd* [1964] 2 QB 480; and *British Bank of the Middle East v Sun Life Assurance Co of Canada (UK) Ltd* [1983] 2 Ll Rep 9.

## Resolution of dispute

**5.17** Where there is a potential dispute over a retention of title claim the receiver or his solicitors frequently write a standard form of letter indicating that in the receiver's view the company in receivership has title to the goods in question and that, as part of the receiver's general powers of sale, it is his intention to dispose of the goods in the normal course of business or otherwise. It is, clearly, important from the receiver's point of view to put on record his general intentions so that the supplier, if he feels that he has a reasonable case to put forward, can take suitable proceedings to protect his interests. In many cases, where the supplier feels so justified, interdict proceedings are commenced under which the supplier seeks interim interdict preventing the receiver from disposing of the goods in question pending a resolution of the disputed retention of title claim, either by negotiation or by the court. As mentioned in Chapter 4[1] and paragraph 5.05 where there are suppliers claiming retention of title, the receiver usually lodges caveats in the Court of Session and the appropriate sheriff court to prevent such suppliers obtaining interim interdict without the receiver having an opportunity of being heard and having had an opportunity to put a proposal which allows him to deal with the goods and settle in due course if he cannot resist the retention of title claim.

1 Paragraphs 4.69.

**5.18** It is often the case that where a real dispute does exist, a practical short-term solution is negotiated along the lines of the receiver:
(1) either giving some form of written undertaking that if it should be established by the court that the goods in dispute are subject to a valid retention of title clause, then he will return the goods or pay for them at their invoice value; or
(2) reaching some other form of extra-judicial settlement with the supplier which avoids further delay and expense in resolving the dispute.

In *Leyland DAF Ltd v Automotive Products plc*[1] the supplier of components refused to continue supplies to the administrative receivers of Leyland unless an outstanding invoice of some £750,000 was met in full. The Court of Appeal held that there was no legal obligation on Automotive Products to continue to supply Leyland. At common law in the absence of a contractual or statutory obligation there was no obligation on one person to continue to trade with another. Further, even if there was a long-term contract in existence, the supplier (in the absence of contractual terms to the contrary) was not obliged to continue to supply once there had been default even though he may have agreed to supply the goods on credit. Finally, the refusal of Automotive Products to continue to supply components to Leyland did not constitute a violation of Article 86 of the EEC Treaty since Automotive Products was not in a dominant position and, even if it were in a dominant position, its refusal to supply components did not constitute an abuse of that position but was no more than a commercial decision taken in its interests.[2]

1 *Leyland DAF Ltd v Automotive Products plc* [1994] 1 BCLC 245.
2 [1994] 1 BCLC 245.

## Validity of retention of title conditions and trusts over funds

**5.19** Suppliers of goods in attempting to gain the maximum protection for their interests have imposed retention of title conditions in varying terms and, as part of such conditions or independently, creditors have purported to establish trusts over moneys held by or on behalf of the company all of which have been subject to review by the Scottish courts in recent years. As a result the following principles appear to have emerged in relation to the validity or otherwise of such conditions and/or trusts:
(1) A simple clause of retention of title which is separable from other ancillary clauses related to retention of title will be effective but if the retention of title provision is included as part of a larger clause incorporating other concepts

which are unacceptable under the law of Scotland, then the whole clause will be ineffective.[1] While the *Emerald Stainless Steel* and *Deutz Engines* cases have been overruled by the decision in *Armour v Thyssen Edelstahlwerke AG*[2] in relation to the specific point of seeking to secure the payment of all outstanding monies by a retention of title clause over particular goods, both cases appear to be good law for the proposition stated within this paragraph (1).

(2) If it is agreed between the parties in a contract for sale that property should not pass until all debts due by the purchaser to the seller have been paid, the courts in Scotland will enforce such a clause.[2]

(3) Trust moneys credited to a bank account, without notice being given to the bank of the existence of a trust, may be protected if such moneys are clearly distinguishable from other moneys of a company[3] and a condition imposed on a purchaser to set up a trust fund for any moneys received by that purchaser in the event of a further sale will not be effective unless positive steps have been taken by the purchaser to place the trust proceeds outwith the purchaser's control and so to set up a valid trust.[4] An invoice discounting agreement whereby a company agrees to sell and a third party agrees to buy all book debts owed to the company whether present or future creates a trust sufficient to divest the company of the beneficial right to the debts and ranks in priority to the holder of a floating charge.[5]

(4) If a purchaser acquires materials from a supplier and uses these to create a new species of goods from them, then the ownership of the new goods vest with the purchaser under the doctrine of specification.[6] The decision of the House of Lords in the *Armour* case[2] did not disturb the finding of the Court of Session in respect of the doctrine of specification. The manufacturer, however, of the new goods must have acted in good faith.[7]

(5) A supplier of goods will have no rights against a receiver of the purchaser if the purchaser prior to the receiver's appointment sells the goods to a sub-purchaser, on the grounds that the law of Scotland does not recognise the doctrine of tracing in the case of sale proceeds being received either before or after such appointment.[8]

(6) Where goods are sold by a person who is not their owner and who sells them without the authority or consent of the owner, the buyer acquires no better title to the goods than that of the seller unless the owner of the goods is by his conduct precluded from denying the seller's authority to sell.[9]

(7) Where goods with the owner's consent are in the possession of a party other than the owner and such party disposes of such goods to a third party, the third party without notice of a retention of title clause will obtain a good title to such goods.[10]

(8) The *lex situs* governs the interpretation of a retention of title clause expressed to be subject to the law of a foreign jurisdiction.[11] The decision of the House of Lords in the *Armour* case[2] did not disturb the finding of the Court of Session in respect of the rules governing the *lex situs*.

1 *Emerald Stainless Steel Ltd v South Side Distribution Ltd* 1983 SLT 162; *Deutz Engines Ltd v Terex Ltd* 1984 SLT 273; *Hammer and Sohne v HWT Realisations Ltd* 1985 SLT (Sh Ct) 21.
2 *Armour v Thyssen Edelstahlwerke AG* [1990] 3 WLR 810.
3 *Smith v Liquidator of James Birrell Ltd* 1968 SLT 174.

4 *Export Credits Guarantee Dept v Turner* 1981 SLT 286; *Clark Taylor & Co Ltd v Quality Site Development (Edinburgh) Ltd* 1981 SLT 308.
5 *Tay Valley Joinery Ltd v CF Financial Services Ltd* 1987 SLT 207.
6 *International Banking Corpn v Ferguson Shaw & Sons* 1910 SC 182; *Armour v Thyssen Edelstahlwerke AG* 1986 SLT 452.
7 *McDonald v Provan of Scotland Street Ltd* 1960 SLT 231.
8 *Michelin Tyre Co Ltd v Macfarlane (Glasgow) Ltd* 1917 2 SLT 205.
9 Sale of Goods Act 1979, s 21(1); and the *Liquidator of Brechin Auction Co Ltd v Reid* 1895 22 R 711.
10 Sale of Goods Act 1979, s 25(1); *Thomas Graham & Sons Ltd v Glenrothes Development Corpn* 1968 SLT 2; and *Archivent Sales & Development Ltd v Strathclyde Regional Council* 1985 SLT 154.
11 *Hammer & Sohne v HWT Realisations Ltd* 1985 SLT (Sh Ct) 21; *Armour v Thyssen Edelstahlwerke AG* 1986 SLT 452; but see *Zahnrad Fabrik Passau GmbH v Terex Ltd* 1986 SLT 84.

**5.20** The facts in *Emerald Stainless Steel Ltd v South Side Distribution Ltd*[1] were that suppliers sold certain goods under terms and conditions of sale which the parties agreed had been validly incorporated into the contract. One of the points in issue and, it is believed still relevant under the law of Scotland, was whether the court could divide up a long clause purporting to retain title into separate parts. Lord Ross took the view that the clause could not be broken down in this way. However, Lord Ross was prepared to accept in *Deutz Engines v Terex Ltd*[2] that, if the clause were properly punctuated, it was possible for the court to apply certain clauses which were valid under the law of Scotland and ignore other sub-clauses which would be incompetent under the law of Scotland.

1 1983 SLT 162.
2 1984 SLT 273.

**5.21** In *Smith*'s case,[1] some months prior to its liquidation, a company received the proceeds of certain policies of assurance which had been arranged under a pension and life assurance scheme for the benefit of its employees. The scheme was being discontinued and the sums were received by the company for behoof of its employees. The company paid the proceeds of the policies of assurance into a No 2 account with its bank but the bank was not on notice of the trust affecting the proceeds. At all times, from the date when the proceeds were credited to the No 2 account until the date of liquidation, there was always a sum in excess of the amount received under the policies of assurance and, at the same time, the company's No 1 account was continuously overdrawn to an amount in excess of the funds in the No 2 account. The court held that the proceeds received in respect of the assurance policies were clearly distinguished and capable of being disentangled from the company's own funds and that such sum should be credited for behoof of the company's employees.

1 *Smith v Liquidator of James Birrell Ltd* 1968 SLT 174.

**5.22** The case of *Tay Valley Joinery Ltd v CF Financial Services Ltd*[1] has excited considerable interest both from the point of view of consideration by the court of factoring or invoice discounting of debts but also because of its interest that a trust may prevail against a receiver without necessarily following the strict rules under the law of Scotland relating to the assignation of debt and intimation to the third party. The facts in the case were that a company entered into an invoice discounting system with a factoring company whereby the factoring company agreed to purchase the book debts of the company, both presently existing and also those which would be created in the future. No formal assignation of the debts took place as they arose and there was no intimation to the debtors of the company of the factoring company's interests. At regular intervals in terms of the invoice discounting agreement, a statement was prepared which set out a note of the debts which had arisen and recorded that the interest in these debts had passed to the factoring company. The question was whether the debts due to the company had been validly assigned to the factoring company or were caught as part of the property and undertaking of the company following upon the appointment of receivers. The court held that the terms of the agreement had effectively created a trust over the book debts and that the beneficial interest in them had passed to the factoring company. The company had divested itself of its rights in the debts. While there has been keen academic interest in the *Tay Valley Joinery* decision,[1] it is suggested that the decision is correct and fits happily with the decisions in the cases of — *Smith*,[2], *Export Credits Guarantee*[3] and *Clark Taylor*.[4] While there has always been resistance to the introduction of equitable principles into the law of Scotland, it seems clear that the courts in Scotland will be prepared to examine the reality of the transaction. If the right to payment of debts is truly vested in another person, even although a formal assignation of that interest has not been intimated to the third party, the court will apparently be prepared to give effect to the arrangement.

1 1987 SLT 207.
2 1968 SLT 174.
3 1981 SLT 286.
4 1981 SLT 308.

**5.23** The liquidator admitted the claim of ECGD in the *Export Credits* case to an ordinary ranking in the liquidation but ECGD claimed that the delivery of the recourse agreement to them as sole beneficiaries set up an irrevocable trust. It maintained that all sums received by the company or its liquidator and the right to all debts incurred by overseas customers as soon as these were constituted were caught by the terms of the trust and that all such moneys were truly held for behoof of ECGD. The court held[1] that a trust had not been constituted prior to the liquidation by the delivery of the recourse agreement since intimation, where necessary to constitute the trust, would require to take place simultaneously with the coming into existence of a trust fund and no such trust fund was in existence at that time. There was only a contractual obligation on the company to hold payments in trust and such an obligation was not binding on the liquidator.

1 *Export Credits Guarantee Dept v Turner* 1981 SLT 286.

**5.24** The facts in *Clark Taylor & Co Ltd v Quality Site Development (Edinburgh) Ltd*[1] were that Clark Taylor sold bricks to Quality Site subject to a condition in the following terms which had been validly incorporated into the contract between the parties:

> 'In the event of the buyer re-selling or otherwise disposing of the goods or any part thereof before the property therein has passed to him by virtue of clause 11(a) hereof, then the buyer will, until payment in full to the seller of the price of goods, hold in trust for the seller all his rights under such contract of resale or any other contract in pursuance of which the goods or any part thereof are disposed of or any contract by which property comprising the said goods or any part thereof is or is to be disposed of and any money or any other consideration received by him thereunder.'

1 1981 SLT 308.

**5.25** Quality Site used the bricks sold by Clark Taylor in carrying out a number of contracts and, in due course, payment in respect of the bricks supplied by Quality Site was duly made by the ultimate customer. As soon as each payment was received by Quality Site, it was immediately remitted to the current account of Quality Site with the Bank of Scotland. The issue in the case was solely concerned with the sub-clause which purported to create the obligation to 'hold in trust' all their rights under any contract of free sale and any other contract in pursuance of which disposal of the bricks was involved.

**5.26** The First Division of the Court of Session held[1] firstly, that Condition 11(b) purported to secure the freezing of the defined subjects regardless of their value under an alleged trust which gave no beneficial interest to the supposed beneficiary until they received the price of the bricks which they sold to Quality Site; the essential ingredients of a trust were entirely lacking and condition 11(b) was no more than an attempt, under the guise of an alleged trust, to keep valuable assets of the company out of the hands of its other creditors. Secondly, where the truster and trustee are the same persons, there must be in existence an asset, there must be a dedication of the asset to defined trust purposes, there must be a beneficiary with defined rights in the trust estate, and there must also be delivery of the trust deed or subject of the trust or a sufficient and satisfactory equivalent to delivery, so as to achieve irrevocable divestiture of the truster and investiture of the trustee in the trust estate. Finally, a contractual obligation to constitute a trust is not sufficient to have the effect of constituting a trust in favour of one contracting party, particularly where the party undertaking the obligation is himself to discharge the office of both truster and trustee. Clearly, some form of delivery was essential before a valid trust could be created.

1 *Clark Taylor & Co Ltd v Quality Site Development (Edinburgh) Ltd* 1981 SLT 308.

**5.27** The facts in *International Banking Corpn v Ferguson Shaw & Sons*[1] were that oil had been stolen and sold to the defenders who were bona fide purchasers and as such, converted the oil with other materials into lard or cooking fat. The lard or cooking fat was then sold to customers in the ordinary course of business. The court held that this was a proper example of specification; the defenders had the exclusive right of property in the lard but had to account to the pursuers for the value of the oil which had been used.

1 1910 SC 182.

**5.28** In the case of the *Armour v Thyssen Edelstahlwerke AG*[1] the issues of specification and *lex situs* were fully considered and appear to be unaffected by the House of Lords decision.[2] In the case, the joint receivers of Carron Company Limited sought a declarator that a quantity of steel amounting to 67,423 kilograms, for which no payment had been made and which was delivered to the company's premises prior to the date of appointment of the joint receivers by the defenders, belonged to the company and could be sold by the joint receivers. Alternatively, the proportion of steel which had been cut into pieces before the appointment and could not be returned to its original state belonged to the company in accordance with the principle of specification. The defenders relied on the defenders' general conditions of delivery and payment which expressly provided that the law of the Federal Republic of Germany was to be applied to the contracts between them and the company.

Clause I No 3 of the general conditions of delivery and payment stated:

> 'Reservation of Ownership (Retention of Title)
> (1) All goods delivered by us remain our property (goods remaining in our ownership) until all debts owed to us, including any balances existing at relevant times – due to us on any legal grounds – are settled. This also holds good if payments are made for the purpose of settlement of specially designated claims. Debts owed to companies, being members of our combine, are deemed to be such debts.
> (2) Processing of the goods remaining in our ownership is effected on our behalf as manufacturer, according to section 950 of the Civil Code, but without putting us under any obligation. Goods so processed are deemed to be goods remaining in our ownership according to paragraph (1).'

1 1986 SLT 452.
2 [1990] 3 WLR 810.

**5.29** There were in fact eleven separate sub-clauses under Reservation of Ownership which came before the court but the quoted sub-clauses are essentially the critical ones for the purpose of the issues raised. The above translation from the German was agreed by a joint minute to be an accurate translation into English. It was maintained by the joint receivers that property in all steel strip passed to Carron at latest on delivery of such strip to their premises in Scotland. There was no dispute that delivery was actually carried out and invoices were produced. It was maintained by the joint receivers that the provisions of the defenders' general conditions of delivery and payment had no bearing on the ownership of the steel strip once it had been delivered to Carron's premises by the defenders. The joint receivers maintained that the steel strip was situated in Scotland thereafter and the parties' property rights in it were governed by Scots law. They therefore maintained that Clause I No 3 of the defenders' general conditions was invalid under Scots law in that it was an attempt to create security over moveable property in circumstances where Scots law did not recognise such a security. The defenders, on the other hand, maintained that Clause IV No 5 of the said conditions provided that the law of the Federal Republic of Germany should apply and under such law Clause I No 3 was valid as a simple retention of title.

**5.30** The Lord Ordinary decided at procedure roll that a proof before answer was appropriate on the grounds that there had been no agreement as to translation from German to English in relation to the various documents; that the defenders sought to prove that the law of the Federal Republic of Germany applied and that it was appropriate that there should be investigation into the averments to specification. At the conclusion of the proof, the joint receivers' counsel maintained his plea to the relevancy and sought decree. Alternatively, he submitted that the evidence on the law of the Federal Republic did not support or, at any rate, sufficiently support the conclusion that Clause I No 3 was a simple retention of title clause. Further, and in any event, the property in a portion of the steel had passed to Carron when it was converted into manufactured goods under Scots law relating to specification. It was averred that after cutting the steel, it was impossible to return the steel strip to its original state. Having heard the evidence of three witnesses involved in the steel trade, the court concluded that once the steel was cut it was not easily resaleable and, in any event, only in a different market. Similarly, when the steel was cut into shapes. On melting, the resulting steel changed in its chemical composition and was not in its original state and would only command scrap value. Lord Mayfield in his review of the authorities on specification considered the authorities, namely *Wylie & Lochhead v Mitchell*,[1] *International Banking Corpn v Ferguson Shaw & Sons*[2] and *McDonald v Provan*.[3] Reference was also made to *Bell's Principles* and *Erskine's Institutes*. His Lordship stated that he found the rules difficult to apply to modern industrial and manufacturing processes. The evidence, however, led him to the view that, as a result of cutting, and if melting were carried out, the result would be steel in a different form. After melting, the steel would be in a different form because of the change in chemical composition. Its state was altered and to return it to its former state an element would have to be added. His Lordship, therefore, concluded that the evidence suggested a recognition by the steel trade that the steel, in fact, was in a different form and thus, in a manufacturing sense, a new species.

1 (1870) 8M 552.
2 1910 SC 182.
3 1960 SLT 231.

**5.31** In *McDonald v Provan of Scotland Street Ltd*,[1] the front part of a stolen motor vehicle including half the chassis, the engine and the gears was welded to the rear portion of another similar motor vehicle. The composite vehicle was then sold to a third party who acquired it bona fide before they, in turn, resold it. Three months after the resale, the police removed the motor vehicle from the possession of the eventual purchaser who raised an action of damages for breach of warranty against its seller. The court held that the doctrine of *specificatio* (pleaded by the seller) can only be invoked where there was absolute bona fides on the part of the manufacturer and could not be applicable where part of the composite subjects was constructed from stolen property.

1 1960 SLT 231.

**5.32** The facts in *Michelin Tyre Co Ltd v Macfarlane (Glasgow) Ltd*[1] were that tyres were supplied to Macfarlane who were motor agents by Michelin under what might be termed a simple retention of title clause. On Macfarlane's liquidation the question which arose was whether Michelin were entitled to recover the moneys in respect of tyres sold by Macfarlane (but not paid for) to customers before the appointment of the liquidator. It was conceded by Michelin that they were not entitled to recover, except as ordinary creditors, the moneys received by Macfarlane prior to their liquidation and Macfarlane's liquidator conceded that Michelin were entitled to recover tyres remaining unsold as at the date of liquidation. This left the question of the moneys received by the liquidator after the commencement of the company's winding up. The House of Lords were clear in their judgments: the Lord Chancellor said that the suggestion that Michelin should be entitled to the sale proceeds by virtue of the doctrine of subrogation in respect of a notional property in the goods remaining in Michelin after the actual property had passed to a purchaser from Macfarlane was untenable.

1 1917 2 SLT 205

**5.33** In the *Brechin Auction* case,[1] a purchaser of cattle agreed with an auction company who paid for the cattle and therefore acquired title thereto that title to the cattle would pass to the purchaser whenever he should choose in the future. The purchaser was in possession of the cattle and thereafter he sold the cattle to a third party without informing the auction company. In an action by the liquidator of the auction company against the sub-purchaser, the court held that the liquidator was personally barred by what is now section 21 of the Sale of Goods Act 1979.

1 *Liquidator of Brechin Auction Co Ltd v Reid* (1895) 22 R 711.

**5.34** The *Thomas Graham*[1] case which was approved in the subsequent *Archivent*[2] case both involved the supply of materials to a building company which sold those materials in the case of *Thomas Graham* in the construction of houses and garages and in the *Archivent* case, subject to a retention of title clause for the purposes of building a school. When in the *Thomas Graham* case, the contractor went into voluntary liquidation and in the *Archivent* case, the contractor went into receivership, the supplier in each case sued direct the eventual purchaser. In both cases, the defenders argued and succeeded in showing that the circumstances fell within the provisions of section 25 of the Sale of Goods Act 1979 (or, in the earlier case, the equivalent section of the Sale of Goods Act 1893) and in each case, the court held that property in the materials had been transferred by the contractor as a mercantile agent under the Factors Act 1889 to the respective purchaser in good faith.

1 *Thomas Graham & Sons Ltd v Glenrothes Development Corpn* 1968 SLT 2.
2 *Archivent Sales & Development Ltd v Strathclyde Regional Council* 1985 SLT 154.

**5.35** In the *Hammer and Sohne* case,[1] the pursuers founded on a contractual provision which purported to allow them to retain title to the goods until all the defenders' liabilities to the pursuers had been discharged. As part of these conditions, the law governing the conditions was stated to be West German law. The defenders who were in receivership argued that the clause in question was an attempt to create a security over moveables which was unacceptable under the law of Scotland and, in any event, while the proper law of the contract might be West German, the proper course was to apply the *lex situs* of the present location of the goods in question, namely Scots law. It was recognised at the time that if Scots law applied to the transaction, the clause would be rejected on the basis of the law existing at the time on the grounds that the clause was an attempt to create a security without possession. However, as previously noted, the position would be different under present law.[2]

1 *Hammer & Sohne v HWT Realisations Ltd* 1985 SLT (Sh Ct) 21.
2 *Armour v Thyssen Edelstahlwerke AG* [1990] 3 WLR 810.

**5.36** The learned sheriff in the *Hammer & Sohne* case[1] said at 22:

> 'In *Cheshire and North on Private International Law* (Tenth Edition) Page 195, the expression "the proper law of the contract" is referred to as being "a convenient and succinct expression to describe the law that governs many of the matters affecting a contract". Determination of this may depend on ascertaining whether or not the parties have expressed any choice of system within the terms of their contract and/or whether the contract is most closely associated with a particular system of law. On such criteria, I would not be disposed to question whether West German law is the "proper law" in that restricted sense and in the circumstances of the present case. In my belief, however, that is not the appropriate way by which to approach the present issues – at least not initially. I consider that the course is rightly charted by *Cheshire and North* (Supra at Page 195), where it is said:
>
> > "the correct inquiry is not – what law governs a contract question? It is – what law governs the particular question raised in the instant proceedings?"

for, as was said in *Re United Railways of Havanna and Regla Warehouses Ltd* [1960] Ch 52 at Page 92 (quoting *Cheshire* 5th Edition), "the fact that one aspect of a contract is to be governed by the law of one country does not necessarily mean that that law is to be the proper law of the contract as a whole".'

1 *Hammer & Sohne v HWT Realisations Ltd* 1985 SLT (Sh Ct) 21.

**5.37** It may, however, be wrong to regard the *lex situs* as being an inflexible corpus of law. In another case,[1] the pursuers' Terms and Conditions provided inter alia that contracts were subject to German law. The judge drew a distinction between the interpretation of personal contractual rights as opposed to proprietary rights: the case being concerned with the latter. His Lordship approved a passage from an opinion of Lord Chancellor Herschell in *Hamlyn & Co v Talisker Distillery*[2] as follows:

> 'I should be prepared to admit that an agreement which was opposed to a fundamental principle of the law of Scotland founded on conditions of

public policy could not be relied upon and insisted upon in the Courts of Scotland ...'

1 *Zahnrad Fabrik Passau GmbH v Terex Ltd* 1986 SLT 84.
2 (1894) 21 R (HL) 21 at 23.

**5.38** Lord Davidson concluded in the case[1] that there was no reason why one of the parties should not incorporate into a contract one or more provisions of a foreign legal system subject always to the qualification that if such provisions were opposed to a fundamental principle of the law of Scotland, there could be a challenge. However, any such challenge would not be successful if the difference was one of degree and could not be regarded as fundamental.

1 *Zahnrad Fabrik Passau GmbH v Terex Ltd* 1986 SLT 84.

**5.39** In the *Carron* case,[1] Lord Mayfield in his consideration of the *lex situs* issue reviewed a number of the authorities[2] and concluded that there was clear authority that the *lex situs* governs the creation of real rights in corporeal moveables. He considered it was also clear that whether or not a security has been created the effectiveness or otherwise has to be determined by the law of the place where the goods are actually located. In his view, that finding was supported by *Mitchell v Burnett & Mouat* and subsequent authorities.[2]

1 *Armour v Thyssen Edelstahlwerke AG* 1986 SLT 452.
2 *Mitchell v Burnett & Mouat* (1746) Mor 4468; *Hamlyn & Co v Talisker Distillery* (1894) 21 R (HL) 21 and *Hammer and Sohne* 1985 SLT (Sh Ct) 21.

**5.40** One area which has not yet been mentioned is the difficult one where goods supplied have been inmixed with other goods. Due to the fairly strict attitude of the Scottish courts in relation to retention of title clauses, it is thought that the Scottish courts would be unlikely to uphold a retention of title clause which purported to retain ownership in a seller of materials until the price had been paid once such materials had been inmixed with other goods. However, there may be certain circumstances where the supplier of materials converted into manufactured goods which contain various materials inmixed may have some protection under the law of Scotland.

## Accession and specification

**5.41** Accession occurs where two items are combined permanently (such that there can be no separation) with one (the accessory) being subsumed into the other (the principal). The accession can be by two moveables being combined or by a moveable being fixed to land. For a moveable to become attached to land requires more than that it is fixed to a building or ground [1]. Specification is the creation of a new *res* with materials belonging to another and stems from the original Roman law concept of specification. An obvious example of specification would be grapes turned into wine: the *res* cannot be changed back into its original state.

In *Bell's Principles* (10th edn) at para 1298(1), the rules for determining ownership are set out as follows:

> 'That, if the materials, as a separate existence, be destroyed in bona fide, the property is with the workman, the owner of the materials having a personal claim for a like quantity and quality, or for the price of the materials; that, if still capable of restoration to their original state, the property is held to be with the owner of the materials, a claim against him for work and indemnity in quantum lucratus being competent to the workman.'

As has already been noted the rules quoted by Bell were followed in the *International Banking Corpn* case[1] and the *Carron* case.[2]

1 *International Banking Corpn v Ferguson Shaw & Sons* 1910 SC 182.
2 *Armour v Thyssen Edelstahlwerke AG* 1986 SLT 452.

**5.42** An interesting discourse on the limits of specification took place in *Kinloch Damph v Nordvik Salmon Farms*[1] where Lord Macfadyen refused to accept that quantities of salmon smolts which later matured into fully-developed salmon could possibly fall within the doctrine of specification. His Lordship relied on expert evidence which established:

(1) the species name of the Atlantic salmon is *salmo salar* and there is no change in the species name whether the fish are in fresh or salt water. The species is a reflection of the genetic identity of the animal and does not change with changing environment;
(2) the changes that take place in the fish from parr to smolt to salmon are physiological changes principally affecting the gill and kidney which allow the fish to adapt to changing salinity conditions and have no bearing on the species of the animal which remains constant.

This case is to be contrasted with the English decision in *Chaigley Farms Ltd v Crawford, Kaye & Grayshire Ltd*[2] where it was held that a distinction could be drawn between 'livestock' and 'goods' and animals which had been slaughtered on the principle that clearly slaughtered animals could not be put back into the position of being live animals.

1 [1999] Scot CS 162 (30 June 1999).
2 [1996] BCC 957.

## Confusion

**5.43** Confusion is the mixing of liquids and commixtion is a mixing of solids. An example of confusion might be the mixing of motor oils and an example of commixtion might be the mixing of bricks of the same type.

**5.44** In *Bell's Principles* at para 1298(2), the rules for determining ownership where liquids or solids belonging to different persons are inmixed are set out as follows:

> 'Confusion or commixtion raise a common property, if the commodities be of the same kind; and of such property *pro indiviso* the shares are in proportion to quantity and value; where either the union is by common consent, or where, having been made by accident or without fault, the commodities are inseparable. The property is unchanged if the articles be capable of separation. If the union be of substances different, so as to create a *tertium quid*, the property is (according to the rule in specification) with the owner of the materials, or with the manufacturer, according to the possibility or impossibility of restoring the original substances.'

**5.45** The general result is that if the liquids or solids may be separated into their original properties, then the property rights are unchanged but if the various materials are inseparable, then the new *res* may be regarded as common property and the supplier's share would be calculated on the basis of his contribution to the new *res*. If an entirely new *res* has been created, then the specification rules referred to above will apply.

**5.46** There is a further set of circumstances which is worthy of consideration, namely where the item which has been manufactured or is in the process of manufacture cannot be regarded as falling within the rules applicable to specification, confusion or commixtion. In the case of *Wylie & Lochhead v Mitchell*[1] the defender had contracted to build a hearse for a firm of undertakers. Wylie & Lochhead supplied a number of the materials but the defender became bankrupt before completion of the hearse. The court held that the hearse was the result of neither specification nor confusion. The materials, skill and labour of the contributions were voluntarily and inseparably combined and the court applying general principles of equity said that the parties were joint proprietors of the subject produced in proportion to the value of their respective contributions.

1 (1870) 8 M 552.

**5.47** Following the publication of a joint report by the Law Commission and The Scottish Law Commission[1], a perceived inadequacy under the Sale of Goods legislation has been rectified. Section 16 of the Sale of Goods Act 1979 provided that:

> 'Where there is a contract for the sale of unascertained goods no property in the goods is transferred to the buyer unless and until the goods are ascertained.'

If the seller was paid for the goods, but became insolvent before the goods were ascertained, then the insolvency practitioner would retain title to the goods, albeit that the company had been paid.

The result has been the passing of the Sale of Goods (Amendment) Act 1995 which came into effect on 19 September 1995 and deals with the sale of unascertained goods forming part of an identified bulk and the sale of undivided shares in goods. There are two key parts of the new Act. The first creates a new rule on sale of goods out of a bulk which enables property in an undivided share in the bulk to pass before ascertainment of goods relating to specific sale contracts. It puts into law the doctrine of 'ascertainment by exhaustion' whereby stock from which goods are drawn is depleted successively by withdrawals until all that is left will satisfy the contract in question. The second is a new concept whereby the buyer will become the co-owner with others having a claim on the entire bulk. Bulk is defined to mean a mass or collection of goods of the same kind which (a) is contained in a defined space or area; and (b) is such that any goods in the bulk are interchangeable with any other goods therein of the same number or quantity.

1 Sale of Goods Forming Part of a Bulk in July 1993 (Scot Law Com No 145).

CHAPTER 6

# Receivership as it affects officers of company and its employees

## Effect on officers of company and their powers

**6.01** The appointment of a receiver does not affect the position of the officers of the company, namely its directors and secretary. Their tenure of office as such is not terminated by the receiver's appointment and accordingly they remain subject to their statutory duties. While there is nothing to prevent any director or the secretary subsequently resigning office as such, this does not, for example, necessarily relieve the person resigning from his obligations in relation to the statutory statement of affairs to be submitted to the receiver.[1] Tenure of office as a director or secretary is to be distinguished from executive employment however and, as regards the latter, the effect of the appointment of a receiver is no different from that on other employees.[2] As to whether or not an officer is also an employee, and entitled to remuneration as such see 6.04 below.

1 IA 1986, s 66.
2 See para 6.07.

**6.02** The powers of the company's officers as such are, however, affected by a receiver's appointment[1]. While they can still exercise certain powers, such as the power of the directors to convene a general meeting of the company, for example, to place the company in voluntary liquidation their general powers of management and ability to deal with the assets covered by the charge are suspended. In the first Scottish case to consider the effect of receivership on directors' powers, it was held[2] that where a receiver is appointed over the whole assets of a company the directors of the company are not entitled to deal in any way with the property of the company. In a subsequent case[3] however the court differed from this view after considering an intervening English decision,[4] stating that the views expressed in it were capable of general application and did not in principle conflict with the provisions of the then Scottish statutory provisions. The decision in the *Newhart Developments* case has been confirmed in subsequent cases.[5]

1 Reference is made to paras 2.21-2.28 above.
2 *Imperial Hotel (Aberdeen) Ltd v Vaux Breweries Ltd* 1978 SLT 113.

3 *Shanks v Central Regional Council* [1987] ALT 410.
4 *Newhart Developments Ltd v Co-operative Commercial Bank Ltd* [1978] QB 814.
5 *Tudor Grange Holdings Ltd v Citibank NA* [1991] BCLC 1009 and *Independent Pension Trustee Ltd v LAW Construction Co Ltd* 1997 SLT 1105.

**6.03** In the *Independent Pension Trustee* case[1] the court followed *Gomba Holdings UK Ltd*[2], doubted *Shanks*[3] and agreed with *Tudor Grange*[4] that *Newhart*[5] needed to be narrowly construed. It held that it would be contrary to principle and wholly impractical if there was some kind of diarchy over a company's assets, and accordingly, during the currency of a receivership, the directors had no power over assets in the possession or control of the receiver. The opinion was expressed that where a receiver was disabled from exercising a right or power of the company because of a conflict of interest, the company directors might be entitled to exercise that right or power. Assets would include not only the company's property, but its rights and powers, in so far at least as these have commercial value or significance.

1 *Independent Pension Trustee Ltd v LAW Construction Co Ltd* 1997 SLT 1105.
2 *Gomba Holdings UK Ltd v Homan* [1986] 1 WLR 1301.
3 *Shanks v Central Regional Council* 1987 SLT 410.
4 *Tudor Grange Holdings Ltd v Citibank NA* [1991] BCLC 1009.
5 *Newhart Development Ltd v Co-operative Commercial Bank Ltd* [1978] QB 814.

## Position of directors

**6.04** There has always been a debate about how a working director ought to be treated when he claims to be an employee in any insolvency. Reference is made to Statement of Insolvency Practice 6 issued by R3 (formerly the Society of Practitioners of Insolvency).[1] As background, section 230(1) of the 1996 Act defines an 'employee' as 'an individual who has entered into or works under (or, where the employment has ceased, worked under) a contract of employment'. Section 230(2) of the 1996 Act defines 'contracts of employment' as a 'contract of service or apprenticeship whether express or implied, and (if it is expressed) whether oral or in writing'. In *SSTI v Bottrill*[2] the EAT opined that facts indicating employment were:
(a) whether tax and NIC were paid on that basis;
(b) the employee had no other employment;
(c) the contract of employment was signed and dated and indicated that the position was that of an employee;
(d) the employee was entitled to holidays and sick pay;
(e) the employee worked every day from 8.30 am until 5.30 pm;
(f) the employee was paid by salary and did not receive director's fees.

The court took the view that factors which mitigated against employee status were:
(1) theoretical control over the company;
(2) the fact that in that case the employee had taken only 8 out of 16 days' holiday in the last year; and

(3) that the employee had not received pay for the last month (because the chequebook was not available).

The Court of Appeal in the *Bottrill* case upheld the decision of the EAT and stated that:

> 'Whether or not an employer/employee relationship exists can only be decided by having regard to all the relevant facts. If an individual has a controlling shareholding, that is certainly a fact which is likely to be significant in all situations and in some cases it may prove to be decisive. However, it is only one of the factors which are relevant and certainly it is not to be taken as determinative without considering all the relevant circumstances.'

The Court of Appeal specifically approved the earlier decision of the Court of Session in *Fleming v SSTI*[3].

1 See Appendix 15 for Technical Release 6 and generally Technical Release 5.
2 [1998] IRLR 120.
3 [1997] IRLR 682.

**6.05** Where a floating charge does not extend over the whole assets of a company, the powers and duties of the directors in relation to the excluded assets (including assets held in trust) remain intact.

## Position of employees

**6.06** The general rule is that, except in certain special circumstances mentioned below, the appointment of a receiver does not of itself terminate then existing contracts of employment between the company and its employees.[1] The special circumstances in which the appointment of a receiver results in termination of such contracts were enunciated in an English decision[2] involving the appointment out of court by holders of a debenture of a receiver and manager to act as agent of the company and are as follows:

(1) the appointment was accompanied by the sale of the business of the company (but note now the effect of the 1981 Regulations); or
(2) simultaneously with, or very soon after, the appointment, the receiver entered into a new agreement with a particular employee which was inconsistent with the continuation of his previous contract of service; or
(3) the continuation of a particular employee's employment was inconsistent with the role and function of the receiver and manager.

There will however be a dismissal if the company ceases to trade.

1 *Re Foster Clark Ltd's Indenture Trusts, Loveland v Horscraft* [1966] 1 WLR 125; *Re Mack Trucks (Britain) Ltd* [1967] 1 WLR 780; *Griffiths v Secretary of State for Social Services* [1974] QB 468; *Nicoll v Cutts* [1985] BCLC 322.
2 *Griffiths v Secretary of State for Social Services* above.

**6.07** That case [1] involved the company's managing director and in relation to the last of these special circumstances it was held that the mere fact that he held such position did not mean that his continued employment in that capacity was inconsistent with the role and function of the receiver in that, firstly, he had, in fact as well as in theory, been under the fairly stringent control of the Board and, secondly, the receiver had not been appointed to work full-time in the conduct of the company's business but merely to exercise supervision and control over the way in which the company's business was run with particular regard to the financial implications.

1 *Griffiths v Secretary of State for Social Services* [1974] QB 468.

**6.08** The general rule in relation to employees' contracts of service as stated by the court in England is consistent with the statutory provision[1] that any contract entered into by or on behalf of the company prior to the receiver's appointment shall, subject to its terms, continue in force notwithstanding such appointment. As a practical matter, however, if the receiver wishes to continue any such contract (or for that matter enter into new contracts of employment) he will in order to maintain the employee's goodwill ensure that the employee is paid as such payments will be a proper expense of the receivership. The effect of the general rule as to pre-receivership contracts of employment is that the employees in question have, for the purposes of the 1996 Act continuity of employment.

1 IA 1986, s 57(7).

**6.09** Prior to the coming into effect of section 58 of the IA 1985 (now consolidated in section 57 of the IA 1986) a receiver incurred no personal liability merely by continuing to employ existing employees of the company.[1] This was thought by the government to put at risk the interests of such employees and that section accordingly made amendments to the statutory provisions governing the agency and liability of a receiver for contracts so as to render a receiver personally liable for contracts of employment adopted by him[2] although he is given a fourteen day period of grace to decide whether or not to adopt any such contract[3] in that it is provided that the receiver is not to be taken to have adopted a contract of employment by reason of anything done or omitted to be done within fourteen days after his appointment. The liability was further amended by the amendment of section 57 of the IA 1986 by the introduction of the concept of 'qualifying liabilities' by the IA 1994. The IA 1994 was passed as a direct result of the implications of the *Paramount Airways* case which the Government perceived would have a detrimental effect on receiverships as a whole. Although the Act was introduced after the Court of Appeal's decision in *Re Paramount Airways Limited (No 3)*[4] the Court of Appeal's decision was affirmed by the House of Lords as *Powdrill v Watson*[5]. The *Paramount* cases held that where employees were retained beyond 14 days their contracts of employment were effectively adopted in full by an administrator. When subsequently dismissed the employee was entitled to all his entitlements under his employment contract including the unexpired notice period and other very significant claims which would rank as an administrator's outlay rather than as an ordinary claim.

Although *Paramount* was an administration case *Lindop v Stuart Noble & Sons Ltd*[6] held this would also apply in a receivership. The IA 1994 introduced the concept of qualifying liabilities to restrict such claims to what was perceived to be a more acceptable level. Section 57(2)[7] provides that a receiver is personally liable on any contract of employment adopted by him to the extent of any qualifying liability. Section 57(2A)[8] defines a liability to be a qualifying liability if:

(a) it is a liability to pay a sum by way of wages or salary or contribution to an occupational pension scheme;[9]
(b) it is incurred while the receiver is in office, and
(c) it is in respect of services rendered wholly or partly after the adoption of the contract.

Where the services are rendered partly before and partly after the adoption of the contract, liability only extends to so much of the sum as is payable in respect of services rendered after the adoption of the contract.[10] Wages or salary payable in respect of a period of holiday or absence from work through sickness or other good cause are deemed to be wages or salary in respect of services rendered in that period, and a sum payable in lieu of holiday is deemed to be wages or salary in respect of services rendered in the period by reference to which the holiday entitlement arose.[11] Reference to wages or salary payable in respect of holiday includes any sums which, if they had been paid, would have been treated for the purposes of the enactments relating to social security as earnings in respect of that period.[12]

1 *Nicoll v Cutts* [1985] BCLC 322.
2 See now IA 1986, s 57(2).
3 Ibid, s 57(5).
4 [1994] 2 All ER 513.
5 [1995] 2 AC 394.
6 1999 SCLR 889.
7 IA 1986.
8 IA 1986.
9 For what is an occupational pension scheme the position is more complex than might be imagined and reference is made to a specialist work such as David Pollard's excellent *Corporate Insolvency: Employment and Pension Rights* (2nd edn, 2000).
10 IA 1986, s 57(2B).
11 IA 1986, s 57(2C).
12 IA 1986, s 57(2D).

## Rights of employees on receivership

### *Preference for wages*

**6.10** Where a receiver is appointed, debts which would have ranked as preferential debts in a winding up require to be paid from the assets in the receiver's hands in priority to the floating charge creditor's debt provided such preferential debts have been intimated, or otherwise become known to him, within six months of advertisement by him for claims in the Edinburgh Gazette and a local newspaper.[1] While section 59(1) of the IA 1986 provides for such priority where a receiver is appointed 'and the company is not at the time of the appointment in course of being wound up' this does not necessarily preclude the payment of these debts by the receiver even where his appointment is subsequent to the commencement of a winding up.[2]

1 IA 1986, s 59(1) and (2).
2 *Manley Petitioner* 1985 SLT 42.

**6.11** The debts which rank as preferential debts in a winding up are those which so rank under sections 175 and 386 of the IA 1986 and Schedule 6 thereof (read with Schedule 4 to the Pension Schemes Act 1993) and there is a right of relief in respect of any such debts so paid from the assets of the company available for the payment of ordinary creditors. These debts include inter alia:

(1) so much of any amount which is owed by the company to an existing or past employee and is payable by way of remuneration in respect of the whole or any part of the period of four months up to the receiver's appointment, subject to such limit as may from time to time be prescribed by order of the Secretary of State;[1] and
(2) any accrued holiday remuneration in respect of any period of employment prior to the receiver's appointment owed to an employee whose employment has been terminated before, on or after the receiver's appointment.[2]

1 IA 1986, Sch 6, para 9 and s 387(4)(b): the present limit is £800.
2 Ibid, para 10 and s 387(4)(b).

**6.12** An amount is payable by way of remuneration if it is paid as wages or salary whether for time or piece work or earned wholly or partly by way of commission.[1] It does not include remuneration payable to a director by way of fees. Holiday remuneration is deemed to have accrued in respect of any period of employment if, by virtue of the contract of employment or any enactment, that remuneration would have accrued in respect of that period if the employment had continued until the employee became entitled to be allowed the holiday and includes sums which for social security purposes would have been treated as earnings for such period.[2] Likewise, remuneration in respect of absence from work through sickness or other good cause is deemed to be wages or salary for the period of absence.[3]

1 IA 1986, Sch 6, para 13(1)(a).
2 Ibid, paras 14(2) and 15(b).
3 Ibid, para 15(a).

**6.13** In addition certain other entitlements of employees principally under the employment protection legislation, each of which is dealt with later in this chapter, are deemed to be wages in respect of the periods for which they are payable.[1] These are:

(1) guarantee payments under Part III of the 1996 Act (employees without work to do);
(2) remuneration on suspension on medical grounds, or on maternity grounds, under Part VII of the 1996 Act;

(3) payments for time off work for trade union activities, to look for work or to arrange training or ante-natal care; and
(4) remuneration under a protective award.

These entitlements are deemed to be wages in respect of the period for which they are payable. As a result there is a problem in the case of protective awards as to how such awards in so far as relating to a period after a receiver's appointment should be treated. This problem is in practice resolved by the payment of such an award being made to the employee by the Secretary of State for Employment out of the National Insurance Fund.[2]

1 IA 1986, Sch 6, para 13(2), incorporated in by the ERA 1996, s 240, Sch 1, para 29.
2 ERA 1996, s 122(3)(d) and see para 6.26.

## *Entitlements under employment protection legislation*

**6.14** In addition to the preferential statutory rights on receivership in respect of arrears of wages, or salary etc, employees also have other statutory entitlements introduced by the employment protection legislation which, while generally unaffected by the receivership of their company employer, are paid not by the receiver, but by the Secretary of State for Employment out of particular statutory funds. Before dealing with the treatment of such entitlements on receivership it is necessary to describe them. As it is not within the scope of this work to describe these comprehensively the descriptions in the following paragraphs are of necessity brief and reference should be made to the relative statutory provisions for more detail.

## *Redundancy payments*

**6.15** An employee made redundant is entitled to a redundancy payment calculated in accordance with the 1996 Act. In most cases the calculation is based on 1 week's pay for each year's service under the age of forty-one and 1.5 weeks' pay for each year's service over the age of forty-one with a maximum of twenty years' service being allowable. The maximum weekly pay is currently capped at £280.

## *Notice*

**6.16** While at common law employees have always been entitled to contractual notice where so provided by the contract or reasonable notice in the absence of a contractual provision, section 86 of the 1996 Act lays down statutory minimum periods of notice which may be summarised in most cases as one week's notice for each year of service up to a maximum of twelve. Under the 1996 Act employers are obliged to pay employees during the statutory notice period.

## Protective award

**6.17** There are statutory requirements laid down in the TULRCA 1992 as extended by the Collective Redundancies and Transfer of Undertakings (Protection of Employment) Regulations 1995 and the Collective Redundancies and Transfer of Undertakings (Protection of Employment) Regulations 1999 for handling redundancies which require employers to consult either with a trade union or with elected representatives of the employees affected. These requirements are, shortly, that an employer must consult about proposed redundancies in good time and not later than 30 days before the first redundancy in the event of between 20 and 99 employees being involved in such redundancies and not later than 90 days in the event of 100 or more employees being so involved. Failure to fulfil these requirements entitles the trade union or the elected representatives (not the individual employees) to apply to an industrial tribunal for a protective award and, in the absence of special reasons justifying failure to consult, such an award will be made. The award, if made, entitles the employees to payment during the protective period which will be a period of up to 90 days in all cases. The protective period commences on the day on which the first dismissals by reason of redundancy take effect. There is no limit to pay for this purpose. The entitlement of any employee included in such an award is abated by any remuneration actually received or due for services rendered by the dismissing employer and by payments in lieu of notice. In the case of receivership for obvious practical reasons, it is more often than not impossible for the receiver to comply with these statutory requirements as to consultation. The TULRCA 1992 sections 188(7) and 193(7) does provide that the minimum time limits are subject to reduction if there are special circumstances which make it not reasonably practical for the employer to comply, provided the employer takes all such steps towards compliance as are reasonably practical in the circumstances. Insolvency or the appointment of a receiver is not of itself a special reason justifying failure to comply with these statutory requirements [1] as the events leading to insolvency and/or the appointment of a receiver will generally be foreseeable by the company. There have, however, been circumstances which, in conjunction with insolvency, have been considered to be special reasons.[2]

1 The *Baker's Union v Clarks of Hove Ltd* [1978] IRLR 366 and *Smith and Moore v Cherry Lewis Ltd (in receivership)* November 2004 EAT (appeal No UKEAT/0455/04DM).

2 *Association of Pattern Makers and Allied Craftsmen v Kirvin Ltd* [1978] IRLR 318; *Union of Shop, Distributive and Allied Workers v Leancut Bacon Ltd* [1981] IRLR 295; *GMB v Rankin and Harrison* [1992] IRLR 514; *Angus Jowett & Co v NUTGW* [1985] IRLR 326; and *AEEU and GMB v Clydesdale Group plc* [1995] IRLR 527.

## Maternity pay

**6.18** Statutory maternity pay is paid by employers but is normally recoverable by the employer by deduction from National Insurance Contributions.[1] To be eligible an employee must have a minimum of twenty-six weeks of continuous employment ending with the week immediately preceding the fourteenth week before the expected week of confinement and fulfil certain other criteria with regard to earnings level, notice to employer etc. The maximum period during which statutory maternity pay is paid is twenty-six weeks.

1 Social Security Contributions and Benefits Act 1992, ss 164-166 as amended.

## *Unfair dismissal*

**6.19** If an employee is found to have been unfairly dismissed he or she is entitled under the employment protection legislation to an award assessed under one or more of the following headings:

### (a) Basic award[1]

This is calculated in a similar way to a redundancy payment.

### (b) Compensatory award[2]

This is the amount the tribunal considers just and equitable in all the circumstances having regard to the loss sustained by the complainant in consequence of the dismissal in so far as that loss is attributable to action taken by the employer, but subject to a maximum amount of which from 1 February 2004 stands at £55,000. The maximum figure is usually increased each year by Statutory Instrument. There are certain circumstances where the maximum will not apply and these include where there has been discrimination under the Sex Discrimination Act 1975, the Race Relations Act 1976, the Disability Discrimination Act 1995, the Employment Equality (Sexual Orientation) Regulations 2003 and the Employment Equality (Religion or Belief) Regulations 2003.

### (c) Enhancement on failure to obey a tribunal order to reinstate or re-engage[3]

In the ordinary case this amounts to an extra 26 to 52 weeks' pay.

1 ERA 1996, ss 118-122 and 126.
2 Ibid, ss 123, 124A and 126.
3 Ibid, s 13(2).

## *Guarantee payment*

**6.20** Employees who are laid off are entitled to a guarantee payment calculated in accordance with sections 28-35 of the 1996 Act, this payment being subject to a maximum of £18.40 per day as from 1 February 2005 and five days' pay in any period of three months.[1]

1 ERA 1996, s 31 as increased usually each year by statutory instrument.

## *Suspension on medical grounds*

**6.21** Employees suspended from work to comply with any enactment or instrument or to comply with the Health and Safety at Work etc. Act 1974 are entitled to a week's pay for each week's absence up to a maximum of 26 weeks.[1]

1 1996 Act, s 64.

## *Time off for trade union or employee representative activities*

**6.22** Employees who are union officials[1] or employee representatives[2] are entitled to what may simply be described as usual remuneration when engaged in carrying out their duties as such officials or in relevant training.

1 TULCRA 1992, s 169.
2 ERA 1996, s 62.

## *Time off to look for employment or arrange training*

**6.23** Employees who are under notice of redundancy are entitled to be paid for absence from employment either to look for alternative employment or arrange training.[1]

1 ERA 1996, s 52.

## *Time off to act as a pension trustee*

**6.24** Employee who have time off to act as a pension scheme trustee are entitled to be remunerated for this[1].

1 ERA 1996, s 59.

**6.25** Where reference is made to a 'week's pay' in relation to an award of compensation, a basic award of compensation an additional award or a redundancy payment, this is calculated in accordance with ss 220 to 229 to the 1996 Act. A 'week's pay' is presently (from 1 February 2005) subject to a maximum limit of £280.[1]

1 ERA 1996 as increased usually every year by statutory instrument.

### *Treatment of employees' claims including statutory preferential rights and employment protection entitlements on receivership*

**6.26** The claims of employees in respect of unpaid salary or wages (as defined for this purpose) and their entitlements under the employment protection legislation may be dealt with in the three following ways, each of which may overlap the other:

(1) If it is a claim for wages or salary or for deemed wages and/or for accrued holiday pay it is entitled, within the statutory limits, to a preferential ranking.

(2) It may be paid by the Secretary of State for Employment out of the National Insurance Fund or other appropriate fund.

(3) To the extent that it is not paid out as a preferential claim or by the Secretary of State, it will be entitled to an ordinary ranking in the liquidation of the company if any surplus assets are available for ordinary creditors. For example, a compensatory award for unfair dismissal is only entitled to an ordinary ranking. As regards payments by the Secretary of State he will on receivership pay such claims from the National Insurance Fund or other appropriate fund where all or part of the claim in question is due to the employee on the later of:
   (i) the date of insolvency which includes the date of the appointment of the receiver;[1] or
   (ii) the date of termination of employment; or
   (iii) in the case of a Protective Award or a basic award for unfair dismissal, the date of the award.[2]

1 ERA 1996, s 183.
2 Ibid, s 185.

### *Occupational pension schemes*

**6.27** Included amongst preferential debts in a winding up and so in the preferential debts which a receiver must pay in priority to the floating charge creditor's debt is any sum owed by the company to which category 4 of IA 1986 Schedule 6 as amended by the Pension Schemes Act 1993 applies, namely certain contributions to occupational pension and state scheme premiums. An occupational pension scheme is defined in s 1 of the Pension Schemes Act 1993.[1] Generally these are:

(i) contributions from the employee to an occupational pension scheme (not a personal pension scheme) that have been deducted by the employer from earnings paid to the employee during the four months preceding the relevant date but not paid to the pension scheme;

(ii) contributions due from the employer to an occupational pension scheme which is contracted out of SERPS but only in respect of the 12-month period preceding the relevant date and only where they are attributable to the provision of guarantee minimum pensions or protected rights under the scheme;

(iii) state scheme premiums payable by the employer in relation to service in the 12 months prior to the date of fixing the amount of the premium.

Trustees or administrators of an occupational pension scheme or a personal pension scheme may apply to the National Insurance Fund where there are payments due from the company to such a scheme in terms of section 124 of the Pension Schemes Act 1993 as amended by section 90 of the Pensions Act 1995. On such an application being made the National Insurance Fund will process the application and pay the schemes direct and take over the claim that there would be in the receivership. Such subrogated claim will not always however rank, due to inconsistencies in the legislation, at the same level as the original claim would have ranked in the receivership.

1 'Occupational pension scheme' means any scheme or arrangement which is comprised in one or more instruments or agreements and which has, or is capable of having, effect in relation to one or more descriptions or categories of employment so as to provide benefits, in the form of pensions or otherwise, payable on termination of service, or on death or retirement, to or in respect of earners with qualifying service in an employment of any such description or category.

## Sale of the business

**6.28** The receiver of a company's whole undertaking and assets in order to maximise his realisations will normally endeavour to dispose on a going concern basis of the company's business or parts of it or, where the company has several businesses, some of them. Any such disposal will be a transfer to which the 1981 Regulations[1] will apply. The 1981 Regulations were introduced in the UK to implement the Acquired Rights Directive (EC Directive 77/187). Although the Acquired Rights Directive has been amended by Council Directive 98/50/EC which allows member states to incorporate changes into their law to preclude the transfer provisions from applying in a liquidation, these will not extend to receiverships.

The introduction of the 1981 Regulations had a significant effect on the sale of businesses by receivers. The principal provisions of the 1981 Regulations provide that a relevant transfer shall not operate so as to terminate the contract of employment of any person employed by the transferor in the undertaking or part transferred but any such contract which would otherwise have been terminated by the transfer shall have effect after the transfer as if originally made between the person so employed and the transferee. For the purposes of the 1981 Regulations, a 'relevant transfer' is a transfer from one person to another of an undertaking situated immediately before the transfer in the United Kingdom or a part of one which is so situated and any reference to a person employed in an undertaking is a reference to a person so employed immediately before the transfer.

1 SI 1981/1794.

**6.29** The provisions of the 1981 Regulations of primary relevance in the context of a receivership situation are, with the exception of the special provisions to cover transfers by receivers and liquidators referred to later, those which refer to a person employed in an undertaking or any part of it immediately before its transfer under a contract which, but for the provisions of the 1981 Regulations, would be terminated by the transfer of the undertaking or its relative part. The 1981 Regulations were made to implement Council Directive No 77/187/EEC and that Directive refers to contracts of employment or an employment relationship 'existing on the date of transfer'. The House of Lords' decision[1] in *Litster* is the leading case on what is a relevant transfer. The circumstances were that the Forth Dry Dock Co Ltd went into receivership in September 1983. A company proposed to purchase all the assets of the company in receivership and to take a new lease of the dock which it occupied. The purchaser insisted on the employees of the company in receivership being dismissed so as to avoid taking on liability for them. It was, accordingly, arranged between the purchaser and the receiver that all the employees would be dismissed approximately one hour before completion of the sale. Following completion, the purchaser re-employed many of the dismissed employees. The employees argued their case, ultimately to the House of Lords which held

(1) where dismissal of employees takes place before a business transfer for a reason connected with the transfer, these employees are deemed to be employed right up to the point before transfer;
(2) consequently, the 1981 Regulations apply and the liability for employees' rights are deemed to be transferred to the purchaser, thus negating the introduction of a break in time;
(3) United Kingdom courts are obliged to construe European Directives and Regulations issued under them in such a way as to give them their intended effect, not their literal meaning;
(4) the purpose of the Directive and, by implication the 1981 Regulations, was to transfer liability for employees' rights to purchasers in all business transfer situations;
(5) the 1981 Regulations have to be construed in a purposive fashion but without prejudice to the right of the new owner to show that an employee had been dismissed for 'an economic, technical or organisational reason entailing changes in the work force', ie the one defence open to employers according to both the Directive and the 1981 Regulations. As no such argument could be advanced in the *Litster* case, that defence could not apply. The effect of the *Litster* decision is that the arrangements previously made on many occasions between receivers and prospective purchasers in relation to the dismissal of employees not required by the purchaser prior to completion of a sale will be ineffective in protecting the purchaser against liability which will almost certainly include liability not simply for redundancy but also for unfair dismissal. Where a receiver before the transfer for a reason unconnected with the transfer, fairly or unfairly dismisses an employee, no liability will transfer to the purchaser.

1 *Litster v Forth Dry Dock Engineering Co Ltd* [1990] 1 AC 546, [1989] 1RLR 161.

**6.30** Regulation 8(1) of the 1981 Regulations states that where, either before or after a relevant transfer, any employee of the transferor or transferee is dismissed, that employee should be treated as being unfairly dismissed if the transfer or a reason connected with it is the reason or principal reason for the dismissal. Regulation 8(2) however provides that regulation 8(1) will not apply to the dismissal where an economic, technical or organisational ('ETO') reason entailing changes in the workforce of either the transferor or the transferee before or after a relevant transfer is the reason or principal reason for the dismissal. It is highly likely that a receiver immediately on appointment will wish to reduce costs and consider dismissals. Indeed the framework of the IA 1986 puts pressure on him to make decisions within 14 days and negotiations may well not have started with any prospective purchaser by that time. If the intention is to make a business more attractive for a purchaser then that is likely to be a reason connected with a future transfer whereas reducing the size of the workforce because the receiver cannot afford to retain staff would not be. The Tribunal will need to decide as a question of fact which is the principal reason. Regulation 8(2) does however provide the exception where the reason or principal reason for dismissing an employee is an ETO reason entailing changes in the workforce. In *SCS Consulting Ltd v Thompson*[1] the EAT emphasised that the decision as to whether the dismissal was an ETO dismissal is a question of fact for the Tribunal. In that case the Tribunal concluded that the business was overstaffed, inefficient and insolvent. The only way that it could be viable for the future and continue as a going concern was for the workforce to be reduced in size. In *Wheeler v Patel*[2] the word 'economic' was interpreted to relate to the conduct of the business not just to some potential or actual financial effect on the selling price for it. The reference to entailing changes in the workforce concentrates on the effect of the ETO reason and accordingly must 'entail' a change in the workforce. The dismissal of one employee followed by the engagement of another in his place does not constitute a change in the workforce. The ETO defence does not mean that the dismissal will have been fair but simply that it is not automatically unfair. The employer must have acted reasonably and have followed proper procedures as in any other unfair dismissal case.

1 (2001) IRLR 801.
2 (1987) IRLR 211.

**6.31** Where there has been a pre-transfer dismissal and the ETO defence does not apply then any liability will pass to the transferee. If the ETO defence does apply or the dismissal was not in contemplation of a sale then no liability will pass to a transferee. In *Longden and Paisley v Ferrari Ltd and Kennedy International Ltd*[1] it was held that giving a receiver a list of employees to be retained did not amount to a request from the transferee to dismiss the others. This must however be viewed as a dangerous practice and not to be recommended. The normal qualification period of one year's continuous employment applies as a result of the Collective Redundancies and Transfer of Undertakings (Protection of Employment) (Amendment) Regulations 1995 (SI 1995/2587).

1 (1994) IRLR 157.

**6.32** Regulations 10 and 11 of the 1981 Regulations contain obligations to inform the appropriate representatives of any employees of:

(a) the fact that the relevant transfer is to take place, when, approximately, if it is to take place and the reasons for it;

(b) the legal, economic and social implications of the transfer for the affected employee;

(c) the measures which he envisages he will, in connection with the transfer, take in relation to those employees or, if he envisages that no measures will be so taken, that fact; and

(d) if the employer is the transferor, the measures which the transferee envisages he will, in connection with the transfer, take in relation to such of those employees as become employees of the transferee after the transferor and, if he envisages that no measures will be so taken, that fact.

Regulation 10(7) provides that in any case where there are reasonable circumstances which render it not reasonably practicable for an employer to perform a duty imposed on him to inform and consult he shall take all such steps towards performing that duty as reasonably practicable in the circumstances. On an application an Employment Tribunal may award appropriate compensation, meaning such sum not exceeding 13 weeks' pay for the employee in question as the Tribunal considers just and equitable having regard to the seriousness of the failure of the employer to comply with his duty. It is no defence to this obligation that the company is in receivership. The *Alamo* case[1] confirmed that liability for failure by the transferor to consult before transfer passes on transfer to the transferee.

1 *Alamo Group (Europe) Ltd v Tucker* [2003] ICR 829, but see fn 3 to para 6.33 for an earlier contrary Scottish decision.

## Liabilities that transfer or do not transfer on a relevant transfer

**6.33** The following rights and liabilities will be retained by the company in receivership:

(i) criminal liabilities in terms of Regulation 5(4);

(ii) Regulation 5(5) entitles an affected employee to terminate the contract of employment where the transfer involves a significant change which is to the employee's detriment;

(iii) an employee may object to the transfer under Regulation 5(4A) on the basis of a substantial change in working conditions to his detriment and will remain employed by the transferor. In *University of Oxford (Chancellor, Master and Scholars) v Humphries*[1] Mr Humphries prior to the transfer was entitled to remain employed until the age of 67. The transferee sought to amend this and he resigned claiming unfair dismissal. The Court of Appeal upheld his view;

(iv) Regulation 7 excludes so much of a contract of employment as relates to an occupational pension scheme other than provisions of an occupational pension scheme which do not relate to benefits for old age, invalidity or survivors, the proviso having been added by section 33(5) of the Trade

Union Reform & Employment Rights Act 1993. But the Pensions Act 2004 will amend this from 6 April 2005.

Under the 1981 Regulations the contract of employment will be treated as if it had been originally made between the person so employed and the purchaser, subject to certain exceptions, and in accordance with Regulation 5(2)

(a) all the transferor's rights, powers, duties and liabilities under or in connection with any such contract shall be transferred by virtue of this Regulation to the transferee; and
(b) anything done before the transfer is completed by or in relation to the transferor in respect of that contract or a person employed in that undertaking or part shall be deemed to have been done by or in relation to the transferee.

In *Bernadone v Pall Mall Services Group*[2] it was confirmed that following a transfer the transferee takes on liability for personal injuries previously suffered by an employee in the business; and the transferee takes over rights of indemnity in respect of those injuries under the previous employer's liability insurance policy. The rights against the transferor's insurers is a right arising from or in connection with the employee's contract of employment in accordance with Regulation 5(2)(a). Where a transferor has failed to consult adequately before the transfer in breach of Regulations 10 and 11, there are conflicting decisions on whether the liability for failure to consult passes on transfer to the transferee. In Scotland the EAT in *Transport & General Workers' Union v James McKinnon*[3] held that it did not whereas an English EAT in *Alamo Group (Europe) Ltd v Tucker*[4] held that it did.

Although there is the general provision excluding rights under or relating to occupational pension schemes this has been strictly interpreted under *Beckmann v Dynamco Whicheloe McFarlane Ltd*[5] which was approved in *Martin v South Bank University*[6]. In *Beckmann* the ECJ held that only benefits paid from the time when an employee reaches the end of his normal working life as laid down by the general structure of the pension scheme can be construed as 'old age benefits'. Accordingly where there are any benefits, whether administered through a pension scheme or not, which provide for early retirement pensions, enhanced pensions on a redundancy or enhanced redundancies for people over a specific age, then these are not old age benefits and accordingly transfer. There will need to be case law to set out exactly how this is to be administered, since the experience of the writers is that there are various ways of dealing with such rights following a transfer and subsequent redundancies.

Finally the Pensions Act 2004 will to some extent bring pensions within the scope of the 1981 Regulations. The transferee will either have to offer membership of an occupational pension scheme or pay 'relevant contributions' (yet to be defined but likely to be an amount equal to the amount of the employee's contribution, up to a maximum of 6%) to a stakeholder scheme.

1 (2000) IRLR 183.
2 (2000) IRLR 487.
3 (2001) IRLR 597.
4 (2003) IRLR 266.
5 (2003) ICR 50.
6 (2004) IRLR 74.

**6.34** As already mentioned the 1981 Regulations contain special provisions, introduced by Parliament as a result of representations made by or on behalf of insolvency practitioners in the United Kingdom, relating to transfers by receivers and liquidators against the background of the then prevalent practice in the United Kingdom of hiving down by such receivers or liquidators. The effect of the provisions in question, which are contained in Regulation 4, is, in the event of the transfer by inter alia a receiver of a company to a wholly-owned subsidiary, to postpone the transfer until immediately before either the subsidiary ceases, otherwise than by liquidation, to be such a subsidiary or the undertaking (or relevant part) is transferred by such subsidiary to a third party. These provisions put the receiver in the same position as if had he at that later date sold the undertaking (or relevant part) directly to a purchaser and gives him the opportunity both before and after any such hiving down to reduce employment levels without necessarily passing liability arising thereby to the purchaser. The same end result will apply even if some employees are dismissed before the hive down takes place on the basis that the courts will treat such a series of transactions in a purposive way.[1]

1 *Re Maxwell Fleet & Facilities Management Ltd (in administration)* (2000) IRLR 368.

Chapter 7

# Sale of receivership assets

## Introductory considerations

**7.01** One of the most urgent matters for consideration by a receiver after his appointment is the investigation and evaluation of the business carried on by the company and its saleability as a whole or in parts. If he is fortunate, the receiver will have had an opportunity of considering a financial report prepared prior to and resulting in his appointment in which in all probability valuations will have been specified either on a going concern basis or a break-up basis. One of the unfortunate consequences of receivership is that valuations on a going concern basis (depending upon the economic climate) can be for practical purposes of limited value in a receivership context. As a very rough guideline, sales by a receiver at approximately one-third to one-half of a going concern valuation have not been unusual and, while most receivers will endeavour to sell more advantageously, a receiver will probably be reasonably satisfied with the consideration if, firstly, it reflects the best value which the receiver could reasonably have hoped to achieve in the circumstances and secondly, such consideration is equal to an amount in excess of an estimated break-up figure. It is emphasised, however, that each sale by a receiver carries with it different problems and characteristics and there is no such thing as a 'standard' sale of a business or its individual assets. In assessing whether the consideration properly reflects the best value which a receiver could reasonably hope to achieve, account will be taken of the extent of advertisement of the business or assets in the press and specialist publications and also of the general market conditions both as regards the general location of the business and assets and the state of the particular trade nationally and internationally.

**7.02** There are, in practice, two principal courses open to a receiver in disposing of assets belonging to a company in receivership: he can either sell the business or separate businesses with their assets on a going concern basis in whole or in part or he can dispose separately of individual assets without continuing the trade. A combination of both is, of course, possible in the appropriate circumstances. It has been suggested[1] that a receiver can arrange to sell the issued share capital of the company in receivership on a basis which ensures creditors are taken on and which leaves something for the shareholders or arrange for a scheme of reconstruction but it is respectfully submitted that it will only be in exceptional circumstances that either of these courses of action will be either appropriate or possible.

1 *Tolley's Receivership Manual* (1987, 3rd edn) para 7.1.

**7.03** Depending on the size and type of business, the receiver may decide to prepare and circulate an information brochure about the activities and particulars of the company including, for example, details of the latest accounts and trading results, the business itself and employees and information about the fixed assets and stock and work-in-progress. Most receivers who prepare such an information brochure will normally insert a disclaimer of liability in relation to any matters contained therein. Such a disclaimer will be in a form similar to the following:

> 'The following particulars are set out as a general outline only for the guidance of intending purchasers or their advisers and do not constitute either in whole or in part an offer or contract.
>
> All references to descriptions, dimensions, references to condition and necessary permissions for use and occupation and other details, while given in good faith and believed to be correct should not be relied upon as statements or representations of fact by intending purchasers or their advisers all of whom should satisfy themselves by inspection or otherwise as to the accuracy of all such references. No warranty or representation whatsoever is given as to the accuracy of any such references. The Receiver acts only as agent of the company and without personal liability. Neither the Company nor the Receiver, nor the firm of which the Receiver is a partner, nor associated entities nor the directors, shareholders, employees, managers, partners or agents of any of them make any warranty or representation, express or implied, as to the reasonableness, accuracy or completeness of the information construed herein for any purpose whatsoever. None of these parties accept any responsibility or liability for any information herein or for any errors or omissions herefrom or any use you may make of any part of it. Any intending purchaser who relies on these particulars does so at his own risk. No employee, agent or any other person is authorised to make offers for sale or accept offers for purchase in respect of any assets of the business on behalf of the company or the Receiver, who will only be bound by a formal written contract signed by the Receiver. The Receiver has not sought to independently verify any of the information contained herein which has been compiled from information supplied by management of the Company and derived from the records of the Company.'

## Duties of receiver

**7.04** Turning briefly to the duties of a receiver, it is generally accepted that the primary duty of a receiver is owed to the holder of the floating charge by whom he was appointed to realise the property subject to the charge with a view to satisfying such holder's secured claim. In preparing his information brochure the receiver should be very careful to avoid offering securities for sale, for example in the case of the issued share capital of a hive down subsidiary, as he may commit an offence under the Financial Services and Markets Act 2000 and subordinate legislation. The duties of a receiver are considered more fully in Chapter 3 but, in relation to the disposal of assets generally, a receiver has a duty to exercise reasonable care in their disposal.[1]

1 *Standard Chartered Bank v Walker* [1982] 3 All ER 938; *Forth & Clyde Construction Co Ltd v Trinity Timber & Plywood Co Ltd* 1984 SLT 94; *American Express International Banking Corpn v Hurley* [1985] 3 All ER 564.

## Form of agreements

**7.05** There are set out in Appendices 9 and 10 of this book suggested forms of hive down agreement and agreement for the sale of a business and the first point to emphasise is that a clear and concise definition of the constituent elements in the particular business is essential.

**7.06** A typical definition of a particular manufacturing business may include the business and undertaking of the Vendor relating to the manufacture, distribution and sale of space invaders and associated products carried on by the Vendor at Pitlochry including (without prejudice to the generality of the foregoing) the specific assets. It is prudent to describe various specific assets in detail (both those included and excluded from the sale) as well as dealing with third party assets which may be crucial for the continuance of the business.

**7.07** In some transactions the parties will have agreed an aggregate consideration for the Business or various individual assets and the necessity for valuations of, for example, stock and work-in-progress will not arise: however, in other cases this is not the position. If a valuation of such assets is required, it will be necessary for a stocktaking to be carried out at or as near as possible to the Transfer Date (normally the opening or close of business on a particular date) by representatives of the receiver and the purchaser. It is vitally important that the basis of valuation should be clearly specified whether in terms of standard accounting principles or otherwise eg the lower of cost or net realisable value using the principles and bases of accountancy consistent with those used in the preparation of valuations for the balance sheet of the company in receivership over the previous two or three years. It is often provided (but depends on the circumstances) that no account shall be taken of, or direct allowances made for, obsolete, damaged or slow-moving stock.

**7.08** As one would expect those involved in stocktakings to be both experienced and responsible one would always hope that the provision of some firm basis of valuation (such as described) would prevent disputes arising between the parties. However, it is prudent to provide that in the event of a dispute arising as to any aspect of the stocktaking and/or the valuation, the same should be referred to an arbiter, acting as an expert and not as an arbiter and appointed by agreement between the parties or, failing agreement, as nominated by the holder of some office such as the President for the time being of the Institute of Chartered Accountants of Scotland whose decision shall be final and binding on the parties. There should also be provision for payment of the arbiter's fees and outlays either in the reference to arbitration or as may be directed by the arbiter.

**7.09** Finally on valuations, it is recommended (if acting for a receiver) that a clause be inserted in the agreement to the effect that the parties will all use their best endeavours to ascertain the valuation of such stock and work-in-progress as soon as practicable and within a reasonable and definite period: otherwise a purchaser may delay completion of the stocktaking for his own benefit.

## *Status of finished goods*

**7.10** Questions sometimes arise as to the status of finished goods: for example, whether some items form finished goods sold to customers and, therefore, are not included in the sale or whether they form other unsold finished goods or work-in-progress and are so included. It is suggested that items which have been completed through all their manufacturing and production processes and are clearly identifiable as goods already sold to a particular customer (even although still physically within the company's premises) should always be regarded as finished goods sold to customers and not included in the sale: in other words, finished goods are goods which are in a deliverable state and in this context have already been sold.[1] Problems can arise, particularly in relation to sales for an agreed aggregate consideration, where over-zealous receivers produce and sell finished goods immediately prior to the Transfer Date, thereby diminishing the value of stock and work-in-progress. It is obvious that the agreement should endeavour to be clear and precise on such matters to avoid misunderstanding and dispute.

1 See the Sale of Goods Act 1979, s 61(5).

## *Assignation of rights and obligations under contracts*

**7.11** In certain receiverships the assignation or transfer of the rights and obligations under contracts will be vitally important as the rights and obligations under such contracts may form a significant element of the Business for which the purchaser is paying. In other types of receivership, contracts will be essentially short-term and formal assignation will not be necessary. Care should be taken to check the text of all contracts of any importance to ensure that the appointment of a receiver does not allow or result in automatic termination of any such contracts or otherwise adversely affect their value. If an assignation is required and is duly executed both by the company in receivership and the purchaser, it will, to be effective, require to be intimated to the third party in terms of the Transmission of Moveable Property (Scotland) Act 1862. As a practical consideration, if the contracts are a vital element of the business, the purchaser will not proceed unless at the very least he has reached an informal understanding with the third party or parties whereby agreement is reached with the purchaser taking over the particular contracts in question.[1]

1 For a general discussion on assignation of contracts reference should be made to WW McBryde *The Law of Contract in Scotland* (2nd edn, 2001), ch 12.

**7.12** It should be borne in mind that contracts forming part of the Business often carry with them a strong element of *delectus personae* and a third party may not be agreeable to the assignation of the rights and obligations under a contract. Indeed, in certain cases, the contract may specifically prohibit assignation of rights without the prior permission of the third party. One of the areas where this problem commonly arises is building and other construction contracts[1]. Although most receivers will be reluctant to become involved in such contracts for obvious reasons of general personal liability and liability for defects, circumstances do arise where, in the early stages of a receivership, a receiver will see an opportunity to collect a substantial amount of money if he can assign the rights and obligations under one or more contracts to another construction company. A deed of novation is often entered into in these circumstances between the company in receivership, the employer and the new contractor.[2] At the same time, a side agreement is usually entered into between the parties to deal with such matters as moneys lying in the hands of the employer, retention moneys and the exclusion by the company in receivership and the receiver of all liability for latent defects. The receiver will obtain a payment from the new contractor, the employer will have his contract performed more quickly and less expensively and the new contractor will collect the balance of sums due on the contract, presumably on terms advantageous to him.

1 See 4.05-4.07 above.
2 Note that in January 2001 the Scottish Building Contract Committee produced the most recent version of their Insolvency Practice Guide intended for employers and their professional advisers in the event of the insolvency of a main contractor while carrying out work under a Scottish Building Contract. It has a 'Style of Conditional Novation Agreement' annexed.

## Supplies on or about the Transfer Date

**7.13** It is usual to provide that pre-payments made by the Vendor prior to the Transfer Date in respect of goods to be supplied to the Business but not delivered prior to the Transfer Date and not forming part of the Business at the Transfer Date shall be refunded by the purchaser within a period (normally seven days) after delivery of such goods.

**7.14** The agreement should also make it clear that the purchaser will assume and fulfil all debts, liabilities and obligations relating to the Business arising or accruing after the Transfer Date and will take over all outstanding contracts, engagements and orders relating to the Business disclosed to it at or prior to the Transfer Date. A receiver should obtain an indemnity from the purchaser in respect of all losses arising out of the purchaser's failure to perform these obligations. Care should be taken to cover the position where goods are due to be supplied after the Transfer Date but which are delivered early by the supplier on or prior to the Transfer Date. In these circumstances, the purchaser should be responsible for payment but in a case where valuations of stock are required, the early arrival of goods could involve the purchaser in paying twice. Accordingly, such goods should be excluded from any valuation of stock.

## *Books and records of the company*

**7.15** The beneficial ownership of the books and records of the company is usually retained by the company in receivership and if required, photocopies of such books and records are usually made available to both the receiver and the purchaser although physical delivery of such books and records has already been made to the purchaser. The possibility should always be covered of the appointment of a liquidator who in terms of section 144 of the IA1986 takes into his custody or under his control all the property of the company to which the company is or appears to be entitled. If the books and records have been delivered by the receiver to the purchaser and the beneficial ownership of such books and records also transferred to the purchaser, the liquidator would not be in a position to recover them. In addition, the receiver or the liquidator may require the books and records of the company to deal with creditors generally or in connection with possible offences by officers of the company. It should be noted that the normal rules for the retention of VAT records state that such records should usually be retained for six years[1]. However, the liquidator of an insolvency company may destroy the books, papers and records, including VAT records, one year after the date of dissolution of the company[2]. Similarly, by concession, official receivers may also, on request, destroy the books and records of a company after a year.

1 VAT Notice 700/56102, para 19.1.
2 SI 1994/2507, reg 16.

## *Patents and trade marks*

**7.16** In acquiring rights to patents and trade marks, a purchaser will require a formal assignation of all such rights and will thereafter require to apply to the Patents Office or Trade Mark Registry (in the case of registered marks) to complete the appropriate registration formalities.

## *Premises*

**7.17** In relation to heritable and leasehold property being acquired by the purchaser the normal conveyancing procedures will obviously require to be carried out but this aspect is considered at paragraphs 7.44 et seq.

## Book debts

**7.18** As a general rule, the definition of the Business will not include the right to collect all book debts up to and including the Transfer Date. Most receivers will wish to retain the right to collect outstanding debts of the company in receivership and will only be interested in selling physical assets. However, circumstances may arise where the purchaser wishes to maintain sole contact with customers as a result of his purchase of the Business and it may be convenient for the receiver to allow the purchaser to collect on his behalf as agent certain or all of the outstanding book debts, on the basis of a commission (incorporating expenses incurred) being charged by the purchaser to the receiver.

**7.19** Again, arrangements of this nature may form part of a total package with the purchaser and the only warning note which might be sounded relates to the financial standing of the purchaser. It would be ironical, indeed, for a receiver to appoint the purchaser to act as his agent and for the purchaser, during the period of the engagement, to go into receivership or liquidation or become bankrupt, without clearly establishing a valid trust over the funds collected on behalf of the receiver and remitting such funds into a separate account as required pursuant to the decision in *Clark Taylor & Co Ltd v Quality Site Developments (Edinburgh) Ltd*.[1] It is obviously a question of judgment for the receiver in the particular circumstances. A suggested form of letter regulating the terms of any such agreement for the collection of debts is given in Appendix 11.

1 1981 SLT 308; but see also *Tay Valley Joinery Ltd v CF Financial Services Ltd 1987* SLT 207 where a trust may be created sufficient to divest the beneficial rights to debts in certain circumstances.

## Liabilities prior to the Transfer Date

**7.20** The purchaser will be anxious to ensure that he does not take over or in any way become responsible for any of the debts and liabilities of the Business incurred by the company in receivership prior to the Transfer Date. As the purchaser is acquiring only assets, the purchaser will not normally in any event be concerned with debts and liabilities except perhaps in the case of liabilities to employees.[1] The purchaser should, if he can, however, obtain an indemnity from the company in receivership and the receiver from and against all such debts and liabilities.

1 The 1981 Regulations.

## Goodwill

**7.21** Goodwill is rarely included as part of the constituent elements in the sale by a receiver of the business. It is, of course, a very intangible asset in the case of solvent businesses and even more so in a receivership context. For that reason a value is rarely placed on the goodwill of the business of a company in receivership and if it is included as an asset, its value will usually be nominal. In a sale, goodwill also formerly suffered from the disadvantage of attracting *ad valorem* stamp duty on the value attributable to it as part of the consideration payable by the purchaser, but this is no longer the case since the enactment of section 116 of and Schedule 37 to the Finance Act 2002.

## Early transfer of the Business

**7.22** It will be readily appreciated that although agreement in principle may have been reached quickly between the receiver and the prospective purchaser, there are many and detailed arrangements to be discussed before a formal agreement can be finally concluded between the parties. Many solicitors engaged in insolvency work experience some anxiety when it is suggested by the purchaser and the receiver that notwithstanding the wording of a formal agreement has still to be concluded, they wish to enter into some form of interim arrangement pending completion of such an agreement whereby the purchaser takes over the effective management and operation of the business. From a commercial point of view, such a course of action may be sensible for the future success of the Business in the hands of the purchaser but the encapsulation of a suitable form of wording may create problems. In the final analysis, such an arrangement can really only be contemplated where the receiver is satisfied with the good faith and standing of the purchaser, financial and otherwise. A suggested form of wording is given in Appendix 12 but it is emphasised that such wording is an outline only and requires to be adapted to suit the particular circumstances of the case.

## Mechanics of sale of the Business-form of sale

**7.23** There are basically two methods of disposing of a business. It can be implemented either (1) by way of an agreement for the sale of the business between the company in receivership and the purchaser (a suggested style of which is given in Appendix 10) or (2) by way of a hive down agreement between the company in receivership and a new subsidiary of the company in receivership followed, after an interval of at least a few days, by a share purchase agreement between the company in receivership and the eventual purchaser for the sale to the purchaser of the issued share capital of the new subsidiary (suggested styles of which are given in Appendices 9 and 13).

## Missives

**7.24** While consideration will be given principally to formal agreements, there is nothing to prevent the sale of the Business or of individual assets being effected through an exchange of missives between the solicitors for the respective parties. However, all solicitors involved in missives of this nature should be encouraged to agree the form of words between them prior to delivering executed letters: otherwise the process of comprehending five or six letters constituting missives can become very tedious and cumbersome. In general, where the particular business is of some substance, it would be more usual practice for a formal agreement to be concluded between the parties.

## Designation of vendor and liability of receiver

**7.25** Before dealing with the main clauses of these types of agreement, a few words should be said about the designation of the company in receivership. Any sale of a business or its individual assets is essentially a sale by the company albeit that the receiver negotiates, authorises and effects any such sale under the power given to him in terms of Schedule 2 to the IA 1986: the receiver having been appointed by the holder of the floating charge acts in terms of section 57(1) of that Act as an agent of the company in realising the assets attached by such floating charge. It is often helpful, however, to design the company in receivership as the vendor acting by its receiver followed by the designation of the receiver (thereafter defined as 'the receiver') because certain obligations may fall to be performed by the vendor and the receiver will wish to ensure that as few obligations as possible fall upon him.

**7.26** All receivers will seek to exclude completely personal liability (bearing in mind the provision of section 57(2) of the IA 1986 which states that a receiver is personally liable on any contract entered into by him except in so far as the contract otherwise provides) but if compelled to grant some personal obligations a receiver will wish a clause inserted to the effect that he will only be liable to the extent of any free proceeds available after all categories of persons described in section 60(1) of the IA 1986 (which includes the holder of the floating charge by virtue of which he was appointed) have been satisfied. If any liability falls upon the receiver in terms of such a clause, the receiver, by virtue of section 57(3) of the IA 1986, is entitled to be indemnified out of the property in respect of which he was appointed. The effect of these provisions is that if a claim is competent against the receiver personally out of the free proceeds available to the liquidator, the provision for the receiver's liabilities under section 60(1)(d) of the IA 1986 will be increased by the extent of such claim. As liquidation may follow at an early date there is a strong case for inserting a time limitation of, say, six months for the intimation of any claim under the agreement against the receiver otherwise the receiver may not be in a position to release all the surplus funds to the liquidator.

## Terms of agreement for sale of business

**7.27** The main clauses of an agreement for the sale of a business (not previously considered) are set out below.

## Recital

**7.27A** A recital is normally included which sets out the provisions of the floating charge by virtue of which the receiver was appointed and details of his appointment. If acting for the purchaser, a copy of the receiver's appointment should be obtained together with copies of the floating charge under which the receiver was appointed and the certificate of registration of the charge. Section 55(4) of the IA 1986 provides that a person dealing with a receiver in good faith and for value shall not be concerned to inquire whether the receiver is acting within his powers. It appears, therefore, that a purchaser in dealing with a receiver is under no obligation to inquire into the regularity or otherwise of a receiver's appointment or whether he is acting within his powers and it will only be in cases where the purchaser is on notice of an irregularity in the receiver's appointment or restraint in his powers that the onus will shift to the purchaser to satisfy himself further, otherwise he will be deprived of the benefit of the protection of section 55(4).

## Interpretation

**7.28** An interpretation clause should contain definitions of the business (encompassing the principal assets) or of the assets (in the case of a sale of assets), the Transfer Date and normally a completion date if different from the Transfer Date.

## Consideration

**7.29** The consideration in the agreement will either be a fixed aggregate amount or a variable amount depending, for example, on the result of a stocktaking. In either case it is advisable to have a proper allocation of the consideration as against particular assets. From the point of view of the receiver, he will wish to ensure that the allocation compares favourably with any valuations obtained by him of assets such as heritable property and plant and machinery and that such allocations will stand scrutiny by a liquidator who will wish to see an allocation in excess of break-up. The figure for any heritable property will also be important in determining the amount to which a holder of a standard security over such property is entitled although the prior approval of the heritable creditor to such allocation is not only advisable but essential if such creditor's claim will not be satisfied in full from the amount allocated to such heritable property. From the point of view of the purchaser, he will wish to see sensible values taking into account, principally, possible stamp duty land tax on the conveyance of heritable property, capital allowances on fixed assets (though this is less important since the changes to the structure of capital allowances) and also the availability of possible government assistance in respect of fixed assets.

## *Exclusion of warranty*

**7.30** A useful clause if acting for a receiver is one stating that the purchaser, having inspected the assets comprised in the Business as they stand, shall take the same in the condition in which they are and no warranty or assurance is given or implied as to the condition, quality or fitness of such assets. It is however questionable the extent to which a receiver can completely contract out of all liabilities. Section 6 of the Health & Safety at Work etc Act 1974 specifies that someone who supplies machinery or equipment (new or second hand) by way of sale, lease, hire purchase or otherwise as principal or agent is required to ensure that the equipment is to a certain standard. Auctioneers have been advised by counsel that they are not able to contract out of this obligation. Accordingly, it is difficult to see how a receiver would not have the potential for both civil and criminal liability in certain situations.

## *Good title*

**7.31** It is normal in a clause dealing with completion of the sale to insert wording that the vendor shall deliver full and free possession of the Business free from all liens, restrictions, options, encumbrances, mortgages and charges of any kind. In this connection if any of the parties have knowledge of a retention of title claim, suitable arrangements should be made in case the claim is upheld. If the purchaser proceeds without knowledge of a particular claim, there is a strong argument that he has purchased in good faith and obtained a good title,[1] thereby giving to the supplier, in the event of the retention claim being upheld, a claim in damages against the receiver. As a practical solution where a retention of title claim has been intimated but not accepted, the receiver can attempt to negotiate with the supplier for an amount equal to the invoice value of the goods the title of which is in dispute to be placed in a separate bank account pending resolution of the dispute or can arrange for the supplier to buy back the goods in dispute at a discounted figure (probably the likely realisation figure at an auction). If the latter method is employed, then if the supplier is successful in his claim, he will obtain full payment of the value of the original goods irrespective of any arrangements made for the return of the goods at a discounted figure. If he is unsuccessful, at least he will have obtained the return of the goods at the discounted figure. Most receivers will procure that they have an unchallengeable title to the assets which they are purporting to sell and will normally make some arrangements with suppliers who are maintaining a retention of title claim.

1 Sale of Goods Act 1979, s 25(1); *Thomas Graham & Sons Ltd v Glenrothes Development Corpn* 1968 SLT 2; and *Archivent Sales and Development Ltd v Strathclyde Regional Council* 1985 SLT 154.

## Miscellaneous provisions

### *VAT*

**7.32** It should be borne in mind that VAT may be payable on the sale of certain assets unless it can be shown that a business or a part of a business is being sold. Where the purchaser is taking over a business or is substantially carrying on such business hitherto carried on by the company in receivership, liability for VAT is avoided by reliance on the Value Added Tax (Special Provisions) Order 1995[1] and subject to compliance with the requirements set out in paragraph 5 thereof. In cases of doubt, where prior clearance from HM Customs and Excise cannot be obtained, it is recommended that VAT should be charged and should be recovered at completion from the purchaser. In addition, it is advisable to state that the consideration is exclusive of VAT (if any) otherwise the purchaser may seek to claim that the consideration was VAT inclusive and thereby leave the receiver with a potential liability for an apparent VAT element on the sale. If VAT is payable, the receiver will require to deliver to the purchaser a VAT invoice to enable the purchaser to recover the VAT in due course. It has been held[2] in the context of insolvency that the ultimate intentions of the transferee as to the type of goods or services that it would supply were irrelevant for VAT purposes as was the transferor's insolvency. The vital consideration was whether the transferee had been put in possession of a going concern business at the time of transfer.

1 SI 1995/1268, reg 5.
2 *Customs and Excise Comrs v Dearwood Ltd* [1986] STC327 as applied in *A One Fashions v Customs & Excise Comrs* (12 July 2003, unreported) and in *Comrs of Customs & Excise v Padglade Ltd* [1995] STC 602 and followed in *Bags More Ltd v Customs & Excise Comrs* (No 16124) (1999) Lawtel (22 August 2000, unreported).

### *Stamp duty*

**7.33** On 1 December 2003 stamp duty was abolished other than for instruments relating to stocks, shares and marketable securities. From that date stamp duty land tax replaced ad valorem stamp duty on land transactions.[1] This continued the trend started in 2000[2] abolishing stamp duty on the transfer of intellectual property (eg patents, trade marks. etc.) and followed in 2002[3] for the disposal of goodwill. A discussion on stamp duty land tax is outwith the scope of this book.

1 FA 2003, ss 42-124 and Schs 3-19 and FA 2004, ss 296-305 and Sch 39-41.
2 FA 2000, s 129 and Sch 34.
3 FA 2002, s 116 and Sch 37.

## Section 61 petition

**7.34** What happens if a standard security holder refuses to grant a discharge because he will not receive the full amount of indebtedness due to him or as happened in the petition of *Armour and Mycroft*[1] the company in receivership is inhibited prior to the appointment of the receiver and the inhibitors refuse to discharge the inhibition? The answer is that the receiver requires to petition the court pursuant to section 61 of the IA 1986 for the discharge of the security or encumbrance. Fortunately, the number of occasions when difficulties of this nature arise are thought to be infrequent and the *Armour and Mycroft* petition[1] was the first reported case which invoked the provisions of section 21 of the 1972 Act.[2]

1 1983 SLT 453.
2 See now the IA 1986, s 61.

**7.35** The facts in the *Armour and Mycroft* petition[1] were that the petitioners as the joint receivers of Carron Company Limited were about to sell the first of the Carron businesses when it was discovered that a creditor, Buccleuch Engineering Limited, had, on the day before the appointment of the joint receivers, raised an action for payment of a debt and had inhibited on the dependence of the action. The practical short-term solution involved the payment into court of an amount equal to the debt and the execution by Buccleuch of a partial discharge of the inhibition in relation to the heritable property forming part of the Carron business about to be sold together with an application by the joint receivers under section 21 of the 1972 Act.[2] As was appreciated at the time, the joint receivers were likely to be selling various businesses and properties over the immediately following weeks and months thereafter and a motion to the court for further partial discharges of the inhibition as and when required was felt to be impractical. It was, therefore, agreed by the parties concerned that an application should be made pursuant to the provisions of section 21.[2] On the application being heard, Buccleuch contended that authority for the sale should only be given on condition that their debt was satisfied before that of the floating charge holders or, alternatively, that they should be paid before the company received any part of the proceeds of sale.

1 1983 SLT 453.
2 See now the IA 1986, s 61.

**7.36** The court held (1) that except in exceptional circumstances the court should not impose conditions on a sale whereby creditors who had not effectually executed diligence – such as the respondents – would obtain the same favourable treatment as if they had; but (2) that it was equitable that the respondents should be paid after the holder of the floating charge but before the ordinary creditors, since by their inhibition they could have successfully prevented the company from selling its heritable property but for the intervention of the receivers; and the approval of the sales was authorised subject to this condition.

## Hive down agreements

**7.37** A few observations in general should be made about hive down agreements.

### *Nature of hive down agreements*

**7.37A** In relation to a business, a hive down agreement itself is essentially an agreement between a company, including one in receivership and a new wholly owned subsidiary for the sale of the Business to that new subsidiary, the reasons for which are more fully set out in paragraph 7.38. The consideration is normally stated as an inter-company loan repayable on demand. It used to be very important for tax reasons from the eventual purchaser's point of view that the new subsidiary should carry on the same trade, normally for a few days, under the control of the receiver before the next stage was reached: namely, the sale by the company in receivership to the eventual purchaser of the issued share capital of the subsidiary. It was equally important that during the whole stages of hive down and subsequent sale there should be a continuity of ownership of the trade.[1] However, the taxation advantages of hive downs in receivership situations have been severely curtailed by the provisions of the Finance Act 1986[2] and hive downs are much less used as a convenient vehicle in the context of receivership.

1 Income and Corporation Taxes Act 1988, s 393.
2 Finance Act 1986, s 42 and Sch 10.

### *Reasons for hive down agreement*

**7.38** The main reason for hiving down in current circumstances is likely to be to seek to avoid the consequences of liquidation by transferring the whole of the business to a separate legal persona, thereby avoiding uncertainties in respect of (a) the receiver's position as agent of the company in receivership, (b) his ability to carry on the Business and (c) his liability on contracts entered into after the appointment of a liquidator.

## Management buy-outs

**7.39** Reference should also be made to the fact that the sale of the Business (or part of it) may take the form of a management buy-out. The usual scenario involves three or four directors of the company in receivership or in larger receiverships a group of middle managers who are well acquainted with the manufacturing and production aspects of the business but who normally lack financial experience. Frequently, these are the vital personnel who perform a very important role in advising and assisting the receiver on a day to day basis particularly in the early days of receivership and, if they indicate a wish to purchase the Business, the receiver will normally encourage the managers to seek independent professional advice. It should be emphasised that, however anxious the receiver may be on a personal level to sell the Business to the managers, he must bear in mind his duties and properly advertise and expose the Business for sale to ensure that the optimum realisation is attained. For a more detailed consideration of problems relating to an MBO, reference should be made to SIP13 (Scotland) 'Acquisition of Assets of Insolvent Companies by Directors'.[1] Where directors of the company are involved in the purchase section 320 of the CA 1985 needs to be considered following the decision in *Demite Ltd v Protec Health Ltd*[2] that the section applies to the sale of assets, even by a receiver. For a more detailed consideration of this, reference is made to an article by Shashi Rajani.[3]

1 See Appendix 15, issued September 1998.
2 *Demite Ltd v Protec Health Ltd* [1988] BCC 638.
3 *Insolvency Law & Practice* Vol 14, No 5, 1998, p 275.

## Preparation of financial package

**7.40** Accountancy and general financial advice is readily available to a prospective management buy-out group from the accountancy profession and they, in suitable cases, are in a position to present to suitable institutions a financial package incorporating projected capital expenditure, working capital and cash flow requirements as well as marketing trends within the particular industry. Institutions such as the merchant banks, the clearing banks and private equity institutions are frequently involved and the managers, if properly advised, can normally hope to obtain grant assistance from Governmental bodies. The institutional investment often takes the form of part loan and part equity and frequently involves participating preference shares which may, at the option of the institution concerned, be converted into equity capital. In the case of loans, the institution will normally wish some security in the form of standard securities and/or floating charges or, if the managers are prepared to grant them, personal guarantees.

## Finalising documentation

**7.41** If acting for a team of managers, the importance of speed and professionalism in putting together all the parts of a complex jig-saw cannot be over-estimated. The solicitor acting for the managers must be negotiating and settling the form and content of the documentation with the institution's solicitors as well as dealing with the receiver's solicitors on the form of the agreement for the sale of the Business. It is not appropriate in this book to deal in any detail with the documentation required by an institution but usually a form of subscription agreement will be settled whereby the institution takes up ordinary shares or preference shares as the case may be in the shelf company which will have been acquired by the managers. The form of the subscription agreement will be largely regulated by the terms of the offer letter issued to the managers by the institution.

## Employees

**7.42** The position of employees is considered in detail in Chapter 6. It is sufficient here to restate the broad principles relevant to the sale of a business. The 1981 Regulations will apply to a sale of a business where all the employees being transferred are dismissed some time prior to the effective date which, on the basis of *Litster*[1], means that the Regulations will apply to a contract of employment that was subsisting at any stage prior to the moment of a transfer of the undertaking.[1] Especially in view of *Litster*[1] and to avoid any possible problems for the receiver, it is very important that the receiver obtains a full indemnity from the purchaser of the business in respect of any potential claims from employees.

1 *Litster v Forth Dry Dock Engineering Co Ltd* [1990] 1 AC 546, [1989] IRLR 161.

**7.43** In a hive down transaction, the effective sale date is the date when the company in receivership ceases to be registered as the holder of the entire issued share capital of the subsidiary – it is not the effective date of the hive down. During the period from the effective date of the hive down to the date of acquisition of the share capital of the subsidiary by the purchaser, the employees should remain the employees of the company in receivership and should be sub-contracted by the company in receivership to the subsidiary, the subsidiary normally being obligated in terms of the hive down agreement to indemnify the company in receivership in respect of wages, PAYE, national insurance contributions and like obligations.

## Property matters

**7.44** Consideration will now be given to the conveyancing formalities involved in the sale of heritable property forming part of the Business before giving consideration to the question of letters of obligation to be given by the vendors' solicitors. It is recommended that the obligations of the receiver in relation to detailed property matters (including letters of obligation) should be discussed and agreed before any agreement is executed. In the case of a disposition of heritable property, it is suggested that the narrative should describe the company in receivership as 'Galaxy Products Limited incorporated under the Companies Acts and having its registered office at 10 Heavenly Mansions, Pitlochry acting by Frederick Galileo, Chartered Accountant, Saturn House, Pitlochry, as receiver thereof conform to instrument of appointment in his favour dated 11th November 2003.' The warrandice clause *quoad* the receiver should be qualified to fact and deed only and it is submitted that there should be inserted *in gremio* a clause excluding the personal liability of the receiver. The safe course is to make provision for these terms in the agreement for the sale of the Business. Execution of documents relating to property should accord with the provisions of the Requirements of Writing (Scotland) Act 1995. If there are joint receivers, the signature of both receivers is required unless, in terms of section 56(3) of the IA1986, the instrument of appointment permits them to act individually in which event the signature of one receiver is sufficient.

**7.45** If the receiver of a Scottish company is selling property situated in England, the accepted mode of execution in England follows the provisions of section 42(1) of and paragraph 8 of Schedule 1 to the IA 1986 which provide that except in so far as may be inconsistent with the debenture by virtue of which he was appointed, the receiver is now specifically entitled to use the company's seal. In practice, an English receiver will execute an appropriate document as a deed.

### *Power of execution by receiver after appointment of liquidator*

**7.46** From time to time, the question arises as to the competency of a receiver executing a disposition of heritable property after a liquidator has been appointed. Cautious conveyancers have been known to seek the consent (either by separate letter or *in gremio* of the disposition) of the liquidator. While the agency of the receiver may have been terminated by the appointment of a liquidator, it is submitted that it is still valid and competent for the receiver to dispose of property subject to the floating charge including heritable property, without recourse to the liquidator for the following reasons:

(1) under paragraph 2 of Schedule 2 to the IA 1986, the receiver has the power to sell heritable property provided he is still the receiver; and
(2) under paragraphs 8 and 9 of Schedule 2 to the IA 1986, the receiver has power to use the seal and execute any deeds on behalf of the company.

In addition, section 127 of the IA 1986 (avoidance of dispositions of property after the appointment of a liquidator) does not apply to a sale by a receiver because in granting the charge the company disposed of the property and as was explained in the case of *Barrows v Chief Land Registrar*,[1] the rights and powers given to the receiver were those specified in the debenture and as such the property of the debenture holder rather than the company. The receiver's power in Scotland to deal with the property is not affected by the liquidation.

1 (1977) Times, 20 October.

## Letters of obligation

**7.47** All firms of solicitors in Scotland are engaged almost daily in giving their personal obligations to deliver or exhibit clear searches and the historical development of letters of obligation and their necessity in settling property transactions in Scotland is well known. What is, however, increasingly being realised is the fact that in the context of receivership where the receiver normally excludes his liability totally, his solicitor may well undertake personally an unduly burdensome liability relating to some matter which may well have occurred some time prior to the appointment of the receiver. Against the background of a sale of heritable property by a receiver, an unguarded and unqualified letter of obligation in respect of heritage may read as follows:

> 'With reference to the settlement of this transaction today and provided that the disposition in favour of your clients is recorded within 7 days of today's date, we hereby undertake to deliver to you within 6 months of this date Search in the Property, Personal and Companies Charges Registers brought down in terms of the Memorandum adjusted between us and showing the records clear of all incumbrances and diligences prejudicial to our clients' title.'

The wording is considered as follows.

## *Personal obligation*

**7.48** The obligation is the personal obligation of the selling solicitors. Occasionally, the form is encountered ... 'On behalf of our clients [Name and Designation of clients], we hereby undertake ...'. In these circumstances, the law of agency ensures that the principal will be bound where the agent is acting for a disclosed principal.[1] If it is desired to enforce the obligation against the selling solicitors the words 'on behalf of our clients etc ...' should be deleted.

1 *Bell's Principles* 224A; *Miller v Mitchell* (1860) 22 D 833.

## *Property, Personal and Charges Registers*

**7.49** It is probably accepted that on a settlement date, the Property Register may be in arrears, while the Personal Register can be checked up to 10 am on that date and the Companies Charges Register can be checked right up to the last moment. What happens, however, if unknown to the receiver's solicitors, the company some weeks pre-receivership disponed to a neighbouring proprietor part of the property which the receiver is purporting to sell and the disposition has not yet been recorded or does not appear in the Property Register? What happens, firstly, if the company pre-receivership or secondly, post-receivership, was inhibited and this fact is only discovered after conclusion of a contract but before settlement or thirdly, if the company in receivership is inhibited the day after settlement but before the disposition in favour of the purchaser is recorded? What happens if a floating charge (apart from the floating charge under which the receiver was appointed) already on the Register crystallises the day before settlement but intimation in the Register is not given of the appointment of a receiver until several days after settlement? Consideration of these matters is given in the succeeding paragraphs.

### *Our client's title or our clients' title*

**7.50** A great deal of potential trouble could be avoided by carefully specifying for which client the granter of the obligation is acting viz the company in receivership or simply the receiver. It is obviously very much easier to control the activities of the receiver than a company in receivership which in all probability faced financial problems in the period immediately preceding receivership with consequent inhibitions, arrestments and other forms of diligence.

## Proposals

**7.51** It is suggested that in the case of transactions involving receivers the following matters may be considered as qualifying the extreme limits of the typical letter of obligation to which reference has already been made.

### *Property Register*

**7.51A** So far as the Property Register is concerned, the position will be known down to the latest date disclosed by the interim report. In cases involving property subject to registration of title, less difficulty is encountered as the Land Register reports are more up to date. In a typical receivership, the receiver's solicitors will normally have taken delivery of title deeds and other documents from the company's solicitors and in these cases the company's solicitors will be required pursuant to section 236 of the IA 1986 to provide a report of the company's transactions including recent transactions up to the time of the receiver's appointment. Although there is a theoretical possibility that some of the company's property may have been conveyed prior to the appointment of the receiver without as yet an entry appearing on the Property Register, it is suggested that the risk of the receiver's solicitors being unaware of that fact is, in the normal course of events, minimal. It is therefore proposed that, notwithstanding the point made in paragraph 7.47 and pending change in Scottish legal practice in this area, an undertaking by the receiver's solicitors to provide a clear search in respect of the period from the date of the interim report to the date of settlement could normally be given in the usual terms.

### *Personal Register*

**7.52** So far as the Personal Register is concerned, the receiver's solicitors should not conclude any agreement involving heritable property until a search in the

Personal Register has been carried out: otherwise a purchaser, on finding an inhibition, could decline to proceed (*Dryburgh v Gordon*).[1] Any inhibition prior in date to the date of creation of the floating charge under which the receiver was appointed will have to be cleared before a purchaser can receive a good title and, consequently, before any moneys are paid out in terms of the floating charge. If the inhibition is registered after the date of creation of the floating charge, then on the *Armour and Mycroft*[2] principle, a sale can only proceed if the inhibitor is paid the amount of his debt after the floating charge creditor but before the claims of ordinary creditors. An inhibition registered after the date of appointment of a receiver will be ineffective in a question with the receiver on the ground that the floating charge has already crystallised on the assets of the company and has become a fixed security in terms of section 70 of the IA 1986.[3]

1 (1896) 24 R 1.
2 1983 SLT 453.
3 See paras 2.16-2.18.

**7.53** It is suggested that it would be appropriate for the receiver's solicitor to undertake to deliver a clear search in the Personal Register but subject to any rights of inhibitors who have inhibited firstly, prior to the date of creation of the floating charge (which inhibition will rank before the floating charge) and secondly, prior to the appointment of the receiver. Such a course may be unsatisfactory to the purchaser's solicitors but the alternative, in the case of a pre-floating charge inhibition, involves either a discharge of the inhibition (if one can be obtained) to free the heritable property from the scope of the inhibition or depending on the amount due to the inhibiting creditor a partial discharge of the inhibition releasing the heritable property the receiver wishes to sell provided other heritable property exists to safeguard the inhibiting creditor's position and/or a section 61 petition under the IA 1986 (or going back to the court which authorised the inhibition under the *Taymech v Rush and Tompkins* principle[1]). None of the alternatives is very attractive from the point of view of speed. If the inhibition is past the date of creation of the floating charge but pre-dates the date of appointment of the receiver, it is, nevertheless, suggested that the purchaser's solicitors should seek a partial discharge or failing that insist on a section 61 petition and settle the transaction based on present law viz *Armour and Mycroft*.[2] If practical in the scale of value of the transaction, at the same time there should be placed on deposit receipt an amount equal to the debt owed to the inhibitor pending the result of the section 61 petition. This latter suggestion may of course be impractical in that the amount of the debt owed to the inhibitor may exceed the consideration payable by the purchaser. It is accepted that in view of the *Armour and Mycroft*[2] decision the receiver may decide to petition for the immediate appointment of a liquidator with the prospect of cutting down an inhibition in terms of section 185 of the IA 1986. An early appointment of a liquidator is, however, often unhelpful to a receiver in his general conduct of the receivership and can be very disadvantageous from the point of view of taxation.[3]

1 *Taymech Ltd v Rush & Tompkins Ltd* 1990 SLT 681.

2 1983 SLT 453
3 See *Tolley's Taxation in Corporate Insolvency and Rescue* (5th edn) para 5.13.

## *Companies Charges Register*

**7.54** From time to time certain solicitors will require a clear search in the Companies Charges Register. Such a requirement is usually impossible because (A) the floating charge creditor may never be fully satisfied and (B) full satisfaction is rarely achieved immediately following the sale of one particular property. There is a school of thought that insists that a memorandum of partial or full satisfaction should be executed to release the particular property from the charge on the ground that the floating charge has become equivalent to a fixed security in terms of section 70 of the IA 1986 and it is, therefore, necessary for the floating charge holder to discharge such fixed security in a similar way as a heritable security would be discharged under and in terms of the Conveyancing and Feudal Reform (Scotland) Act 1970. The argument by the receiver is that he has been appointed by the holder of the floating charge to realise on his behalf the property subject to the charge and that as in terms of Schedule 2 to the IA 1986 he has full power of sale over such property, it is not necessary either for a discharge to be given by the floating charge creditor or for the receiver to provide a clear search in the Companies Charges Register. In relation to any prior ranking floating charge which has not crystallised, it is suggested that a letter of non-crystallisation is obtained from the holder of such prior ranking floating charge and delivered to the purchaser.

**7.55** For practical purposes, it is suggested that the purchaser's solicitors should rely exclusively on the receiver's statutory power of sale. Any other floating charges do not automatically crystallise by the appointment of a receiver but can do so by the operation of section 52(1)(d) of the IA 1986 or of a provision in the floating charge, or any ancillary documents to that effect, entitling the holder thereof to appoint a receiver and such holder in these circumstances appointing a receiver. Accordingly, it should not be necessary to require a Companies Charges obligation from the receiver's solicitors.

**7.56** From what has been said, it will be readily appreciated that a clear understanding between the receiver's solicitors and the purchaser's solicitors should be reached before any sale agreement relating to or including heritable property is concluded. It is much easier to agree the form and content of a letter of obligation before concluding an agreement than at a later stage.

## Pension matters

**7.57** As part of the overall arrangements for the sale of a business, the purchaser, if an established company of any size, in all probability may wish to make suitable arrangements to transfer the benefits (if it is possible to do so) of the pension scheme of the company in receivership to the pension scheme operated by the purchaser although the stock market crash of the early 21st century and crisis in the pensions industry has severely affected the confidence of a purchaser to take on the liabilities of a pension fund whose principal employer has become insolvent. There have been some hard cases and attention is drawn to the *T&N* case[1] which, although an administration case, illustrates some of the problems.

1 *T&N Ltd* [2004] EWHC1680, Ch D.

**7.58** However, it is very important to note that the assets belonging to a pension scheme are not assets of the company in receivership and, accordingly, when a floating charge crystallises over the assets of the company, pension scheme assets will fall outwith the scope of the charge. Nonetheless, any surplus (however unlikely a surplus may seem at the date of publication of this book!) arising after all proper benefits have been provided for, may form an asset available to the receiver subject always to the terms of the relevant pension documentation. The scheme rules may provide for any such surplus to be paid over to the company in receivership as the employer under the pension scheme documentation or the fate of the surplus may be a matter entirely within the discretion of the trustees or, indeed, there may be other possibilities. It is therefore of supreme importance to establish at an early stage the provisions in the relevant pension scheme documentation to enable a view to be properly taken. Since it is usually impossible to finalise the pension aspects of the sale before completion it is sometimes agreed that if the trustees of the pension scheme of the company in receivership are agreeable and subject to the purchaser becoming an 'employer' for the purposes of such scheme within a period of not more than twelve months from the completion date, then subject to Inland Revenue approval, the trustees of such pension scheme will discuss with the trustees of the purchaser˜'s pension scheme appropriate transfer values for those employees being transferred to the purchaser's pension scheme. Although a receiver is not really affected by such pension arrangements, it is usual to arrange for the receiver to consent in a formal deed of adherence for any right, title and interest he may have thereto.

**7.59** The provisions of paragraphs 7.57 and 7.58 are subject to the important requirement imposed by the Pensions Act 1995 on an insolvency practitioner (which would include a receiver) to satisfy himself that at all times at least one of the trustees of a pension scheme is an independent person and if, at any time he is not satisfied, to appoint or to secure the appointment of an independent person as a trustee of the relevant scheme. It is not at all unusual to find that in pension schemes the trustees are some or all of the executive directors of the principal employer without an independent trustee. A better approach is for companies to procure that as well as a few of the executive directors, there is also one or more of an insurance broker, independent chartered accountant or independent solicitor as an additional trustee or trustees. However, the receiver in terms of the 1995 Act must ensure that there is an independent person as a trustee of the scheme within three months after he is appointed. Certainly, he should not consider reaching any form of agreement in relation to the affairs of the pension scheme until he has complied with his obligations under the 1995 Act. If the independent trustee resigns or ceases to be independent the obligation remains with the receiver to appoint another independent trustee. For a more detailed consideration of this and the changes to take place on the implementation of the Pensions Act 2004, see para 3.53.

## Change of name

**7.60** In many receiverships and particularly larger cases, the company name will be perceived by a purchaser as a valuable asset in an ongoing business. For this reason, arrangements are often made as part of an agreement for the purchaser to be entitled to use the name of the company in receivership.

**7.61** Taking as an example Galaxy Products Limited (Galaxy), a holding company of several subsidiaries and Rococo Cocoa Co Limited (Rococo), its principal trading subsidiary, the following points should be noted:

(1) Any change of name of Galaxy will require the members of Galaxy to pass an appropriate special resolution and the cost of convening the necessary extraordinary general meeting may or may not be an acceptable cost to a purchaser who would normally be expected to meet such cost. In the case of a public listed company in receivership the cost is unlikely to be acceptable.

(2) On the other hand, the prospective purchaser of the business of Rococo will probably only wish the use of the corporate name of Rococo and if Rococo is a wholly owned subsidiary of Galaxy it should in most cases be possible for the receiver acting as receiver of Galaxy to require Rococo to change its name while at the same time the purchaser passes a special resolution to change its name to Rococo. In most cases the costs involved in changing names, while a matter for negotiation, will be borne by the purchaser.

(3) As the main function of a receiver is to realise assets, it has become customary in many cases to change the name of the company in receivership to a name embodying the function of realisation. In normal circumstances Rococo could expect to become RCC Realisations Limited. Difficulties have sometimes been experienced in a subsequent liquidation when creditors of the old Rococo do not recognise in statutory liquidation notices the name RCC Realisations Limited. The practice has therefore developed in many instances of showing the former name of RCC Realisations Limited while at the same time to avoid embarrassment to the purchaser of the business of the old Rococo, inviting such purchaser, at his own cost, to insert an intimation beside any such statutory liquidation notice making it clear that the purchaser is not associated in any way with the company in liquidation.

CHAPTER 8

# Extent and ranking of securities, guarantees and related matters

## General position

**8.01** It is advisable in all receiverships that as soon as possible after the appointment of the receiver, detailed enquiries should be made by carrying out a search at the Companies Registry as to any existing fixed securities and other floating charges and their respective rankings. As regards ranking of floating charges, section 464(1) of the 1985 Act provides that, subject to section 464(2), the instrument creating a floating charge over all or any part of the company's property may contain:

(a) provisions prohibiting or restricting the creation of any fixed security or any other floating charge having priority over, or ranking *pari passu* with, the floating charge: or
(b) provisions regulating the order in which the floating charge shall rank with any other subsisting or future floating charges or fixed securities over that property or any part of it.

**8.02** Section 464(2) provides that where all or any part of the property of a company is subject both to a floating charge and to a fixed security arising by operation of law, the fixed security shall have priority over the floating charge. This means, that a fixed security arising by operation of law such as a landlord's hypothec would rank prior to a floating charge.[1] It should also be noted that the rights and remedies of the holders of fixed securities such as standard securities are unaffected by the appointment of a receiver and such holders while in many cases working in co-operation with the receiver are nonetheless free to exercise their rights independently. In the absence of any agreement with regard to the ranking of various securities, section 464(4)(a) of the 1985 Act provides that a fixed security, the right to which has been constituted as a real right before a floating charge has attached to all or any part of the property of the company, shall have priority of ranking over the floating charge. Floating charges rank with one another according to the time of registration in accordance with Chapter II of Part XII of the 1985 Act.[2] In addition, floating charges which have been received by the Registrar of Companies for registration by the same postal delivery rank with one another equally.[3] In September 2004 the Scottish Law

Commission issued a Report[4] on 'Registration of Rights in Security by Companies'. The key recommendations of this are:

(1) An advance notice may be registered and if the floating charge is registered within 21 days thereof, it will be deemed to have been registered on the date of registration of the advance notice.
(2) Floating charges should rank with other securities, whether fixed or floating, by date of creation.
(3) Registration of floating charges should be in a Register of Floating Charges to be maintained by the Keeper of the Registers of Scotland and the text of the deed ought to be registered.
(4) Constitution of a floating charge should take place on registration.
(5) There should no longer be any requirement to register particulars of a security granted by a company with the Registrar of Companies.
(6) A floating charge granted by a company incorporated in England and Wales and intended to be effective in Scotland as respects assets located in Scotland should require to be registered in the Register of Floating Charges.
(7) A floating charge granted by an overseas incorporated company and intended to be effective in Scotland as respects assets located in Scotland should require to be registered in the Register of Floating Charges.

1 *Grampian Regional Council v Drill Stem (Inspection Services) Ltd (in receivership)* 1994 SCLR 36, but see *Cumbernauld Development Corpn v Mustone Ltd* 1983 SLT (Sh Ct) 55; see para 2.19.
2 CA 1985, s 464(4)(b).
3 Ibid, s 464(4)(c).
4 Scot Law Com No. 197.

## Ranking agreements and related problems

**8.03** In practice, where a number of securities have been constituted by the borrowing company, the normal course is for a formal ranking agreement to be concluded between the borrowing company and its various secured creditors so that the order and extent of ranking of all such securities is clearly laid down.

## Running account

**8.04** Difficulties can arise in relation to section 464(5) of the 1985 Act in the case of a clearing bank or other secured creditor having a floating charge over the assets and undertaking of the borrowing company and which has made available a running account overdraft or otherwise to the borrower. Section 464(5) provides that where the holder of a floating charge, in such circumstances, has received intimation in writing of the subsequent registration in accordance with Chapter II of Part XII of the 1985 Act of another floating charge over the same property or any part thereof, the preference in ranking of the first mentioned floating charge shall be restricted to security for (a) the holder's present advances; (b) future advances which he may be required to make under the instrument creating the floating charge or under any ancillary documents; (c) interest due or to become due on all such advances; and (d) any expenses or outlays which may reasonably be incurred by the holder. As a result, all clearing banks and other creditors holding securities from a borrowing company in respect of a running account normally always insist on a 'fluctuating advances' clause being agreed with the borrowing company and other such creditors. The effect of a form of 'fluctuating advances' clause is to protect the ranking of the holder of a floating charge in terms of the ranking agreement notwithstanding that such holder may advance further moneys to the borrower after intimation of the registration of another floating charge, the effect of which would normally cause such holder to be restricted in his preference in ranking to security for the sums specified in section 464(5).

## Interest and additional interest

**8.05** From time to time, questions have arisen as to the right of loan creditors to charge certain additional interest on amounts outstanding by a borrower. Normally, the documentation setting up the loan facilities will provide for interest to be fixed, for example, in accordance with the particular lender's rates for the time being with power to the lender to give a certificate indicating the amount due together with interest at any particular time. A problem may arise where a lender inserts in loan documentation that in certain circumstances the borrower will, in addition to all other interest chargeable in terms of the loan facility, also be required to pay, for example, one year's interest on the amount of the loan then outstanding. The point arises as to whether the additional interest is validly chargeable by the lender or whether it is to be regarded as a penalty and so unenforceable.

**8.06** In considering the question of additional interest charges in these circumstances, careful examination of the precise wording in the loan documentation is very important. If the documentation states that such additional interest will be payable on the happening of certain events none of which involves a breach of contract, the provision for additional interest will be enforceable.[1] In that case Lord Keith reviewed the authorities and concluded:

> 'I am unable to accept that the law about penalty and liquidated damages has any application in a case which is not a case of breach of contract and I consider that *Bell Bros (HP) Ltd v Aitken*[2] is authority binding upon me for the view that it has no application.'

On the other hand, if the additional interest is stated to be payable in the event of a breach of contract, the clause in the loan documentation to that effect will be subject to the tests set out in the leading case on the subject.[3] Lord Roskill summarised the position in a later case[4] as follows:

> '... one purpose, perhaps the main purpose, of the law relating to penalty clauses is to prevent a plaintiff recovering a sum of money in respect of a

breach of contract committed by a defendant which bears little or no relationship to the loss actually suffered by the plaintiff as a result of the breach by the defendant. But it is not and never has been for the Courts to relieve a party from the consequences of what may in the event prove to be an onerous or possibly even a commercially imprudent bargain.'

1 *Granor Finance Ltd v Liquidator of Eaststore Ltd* 1974 SLT 296.
2 *Bell Bros (HP) Ltd v Aitken* 1939 SC 577.
3 *Clydebank Engineering and Shipbuilding Co Ltd v Don Jose Ramos Yzquierdo y Castaneda* [1905] AC 6, HL.
4 *Export Credits Guarantee Department v Universal Oil Products Co* [1983] 1 WLR 399.

**8.07** It is sometimes the case that the additional interest provisions in loan documentation refer to other provisions which set out the circumstances in which the additional interest becomes payable and/or circumstances constituting a breach of the loan agreement. Clearly, careful drafting of the loan agreement will avoid ambiguity but in the final analysis the enforceability of additional interest provisions may depend on the severability of the provisions relating to the breach from those under which the additional interest becomes payable. In *Alloa Brewery Co Ltd v Investors in Industry plc* the court held that early repayment compensation fell to be included as a 'charge', giving priority to the creditor not only in respect of principal and normal interest etc secured by the standard security but also the interest forming the early repayment compensation.[1]

1 1992 SLT 121.

## Wages preference

**8.08** Consideration requires to be given to the situation where a floating charge holder has a claim for a wages preference and a ranking agreement exists with other floating charge holders. The usual situation involves a clearing bank having made available to the borrowing company an overdraft facility on current account and also operating a separate wages account. On the appointment of a receiver, the clearing bank will be due a certain amount on current account overdraft as well as a further amount which may be entitled to a preferential ranking as sums advanced for the payment of wages. In the absence of any discussion (save for a standard form of ranking agreement providing for *pari passu* ranking to some extent) with another secured creditor, who perhaps has made available a fixed loan secured also by way of a floating charge, what is the position with regard to the clearing bank's claim for preferential ranking in the company's overall aggregate indebtedness?

**8.09** Firstly, the clearing bank would be entitled to a preferential ranking in respect of its wages account, subject to the receiver being satisfied that its claim qualifies for a preferential ranking under and in terms of section 386 of the IA 1986 as applied by section 59 of that Act and also to the limits imposed from time to time by statutory instrument. The more difficult question is whether, in the absence of previous written agreement between the parties, in the *pari passu* ranking between the clearing bank and the other lender, the amount of the admitted wages preference should be deducted from the overall indebtedness to the clearing bank or should the clearing bank be entitled to argue that the aggregate indebtedness due by the borrowing company is the figure which should be fixed insofar as the *pari passu* ranking is concerned? It is thought that the amount of any claim to preferential ranking must be deducted from the total aggregate indebtedness of the clearing bank on the basic principle that a creditor cannot rank more than once. When the clearing bank has been paid the amount of its preference, the clearing bank and the other lender are in the position that there is still an aggregate total indebtedness, albeit that in the case of the clearing bank the amount of the wages preference has already been paid.

## Option in loan documentation to heritable creditor

**8.10** A heritable creditor may attempt to improve his position by the use of an option arrangement whereby on the happening of certain events (eg the sale of the security subjects) such creditor is entitled to exercise an option to purchase part of the security subjects for a consideration specified in the original loan agreement. To further protect his position, the standard security over the security subjects in favour of the heritable creditor will have specified that the security being granted is 'in respect of all sums due or to become due and in respect of all obligations contained in the loan agreement'. In a question with a receiver who has been appointed over the whole property of the borrowing company, is the option arrangement valid?

**8.11** As a general rule, obligations such as those specified above are not usually enforceable against a receiver.[1] However, for the following reason, it is thought that such an option arrangement may be binding on a receiver. If the standard security states that all obligations contained in the loan agreement are secured, in the absence of acceptance by the receiver of the option arrangement, the heritable creditor would be justified in withholding its consent to a sale to a third party and in declining to deliver an executed discharge of the standard security. The obligations to grant consent to the sale in exchange for an acceptance by the receiver that he will honour the option arrangement are interdependent. If the receiver wishes the sale to proceed to the third party, he may be required in practice to honour the option arrangement otherwise, in the absence of an executed discharge of the standard security, the sale cannot proceed.

1 *MacLeod v Alexander Sutherland Ltd* 1977 SLT (Notes) 44; but see *Freevale Ltd v Metrostore (Holdings) Ltd* [1984] 1 All ER 495 and *Telemetrix plc v Modern Engineers of Bristol (Holdings) Ltd* [1985] LS Gaz R 1561 and paras 4.39-4.41.

**8.12** It could be argued that the provisions of section 61 of the IA 1986[1] could be invoked to deal with the situation where the receiver wishes to sell a heritable property which is subject to a secured obligation. However, it is suggested that the court, on hearing an application under section 61, would reject the receiver's case on the ground that a valid, binding and secured obligation existed and that the heritable creditor would be entirely justified in refusing to discharge a standard security where an option arrangement clearly formed part of the secured obligations of the company in receivership. The receiver could hardly be said to be unable to obtain the consent of the heritable creditor: on the contrary, in most cases, the heritable creditor would give his consent provided his rights under the option arrangement were preserved.

1 Further consideration of this section is given in paras 3.36-3.39 and paras 7.34-7.36.

## General duty to guarantors

**8.13** In the context of ranking of securities and guarantees, serious consideration should be given to the position of guarantors in the light of the decision in *Standard Chartered Bank Ltd v Walker*.[1] A detailed discussion of the position of guarantors is contained in Chapter 3 paragraphs 3.49 to 3.50.

1 [1982] 3 All ER 938 and *Silven Properties Ltd v Royal Bank of Scotland plc* [2003] BCC 1002.

## Position of inhibitions in ranking

**8.14** The petition of *Armour and Mycroft*[1] has been the subject of much discussion in the general context of diligence and reference is made to paragraphs 2.17 and 2.18.

1 1983 SLT 453.

**8.15** What principles derive from both the general law and in particular the *Armour and Mycroft* decision[1] as regards the ranking of inhibitions in relation to floating charges? It is thought these are as follows:

(1) An inhibition which pre-dates the creation of a floating charge ranks prior to any claim by the holder of the floating charge.
(2) An inhibition which post-dates the creation of a floating charge but pre-dates the receiver's appointment is not thought to be an effectually executed diligence and on the basis of *Armour and Mycroft*, such an inhibiting creditor is entitled to be paid out after the floating charge has been satisfied but before the claims of ordinary creditors.
(3) An inhibition taken out after the appointment of a receiver is completely ineffective *quoad* the receiver on the ground that the floating charge will already have crystallised on the assets of the company and become a fixed security in terms of section 70 of the IA 1986.[2]
(4) Faced with the circumstances of *Armour and Mycroft*,[3] a partial discharge should be obtained (if possible). Counsel for the inhibitors in *Armour and*

*Mycroft*[3] refused to allow a full discharge in exchange for a payment into court of the whole amount of the debt due to the inhibitor on the ground that such an arrangement might not be binding on a liquidator. Liquidation might well be a convenient route in appropriate cases to nullify an inhibition by virtue of the provisions of section 185 of the IA 1986. However, it is appreciated that the immediate appointment of a liquidator can be unhelpful to a receiver in his general conduct of the receivership and can in certain circumstances be disadvantageous from the point of view of taxation. Considerations of whether it is appropriate to recall an inhibition where there is no adjudication are usefully set out[4] in Lord Coulsfield's opinion in *Taymech Ltd v Rush & Tompkins Ltd*. It is also instructive to consider the case of *Hawking of Hafton House Ltd*[5] in which it was held that funds consigned with the clerk of court prior to the appointment of a receiver were removed from the 'property of the company' and therefore not available to the receiver.

1 1983 SLT 453.
2 See also *Forth & Clyde Construction Co Ltd v Trinity Timber & Plywood Co Ltd* 1984 SLT 94.
3 See n 1 above.
4 1990 SLT 681.
5 1990 SC 198.

**8.16** The practical realities of the circumstances with which the receivers were faced in *Armour and Mycroft*[1] are also relevant. As has been stated,[2] whatever the strengths of the receivers' position in a question as between them and the inhibitors as a matter of strict law, the fact remained that there was an inhibition standing on the register and the purchasers to whom the receivers were anxious to sell certain properties were not being offered a clear title. It is well settled in law that a title which is subject to an inhibition is not a title which a purchaser is bound to accept.[3] If no agreement can be reached then the only remedy is to petition the court under section 61 of the IA 1986 although as a speedy remedy it is not attractive. Therefore, as a practical matter, some form of arrangement must, if at all possible, be negotiated with an inhibiting creditor as happened in *Taymech v Rush and Tompkins*.[4]

1 1983 SLT 453.
2 JADH 1983 SLT (News) 177.
3 *Dryburgh v Gordon* (1896) 24 R1.
4 *Taymech Ltd v Rush & Tompkins Ltd* 1990 SLT 681.

## Position of arrestors in ranking

**8.17** What is the position if a receiver is appointed over the whole assets and undertaking of a company and the day after the receiver's appointment, a creditor of the company arrests funds in the hands of a third party? It could be argued on the one hand that the arrestment falls to be settled on the basis of the decision in the *Lord Advocate v The Royal Bank* case[1] and, in any event, the charge has crystallised over the assets of the company before the arrestment was made.

Reference is made to the opinion of Lord Cowie in *Forth & Clyde Construction Co Ltd v Trinity Timber & Plywood Co Ltd*[2] which case was the subject of an appeal to the First Division of the Court of Session who upheld the interlocutor of the Lord Ordinary. Lord Cowie decided in the Outer House that a receiver had power by virtue of section 15(1)(a)[3] to ingather the property attached by the floating charge and if that property consists of the whole property of the debtor the receiver cannot be prevented from exercising his power by an arrestment whether or not the value of the company's other assets exceeds the company's total liabilities; and the arrestment was accordingly recalled. Consideration should be given to *Iona Hotels Ltd (in receivership) v Craig*[4] which is discussed in more detail in paragraph 9.09 and to *Hawking v Hafton House Ltd*.[5] Reference is also made to paragraph 2.16 et sequentia.

1 *Lord Advocate v Royal Bank of Scotland Ltd* 1978 SLT 38.
2 1984 SLT 94.
3 Now enacted as IA 1986, Sch 2, para 1. See also *Hawking v Hafton House Ltd* 1990 SC 198 where after arrestments without a forthcoming and inhibitions without adjudication were withdrawn, the court held that funds consigned with the clerk of court prior to the appointment of a receiver were removed from the 'property of the company' and therefore not available to the receiver.
4 1991 SLT 11.
5 1990 SC 198.

## Fixed charge by an English registered company over book debts

**8.18** Consideration should also be given to the position where an English registered company with a place of business in Scotland has granted in favour of the holder of a floating charge also a first fixed charge over book debts. It is submitted that unless a valid assignation of each and every debt had taken place and after being duly stamped, has been intimated, in terms of the Transmission of Moveable Property (Scotland) Act 1862, to each debtor, no valid security over the book debts of the company would have been created under the law of Scotland. It has been held in Scotland that the beneficial ownership of book debts may be transferred to a purchaser under an invoice discounting agreement.[1] In England, the following wording for several decades has provided an effective assignment of all book debts of the company:

> 'The Company as beneficial owner and to the intent that the security shall rank as a continuing security for all indebtedness and liabilities from time to time due and to become due hereby charges by way of a first fixed charge all book debts both present and future (and the proceeds of realisation thereof) due or owing to the Company.'

However, there is a clear line of authority[2] suggesting that to be effective, such a clause should ensure that not only is there an obligation on the company to open a separate account to deal solely with receipt of book debts but also there should be an express obligation on the company that such an account be used for no other purpose. These authorities[2] have been called into question by the Privy Council decision in *Brumark*[3] and the subsequent Court of Appeal decision in *Spectrum*[4]. Suffice to state here that, in spite of considerable anxieties, the present English position may be stated by reflecting that the rules set out in *Siebe Gorman*[2] live on perhaps subject to possible future views of the House of Lords during the course of 2005.

1 *Tay Valley Joinery Ltd v CF Financial Services Ltd* 1987 SLT 207: the stamping requirement is necessary for enforceability but may not be strictly necessary at the time of intimation.
2 *Siebe Gorman & Co Ltd v Barclays Bank Ltd* [1979] 2 Lloyds Rep 142; *Re Armagh Shoes* [1982] NI 59; *Re Keenan Bros Ltd* [1984] 2 ILT 205.
3 *Agnew v IRC* [2001] AC 710.
4 *Re Spectrum Plus Ltd* [2004] 1 All ER (D) 390.

**8.19** It is generally accepted that it is the *lex situs* which governs questions relating to securities over incorporeal moveable property which includes debts and that the *situs* of a normal contract debt will be the place where the debtor resides.[1] It therefore appears that a charge over book debts created by an English registered company with a place of business in Scotland will be valid without intimation in respect of debtors residing in England but, on a strictly Scottish basis, will be invalid in respect of debtors residing in Scotland unless followed by intimation to each and every debtor.

1 See Chap 5 paras 5.19(8) et seq.

**8.20** However, attention is drawn to the Civil Jurisdiction and Judgments Act 1982 as amended[1] which provides that, for a commercial debt, jurisdiction may be founded on (a) where the debtor is in the UK, in the course of the place of performance of the obligation in question, the place of payment being the place of performance, or (b) where the debtor is domiciled in another contracting state, in the place where the goods were delivered (England not being another contracting state, but the same one). In these circumstances, it would appear as a result of that Act to be possible for a Scottish debtor to be sued in England in a Scottish receivership if the contract provides for England to be the place of payment and for the proceeds thereof in a question between the receiver and the liquidator of the company in receivership to be caught within the fixed and floating charge as a fixed charge over the relevant book debt. For consumer debts, a person may only be sued in the courts of the place of residence of the consumer.

1 The Civil Jurisdictions and Judgements Order 2001 (SI 2001/2939).

## Directors' borrowing limits exceeded

**8.21** In the first and second editions of this book, much attention was devoted to the possibility of directors' borrowing limits being exceeded.[1] It is suggested that, in respect of loans granted on or after 4 February 1991,[2] if a company enters into a transaction which has been decided on by its directors and the transaction infringes a limitation on the powers of the directors contained in the memorandum and articles of association, the other party to the transaction may nonetheless treat the company as bound by it if he enters into it in good faith.

1 See 2nd edn, paras 8.21 – 8.33.
2 Section 35 of the 1985 Act.

## Unlimited guarantees and letters of set-off

**8.22** A floating charge creditor lending money to a number of companies in a group normally insists at the outset that each of the borrowing companies execute a joint and several unlimited guarantee in respect of its own borrowings and those of any other company in the group. In addition, it is also usual for each of the borrowing companies to execute a letter of set-off which entitles the lender to apply any sums at credit of any accounts in the name of any of the borrowing companies against any debt of whatsoever nature owed by any of the other companies in the group. Examples of a form of a joint and several unlimited guarantee and a letter of set-off are contained in Appendix 16 and Appendix 17 respectively. It is important for a receiver to check that all such forms of joint and several unlimited guarantee and letters of set-off have been validly executed by each of the borrowing companies, otherwise the guarantors may not be bound under their terms.

## Suggested approach of receiver

**8.23** As to how a receiver should deal with a situation where there are joint and several unlimited guarantees and letters of set-off, the following is a typical example of the outcome of the receivership of a group of companies. It is assumed that there are five companies in the group:

| | | |
|---|---|---|
| Galaxy Products Limited | (the holding company) | (Galaxy) |
| Rococo Cocoa Co Limited | (a trading subsidiary of Galaxy) | (Rococo) |
| Rococo Cocoa Co (Scotland) Limited | (a trading subsidiary of Galaxy) | (Rococo (Scotland)) |
| Orinoco Cocoa Co Limited | (a trading subsidiary of Galaxy) | (Orinoco) |
| Orinoco Cocoa Co (Scotland) Limited | (a dormant subsidiary of Galaxy) | (Orinoco (Scotland)) |

**8.24** Shortly before the appointment of the receiver, if the holder of the floating charge executed by each company in the group (for the purposes of the remainder of this chapter known as 'the lender') applied the terms of a letter or letters of set-off while at the same time consolidating all the accounts of Galaxy and its subsidiaries, the result would have been that at the date of the appointment of the receiver only Galaxy to the extent of £2.75 million was indebted to the lender. The reason for such setting-off and consolidation might be on account of the desire of the lender to treat the indebtedness of Galaxy as a group facility for the purpose of strengthening its arguments if there were any questions relating to the validity of any constitutional elements of the indebtedness of the group companies. In fact, the letters of set-off were only applied by the receiver to the extent that there were credit balances in some of the bank accounts after his appointment. The indebtedness of the companies to the lender on the receiver's appointments secured over the respective property and assets of each company in the group is as follows:

| *Company* | *Amount* £ |
|---|---|
| Galaxy | 1,500,000 |
| Rococo | 250,000 |
| Rococo (Scotland) | 75,000 |
| Orinoco | Nil |
| Orinoco (Scotland | Nil |

**8.25** Let it also be assumed that Galaxy is hopelessly insolvent and not able to pay off any of its indebtedness to the lender, that Rococo and Orinoco have substantial assets (most of which have been realised, realisations to date being in the case of Rococo £1.5 million and being in the case of Orinoco £1 million) and that Rococo (Scotland) is in a position to pay off some £50,000 of its own total indebtedness of £75,000, although not able to contribute to group indebtedness. Orinoco (Scotland) has no assets or liabilities.

**8.26** Galaxy owns heritable properties in Pitlochry which were acquired shortly before the appointment of the receiver and before the lender could take standard securities from Galaxy and which, at the date of the first distribution by the receiver, remain unsold. While the value of such properties cannot be accurately assessed, it is likely on the basis of valuations provided to the receiver that an aggregate figure in the region of £100,000 might be achieved. Orinoco owns heritable property and moveable plant and machinery in Edinburgh which is, as yet, unrealised but is thought to have a value in the region of £50,000, the heritable property being subject to a standard security in favour of the lender and all such property also being subject to a floating charge in favour of the lender. Given these facts, how should the receiver allocate the realised assets against the respective liabilities?

**8.27** The indebtedness, realisations to date and liabilities of the various companies as at the date of the first distribution by the receiver are as follows:

**Indebtedness at date of first distribution**

| | Galaxy | Rococo | Rococo | Orinoco (Scotland) | Orinoco (Scotland) |
|---|---|---|---|---|---|
| | £ | £ | £ | £ | £ |
| Indebtedness | 1,500,000 + interest | 250,000 + interest | 75,000 + interest | NIL | – |
| Realisations | 1,000,000 | 1,500,000 | 200,000 | 1,000,000 | |
| *Less:* | | | | | |
| receiver's liabilities incurred to creditors | 100,000 | 200,000 | 50,000 | 150,000 | |
| Receiver's expenses | 50,000 | 50,000 | 25,000 | 50,000 | |
| Preferential creditors | 150,000 | 350,000 | 75,000 | 200,000 | |
| Total deductions | 300,000 | 600,000 | 150,000 | 400,000 | |
| Net realisations | £700,000 | £900,000 | £50,000 | £600,000 | |

Properties valued approx £100,000 but unrealised

Property valued approx £50,000 subject to standard security but unrealised

**8.28** After providing for some contingencies, the receiver wishes to make a payment to account from the realised assets of Galaxy, Rococo and Orinoco in respect of the aggregate indebtedness to the lender. It is suggested that the correct starting point in relation to any repayments to the lender should be that each company in the group should first of all repay its own indebtedness to the lender. As a result, Rococo's debt on its own account, after paying the lender's preferred claim, is extinguished in respect of its own indebtedness.

**8.29** Orinoco had, in fact, no indebtedness of its own to the lender but had instead a credit balance of £50,000 as at the date of the receiver's appointment and in terms of the letter of set-off, the lender is entitled to take such credit balance to extinguish any other liabilities of Galaxy and Rococo. To that extent, Orinoco can be said to have already paid to the lender in respect of its liability to do so under the joint and several unlimited guarantee.

**8.30** In view of the order of priorities of payments laid down under section 60 of the IA 1986, it is suggested that the receiver's own fees and those of his agents should be apportioned between Galaxy, Rococo, Rococo (Scotland) and Orinoco, rather than charging them entirely to Galaxy.

**8.31** In terms of the unlimited guarantees, each of the companies in the group has undertaken jointly and severally to guarantee payment on demand of all sums for which any of those companies and others were or would become liable to pay to the lender. Although it is assumed that the lender will have made formal demands under and in terms of such unlimited guarantees, this should be specifically checked with the receiver as, normally, it would be necessary for the lender, at some stage, to make a formal demand to each guarantor to enable it to recover the balance of Galaxy's indebtedness not satisfied from that company's assets. Formal demands for payment under the guarantees may not, however, be strictly necessary if, for example, the lender at any time prior to the appointment of the receiver, applied the terms of the letters of set off and consolidated all the accounts leaving only Galaxy with any indebtedness to the lender. The formal demand on the other companies in the group will be necessary only if Galaxy's realised assets are less than Galaxy's aggregate indebtedness to the lender.

**8.32** The following points should be kept in mind. Firstly, the unlimited guarantees are joint and several, ie the lender at its option could look to any of the companies in the group for payment of the total indebtedness.

**8.33** Secondly, the companies who contribute under the unlimited guarantees are entitled to recover their contributions from the principal debtor, ie Galaxy. As Galaxy does not have sufficient funds to meet its indebtedness to the lender, this will not be possible.

**8.34** Thirdly, any of the companies which contributes more than its share is entitled to relief from the others. There are, however, two important exceptions to this principle. If any of the co-guarantors are insolvent and unable to contribute their share of the aggregate indebtedness, then the shares of any such co-guarantors are redistributed amongst the remaining co-guarantors. The second exception covers the position where the co-guarantors are in reality guaranteeing the obligations of a principal debtor and, at least in theory, are entitled to recover in full any amounts paid out to a creditor in respect of the obligations of the principal debtor. However, in practice, most forms of joint and several unlimited guarantee currently used by lenders make it clear that all the co-guarantors are liable both as principal debtors and as co-guarantors. It is, of course, still possible to establish the precise principal and guarantee obligations of each co-guarantor.

**8.35** Fourthly, in terms of the unlimited guarantees, none of the companies is entitled in respect of any payments made by it thereunder to require any assignation of the debts or any part thereof until the whole sums due to the lender by all such companies have been paid. As the lender will be paid in full, the lender could be approached by a future liquidator of Rococo or Orinoco (being companies liable to contribute substantially under the terms of the unlimited guarantees) and an assignation of the moneys paid under such contribution be requested to enable Rococo and/or Orinoco to enforce its right of relief against other co-guarantors if these companies had assets from which a right of relief could be satisfied. It is a general principle of the law of cautionary obligations that where a cautioner obtains an assignation of a debt, he also obtains the benefit of any security held for such debt. Therefore, any contributing guarantor would enjoy the status of a floating charge creditor and would clearly rank in front of ordinary creditors, for example, of the company for whom the guarantor had to contribute towards the overall indebtedness. A style of assignation in these circumstances is given in Appendix 18.

**8.36** It is thought that if the same person is receiver of the various companies in the group (which would usually be the case) he should not be subject to criticism provided that the scheme of division necessary in view of the unlimited guarantees is arranged on a fair and equitable basis with each of the guaranteeing companies (in so far as it is in a position to do so) bearing its rateable share of Galaxy's indebtedness to the lender.[1]

1 *Gloag on Contract* (2nd edn) pp 206–208.

**8.37** Working through the example of the Galaxy companies whose particulars are set out in paragraphs 8.23–8.35 the receiver should proceed as follows (and for present purposes ignoring interest liabilities):

| | | |
|---|---|---|
| Galaxy indebtedness | – | 1,500,000 |
| Net realisations to date | – | 700,000 |
| | | (800,000) |
| Unrealised properties | – | 100,000 |
| Rococo indebtedness | – | 250,000 |
| Net realisations to date | – | 900,000 |
| | | 650,000 |
| | | £ |
| Rococo (Scotland) indebtedness | – | 75,000 |
| Net realisations to date | – | 50,000 |
| | | (25,000) |
| Orinoco indebtedness | – | Nil |
| Realisations to date | – | 600,000 |
| Unrealised properties | – | 50,000 |

Rococo should pay off its own indebtedness to the lender and each of Galaxy and Rococo (Scotland) should make a payment to account for their own indebtedness from their respective realisations. Galaxy is still liable to pay £800,000 and Rococo (Scotland) is still liable to pay £25,000. The unrealised properties for present purposes must be ignored and should be part of the final settlement of liability amongst the co-guarantors when all realisations have been completed.

**8.38** The allocation from this stage should be based on the number of co-guarantors able to contribute rather than the amount of their respective funds. Such a course follows the joint and several argument previously discussed and is on the whole a fair and equitable method of settling the liability of each co-guarantor who is able to contribute. The net result is that, from the example above, it will be necessary for Rococo and Orinoco to pay off in equal shares the balance of indebtedness due by Galaxy and Rococo (Scotland) save that Orinoco will be entitled to be reimbursed by Rococo to the extent of £50,000 being the amount already appropriated by the lender in terms of the letters of set-off.

**8.39** The receiver has, as previously noted, no specific statutory duty to ordinary creditors. As soon as the remaining assets of Galaxy and Orinoco are realised, the final payment to the lender and any adjustments can be made to give effect to a final division on the basis set out above. However, this is very much subject to the receiver still acting as receiver and not having repaid the total group indebtedness to the floating charge creditor. If full payment has been made, the receiver has no *locus standi* to deal with ordinary creditors and a final division should in these circumstances be left to a liquidator. Unless there is an obvious conflict of interest, and, subject to the considerations set out in paragraphs 1.07 to 1.09 inclusive, it would be normal for the same person to be appointed as liquidator of each of the companies on petitions to the court by the receiver under section 55 of and Schedule 2 to the IA 1986.

## Proper division of guarantee liability

**8.40** Another problem can arise where, for example, four companies have each been placed in receivership by the same floating charge creditor, and the respective receiverships have been completed with full payment to the holder of the floating charges and the surplus proceeds in each case passed over to a liquidator. The holder of the floating charges as well as holding such a charge from each individual company in respect of its own indebtedness, may also hold a joint and several unlimited guarantee executed by each company in the group. On the appointment of a receiver to each of the four companies the bank accounts of two of the companies could be in credit and the bank accounts of the other two be overdrawn. On the appointment of the receiver the bank (in exercise of its rights under the floating charges and joint and several unlimited guarantees) could immediately freeze the two credit balances but allow compensating interest to be offset on the overdrawn accounts based on the amount standing to the credit of the other two accounts.

**8.41** On completion of each of the receiverships, the bank would have recovered all amounts due to it without recourse to the unlimited guarantee. The question which might exercise the mind of the liquidator is whether the result of the arrangement effected by the bank has been to benefit the ordinary creditors of the two companies whose accounts were overdrawn at the commencement of the receiverships in that these companies did not require to pay overdraft interest on the full amount of the overdrafts in view of the offsetting arrangement operated by the bank to the detriment of the creditors of the two companies with credit balances which suffered some loss in that they were unable to earn interest on the amounts standing to the credit of their accounts until such time as the bank's claims against the other two companies had been satisfied, thus releasing these credit balances.

**8.42** As already mentioned, a guarantor is entitled on making payment in full to obtain from the creditor an assignation of the debt and any security held for it. However, in this instance, far from making payment in full the guarantor has made no payment whatsoever under the guarantee. Accordingly, there is no debt to be assigned. The possibility of course of the bank calling up the joint and several unlimited guarantees and freezing the credit balances was a foreseeable consequence of each of the companies agreeing to execute joint and several unlimited guarantees. Another possible ground for basing a claim might be that the companies with credit balances were entitled to recompense, the claim being based on quasi contract. Any such claim, of course, would only be entitled to an ordinary ranking.

**8.43** It is thought that the two companies whose bank accounts were in credit at the time when the receiver was appointed are entitled to compensation from the two companies whose bank accounts were overdrawn. The two companies with credit balances have suffered loss in that the balances of their bank accounts were frozen and consequently, they were unable to put those sums to use by earning interest on them. The bank would of course normally have no right to freeze these balances were it not for the existence of joint and several unlimited guarantees. The principal debtors, ie the companies with credit balances benefited since the overdraft interest was only charged on the balance of the overdraft over the sums at credit of the other two companies. However, any such claim if upheld would only be given an ordinary ranking in the liquidations of the other two companies.

**8.44** One possibility, it is thought, would be an action against the holder of the floating charges challenging the validity of its actions. The challenge would be based on the fact that the bank by not calling up the joint and several unlimited guarantees, took other action which was injurious to the two companies with credit balances with the consequence that the guarantor thereby prejudiced was free from any further liability under the guarantee. Another possibility, it is thought, would be an argument that by its action in freezing the two credit balances, the bank would be bound to compensate the two companies with credit balances for all loss sustained. In such circumstances, the banks normally rely on the letters of set-off which, it can be argued, are an attempt to create a security. In this context many banks register letters of set-off with the Registrar of Companies in terms of Part XII of the 1985 Act.

## Avoidance of certain floating charges

**8.45** The statutory provisions under which certain floating charges may be avoided have already been referred to in so far as a receiver's appointment may be affected.[1] These provisions[2] are, however, frequently of more relevance to a receiver when considering the extent of the security afforded by the floating charge by virtue of which his appointment was made and any other floating charges created by the company, as it is a rare occurrence for the floating charge under which he was appointed to be rendered completely invalid by these provisions.

1 See paras 1.50-1.55.
2 Section 245 of the IA 1986.

**8.46** Section 245 of the IA 1986 has introduced a qualification related to ability to pay debts and then only in the case of a floating charge created in favour of an unconnected person[1] within 12 months of the date of the commencement of the winding up or the presentation of a petition for an administration order on which such an order has been made or on an administrator being appointed under paragraph 14 or 22 of Schedule B1 following filing with the court of a copy of notice of intention to appoint under that paragraph, the date on which the copy of the notice is filed or on the appointment by any other means of an administrator the date on which the appointment takes effect ('the relevant time'). Such a charge is not avoided under section 245 unless the company:

(a) is unable at the date of creation of the charge to pay its debts within the meaning of section 123 of the IA 1986; or
(b) becomes unable to pay its debts within such meaning in consequence of the transaction under which the charge is created.

1 For definition see para 8.49.

**8.47** A company in Scotland is deemed unable to pay its debts in terms of section 123 of the IA 1986 if:

(a) a creditor for over £750 having served a three week demand has not received payment or other satisfaction; or
(b) the induciae on a charge, decree or extract has expired without payment; or
(c) it is proved to the satisfaction of the court that the company is either unable to pay its debts as they fall due or that the value of the company's assets is less than the amount of its liabilities, taking into account its contingent and prospective liabilities.

**8.48** The onus of proving that the company was able to pay its debts or was solvent at the relevant time rests on the holder of the floating charge. For this reason, particularly where no cash is being paid (or where no goods or services are being supplied) it has been the practice of parties taking floating charges from companies to request certificates signed by at least two directors to the effect that the company is solvent and will remain so immediately after the creation of the charge. Such circumstances arise, for example, where subsidiaries are asked to grant floating charges in security of guarantees of the parent company's borrowings. Such a certificate only affords a possible remedy, of course, to the holder of the floating charges and is not in any way conclusive evidence of the company's solvency or ability to pay its debts.

**8.49** In addition to floating charges created in favour of unconnected persons within twelve months of the relevant date, the following other floating charges are open to avoidance under section 245 of the IA 1986:
(a) a floating charge in favour of a person connected with the company within two years of the relevant time;
(b) a floating charge in favour of any person whether connected or not at a time between the presentation of a petition for the making of an administration order in relation to the company and the making of such an order on that petition; and
(c) at a time between the filing with the court of a copy of notice of intention to appoint an administrator under paragraph 14 or 22 of Schedule B1 and the making of an appointment under that paragraph.

A connected person[1] is a director or shadow director (ie a person in accordance with whose directions or instructions the directors are accustomed to act) of the company or an associate of either or an associate of the company as associate is defined in section 435 of the IA 1986. The relevant time for assessing the connection is at the time of creation of the charge. Subsequently becoming connected or ceasing to be connected would have no relevance.

1 IA 1986, s 249.

**8.50** The exclusion of the avoidance provisions of section 245 by proving ability to pay debts only applies in the case of a floating charge created within the relevant twelve month period in favour of an unconnected person. In the cases of such charges created within two years of the relevant date in favour of connected persons or in favour of any person whether connected or not in the period between the presentation of a petition for and the making of an administration order, they do not escape challenge by proving ability to pay debts.

**8.51** Section 245 of the IA 1986 invalidates floating charges created within the periods mentioned (except in the circumstances mentioned where ability to pay debts is proved) except to the extent of the aggregate of:
(a) the value of so much of the consideration for the creation of the charge as consists of money paid, or goods or services supplied, to the company at the same time as, or after, the creation of the charge;
(b) the value of so much of that consideration as consists of the discharge or reduction, at the same time as, or after, the creation of the charge, of any debt of the company; and
(c) the amount of such interest (if any) as is payable on the amount falling within (a) or (b) in pursuance of any agreement under which the money was so paid, the goods or services were so supplied or the debt was so discharged or reduced.

For the purposes of section 245(2)(a), the value of any goods or services supplied by way of consideration for a floating charge shall be the amount in money which at the time of their supply could reasonably have been expected to be obtained for supplying them in the ordinary course of business and on the same terms (apart from the consideration) as those on which they were supplied to the company.

**8.52** Whether or not under section 245 of the IA 1986 the consideration consisted of money paid or goods or services supplied to the company will depend in each case on the facts.[1] In one case Lord Hanworth MR in considering equivalent provisions in the Companies Act 1929 said 'one has therefore to look at the facts and see whether or not in substance there was cash paid to the company'. That case and two other English cases[2] were considered by Lord Kincraig in a Scottish case[3] where he expressed the view that in considering the applicability of these statutory provisions the court is not bound to accept that cash payments to the company are within the exception if in substance the payments were made, and the floating charge granted, in order to give a preference to an existing creditor and that the court will look at the facts in each case in order to discover whether the payments were made truly for the benefit of the company, even if also securing a benefit to an existing creditor. In that case certain payments, claimed to be secured by a floating charge created within twelve months of liquidation, were made not to the company but direct to certain of its creditors and Lord Kincraig held that the exception for cash paid to the company was applicable only to cash so paid and not to any other person albeit on behalf of the company. Had the cash been paid to the company on condition that it was used to pay the debts due to such creditors and there was good reason for holding that this was done for the benefit of the company, the floating charge in Lord Kincraig's view might not have been rendered invalid to the extent of the respective amounts advanced.

1 *Re Matthews Ellis Ltd* [1933] Ch 458.
2 *Re Orleans Motor Co Ltd* [1911] 2 Ch 41 (followed in *Re Fairway Magazines Ltd* (1992) BCC 924) and *Re Destone Fabrics Ltd* [1941] Ch 319.
3 *Libertas–Kommerz GmbH v Johnson* 1977 SC 191, 1978 SLT 222.

**8.53** The decision in the *Libertas–Kommerz* case[1] does not, it is thought, mean that a payment to qualify as cash paid to the company for the purposes of the statutory provisions in question must always go directly to the company to swell its assets. Where, for example, a bank holding a floating charge, at the company's request, makes a payment direct to another creditor of the company (without the money being paid to the company to enable it to make the payment) such a payment constitutes cash paid to the company provided the bank has no liability to such creditor in respect of the debt in question. In the *Thomas Mortimer* case[2] Romer J in considering cheques honoured by the bank after the granting of a debenture in its favour by the company expressed the view that this amounted to the bank paying cash at the request of the company to persons who were creditors of the company, the bank not being liable itself to such creditors. He then went on to say – 'Again, if I may say so with all respect to the argument which has been addressed to me, why that is not a payment in cash by the bank to the company for the purposes of this section passes my comprehension.'

1 *Libertas–Kommerz GmbH v Johnson* 1977 SC 191, 1978 SLT 222.
2 *Re Thomas Mortimer Ltd* [1965] Ch 186; *Re Yeovil Glove Co Ltd* [1965] Ch 148.

**8.54** Companies do from time to time change their bankers and it is not unusual for the new bank in consideration for a floating charge to allow the company to pay off its total indebtedness to the old bank by one cheque drawn on its new account or even for the new bank to telegraphically transfer to the old bank at the company's request the amount necessary to clear such indebtedness. It is thought that on the basis of the two English decisions mentioned above this would qualify as cash paid to the company for the purposes of these statutory provisions.

**8.55** The cash paid or goods or services supplied to the company must be so paid or supplied in terms of section 245 'at the same time as, or after' the creation of the charge. It should also be noted that section 245 of the word 'same' in relation to time will lead to a stricter interpretation by the courts remains to be seen. There is certainly evidence in England[1] to suggest that the courts will take a very strict view of the test of contemporaneity.

1 Court of Appeal decision in *Re Shoe Lace Ltd* [1992] BCLC636 per Sir Christopher Slade at 619B–620F and Ralph Gibson LJ at 624H-625D.

**8.56** Section 245 of the IA 1986 requires the cash paid to be in consideration for the charge to enable the floating charge to be valid on its creation. It has been held[1] that these words are not used in a strict contractual sense and can be applied to payments made in reliance upon and because of the existence of the charge.

1 *Re Yeovil Glove Co Ltd* [1965] Ch 148 at 178.

**8.57** It is often the case that when a bank requests a floating charge from a company its account with the bank is already in overdraft. The bank in these circumstances, if it allows the account to run on in the normal course, is entitled to apply the rule in *Clayton*'s case.[1] This means any credits after the creation of the charge can be applied against pre-charge indebtedness until such time as this indebtedness is extinguished with the result that all post-charge debts are cash payments in consideration for the charge and so secured by the floating charge.[2] The Cork Committee[3] recommended that the decision in *Re Yeovil Glove* should be reversed but this recommendation has not to date been implemented.

1 *Devaynes v Noble* (1816) 1 Mer 572.
2 *Re Yeovil Glove Co Ltd* [1965] Ch 148.
3 Report of the Review Committee on Insolvency Law and Practice (Cmnd 8558) paragraph 1562.

**8.58** It should also be noted that a floating charge may be challenged not only under section 245 of the IA 1986 but also as a gratuitous alienation or unfair preference either under section 242 or 243 of the IA 1986 or at common law.

CHAPTER 9

# Payments and distributions

## Provisions of section 60

**9.01** Section 60(1) of the IA 1986 provides that subject to section 61 of that Act (power of court to authorise a disposal of an interest in property) and to the rights of the following categories of persons (which rights shall, except to the extent otherwise provided in any instrument, have the following order of priority) namely:

(a) the holder of any fixed security which is over property subject to the floating charge and which ranks prior to, or *pari passu* with, the floating charge;
(b) all persons who have effectually executed diligence on any part of the property of the company which is subject to the charge by virtue of which the receiver was appointed;
(c) creditors in respect of all liabilities, charges and expenses incurred by or on behalf of the receiver;
(d) the receiver in respect of his liabilities[1], expenses and remuneration and any indemnity to which the receiver is entitled out of the property of the company; and
(e) the preferential creditors[2] entitled to payment under section 59 of the IA 1986,

the receiver shall pay moneys received by him to the holder of the floating charge by virtue of which the receiver was appointed in or towards satisfaction of the debt secured by the floating charge. Thus, both the category of claimants having rights in priority to that of the floating charge creditor over the assets subject to the charge and the order in which these claimants so rank are clearly defined. The statutory order of ranking of such claimants is, however, now subject to any contrary ranking provided in any instrument. Receivership practice over many years has normally resulted in costs being attributed against the realisation of assets depending upon the character of the asset. For example, the holder of any fixed security over a property would expect to have deducted from the proceeds of sale the cost of realisation, such as land agents' fees, solicitors' fees and a proportion of the receiver's fees relating to time involved in managing the sale perhaps forming part of a larger exercise of selling a business incorporating a property or properties subject to a fixed security.

1 See discussion at para 3,55 and para 6.10 and sequentia and the *Paramount* case [1995] 2 AC 394.
2 There are now no preferential creditors except unpaid contributions to occupational pension schemes, employees remuneration and certain levies on coal and steel production.

**9.02** Section 60(2) of the IA 1986 provides that any balance of moneys remaining after the provisions of sections 60(1) and 61 of that Act have been satisfied shall be paid in accordance with their respective rights and interests to the following persons, as the case may require, namely:
(a) any other receiver;
(b) the holder of a fixed security which is over property subject to the floating charge;
(c) the company or its liquidator, as the case may be.

The most normal occurrence is for a receiver to hand over any surplus funds, after satisfaction of the floating charge creditor's claim, to a liquidator.

**9.03** In terms of section 60(3) of the IA 1986 where any question arises as to the persons entitled to a payment under section 60, or where a receipt or a discharge of a security cannot be obtained in respect of any such payment, the receiver shall consign the amount of such payment in any joint stock bank of issue in Scotland in name of the Accountant of Court for behalf of the person or persons entitled thereto.

**9.04** In the case of receivership where the sole asset is a heritable property subject to a standard security as well as the floating charge, a number of problems may arise. Firstly, whatever the ranking of the charges, if the property is to be sold by the receiver, he should, obtain the prior approval of the standard security holder as well as the floating charge holder (if these are different persons) to the price at which he proposes to sell the property. In most cases where the receiver has adequately advertised the property, such secured creditors will normally accept that the property should be sold to the highest bidder even though a shortfall will ensue and either or both such creditors will not receive the full amount (or any) of the indebtedness due by the company.

**9.05** Secondly, where the standard security ranks in priority to the floating charge in the event of no other assets being available the receiver may experience difficulty in recovering his costs. In such circumstances, the receiver will seek to reach an agreement with a standard security holder whereby the reasonable expenses of realisation (including incidental receivership expenses) will be deducted from the proceeds of sale before accounting to such standard security holder.

**9.06** Thirdly, if the receiver should be successful in clearing off the whole indebtedness due to a floating charge creditor who also holds a prior ranking standard security over the sole asset of the heritable property, simply by advantageously realising such heritable property, there was at one time a school of thought to the effect that he should either resign office having so paid off the floating charge creditor or he should retain a small amount of indebtedness to the floating charge creditor pending payment of the preferential creditors and completion of the other remaining matters in the receivership. However, on the basis of the decision in *Manley Petitioner*[1] in so far as it was held that a receiver was obliged to pay the preferential creditors, it is thought that a receiver in these circumstances should carry on and complete the receivership. It will obviously depend on the type of business and available assets in any particular case but, in most cases, it will be unusual for a receiver by selling a property subject to a fixed charge to be in a position to discharge all indebtedness to such fixed charge holder who also holds a floating charge unless the only business of the company is dealing in property. With the change in the law[2], there are unlikely to be significant preferential creditors and on realisation of the principal assets and satisfaction of the fixed and floating charge holder in full, the receiver will normally then arrange for a liquidator to be appointed.

1 1985 SLT 42.
2 Section 386(1) of and Sch 6 to IA 1986 as amended by the 2002 Act.

**9.07** Fourthly, a standard security holder may not be willing to discharge such security if the full amount of the company's indebtedness is not paid. In these circumstances, if the receiver is satisfied that he has adequately advertised the property, he should apply to the court for authority to sell the property under and in terms of section 61 of the IA 1986.

**9.08** As in the case of the powers of the receiver under section 55 of, and Schedule 2 to, the IA 1986 so also in terms of section 60(1)(b) the distribution of moneys is subject to the rights of any persons who have 'effectually executed diligence'. On the basis of the law as it stands at present it is, therefore, clear that an arrestment not followed by a decree of furthcoming is not effectually executed diligence:[1] It is also possible that an inhibiting creditor who does not succeed in obtaining a decree of adjudication before the appointment of a receiver has not effectually executed diligence.[2] In the case of creditors who have done diligence, only those who have effectually executed diligence are entitled to rank in priority to the floating charge creditor. Where funds were arrested on the dependence of an action and subsequently consigned in joint names of the parties' solicitors, the defender thereafter going into receivership, it was held that the act of prior consignation was, of itself, sufficient to remove the consigned sums from the ambit of the floating charge: the receivers' motion for authority to uplift the consigned funds was refused.[3]

1 *Lord Advocate v Royal Bank of Scotland Ltd* 1978 SLT 38.
2 *Armour and Mycroft Petitioners* 1983 SLT 453.
3 *Hawking v Hafton House Ltd* 1990 SLT 496.

**9.09** Where a creditor of a company raised an action[1] and arrested on the dependence on the action funds held by the Sheriff Clerk (although the action was subsequently dismissed without the funds being returned to the company) and the company subsequently created a standard form of bond and floating charge in favour of the bank over the whole of the property of the company, it was held that the arrestment, being merely a step in diligence, rendered the subject litigious as soon as it was used with the result that the company could not defeat it by any posterior voluntary deed.[2] An arrestment created for the arrester a preference over the only form of fixed security which could be created by the voluntary act of a debtor over moveables, namely an assignation in security. The criterion of preference is the date of arrestment as compared with the date of the intimation of the assignation, on the view that since no assignation could be complete before intimation, intimation was counted as part of the voluntary deed.[3] There was no reason, in principle, why the holder of a duly registered floating charge should be in any better position in regard to prior arrestments than the assignee in security whose assignation has been intimated to the arrestee for, in both cases, the voluntary act of the company had been completed, respectively, by registration which made public the previous floating charge and by intimation. Although the arrested property remained the property of the company to which the floating charge could attach, that was subject to the rights of the arrester whose arrestment was prior to the date of registration of the floating charge.

1 *Iona Hotels Ltd (in receivership) v Craig* 1990 SC 330, 1991 SLT 11.
2 *Iona Hotels Limited:* judgment of Lord President Hope at 14.
3 *Iona Hotels Limited:* judgment of Lord President Hope at 15.

**9.10** Section 60(1)(c) of the IA 1986 requires the claims of all creditors in respect of liabilities incurred by the receiver to rank in priority to the claim of the floating charge creditor. In any case, where the receiver hopes to dispose of the business of the company on a going concern basis, even on the basis of an orderly running down of the business, it will be necessary for liabilities to suppliers, for example, to be incurred and it is perfectly appropriate that any such liabilities should be settled in full prior to any payment to the holder of the floating charge.

## Liabilities, expenses and remuneration of receiver

**9.11** Section 60(1)(d)[1] of the IA 1986 recognises that the receiver's own liabilities, expenses and remuneration rank before the floating charge creditor. The receiver will have incurred certain professional fees (eg to his solicitor or surveyor or other agents) and prima facie the receiver is liable personally to settle such professional fees. Although, in practice, it occurs very rarely, the solicitor's fees may be subject to taxation by the Auditor of either the Court of Session or the Sheriff Court at the instance of the receiver. If the receiver is unfortunate enough to have become liable for some obligation or other matter for which monetary compensation has to be paid, then section 57(3) together with section 60(1)(d) allow him to include such liability within this head.

1 See discussion at para 3.55 and para 6.09 and the *Paramount* case [1995] AC 394.

**9.12** Section 58 of the IA 1986 deals principally with the remuneration of the receiver and it states that the remuneration to be paid to a receiver shall be determined by agreement between the receiver and the holder of the floating charge by virtue of which he was appointed. Most receivers, as partners of firms of chartered accountants, operate time recording and time costing systems and such a basis for fixing the remuneration of a receiver is widely used in discussions with floating charge holders[1]. If the receiver's remuneration cannot be determined in accordance with section 58(1) or where it is so determined but is disputed by the holder of any floating charge or fixed security over all or any part of the property of the company, the company or the liquidator of the company, such remuneration may on the application of the receiver or of any such other persons be fixed by the Auditor of the Court of Session.[2] In certain cases (eg the work involved being out of proportion to the value of the assets), there may be some merit in any event in the receiver formally submitting his account to the Auditor for approval. It is, however, unusual for such a course to be taken in a receivership.

1 IA 1986, s 58(2).
2 In recent years, some floating charge creditors have been much more specific in seeking to limit receivership costs by seeking quotations before the receivership commences. While success has been claimed for this approach, it is respectfully suggested that extreme caution and flexibility has to be exercised as receivership by its very nature can be very varied throwing up all manner of problems which may not be apparent at the outset.

**9.13** Under the provisions of section 58(3) of the IA 1986, where the receiver has been paid or retained for his remuneration for any period before the remuneration has been fixed by the Auditor any amount in excess of the remuneration so fixed for that period, the receiver or his personal representatives shall account for the excess.

## Priority of debts

**9.14** Section 59(1) of the IA 1986 provides that where a receiver is appointed and the company is not at the time of the appointment in course of being wound up,[1] the debts which fall under section 59(2) shall be paid out of any assets coming to the hands of the receiver in priority to any claim for principal or interest by the holder of the floating charge by virtue of which the receiver was appointed.

1 But see *Manley, Petitioner* 1985 SLT 42.

**9.15** The debts referred to in section 59(1) of the IA 1986 are in terms of section 59(2) debts which satisfy the following conditions, that is to say, they are debts:
(a) which are preferential debts within the meaning of section 386 of the IA 1986 and Schedule 6 thereto (read with Schedule 4 to the Pensions Schemes Act 1993); and
(b) which, by the end of a period of six months after advertisement by the receiver for claims in the Edinburgh Gazette and in a newspaper circulating in the district where the company carries on business, either

(i) have been intimated to him; or
(ii) have become known to him.

Preferential creditors in a receivership are thus those who would have a similar right on the liquidation of the company and have become known to the receiver by intimation or otherwise in the six month period following his advertisement for such claims. The effect of this is that the receiver is obliged to advertise for such claims as provided in section 59(2). Major changes to the categories of preferential creditors have been made by the 2002 Act[1]. The primary obligation to make prior payment to the company's preferential creditors is contained in these provisions.[1] For these purposes, the company's preferential creditors are now limited to unpaid contributions to occupational pension schemes, employees remuneration and certain levies on coals and steel production.[2] The preferential status of PAYE, value added tax and social security contributions have all been abolished.[3]

1 The 2002 Act, s 251.
2 Section 386 (1) of and Sch 6 to IA 1986.
3 The 2002 Act, s 251.

**9.16** Section 387(4)(b) of the IA 1986 provides that, for the purposes of Schedule 6 to that Act (the provisions relating to preferential creditors in a liquidation) the relevant date is the date of appointment of the receiver under section 53(6) or 54(5) of the IA 1986. Section 59(3) of the IA 1986 further provides that any payments made under the provisions of section 59 shall be recouped as far as may be out of the assets of the company available for payment of ordinary creditors.

**9.17** For a proper understanding of what now constitute preferential debts, it is necessary to examine the provisions of sections 175 and 386 of and Schedule 6 to the IA 1986 which contain definitions of preferential debts.

**Contributions to occupational pension schemes etc**

1 Any sum which is owed by the debtor and is a sum to which Schedule 4 to the Pension Schemes Act 1993 (contributions to occupational pension scheme and state scheme premiums) applies.

**Remuneration of employees etc**

2 (1) So much of any amount which:
(a) is owed by the debtor to a person who is or has been an employee of the debtor; and
(b) is payable by way of remuneration in respect of the whole or any part of the period of four months next before the relevant date,

as does not exceed such amount as may be prescribed by order made by the Secretary of State. The current prescribed amount is £800 in the case of any one employee.

(2) An amount owed by way of accrued holiday remuneration, in respect of any period of employment before the relevant date, to a person whose employment by the debtor has been terminated, whether before, on or after that date.

(3) So much of any sum owed in respect of money advanced for the purpose as has been applied for the payment of a debt which, if it had not been paid, would have been a debt falling within sub-paragraph (1) or (2) above.

3 **So much of any amount which:**

(a) is ordered, whether before or after the relevant date, to be paid by the debtor under the Reserve Forces (Safeguard of Employment) Act 1985; and

(b) is so ordered in respect of a default made by the debtor before that date in the discharge of his obligations under that Act,

as does not exceed such amount as may be prescribed by order made by the Secretary of State.

**9.17A** As already mentioned in the interpretation of Schedule 6 to the IA 1986, in the context of receivership, the relevant date means the date of the appointment of the receiver. The debtor in such context means the company in receivership.

## *Amounts payable by way of remuneration*

**9.18**

(1) For the purposes of paragraph 13(1) of Schedule 6, a sum is payable by the debtor to a person by way of remuneration in respect of any period if:
   - (a) it is paid as wages or salary (whether payable for time or for piece work or earned wholly or partly by way of commission) in respect of services rendered to the debtor in that period; or
   - (b) it is an amount falling within sub-paragraph (2) of paragraph 13 of Schedule 6 and is payable by the debtor in respect of that period.

(2) Sub-paragraph (2) of paragraph 13 of Schedule 6 provides that an amount falls within that sub-paragraph if it is:
   - (a) a guarantee payment under section Part III of the 1996 Act (employee without work to do for a day or part of a day);
   - (b) remuneration on suspension on medical grounds under Part VII of the 1996 Act;
   - (c) any payment for time off under the TULRCA 1992, s 169 (trade union duties), s 62 of the 1996 Act for employee representatives, section 52 of the 1996 Act (looking for work, etc) or section 56 of the 1996 Act (ante-natal care);
   - (d) remuneration under a protective award; See para 6.17 above.

(3) For the purposes of paragraph 14 of Schedule 6 holiday remuneration shall be deemed, in the case of a person whose employment has been terminated

by or in consequence of his employer going into liquidation or being adjudged bankrupt, or in consequence of the appointment of a receiver under section 53(6) or 54(5) of the IA 1986 to have accrued to that person in respect of any period of employment if, by virtue of that person's contract of employment or of any enactment (including an order or direction made under any enactment), that remuneration would have accrued in respect of that period if that person's employment had continued until he became entitled to be allowed the holiday.

(4) Without prejudice to the preceding provisions of paragraphs 13 and 14 of Schedule 6:
   (a) any remuneration payable by the debtor to a person in respect of a period of holiday or of absence from work through sickness or other good cause is deemed to be wages or, as the case may be, salary in respect of services rendered to the debtor in that period; and
   (b) references in paragraphs 13–15 to remuneration in respect of a period of holiday include references to any sums which, if they had been paid, would have been treated for the purposes of the enactments relating to social security as earnings in respect of that period.

## *Orders*

**9.19**

(1) An order under paragraph 9 or 12 of Schedule 6 may contain such transitional provisions as may appear to the Secretary of State necessary or expedient.

(2) An order under the said paragraph 9 or 12 shall be made by statutory instrument which shall be subject to annulment in pursuance of a resolution of either House of Parliament.

## *Money advanced for the purpose of remuneration or accrued holiday remuneration*

**9.20** Paragraph 11 of Schedule 6 to the IA 1986 has preserved the old rule that money advanced by a third party for the purpose of payment of remuneration to employees of the company and so used is preferential although now expressed in much simpler terms. Paragraph 11 provides that so much of any sum owed in respect of money advanced for the purpose as has been applied for the payment of a debt which, if it had not been paid, would have been preferential as employees' remuneration or accrued holiday remuneration will be preferential.

**9.21** This provision can be of benefit to a floating charge holder where such holder is a clearing bank which has provided funds to enable the company to pay its employees. In these circumstances certain conditions must be met, however, before a preferential ranking can be admitted. In considering the equivalent provisions in the Companies Act 1929 Mr Robert Finlayson in his *Law Lectures to Bankers*,[1] at page 152, states as follows:

> 'The money must be advanced "for that purpose" – that is, for the purpose of paying wages or salaries – and it is accordingly necessary to preserve evidence that the advances in question were so made. The simplest method of doing that is to have the cheques which are drawn for the purpose specially marked by the customers as being for wages. They may, for example, be made payable to "Selves for Wages" or as employees' "Wages for bearer". It is not sufficient if the cheques have merely a marking on the back to show numbers and denominations of the notes and coins drawn from the bank or that the banker assumed or understood that the money was required to meet wages. The money, according to the Act, must have been advanced for the specific purpose, and this involves definiteness.'

1 Published by William Blackwood & Sons Limited in 1939 but now out of print.

**9.22** In terms of the previous statutory provisions entitlement to the preference only arose in so far as the employees' priority claims had been diminished by reason of the advances in question having been made. The terms of paragraph 11 of Schedule 6 appear to have the same effect. Mr Finlayson[1] goes on to state:

> 'If the money, although specially borrowed for the purpose, is not actually applied in paying the wages, the position would be that the employees' claim in the liquidation would not have been diminished and they, themselves, would be entitled to a preferential ranking in full. Consequently, the bank, in a case of that kind, could not also obtain a preferential ranking and would require to be satisfied with an ordinary ranking. No doubt, however, any director or officer of the company who obtained advances from a bank for the specific purpose of paying wages, and instead of doing so, applied the money otherwise, would lay himself open to a charge of fraud.'

1 *Law Lectures to Bankers* published by William Blackwood & Sons Limited in 1939 but now out of print.

**9.23** It is accordingly essential that a receiver in considering a claim to a preferential ranking under this head should be satisfied both that the money was advanced and was used for the purposes in question. The claim is of course restricted to the aggregate claims of the employees who received the money advanced which would have been preferential had they not received such money.

**9.24** It can arise that even though a designated wages account has not been opened, a bank can establish that moneys were advanced for the payment of wages, in which event it is entitled to claim a ranking. However, in these circumstances, the bank faces the difficulty of the operation of the rule in

*Clayton*'s case[1] to the effect that any credit received must first be applied in discharging the earliest debit on the account which may have the effect of reducing its potential preferential claim. One of the difficulties of proving in such circumstances that all moneys advanced by the bank in a particular payment are truly for the purposes of paying wages is that there may, for example, be sums included for other expenses and petty cash. Such sums must be clearly excluded in a calculation of the bank's wages preference.

1 *Devaynes v Noble* (1816) 1 Mer 572.

**9.25** In his *Law Lectures to Bankers*,[1] Mr Robert Finlayson at page 121 refers to the unreported case of *National Provincial Bank Ltd v Freedman* where no separate wages account was opened. Shortly before a company went into liquidation, the bank insisted that the debit on the sole account with the company should not exceed a fixed limit. The company required money to pay wages each week and the bank refused to cash wages cheques in favour of the company until it was satisfied that either at the same time or within a few hours cheques in favour of the company would be lodged to reduce the overdraft to such an extent that the wages cheques when drawn would not increase the overdraft beyond the prescribed limit. On the liquidation of the company, the liquidator argued that the bank had advanced no money to meet wages because the cash it had paid out on the wages cheques was merely the same cash which had been lodged around the same time to the credit of the account. The court held, however, that these cheques did not provide the wages but simply reduced the overdraft: the wages cheques were paid by money which was advanced by the bank for that purpose.

1 Published by William Blackwood & Sons Limited in 1939 but now out of print.

**9.26** On the other hand in the *E J Morel* case[1] the normal trading account (the No 2 account) of a company was maintained in credit in excess of the amount to which the wages account was in debit. Wages were drawn monthly and as soon as a debit to the wages account was more than four months old, money was transferred to the wages account from the No 2 account. Buckley J said at 32:

> '... and I think that those two accounts were truly interdependent, so that the bank would never have met a cheque drawn on either one or the other without considering the combined position of those two accounts taken together and, if one reaches that conclusion, the sensible and the right way to regard the matter is to treat those two accounts as though they were in reality one. If that is right, then I think that there is substance in the contention that the bank never did in fact make advances to meet the wages cheques; the company when it drew on its wages account was really drawing its own moneys standing to the credit of the No 2 account ...'

1 *Re E J Morel (1934) Ltd* [1962] Ch 21.

## Right to combine accounts

**9.27** The right to combine the bank accounts of a company in receivership or liquidation depends on the person who wishes to apply such right, the nature of each account and impinges upon the principles of the law of set-off.[1] In many of the cases to which reference is made in the succeeding paragraphs, the extent of a bank's preferred ranking for 'sums advanced for the purpose' depended to some extent on whether or not accounts could be combined and also arose as a separate issue.

1 See paras 4.73-4.89.

**9.28** It has been generally established that a bank is entitled to combine current accounts of a customer in any way it wishes[1] and in a subsequent case[2] combination of a current account and a frozen account of the same customer has been approved. What appears, however, clear is that a receiver or liquidator of a company is not entitled to combine two accounts.[3]

1 In *Re E J Morel (1934) Ltd* [1962] Ch 21; *Garnett v McKewan* (1872) LR 8 Exch 10.
2 *National Westminster Bank Ltd v Halesowen Presswork and Assemblies Ltd* [1972] AC 785.
3 *Bank of Scotland v Purvis Industries Ltd* (unreported) – opinion of Lord Hill Watson dated 21 July 1954.

**9.29** The facts in the *E J Morel* case[1] were that at one stage a company had one bank account which was overdrawn. It was agreed between the company and its bankers that the first account be frozen, a No 2 account be opened to deal with normal business transactions and a No 3 account be opened as a wages account. Thereafter, the No 2 account was maintained in credit in excess of the amount to which the wages account was in debit. Wages were drawn on a monthly basis and as soon as a debit to the wages account was more than four months old, money was transferred to the wages account from the No 2 account. On the winding up of the company, the No 1 account was in debit to the extent of £1,839, the No 2 account was in credit to the extent of £1,544 and the No 3 account was in debit to the extent of £1,623. The bank applied a set-off to the debit and credit balances of the No 1 and No 2 accounts and added the balance of the small debit arising to the debit on the No 3 account. The liquidator argued that only the No 2 and No 3 accounts should be adjusted in this way, no account being taken of the frozen No 1 account. The court held that while the bank could combine several current accounts of a customer as it might choose, it was inappropriate to do so where the accounts were of a different character, such as the frozen No 1 account. As was noted by Buckley J in the course of his judgment[1] at page 30, the case of *Garnett v McKewan*[2] where the bank transferred one account to another branch where the customer also had an account, is authority for the proposition that current accounts of a customer may be combined.

1 *Re E J Morel (1934) Ltd* [1962] Ch 21.
2 (1872) LR 8 Exch 10.

**9.30** The facts in *National Westminster Bank Ltd v Halesowen Presswork and Assemblies Ltd*[1] were that as a result of concern by the bank, the No 1 account of the company was frozen and a new No 2 account was opened for the normal trading business of the company, it being understood that the No 2 account should always be kept in credit. These arrangements were to subsist for a period of four months pending the sale of the company as a going concern and in the absence of materially changed circumstances in the meantime. Within the period of four months the company gave the bank notice of a meeting of creditors for the purpose of appointing a liquidator. On the day of such meeting of creditors, the company paid into the No 2 account a cheque for £8,611 prior to the resolution to wind up the company. The cheque was cleared two days later and the bank claimed to be able to set off the credit of £8,611 against the company's indebtedness on the No 1 account. The bank relied on the terms of section 31 of the Bankruptcy Act 1914 as extended by section 317 of the CA 1948[2] (these sections being applicable only in England), the effect of which was that an account be taken of what is due from the one party to the other in respect of mutual dealings and the balance of the account only should be claimed or paid on either side respectively. The House of Lords held that the terms of section 31 as extended were mandatory and that the bank was entitled to combine a current credit account with a frozen account since the debit on the one account and the credit on the other account amounted to mutual dealings under the section. The arrangements agreed between the bank and the company a few months prior to the appointment of the liquidator ceased on liquidation.

1 [1972] AC 785.
2 Re-enacted as the CA 1985, s 612.

**9.31** One further aspect of the *Halesowen* case[1] should be mentioned from the standpoint of the law of Scotland. At 822 of the report Lord Kilbrandon stated:

> 'An interesting feature of this controversy is that, while by section 318 of the CA 1948 the provisions of the Bankruptcy (Scotland) Act 1913 relating to ranking of claims are imported into the Scottish liquidation code, there is no equivalent to section 31 to be found in the latter Act. The right of set off, or, as Bell calls it in his Commentaries on the Laws of Scotland, 5th ed (1826), vol II, p 124, "the balancing of accounts in bankruptcy," stands on the common law of compensation or retention, expanded in cases of bankruptcy to include debts which would not be susceptible of set off in the case of a solvent creditor. For example, in bankruptcy, the debts need not be of the same nature, or both due at the same time, or both liquid. Bell's Commentaries, vol II, pp 119–121, supply an illuminating account of the parallel development of the law in England and Scotland respectively. It would hardly be possible to maintain in Scotland that set off is mandatory, and independent of the act or agreement of parties, since "it must be pleaded by the debtor who wishes to take advantage of it," and, again:
>
>> "Compensation may be pleaded not only by the primary debtor, but even *illo tacente vel negante*, by anyone having an interest, as a

> cautioner in a bond, or an indorser of a bill of exchange" (*Goudy on Law of Bankruptcy* (4th ed, 1914), pp 551, 552).

So, if set off be mandatory in England, this seems to be one of the fields in which the law relating to companies varies according as they are registered in England or in Scotland.'

1 *National Westminster Bank Ltd v Halesowen Presswork and Assemblies Ltd* [1972] AC 785.

**9.32** The case of *Bank of Scotland v Purvis Industries Ltd*[1] is instructive from the point of view of calculation of a wages preference and also decided that the liquidators of Purvis were not entitled to combine various accounts. It also makes clear that if it is made a condition that a separate wages account be opened and withdrawals are limited to the payment of wages for the statutory period, the bank should experience no real difficulty in establishing a wages preference.

1 Unreported Opinion of Lord Hill Watson dated 21 July 1954.

**9.33** Payments to an employee by way of commission can occasionally cause problems in the context of sums advanced for the purpose of such payments. If an employee is remunerated by the payment of a salary plus a commission based, for example, on the number of products of the company sold by him or based on some other factor clearly linked to the employee's performance, any moneys advanced to the company for the purpose of paying such salary and commission would, it is submitted, be preferential within the usual limits in that payment by way of commission is remuneration. Fees paid to directors do not however qualify as remuneration and so cannot form the basis of a preferential claim by a third party who has advanced the funds to meet such fees.

**9.34** In receivership preferential debts rank equally among themselves and are to be paid in full, unless the assets are insufficient to meet them, in which case they abate in equal proportions.[1]

1 IA 1986, s 175(2).

## 'Gross' or 'net'

**9.35** There has been prolonged and continuing discussion in relation to both an employee's claim in liquidation or receivership to a preferential ranking for unpaid remuneration and even more so to the subrogated claim of a third party who has advanced funds for the purpose of and which were applied in payment of such remuneration. The discussion has arisen from the fact that there is a monetary limit on an employee's preferential claim for unpaid remuneration, the necessity for the company debtor to make certain statutory deductions from employees' remuneration (such as employees' NIC contributions and PAYE) and the practice of banks to advance in some but not all cases the net amount only of the company's wage bill. The arguments are generally known as the 'gross' and 'net' arguments respectively and the authors have read numerous well-reasoned and persuasive opinions of learned counsel on both sides of the border, some arguing strongly for one view and some for the other, particularly in relation to a third party lender's subrogated claim. The Cork Committee[1] acknowledged the problem and recommended in paragraph 1444 of its Report that the question be resolved by legislation. Paragraph 11 of Schedule 6 to the IA 1986 undoubtedly expresses the right to a preferential claim of a third party lender for remuneration payment purposes in much simpler terms but whether the problem is now resolved remains to be seen.

1 Report of the Review Committee on Insolvency Law and Practice (Cmnd 8558).

**9.36** It is not intended to set out at length the competing arguments but to put forward, in reasonably succinct terms, the views of the authors which, as will be seen, support the gross view. These are:

(a) In the case of an employee's claim to a preferential ranking, this is for gross remuneration. In making payment, the receiver is required to deduct and account for, PAYE income tax and employees' NIC contributions.

(b) In the case of the claim of a third party who has advanced funds for the purpose of payment of remuneration which have been so applied and such remuneration had it not been paid would have been preferential, such claim is subject to a simple monetary limit being in respect of each employee involved the maximum amount of the employee's claim to a preferential ranking. The third party's claim is not related to either the net amount actually received by each employee nor to the net amounts advanced during the period in question over which the employee's claim for gross wages would have reached the maximum preferential amount.

CHAPTER 10

# Notification and information where receiver appointed

## Registration and notification of appointment

### *Appointment by holder of floating charge*

**10.01** On the appointment of a receiver by the holder of a floating charge, such holder or person on his behalf must deliver to the Registrar of Companies for registration, within seven days of its execution, a copy (certified in the prescribed manner to be a correct copy) of the instrument of appointment together with a copy to the Accountant in Bankruptcy.[1] Certified in the prescribed manner means certified to be a correct copy by or on behalf of the person making the appointment.[1]

1 Scottish Rules as amended by the Scotland Act 1998 (Consequential Modifications) (No 2) Order 1999, SI 1999/1820, art 4, Sch 2, Pt II, para 142 (1), (2).

**10.02** A notice in the prescribed form requires to be delivered to the Registrar of Companies[1] and to the Accountant in Bankruptcy together with a certified copy of the instrument of appointment and such notice should contain the following information:

(a) details of the appointment;
(b) a statement of the circumstances justifying the appointment;
(c) particulars of the floating charge under which the receiver is appointed; and
(d) the name (or the first-named if several) of the person entitled to the benefit of the floating charge.

On receipt of the certified copy of the instrument of appointment the Registrar requires to enter the particulars of the appointment in the Register of Charges.[2] No registration fee is payable.

1 IA 1986, s 53(1) together with reg 4 and the Schedule to the Scottish Rules.
2 Ibid, s 53(5).

**10.03** The receiver must unless there is already a receiver in office or he has been appointed to replace a deceased or previous receiver who has ceased to act (except where the deceased or previous receiver has not fully complied with the requirements):

(1) forthwith send to the company and publish notice of his appointment (although nowhere does it say where);[1] and

(2) within 28 days after his appointment, unless the court otherwise directs, send such notice of his appointment to all the company's creditors (so far as he is aware of their addresses).

1 IA 1986, s 65(1) and (2), and the Schedule to the Scottish Rules and para 10.06 below.

**10.04** If the company is being wound up, these provisions apply notwithstanding that the receiver and liquidator are the same person subject to any necessary modifications arising from that fact.[1]

1 IA 1986, s 65(3).

**10.05** A person who fails without reasonable excuse to comply with these provisions is liable to a fine and, for continued contravention, to a daily default fine.[1]

1 IA 1986, s 65(4).

**10.06** While there is no requirement to advertise generally the appointment of a receiver (other than the general requirement to publish notice of the appointment in section 65(1)(a) of IA 1986 referred to in paragraph 10.03 above), it is usual to give notice in the *Edinburgh Gazette* and a local newspaper. In addition, there is no provision for the advertisement of such notice within a certain period of the receiver's appointment but this is usually done in practice within a few weeks of his appointment.

**10.07** The lack of information on the appointment of a receiver resulted in many complaints, particularly from ordinary trade creditors, in respect of the absence of provisions for making known at an early date that a receiver had been appointed and also the likely outcome of the receivership. The Cork Committee[1] in its Report stated: 'the most frequent complaint which we have received is of the lack of information once a receiver has been appointed'. As a result the Cork Committee made certain recommendations[2] intended to remedy the position and these have been implemented in the repeal of sections 481 and 482 of the 1985 Act and their replacement by new provisions incorporating the Cork proposals.[3]

1 Report of the Review Committee on Insolvency Law and Practice (Cmnd 8558) paragraph 438.
2 Ibid, paragraphs 476–489.
3 See paragraphs 10.23 to 10.32.

### *Appointment by the court*

**10.08** On the appointment of a receiver by the court, the party who presented the petition or a person on the petitioner's behalf must deliver to the Registrar of Companies for registration, within seven days of its date or such longer period as the court may allow, a copy of the court's interlocutor certified by the clerk of court to be a true copy together with the prescribed form.[1] As in the case of the appointment of a receiver by instrument of appointment, the Registrar of Companies is required on payment of the prescribed fee to enter particulars of a court appointment in the Register of Charges.[2] There is currently no fee payable.

1 IA 1986, s 54(3) and the Schedule to the Scottish Rules.
2 Ibid, s 54(4).

**10.09** The receiver in a court appointment, unless there is already a receiver in office or he has been appointed to replace a deceased or previous receiver except where such requirements have not been fully implemented, has the same duty to notify the company and its creditors of his appointment and publish it.[1]

1 IA 1986, s 65.

## Receiver should seek confirmation of registration

**10.10** While it is the duty of the holder of the floating charge or the petitioner to register particulars of his appointment with the Registrar of Companies, it is suggested that in the interests of prompt notification of his appointment the receiver should always seek confirmation from such holder or petitioner that registration has been effected.

## Non-registration of appointment

**10.11** Failure to deliver to the Registrar of Companies a certified copy of the instrument of appointment or the court interlocutor in the case of a court appointment or the appropriate company form or to notify the company of the appointment does not affect the validity of the receiver's appointment nor the exercise of his powers. The only potential penalty is the imposition of a fine and, for continued contravention, of a daily default fine on any person who without reasonable excuse makes default in complying with the registration requirements:[1] a receiver who fails to notify the company being subject to a similar penalty.[2] There has been criticism of the absence of any other sanctions, particularly as delay or failure to register may result in a party inspecting the Register of Charges being unaware of the appointment. The Cork Committee[3] in considering the effective date of the appointment of a receiver referred to the fact that the Kilbrandon Committee recommended that the appointment of a receiver should take effect only when a duly certified copy of the instrument of appointment had been delivered to the Registrar for registration but the Cork Committee considered that to use the date of registration for filing would introduce an element of uncertainty and would also be unacceptable because speed of appointment is frequently essential. The Cork Committee's own recommendation in relation to the time when a receiver's appointment should run has been implemented by section 53 of the IA 1986[4] but does not alter the position that non-registration of the appointment does not affect its validity. However, the increased notification requirements should go some way to meet the criticism of the absence of sanctions for non-registration other than monetary penalties.

1 IA 1986, ss 53(2) and 54(3), the words in italics being as amended by the CA 1989 ss 107, 212, Sch 16, para 3, Sch 24 as from a day to be appointed.
2 Ibid, s 65(4).
3 Report of the Review Committee on Insolvency Law and Practice (Cmnd 8558) paras 471 and 472.
4 See para 1.40.

## Other publication of receiver's appointment

**10.12** In addition to the increased notification requirements contained in the IA 1986, a receiver still also requires to give the statutory notice under section 59(2) of that Act for preferential claims, such notice requiring to be advertised in the Edinburgh Gazette and in one newspaper circulating in the district where the company carries on business. There is no provision for such notice being advertised within a certain period of the receiver's appointment although in practice this is usually done within a few weeks.

## Notification of appointment on invoices

**10.13** In addition to the registration and notification requirements already mentioned, where a receiver has been appointed, every invoice, order for goods or business letter issued by or on behalf of the company or the receiver or the liquidator of the company on which the company's name appears must contain a statement that a receiver has been appointed.[1] Failure to comply with this requirement can render any officer of the company or any receiver or liquidator who knowingly and wilfully authorises or permits the default liable to a fine.

1 IA 1986, s 64(1).

**10.14** In addition to letters issued by the receiver himself, every letter issued by an agent either on his behalf or on behalf of a liquidator should, in any reference to the company, state that it is in receivership or that a receiver has been appointed and, if appropriate, that it is also in liquidation. The normal practice in Scotland is for a receiver to overstamp on every letter, invoice, order or other document issued by him a notice both intimating the appointment of a receiver and including a general disclaimer of personal liability on the following lines: 'Receiver appointed. The receiver contracts only as agent of the company and without personal liability.'

## Statement to be made to and report to be made by a receiver

### *Statement to be made by officers to receiver*

**10.15** Sections 66–68 of the IA 1986 consolidated provisions governing the information to be supplied to the receiver by the company's management and the information to be disseminated by the receiver to creditors and others, these provisions being designed to meet criticisms of the previous provisions.

**10.16** On his appointment, a receiver must forthwith require some or all of certain specified persons to make out and submit to him a statement in the prescribed form of the affairs of the company.[1]

1 IA 1986, s 66(1) and (3) and the Schedule to the Scottish Rules.

**10.17** The persons specified[1] as requiring to submit a statement of affairs, who must verify it by affidavit, are those:

(a) who are or have been officers of the company;
(b) who have taken part in the formation of the company at any time within a year of the date of the receiver's appointment;
(c) who are or have been within such period employees of or employed under a contract of services by the company and who, in the receiver's opinion, are capable of giving the required information;
(d) who are or have been within such period officers or employees of or employed under a contract of services by a company which within that period was an officer of the company in receivership.

1 IA 1986, s 66(3).

**10.18** A statement of affairs,[1] now verified by affidavit by the persons required to submit it, must show:

(a) particulars of the company's assets, debts and liabilities;
(b) the names and addresses of the creditors;
(c) the securities held by them respectively;
(d) the dates when the securities were respectively given; and
(e) such further or other information as may be prescribed.

1 IA 1986, s 66(2).

**10.19** Where a receiver decides to require from any person or persons a statement of affairs he requires[1] to send to each of those persons (a deponent) a notice in the form[2] set out in Schedule 5 requiring the deponent to make out and submit such a statement of affairs in the prescribed form.[3]

The receiver requires to insert any statement of affairs submitted to him in the Sederunt Book[4] which each insolvency practitioner requires to maintain during his term of office for the purpose of providing an accurate record of the administration of each insolvency proceeding.[5] As regards the expenses of such statement of affairs, a deponent who makes up and submits such statement of affairs is to be allowed and to be paid by the receiver as an expense of the receivership, any expenses incurred by the deponent in so doing which the receiver considers to be reasonable.[6] Any decision by the receiver under this rule is subject to appeal to the court.[7]

The rule expressly provides that nothing in it relieves a deponent from any obligation to make up and submit a statement of affairs or to provide information to the receiver.[8]

1 The Scottish Rules (s 139), r 3.2(1).
2 Ibid, Sch 5, Form 3.1 (Scot).
3 The Scottish Rules, Schedule.
4 The Scottish Rules, r 3.2(3).
5 Ibid, r 7.33(1).
6 Ibid, r 3.3(1).
7 Ibid, r 3.3(2).
8 Ibid, r 3.3(3).

**10.20** Where any persons are required by the receiver to submit a statement of affairs to him, they must do so within 22 days of being given notice of such requirement[1] unless the receiver, at his discretion, either when giving such notice or subsequently extends such period.[2] The court also has a residual discretionary power to extend the period where the receiver has refused to exercise his power to do so.[2]

1 IA 1986, s 66(4).
2 Ibid, s 66(5).

**10.21** The receiver has a discretionary power to release any person either from the requirement to submit to him a statement of affairs or from the obligation to verify or include in such statement any of the specified information[1] with the court again having a residual discretion to exercise this power in the event of the receiver's refusal to do so.[2]

1 IA 1986, s 66(5)(a).
2 Ibid s 66(5).

**10.22** Any person who without reasonable cause fails to comply with any of these obligations relating to the giving of a statement of affairs is liable to a fine and, for continued contravention, to a daily default fine.[1]

1 IA 1986, s 66(6).

## Report by receiver

**10.23** Sections 67 and 68 of the IA 1986 provide that a receiver must make available within three months (or longer period as the court may allow) after his appointment a report to ordinary creditors which will normally be placed before a meeting of such creditors who may at the meeting establish a committee of creditors.

**10.24** On the appointment of a receiver, whether by the holder of a floating charge or by the court, the receiver must within three months (or such longer period as the court may allow) send a report[1] on certain matters to:
(a) the Registrar of Companies;
(b) the holder of the floating charge under which he was appointed;
(c) any trustee for secured creditors (ie creditors holding any security (whether heritable or moveable), any floating charge or any right of lien, retention or preference); and
(d) so far as he is aware of the their addresses, all such secured creditors.

1 IA 1986, s 67(1).

**10.25** The matters to be dealt with in such report are:
(a) the events leading up to his appointment, so far as he is aware of them;
(b) the actual or proposed disposal of any of the company's property;
(c) the actual or proposed carrying on of the company's business;
(d) the total amounts payable to the holder of the floating charge under which he was appointed;
(e) the amounts payable to preferential creditors; and
(f) the amount, if any, likely to be available for the payment of other creditors.

The report must also include[1] a summary of the statement of affairs submitted to the receiver under section 66 and any comments he may have on it.

1 IA 1986, s 67(5).

**10.26** In assessing what sum, if any, is likely to be available for other creditors the receiver will require to take account of the claims of any other secured creditors in addition to that of the holder of the floating charge under which he was appointed and also the estimated costs of the receivership.

**10.27** Within a like period of three months from his appointment (or such longer period allowed by the court) the receiver[1] must either:
(a) send a copy of the report to all unsecured creditors (ie creditors other than secured creditors) in so far as he knows their addresses; or
(b) publish a notice stating an address to which unsecured creditors should write for copies of the report to be sent to them free of charge.

Where a receiver determines to publish such a notice, the regulations[2] provide that the notice shall be published in a newspaper circulating in the area where the company has its principal place of business or in such other newspaper as the receiver thinks most appropriate for ensuring that it comes to the notice of the unsecured creditors of the company.

In addition, whether copies of the report are sent to creditors or they are notified by advertisement where copies can be obtained, the receiver, unless the court otherwise directs, must summon a meeting of the unsecured creditors on not less than fourteen days' notice and lay before such meeting a copy of his report.

1 IA 1986, s 67(2).
2 The Scottish Rules, reg 7.

**10.28** The court cannot direct[1] that the requirement to lay the receiver's report before a meeting of the unsecured creditors be dispensed with unless:
(a) the receiver states in the report that he intends to apply for a direction to that effect; and
(b) not less than fourteen days before the hearing of the receiver's application for a direction to that effect, either a copy of the report containing such statement is sent to all unsecured creditors or there is published notification of where a copy can be obtained.

1 IA 1986, s 67(3).

**10.29** If the company is or goes into liquidation the receiver[1] must send the liquidator a copy of his report within seven days of either sending his report to the Registrar of Companies and the secured creditors mentioned in section 67(1) of the IA 1986 or, if later, the nomination or appointment of the liquidator and if he does so within the period of three months from his appointment (or such longer period allowed by the court) he is relieved of compliance with the requirements to send or make the report available to ordinary creditors and to lay it before a meeting of such creditors.

1 IA 1986, s 67(4).

**10.30** There is a saving provision[1] allowing the exclusion from the receiver's report of any information the disclosure of which would seriously prejudice the carrying out by the receiver of his functions.

1 IA 1986, s 67(6).

**10.31** These obligations on a receiver in relation to the making of a report do not apply[1] where there is already a receiver in office or the receiver has been appointed to replace a deceased or previous receiver who has ceased to act (except where the deceased or previous receiver has not fully complied with the requirements).

1 IA 1986, s 67(7).

**10.32** Any person who without reasonable excuse fails to comply with these provisions in relation to the making of a report is liable to a fine and, for continued contravention, to a daily default fine.[1]

1 IA 1986, s 67(8).

## *Abstract of receipts and payments*

**10.33** The Rules provide[1] that the receiver shall:
(a) within two months after the end of twelve months from the date of his appointment, and of every subsequent period of 12 months, and
(b) within two months after he ceases to act as receiver, send the requisite account of his receipts and payments as receiver to –
 (1) the Accountant in Bankruptcy;
 (2) the holder of the floating charge by virtue of which he was appointed;
 (3) the members of the creditors' committee (if any), and
 (4) the company or, if it is in liquidation, the liquidator.

The two-month period referred to in this Rule may on the receiver's application be extended by the court.[2] The requisite accounts of the receiver's receipts and payments requires[3] to be in the form of an abstract showing –
(a) receipts and payments during the relevant period of twelve months, or
(b) where the receiver has ceased to act, receipts and payments during the period from the end of the last 12-month period to the time when he so ceased (alternatively, if there has been no previous abstract, receipts and payments in the period since his appointment as receiver).

This Rule as to an abstract of receipts and payments is without prejudice to the receiver's duty to render proper accounts required otherwise than in terms of the Rule and if the receiver makes default in complying with the Rule, he is liable to a fine and, for continued contravention, to a daily default fine. [4] Reference is made to the Statement of Insolvency Practice 7 (Scotland), entitled "Preparation of Insolvency Office Holders' Receipts and Payments Accounts"[5].

1 The Scottish Rules, r 3.9(1), and Sch 5, Form 3.2 (Scot) as amended by the Scotland Act 1998 (Consequential Modifications) (No 2) Order 1999, SI 1999/1820, art 4, Sch 2, Pt II, para 141 (1), (2).
2 Ibid, r 3.9(2).
3 Ibid, r 3.9(3).
4 Ibid, r 3.9(4), (5) and Sch 4.
5 See Appendix 15.

# Committee of creditors

**10.34** Section 68 of the IA 1986 entitles unsecured creditors in a receivership situation to establish a committee. Where a meeting of such creditors is convened by the receiver under section 67(2) of the IA 1986 (it would not be only if the court otherwise directed or in certain circumstances when the company is in liquidation), the meeting may, if it thinks fit, establish a committee to exercise the functions conferred upon it by or under the IA 1986. The Rules govern the functions and proceedings of such a committee.[1] Where it is resolved by the creditors' meeting to establish a creditors' committee, the committee will consist of at least three and not more than five creditors of the company elected at the meeting,[1] any creditor of the company who has lodged a claim being eligible to be a member so long as his claim has not been rejected for the purpose of his entitlement to vote.[2] A body corporate or a partnership may be a member of the committee, but it cannot act as such otherwise than by a representative appointed and authorised under section 375 of the CA 1985 to represent the corporation at a meeting of creditors or contributories.[3] A person so authorised must produce to the chairman of the meeting a copy of the resolution from which he derives his authority and such a copy resolution must be executed in accordance with the provisions of section 36B of the 1985 Act or certified by the secretary or a director of the corporation to be a true copy.[4] Presumably in the case of a partnership a resolution by a majority of the partners will be sufficient authorisation with the copy certified by a partner. Reference is made to the Statement of Insolvency Practice 7 (Scotland), entitled "Reporting and Providing Information on their Functions to Committees in Formal Insolvencies".[5]

1 The Scottish Rules, Pt 3, Chap 3, r,3.4(1).
2 Ibid, r 3.4(2).
3 Ibid, r 3.4(3).
4 Ibid, r 3.4(3) and r 7.20(1) and (2) as applied by r 3.6.
5 See Appendix 15.

**10.35** If a committee of creditors is established, it may on giving not less than seven days' notice require the receiver's attendance before it at any reasonable time to furnish it with such information as it may reasonably require relating to the carrying out by him of his functions.[1] Where the committee so requires the receiver's attendance, the Rules provide[2] that the notice to him shall be in writing signed by the majority of the members of the committee for the time being or their representatives. The meeting at which the receiver's attendance is required must be fixed by the committee for a business day and shall be held at such time and place as the receiver determines.[3] Where the receiver attends such a meeting, the members of the committee may elect any one of their number to be chairman of the meeting in place of the receiver or any nominee of his.[4]

1 IA 1986, s 68(2).
2 The Scottish Rules, r 3.7(1).
3 Ibid, r 3.7(2).
4 Ibid, r 3.7(3).

**10.36** As regards the functions of the committee it is provided[1] that in addition to the functions conferred on it by the IA 1986, the creditors' committee will represent to the receiver the views of the unsecured creditors and shall act in relation to him in such manner as may be agreed from time to time.

1 The Scottish Rules, r 3.5.

**10.37** The Rules apply,[1] subject to certain exclusions and modifications, Chapter 7 of Part 4 of the Rules (which deal with the liquidation committee) to the creditors' committee in a receivership and to its members, substituting references to the receiver or to the creditors' committee for references to the liquidator or the liquidation committee and a reference to a creditor for a reference to the creditor member, any references to a contributory member being disregarded.

1 The Scottish Rules, r 3.6.

**10.38** As regards dealings with the company by a member of the committee, membership of the committee does not prevent a person from dealing with the company while the receiver is acting, provided that any transactions in the course of such dealings are entered into on normal commercial terms.[1] The court, however, may, on application of any person interested, set aside a transaction which appears to it to be contrary to the requirements of this Rule and in these circumstances the court may give such consequential directions as it thinks fit for compensating the company for any loss which it may have incurred in consequence of the transaction.[2]

1 The Scottish Rules, r 3.8(1).
2 Ibid, r 3.8(2).

**10.39** The statutory obligations of a receiver in relation to the giving of information do not necessarily relieve him of his duty of accountability to persons to whom he may otherwise be required to account. In an English case[1] decided on the equivalent English provisions prior to the passing of the IA 1985 it was held that a receiver appointed under a debenture providing for him to be the agent of the company was answerable to the company for the conduct of its affairs and was, therefore, under a duty to keep fuller accounts than the statutory abstracts of receipts and payments then required to be compiled and to produce these to the company when required to do so. In that case the receiver was successful in discharging the debenture holder's debt thus enabling the company to continue in business.

1 *Smiths Ltd v Middleton* [1979] 3 All ER 842.

## Enforcement provisions

**10.40** Section 69 of the IA 1986 contains provisions enabling any members or creditor of the company, the Registrar of Companies or a liquidator to apply to the court in appropriate circumstances for an order to enforce compliance by a receiver who is in default with any of his obligations as to filing, delivering or making any return, account or document or giving any notice, which order may include an award of the costs of the application against the receiver.

## Reports on conduct of directors of insolvent companies

**10.41** Administrative receivers (and other insolvency office holders) appointed after 28 April 1986 to companies are obliged to report forthwith to the Secretary of State on the conduct of persons who have been directors or shadow directors[1] of insolvent companies where such conduct makes such persons appear to administrative receivers to be unfit to be concerned in the management of a company.[2] The purpose of such reports is to enable the court on the application of the Secretary of State to make a disqualification order in the appropriate circumstances.

1 For definition see CA 1985, s 741.
2 Company Directors Disqualification Act 1986, ss 6 and 7.

**10.42** Rules were first introduced by two statutory instruments[1] making provision for the manner in which an administrative receiver (and other insolvency office holders) should make such a report. These Rules have now been replaced by those contained in a subsequent statutory instrument[2] which came into effect on 30 September 1996 and which revokes the earlier Rules[3] except to the extent that Rules 2 and 3 of the earlier Rules continue to apply and have effect in relation to:
(a) any report to which the provisions of such Rule 2 apply, and
(b) any interim return required to be made by such Rule 3.[4]

The report in the case of an administrative receiver is to be made in the manner and to the extent provided in Form D2 (Scot).[5]

1 Insolvent Companies (Reports on Conduct of Directors) (Scotland) Rules 1986, SI 1986/626 (s 59); Insolvent Companies (Reports on Conduct of Directors) (No 2) (Scotland) Rules 1986, SI 1986/1916 (s 140).
2 Insolvent Companies (Reports on Conduct of Directors) (Scotland) Rules 1996, SI 1996/1910 (s 154) as amended by the Insolvent Companies (Reports on Conduct of Directors) (Scotland) (Amendments) Rules 2001.
3 Ibid, r 7.
4 Ibid, r 3(2).
5 Ibid, r 4(3).

**10.43** Where it appears to an administrative receiver that the company has at any time become insolvent within the meaning of section 6(2) of the Company Directors Disqualification Act 1986,[1] he may, within six months of the date of his appointment, furnish a return[2] to the Secretary of State with respect to every person who:
(a) was, on the date the administrative receiver was appointed, a director or shadow director of the company, or
(b) had been such a director or shadow director at any time in the three years preceding that date.

The six months' period from the date of the receiver's appointment runs from the original appointment and not from that of a successor in office to a receiver who has vacated office.[3]

1 Rule 3(1) of the Insolvent Companies (Reports on Conduct of Directors) (No 2) (Scotland) Rules 1996, SI 1996/1910 (s 154).
2 Ibid, r 4(2).
3 Ibid, r 4(4).

**10.44** The return in the case of an administrative receiver is made in the manner and to the extent provided in Form D2 (Scot).[1] If an administrative receiver without reasonable excuse fails to comply with this Rule, he is liable on summary conviction to a fine not exceeding level 3 on the standard scale and, for continued contravention, to a daily default fine of one-tenth of level 3 on the standard scale.[2]

1 Rule 4(3) of the Insolvent Companies (Reports on Conduct of Directors) (No 2) (Scotland) Rules 1996, SI 1996/1910 (s 154).
2 Ibid, r 4(7).

**10.45** It is the duty of an administrative receiver to furnish a return to the Secretary of State no later than six months from the date of his appointment where no return has been so furnished up to one week before the expiry of such period, this duty falling on such receiver in office one week before the expiry of that period or, where none is then in office, on the administrative receiver who vacated office nearest to that time.[1] A return does not need to be provided if the administrative receiver has, since his appointment, made reports to the Secretary of State under section 7(3) of the Company Directors Disqualification Act 1986 with respect to the person[2] in question.

1 Rule (5) of the Insolvent Companies (Reports on Conduct of Directors) (No 2) (Scotland) Rules 1996, SI 1996/1910 (s 154).
2 Ibid, r 3(6).

**10.46** The Rules[1] enable the Secretary of State to apply to the court to enforce compliance by an administrative receiver with a requirement by the Secretary of State under section 7(4) of the Company Directors Disqualification Act 1986 to furnish information and books, papers and other records relevant to the conduct of a person as a director.

1 Rule 6 of The Insolvent Companies (Reports on Conduct of Directors) (No 2) (Scotland) Rules 1986, SI 1996/1910 (s 154).

## *Provisions of Rules of general application*

**10.47** Part 7 of the Rules contain provisions of general application in insolvency proceedings. Chapter 1 deals with meetings and its provisions apply to any meetings held in insolvency proceedings other than *inter alia* meetings of a creditors' committee in receivership[1] and so apply subject to any contrary provision in the IA 1986 or in the Rules, or to any direction of the court.[2] Amongst the specific matters dealt with in relation to meetings are:

(a) summoning of meetings[3]
(b) notice of meeting[4]

(c) chairman of meetings[5]
(d) quorum[6]
(e) adjournment[7]
(f) entitlement to vote (creditors)[8]
(g) chairman of meeting as proxy holder[9]
(h) resolutions[10]
(i) report of meeting[11]

1 Rule 7.1(1) of the Scottish Rules.
2 Ibid, r 7.1(2).
3 Ibid, r 7.2.
4 Ibid, r 7.3.
5 Ibid, r 7.5.
6 ibid, r 7.7.
7 Ibid, r 7.8.
8 Ibid, r 7.9.
9 Ibid, r 7.11.
10 Ibid, r 7.12.
11 Ibid, r 7.13.

**10.48** Chapter 2 deals generally with proxies and company representation at meetings of creditors or contributories of the company in insolvency proceedings and in particular:
(a) definition of proxy[1]
(b) form of proxy[2]
(c) use of proxy at meeting[3]
(d) retention of proxies[4]
(e) right of inspection[5]
(f) proxy holder with financial interest[6]
(g) representation of corporations.[7]

1 Rule 7.14 of the Scottish Rules as amended by the Insolvency (Scotland) Amendment Rules 1987, SI 1987/1921 (s 132).
2 Ibid, r 7.15.
3 Ibid, r 7.16 as amended by the Insolvency (Scotland) Amendment Rules 1987 SI 1987/1921(s 132).
4 Ibid, r 7.17.
5 Ibid, r 7.18 as amended by the Insolvency (Scotland) Amendment Rules 1987 SI 1987/1921(s 132).
6 Ibid, r 7.19 as amended by the Insolvency (Scotland) Amendment Rules 1987 SI 1987/1921(s 132).
7 Ibid, r 7.20 as amended by the Insolvency (Scotland) Amendment Rules 1987 SI 1987/1921(s 132).

**10.49** Finally Chapter 3 contains miscellaneous provisions including those dealing with:
(a) giving of notices, etc[1]
(b) sending by post[2]
(c) certificate of giving notice, etc[3]
(d) validity of proceedings[4]
(e) evidence of proceedings at meetings[5]
(f) confidentiality of documents[6]
(g) insolvency practitioners' caution[7]

(h) punishment of offences[8]
(i) fees, expenses etc[9]
(j) power of court to cure defects in procedure[10]
(k) sederunt book.[11]

1 Rule 7.21 of the Scottish Rules as amended by the Insolvency (Scotland) Amendment Rules 1987, SI 1987/1921 (s 132).
2 Ibid, r 7.22.
3 Ibid, r 7.23.
4 Ibid, r 7.24.
5 Ibid, r 7.25.
6 Ibid, r 7.27 as amended by the Insolvency (Scotland) Amendment Rules 1987, SI 1987/1921 (s 132).
7 Ibid, r 7.28.
8 Ibid, r 7.29.
9 Ibid, r 7.31.
10 Ibid, r 7.32.
11 Ibid, r 7.33 as amended by the Insolvency (Scotland) Amendment Rules 1987, SI 1987/1921 (s 132) – note changes introduced by the Insolvency (Scotland) Amendment Rules 2003, SI 2003/2111, r 6, Sch 2, para 10 relating to 'relevant date' meaning the date on which the receiver resigns and the receivership terminates without a further receiver being appointed.

## *Forms*

**10.50** The Rules contain in Schedule 5 certain forms prescribed for use in receivership pursuant to the relative provisions of the IA 1986 and the Rules. These forms are as follows:

| *Number of form* | *Nature of form* | *Section of the IA 1986 and/or Rules prescribed under* |
|---|---|---|
| Form 3.1 (Scot) | Notice Requiring Submission of Receivership Statement of Affairs | Section 66(1) and (4) and Rule 3.2(1) |
| Form 3.2 (Scot) | Receiver's Abstract of Receipts and Payments | Rule 3.9(1) and (3) |
| Form 3.3 (Scot) | Notice of Receiver's Death | Rule 3.10 |
| Form 3.4 (Scot) | Notice of Authorisation to Dispose of Secured Property | Section 61(6) |
| Form 3.5 (Scot) | Notice of Receiver's Report | Section 67(1) |
| Form 4.20 (Scot) | Certificate of Constitution of Creditors' Committee | Rule 4.42 as applied by Rule 3.6 |
| Form 4.22 (Scot) | Notice of Constitution/ Continuance of Creditors' Committee | Rule 4.42 as applied by Rule 3.6 |

CHAPTER 11

# Vacation of appointment of receiver

## General

**11.01** A receiver, whether appointed by the holder of a floating charge or by the court, vacates office if –
(a) he is removed from office by the court (ie the court having jurisdiction to wind up the company) on cause shown on the application by the holder of the floating charge by virtue of which he was appointed;[1] or
(b) he resigns office by giving notice to that effect in the prescribed manner to such persons as may be prescribed;[2] or
(c) he ceases to be qualified within the meaning of the IA 1986 to act as an insolvency practitioner in relation to the company.[3]

1 IA 1986, s 62(3).
2 Ibid, s 62(1).
3 Ibid, s 62(2).

**11.02** In the vast majority of receiverships the receiver will vacate office by resignation after disposing of any surplus funds or assets to the party entitled thereto in terms of section 60 of the IA 1986. The Regulations provide[1] that a receiver, who wishes to resign his office, shall give at least seven days' notice of his resignation to:
(a) the holder of the floating charge by virtue of which he was appointed;
(b) the holder of any other floating charge and any receiver appointed by him;
(c) the members of any committee of creditors established under section 68 of the IA 1986; and
(d) the company, or if it is then in liquidation, its liquidator.

The notice requires to specify the date on which the resignation takes effect.

1 The Scottish Rules (s 141), reg 6.

**11.03** While under the statutory provisions the only way in which a receiver can be removed from office is by an application to the court by the holder of the relevant floating charge, it has been suggested[1] that there may be circumstances in which the Court of Session, in the exercise of its nobile officium, might entertain a petition for removal presented by a person other than the holder of the charge by virtue of which he was appointed, eg by the company or another creditor. The court on presentation of any such application would presumably order the normal advertisement and service appropriate in the circumstances. An action of suspension and interdict may be instigated,[2] but this merely suspends the receiver's powers and an action of reduction would be required to remove the receiver linked to a claim for damages if the wrongful appointment has caused the company any financial loss.[3] In one instance a bank that had lent to an American holding company that had gone into Chapter Eleven appointed a receiver over the assets of a Scottish subsidiary. The US court considered this to be a breach of the Chapter Eleven protection and ordered the bank to seek the removal of the receiver. Problems which arose in relation to preferential creditors where a receiver vacated office and the preferential creditor was not paid in full on a subsequent liquidation are now historic after the abolition of crown preference.

1 *Palmer's Company Law* (24th edn) para 87.17 but not apparently in the 25th edn.
2 *Toynar Ltd v Whitbread & Co plc* 1988 SLT 433. See paras 1.38-1.41.
3 See article by Tom Hughes 'Receivership Recall' in *Insolvency Law and Practice* (Jan/Feb 1989) p 9.

## Remuneration and indemnity

**11.04** Where at any time a receiver vacates office he is entitled[1] to be paid from the property of the company subject to the floating charge in accordance with the priority provisions of section 60(1) of the IA 1986:
(a) his remuneration and any expenses which he has properly incurred; and
(b) any indemnity to which he is entitled out of the company's property.

1 IA 1986, s 62(4).

**11.05** Section 60(1) of the IA 1986 provides that the rights of the categories of persons listed in relation to the distribution of moneys by a receiver shall, except to the extent provided in any instrument, have the order of priority as set out in the section and includes along with the receiver's liabilities, expenses and remuneration any indemnity to which he is entitled out of the company's property.[1]

1 See para 9.01.

## Notification of cessation of appointment

**11.06** The holder of the floating charge by virtue of which a receiver was appointed on the receiver being removed by the court or the receiver himself in a case where the receiver ceases to act as such otherwise than by death must within 14 days of the event notify the Registrar of Companies.[1] The Registrar must enter the notice in the Register of Charges. There is a specific default provision in the subsection to the effect that the receiver or the holder, as the case may require, is liable on default, the penalty being a fine (or a daily default fine in the case of continued contravention).[1]

1 IA 1986, s 62(5) but the daily default provisions are due to be repealed by the CA 1989, ss 107, 212, Sch 15, para 3, Sch 24 as from a day to be appointed. See also the Scotland Act 1998, s 125(1) and Sch 8, para 23(1)–(3).

**11.07** Where a receiver dies, the holder of the floating charge by virtue of which he was appointed requires,[1] forthwith on his becoming aware of the death, to give notice of such death to –

(a) the Registrar of Companies;
(b) the members of the creditors' committee (if any);
(c) the company or, if in liquidation, the liquidator;
(d) the holder of any other floating charge and any receiver appointed by such holder; and
(e) the Accountant in Bankruptcy.[2]

1 The Scottish Rules (s 139), r 3.10 and Sch 5 (Form 3.3 (Scot)).
2 Scotland Act 1998 (Consequential Modifications) (No 2) Order 1999, SI 1999/1820, art 4, Sch 2, Pt II, para 141(1), (3).

**11.08** On vacating office on completion of the receivership or in consequence of the receiver ceasing to be qualified as an insolvency practitioner, the receiver requires[1], in addition to giving notice of so doing to the Registrar of Companies and the Accountant in Bankruptcy under section 62(5) of the IA 1986 to give notice of so doing within fourteen days thereof to the holder of the floating charge by virtue of which he was appointed and to the other parties specified in paragraphs (b) to (d) to Rule 3.10.[2]

1 The Scottish Rules (s 139), r 3.11.
2 Scotland Act 1998 (Consequential Modifications) (No 2) Order 1999 SI 1999/1820, Art 4 Sch 2, Pt II, para 141(1), (4).

## *Ownership of documents*

**11.09** Following the release of receivers appointed to a group of companies, the companies obtained an order requiring the receivers to deliver up all documents relating to the companies' affairs. The receivers delivered up a number of files of documents but refused to deliver others which they claimed had been created by them to advise and inform the debenture holder on the conduct of the receiverships and did not belong to the companies. It was held[1] that the ownership of documents in a receivership situation depended on whether they were created in discharge of the receiver's duties to the company or to the debenture holder. Documents created for the purpose of advising the debenture holder on the conduct of the receivership could not be the property of the company even though they could be said to relate to the company's affairs.

The fact that such documents were created for and on behalf of the receiver who was the agent of the company was not sufficient to confer ownership of the documents on the company.

1 *Gomba Holdings UK Ltd v Minories Finance Ltd* [1989] 1 All ER 261.

## Re-floating of charge

### *Single receiver*

**11.10** If on the expiry of one month following upon the removal of the receiver or his ceasing to act as such no other receiver has been appointed, the floating charge by virtue of which he was appointed:

(a) thereupon ceases to attach to the property subject to it; and
(b) again subsists as a floating charge.[1]

In the event of the company subsequently being wound up the floating charge would again crystallise[2] and in the event of such winding up commencing before the end of the one month period the floating charge presumably does not re-float. It should be noted that for the purposes of calculating the period of one month in this connection, no account is to be taken of any period during which the company is in administration.[3]

1 IA 1986, s 62(6).
2 CA 1985, s 463(1).
3 Enterprise Act 2002 (Insolvency) Order 2003, SI 2003 2096, arts 4-6, Sch, paras 8, 9 except in any case where a petition for an administration order was presented before 15 September 2003.

### *Joint receivers*

**11.11** It is competent for either the holder of a floating charge or the court to appoint joint receivers.[1] On one of such joint receivers ceasing to act either through death, resignation or removal the appointment of the other continues and in that event the floating charge by virtue of which they were appointed would not re-float by reason alone of the former receiver not being replaced.

1 IA 1986, s 51(1), (2) and (6).

## Effect of re-floating of charge

**11.12** If the claim of the holder of the floating charge has been fully satisfied then no debt is secured and the charge is fully satisfied. If such claim has not been fully satisfied then in the normal course no assets of the company will remain to further satisfy the claim secured by the charge unless at a later date assets come to light of which there was no previous knowledge. If the company is not then in liquidation and the holder of the floating charge takes the view that these assets would be attached by it on crystallisation, he could presumably reappoint a receiver.

# Floating Charge

WE, GALAXY PRODUCTS LIMITED, incorporated under the Companies Acts [ Company Number ] and having our registered office at 10 Heavenly Mansions, Pitlochry DO HEREBY BIND and OBLIGE ourselves to pay or discharge upon demand to BANCO ALBINONI plc, [Company Number ] whose registered office is at Corelli Square, Edinburgh ('the Bank') all moneys and liabilities which now are or which may at any time or from time to time be or become due, owing or incurred to the Bank by us and/or for which we now are or may at any time or from time to time be or become liable or responsible to the Bank in any manner of way or in any respect whatsoever, whether alone or jointly with any other person or persons and whether as principal debtors or guarantors or sureties including in particular but without prejudice to the foregoing generality sums of principal, interest, discounts, commissions, charges, costs and expenses, whether on or in connection with or arising out of any current or other account, order, draft, bill, promissory note, letter of credit or guarantee or any one or more of any such or otherwise howsoever; AND IT IS HEREBY PROVIDED AND DECLARED—

## First

That a certificate signed by an authorised signatory shall be sufficient (except in the case of manifest error) to fix and ascertain the whole sums, principal, interest and others, which shall be due by us and/or for which we shall be liable to the Bank as aforesaid and to constitute a balance and charge against us and no suspension of a charge or of a threatened charge for payment of the balance so constituted shall pass nor any sist of execution thereon be granted except on consignation;

## Second

That nothing herein contained shall prejudice or affect any other securities which the Bank already hold or may hereafter hold for any sum or sums due or which may after the date hereof become due by us to the Bank over any other property belonging to us, being always in the power of the Bank to allow all or any part of such securities or the property to which they relate to be disponed or sold or abandoned without applying the same or the proceeds thereof towards payment of any sum to be hereby secured, and the whole obligations hereby undertaken by us shall remain in full force and effect in the same manner and to the same extent as if no such securities had ever existed; and

## Third

That the Bank without prejudice to its rights under these presents and at its discretion, may grant to us or to any other person or persons liable with or for us any time or other indulgence and may compound with us or them, accede to trust deeds and draw dividends, and that all without notice to us or to any other person concerned;

AND IN SECURITY of the said moneys and liabilities mentioned WE DO HEREBY GRANT in favour of the Bank a FLOATING CHARGE over the whole of the property (including uncalled capital) which is or may be from time to time while this Instrument is in force comprised in our property and undertaking DECLARING AS IT IS HEREBY ESPECIALLY PROVIDED AND DECLARED THAT

## (Primo)

Except as may be otherwise agreed in writing by the Bank the Floating Charge hereby created shall rank in priority to any fixed security (other than any fixed security in favour of the Bank which shall rank in all respects in priority and in preference to the floating charge hereby created) as defined in section 70 of the Insolvency Act 1986, or any statutory amendment or re-enactment thereof for the time being in force (which Act as so amended is hereinafter referred to as 'the Act') and any other floating charge being a fixed security or floating charge which shall have been granted or created by us after our execution hereof.

## (Secundo)

At any time after any of the sums secured by the Floating Charge hereby created shall have become due and payable or the breach by us of any of the undertakings given by us in this Floating Charge or after the Bank shall have been requested by us in writing so to do but subject always to applicable law, the Bank shall have power by Instrument in writing to appoint any person or persons to be a receiver or receivers or administrator or administrators of our property and assets, and may in like manner appoint any person or persons to be a receiver or receivers in place of any receiver removed by the Court or otherwise ceasing to act or administrator or administrators in place of any administrator removed by the Court or otherwise ceasing to act. Any receiver or administrator so appointed shall have the powers conferred on a receiver by the Act.

## (Tertio)

We shall be solely responsible for the acts and defaults of any receiver appointed by the Bank hereunder and for his remuneration, costs, charges and expenses and the Bank shall have no liability or responsibility for or in respect of any act or default of any receiver so appointed or for his remuneration.

## (Quarto)

The Bank and every receiver appointed by the Bank hereunder shall be entitled to be indemnified out of the property hereby charged in respect of all liabilities and expenses incurred by them or him in the execution or purported execution of any of the powers, authorities or discretions vested in them or him in pursuance of the Act or these presents and against all actions, proceedings, costs, claims and demands in respect of any matter or thing done or omitted in any way in connection with or relating to the property hereby charged and the Bank and any such receiver may retain and pay all sums in respect of the same out of any moneys received under the powers conferred by the Act or these presents.

## (Quinto)

A demand or notice hereunder shall be in writing signed by an authorised signatory of the Bank and may (without prejudice to any other mode of service or delivery) be served on us by delivery thereof to any office of us at any place or by post addressed to us at our registered office last known to the Bank and a demand or notice so addressed and posted shall be effective twenty four hours after the date and time of such service or delivery notwithstanding that it be returned undelivered.

## (Sexto)

Paragraph 14 of Schedule B1 to the Insolvency Act 1986 (incorporated by Schedule 16 to the Enterprise Act 2002) shall apply to this Floating Charge.

AND WE UNDERTAKE to procure that while this security is in force—

(A) Without prejudice to the provisions hereinbefore contained, unless with the written consent of the Bank we shall not create or allow to come into being any security or charge upon any part of the property (including heritable, real and leasehold property wherever situated) assets, undertakings or uncalled capital of us which is subject to the security hereby created and no debentures, debenture stock or loan capital shall be created or issued and generally no monies shall be borrowed or raised or the payment thereof secured in any manner of way by us or any of our subsidiaries;

(B) (i) The whole property and corporeal assets belonging to us and our subsidiaries shall be insured and kept insured for their full replacement value against loss by fire and such other risks as the Bank may reasonably require, the relative policy or policies being endorsed or noted with reference to the interest of the Bank as the Bank may reasonably require, and we shall produce to the Bank, if so required, within fifteen days after becoming due and payable receipts for any current premiums, failing which the Bank may at our expense effect or renew any such insurances as the Bank shall deem fit; and

(ii) All monies which may at any time be received or receivable under any such insurance or any other insurance covering any of the property and corporeal assets of us or our subsidiaries against such risks as aforesaid shall be applied in replacing, restoring or reinstating the property or assets destroyed or damaged unless the Bank shall otherwise direct in writing;

(C) Except with the written consent of the Bank no part of our heritable, real or leasehold property shall be sold or otherwise disposed of and no lease or sub-lease or licence for a period exceeding three years shall be granted over any of our heritable, real or leasehold property and no other of our property or assets subject to the security hereby created shall be sold or otherwise disposed of unless in the ordinary course of our business or the business of any of our subsidiaries, which course shall not extend to the assigning or sale or in any other way factoring or discounting of debts or securities.

DECLARING that for the purposes of the foregoing undertaking 'subsidiary' shall have the meaning ascribed to it by Section 736 of the Companies Act 1985; And we bind and oblige ourselves for the whole, proper and reasonable expenses of creating and enforcing this security and also for the proper and reasonable expenses of any assignation or discharge thereof; And we warrant these presents at all hands and against all persons; And we consent to the registration hereof and of the aforesaid certificate for preservation and execution.

SIGNED for and on behalf of

GALAXY PRODUCTS LIMITED

and subscribed for it and

on its behalf at

on 20

Director

Director/Secretary

APPENDIX 2

# Extract minute of meeting of directors

EXTRACT from the MINUTES of MEETING of the DIRECTORS of GALAXY PRODUCTS LIMITED held at 10 Heavenly Mansions, Pitlochry on
20

IT WAS RESOLVED that Banco Albinoni plc be asked to appoint a receiver over the whole property comprised in the Company's property and undertaking, including uncalled capital, in terms of the floating charge in their favour dated and registered with the registrar of companies on

Certified a true extract

Director/Secretary

APPENDIX 3

# Letter of request to appoint receiver

*On letterhead of Galaxy Products Limited, 10 Heavenly Mansions, Pitlochry*

[Date]

Banco Albinoni plc,
Corelli Square,
Edinburgh

Dear Sirs,

In accordance with a resolution passed at a meeting of the directors of the Company held today, a certified copy of which is attached, we hereby formally request you to appoint a receiver over the whole property comprised in the Company's property and undertaking, including uncalled capital.

Yours faithfully,

For and on behalf of

Galaxy Products Limited

Director

Appendix 4

# Deed of appointment

WE, BANCO ALBINONI plc, incorporated under the Companies Acts and having our registered office at Corelli Square, Edinburgh, holders of a Bond and Floating Charge granted by GALAXY PRODUCTS LIMITED, [Company Number ] incorporated under the Companies Acts and having their registered office at 10 Heavenly Mansions, Pitlochry ('the Company') in our favour dated 3rd August 1982 CONSIDERING that an event has occurred on the occurrence of which we are entitled to appoint a receiver of the property which is subject to the floating charge created by the said Bond and Floating Charge; NOW THEREFORE in pursuance of the powers conferred on us by the said Bond and Floating Charge and as amended by the Insolvency Act 1986 we do hereby appoint FREDERICK GALILEO, Chartered Accountant, Saturn House, Pitlochry to be receiver of the whole of the property which is or may be from time to time, while the said Bond and Floating Charge is in force, comprised in the property and undertaking of the Company, including their uncalled capital for the time being.

SIGNED for and on behalf of

BANCO ALBINONI plc at

on 20 and

subscribed for it and on its

behalf by:

Director

Director/Secretary

Appendix 5

# Style of letter to debtor

*On letterhead of the company (In Receivership)*

[Date]

Dear Sirs,

Rococo Cocoa Co Limited (In Receivership)

I hereby intimate that I was appointed the receiver of the whole assets and undertaking of Rococo Cocoa Co Limited ('the Company') on [ 20 ].

From the records of the Company it appears that your company owes the Company an amount equal to [£ ] as specified in the enclosed statement of account.

I shall be obliged if you will please make arrangements to settle the outstanding indebtedness within [ ] days of today's date.

Yours faithfully,

Receiver

Note: The Receiver contracts only as agent of Rococo Cocoa Co Limited and without any personal liability.

APPENDIX 6

# Style of letter to creditor

[Date]

Dear Sirs,

*Rococo Cocoa Co Limited (In Receivership)*

I hereby intimate that I was appointed the receiver of the whole assets and undertaking of Rococo Cocoa Co Limited ('the Company') on [ 20 ].

Any supplies of goods or future orders for such goods to the Company as from the date of my appointment will not be accepted unless the order for such supplies or future orders is authorised by my signature or one of my managers a specimen of whose signatures is given below. Any payment for goods will be strictly on a pro-forma or cash basis unless specific arrangements in any particular case are agreed.

You will no doubt appreciate that I am unable to entertain any form of set-off in respect of monies due by you pre-receivership as against monies due by the Company post-receivership to you or vice versa. Before any transaction can be implemented between us, I require the duplicate copy of this letter to be signed by an authorised officer of your company and returned to me as soon as possible.

If you wish to submit a claim against the Company in respect of a pre-receivership transaction, I shall place any such claim for the attention of a liquidator of the Company (should one be appointed).

Yours faithfully,

Receiver

Specimen Signatures

Manager

Manager

Note: The Receiver contracts only as agent of Rococo Cocoa Co Limited and without any personal liability.

*On Duplicate*

To: The Receiver,

Rococo Cocoa Co Limited

[Date]

Dear Sir,

We acknowledge to have received from you a letter dated [ ] of which the foregoing is a duplicate copy and we hereby confirm our agreement to its terms.

Yours faithfully,

Authorised Signatory

Appendix 7

# Style of letter to landlord

*On letterhead of the company (In Receivership)*

Plutocratic Properties Limited,
Golden Egg Lane,
London, EC2

For the attention of [ ]

Dear Sirs,

Rococo Cocoa Co Limited (In Receivership)

[LF]I hereby intimate that I was appointed the receiver of the whole assets and undertaking of Rococo Cocoa Co Limited ('the Company') on [ 20 ].

I understand that a lease ('the Lease') dated [ ] existed as at the date of my appointment between you, as Landlords, and the Company relating to Unit 3 Silverside Industrial Estate, Glasgow ('the Premises'). I am presently [considering the possibility of selling the business of the Company as a going concern] [making arrangements to dispose of various assets belonging to the Company situated at the Premises] and without in any sense adopting the provisions and obligations of the Lease, I am prepared as agent of the Company to pay rent (Check the terms of the lease before sending, as 'rent' is sometimes defined in a lease to include other obligations under the lease. Many leases set out a procedure to follow on a receiver being appointed and it is necessary to determine a property strategy before corresponding with the landlord to ensure the receiver is not drawn into such a procedure which may involve the receiver taking on personal obligations.) in respect of the period of my occupation from the date of my appointment to [ ].

I am writing to you on the understanding that during the period of my occupation you will not irritate the Lease by reason of my appointment or of pre-receivership arrears or in respect of any breach of any conditions of the Lease prior to my appointment.

Please confirm your agreement by arranging for an authorised signatory to sign and return to me the duplicate copy of this letter as soon as possible.

You will appreciate that as receiver, I act as agent of the Company and without any personal liability.

Yours faithfully,

Receiver

*On Duplicate*

To: The Receiver,

Rococo Cocoa Co Limited

[Date]

Dear Sir,

[LF]We acknowledge to have received from you a letter dated [ ] of which the foregoing is a duplicate copy and we hereby confirm our agreement to its terms.

Yours faithfully,

Authorised Signatory

APPENDIX 8

# Caveat

## (a) Against Interim Interdict

Sheriffdom of Drumsheugh and West Edinburgh

CAVEAT
for
Rococo Cocoa Co Limited, incorporated in Scotland under the Companies Acts (registered No [ ]) and having its registered office at Baroque House, Louis XV Avenue, Edinburgh

Should any application be presented at the instance of Macbeth Kilts Limited, 3 Shakespeare Way, Macduff or of any other party against Rococo Cocoa Co Limited for interim interdict against (described activity likely to be complained of) or in respect of any other matter, it is requested that notice be given to the subscriber who will show cause why the application should not be granted.

In Respect Whereof

## (b) Against Liquidation

Should any petition be presented for the liquidation of Rococo Cocoa Co Limited by the Court or by order for the supervision of the Court either with or without the appointment of a provisional liquidator, it is requested that notice is given to the subscriber who will show cause why the petition should not be granted.

In Respect Whereof

## (c) Against both

Should any petition be presented for the liquidation of Rococo Cocoa Co Limited by the Court or by order for the supervision of the Court with or without the appointment of a provisional liquidator, or any application be made at the instance of any party against Rococo Cocoa Co Limited or interim interdict in respect of any matter, it is requested that notice be given to the subscriber who will show cause why the application or the petition should not be granted.

In Respect Whereof

APPENDIX 9

# Hive down agreement

AGREEMENT **dated** **200**

AMONGST

(1) [ ] **LIMITED** (registered number [ ]) incorporated under the Companies Acts and having its registered office at [ ] (**the 'Vendor'**);

(2) [ ] **LIMITED** (registered number [ ]) incorporated under the Companies Acts and having its registered office at [ ] (**the 'Purchaser'**)

(3) [ ] both of [ ] (**the 'Receivers'**);

WHEREAS

(A) The Vendor carries on the business of [ ] and certain other activities ancillary thereto.

(B) The Receivers were appointed joint receivers of the Vendor on [ ] pursuant to powers contained in a Bond and Floating Charge dated [ ] and registered with the Registrar of Companies on [ ] given by the Vendor in favour of [ ].

(C) The Purchaser is a wholly owned subsidiary of the Vendor at the Completion Date (as hereinafter defined).

(D) The Vendor has agreed to sell and the Purchaser has agreed to buy as a going concern such right, title and interest as the Vendor may have in the Business (as hereinafter defined) on the terms and conditions set out in this Agreement.

(E) The Receivers are party to this Agreement merely for the purpose of receiving the benefit of the waivers and exclusions of liabilities and indemnities in their favour in this Agreement.

IT IS AGREED **as follows:-**

## 1 Definitions

1.1 In this Agreement the following expressions shall (unless the context otherwise requires) have the following meanings respectively:-

| | |
|---|---|
| 'Act' | the Insolvency Act 1986; |
| 'Assets' | the Transferred Assets and the Leased Office Furniture. and Equipment but not the Excluded Assets; |
| 'Business' | the business of [ ] carried on from the Premises by the Vendor; |
| 'Commercial Records' | all manuals, personnel records, books of account, sales, purchase and stock records, other records, written information, data and similar items used in and/or relating to the Business; |
| 'Completion Date' | [ ]; |
| 'Contracts' | means the contracts, orders and engagements of the Business (other than the Employment Contracts) entered into or made by the Vendor and/or the Receivers in the course of the Business insofar as they have not been fully performed by the Transfer Date; |
| 'Debts' | all book and other debts and other forms of monetary indebtedness of third parties due or owing to the Vendor at the close of business on the Transfer Date together with the benefit of all rights and securities (if any) of the Vendor in relation to such unpaid amounts; |
| 'Employees' | the employees of the Vendor including those listed in Schedule 3 who will work for the Purchaser upon the transfer of the Business to the Purchaser but only become employees of the Purchaser in terms of Regulation 4 of the Transfer Regulations on the Purchaser ceasing to be a wholly owned subsidiary of the Vendor or the Business being transferred by the Purchaser to another person; |
| 'Employment Contracts' | any contract or arrangement with respect to the employment of the Employees entered into between the Vendor and the Employees whether in writing or otherwise; |
| 'Equipment' | the Fixed Equipment and the Loose Equipment; |
| 'Excluded Assets' | those assets owned by the Vendor listed in Schedule 4; |
| 'Excluded Records' | all documents relating to or created by the Receivers; |
| 'Fixed Equipment' | all plant, machinery, jigs, moulds, fixtures, fittings (not being landlord's fixtures), furniture, equipment and tools of the Vendor physically attached to the Premises at the |

Transfer Date including without prejudice to the generality of the foregoing those listed in Part 1 of Schedule 2;

'General Assets' — all intangible assets and moveable assets (not being Debts or bank accounts) relating to the Business including rights of confidence, and the benefit of Employees' restrictive covenants;

'Goodwill' — the goodwill of the Vendor in relation to the Business, including the benefit of the Vendor's trade connection with its customers and suppliers and the right to carry on the Business in succession to the Vendor from the Premises but provided always that (save as herein provided) nothing in this Agreement shall impose any obligation upon the Vendor or the Receivers to change the name of the Vendor;

'Intellectual Property' — all business names, customer information, patterns, drawings, product names, intellectual property and design rights including (without limitation) trade marks or trade names (whether registered or not) all patents, patent applications, registered designs, copyright, letters patent, service marks, inventions, trade secrets, confidential information and know-how (together with the benefit but subject to the burden of any licences, consents or permissions relating to them) of or used by the Vendor in the Business as at the Transfer Date but only insofar as they can lawfully be assigned without infringing the rights of any third party or breaching any obligations to any third party or breaching any statutory obligation;

'Leased Office Furniture and Equipment' — the office furniture and. equipment leased or hired to the Vendor or on hire purchase to the Vendor, used in the Business and listed in Schedule 1;

'Liabilities' — all and any actions, proceedings, claims, demands, costs, expenses, penalties and liabilities whatsoever brought against or incurred directly or indirectly by the Vendor and the Receivers or any of them;

'Loose Equipment' — all loose plant, machinery, jigs, moulds, equipment, tools, furniture, trade utensils and other moveables owned and used by the

| | |
|---|---|
| | Vendor in connection with the Business as at the Transfer Date whether or not located at the Premises and being part of the items listed in Part 2 Schedule 2; |
| 'Premises' | the property specified in Schedule 5; |
| 'Receivers' Solicitors' | [ ]; |
| 'ROT Stock' | those items of the Stock (if any) in the possession of the Vendor on the Transfer Date which are subject to third party claims including without prejudice to the generality of the foregoing liens and such items which have been supplied to the Vendor pursuant to contracts in respect of which the supplier has claimed reservation of title in those items; |
| 'Purchaser's Solicitors' | ; |
| 'Stock' | all stock in trade and raw materials (other than any items which have been invoiced but not delivered to customers and the ROT Stock) of the Vendor which are situated on the Premises at the Transfer Date; |
| 'Third Party Assets' | assets in the possession of the Vendor immediately prior to the Transfer Date, but to which the Vendor has no entitlement, as against any third party, to transfer under this Agreement; |
| 'Transfer Date' | [ ] hours on [ ]; |
| 'Transferred Assets' | the Stock, the Goodwill, the Equipment, the Premises, the General Assets, the Work in Progress and the Intellectual Property but excluding the Excluded Assets; |
| 'Transfer Regulations' | the Transfer of Undertaking (Protection of Employment) Regulations 1981; |
| 'VAT' | Value Added Tax; |
| 'VATA' | Value Added Tax Act 1994; and |
| 'Work in Progress' | the benefit of the Contracts and all partly completed goods or services allocated by the Vendor or the Receivers to the Contracts. |

1.2 Each reference to a statute or provision of a statute shall be construed as a reference to that statute or provision as amended, extended or re-enacted by any other statute or provision of statute.

1.3 The headings in this Agreement are for convenience only and shall not affect its interpretation.

## 2 Sale of Business

2.1 The Vendor acting by the Receivers shall sell and the Purchaser shall purchase the Business incorporating the Transferred Assets as at and from the Transfer Date.

2.2 The Transferred Assets will be sold by the Vendor subject to any subsisting reservation of title claims, charges, liens, encumbrances or other third party rights whatsoever.

2.3 Failure by the Vendor to pass any title, right or interest to or in any of the Transferred Assets shall not be a ground enabling the Purchaser to rescind or treat the Vendor as in breach of this Agreement or to claim a reduction of the purchase price.

## 3 Consideration

The aggregate consideration (exclusive of VAT and stamp duty land tax) for the sale and purchase pursuant to clause 2 shall be such amount as may be agreed between the Vendor and the Purchaser or such amount as Messrs [ ], Chartered Accountants, acting as experts and not as arbiters shall certify to be a fair and proper consideration, the decision of Messrs [ ] being final and binding on the parties.

## 4 Payment of price

4.1 The consideration together with any VAT and any stamp duty fund tax payable by the Purchaser in terms of or arising out of this Agreement under and in terms of clause 3 hereof shall be entered in the books of the Vendor and the Purchaser as secured debts repayable on demand to the Vendor.

4.2 By way of security for the consideration referred to in clause 4.1, the Purchaser shall, at the expense of the Purchaser, forthwith upon the execution of this Agreement create a floating charge over all its whole undertaking and assets in favour of the Vendor.

## 5 Completion

5.1 Completion of the sale and purchase specified in this Agreement shall take place on the Transfer Date when, unless otherwise agreed between the Vendor and the Purchaser:

- 5.1.1 title to all assets comprised within the Business and sold pursuant to this Agreement which are capable of transfer by delivery thereof and such delivery shall be deemed to have taken place on the Transfer Date;
- 5.1.2 the Vendor will give entry and vacant possession to the Premises and the Vendor and the Receivers shall implement the provisions of paragraph 4 of Schedule 5; and
- 5.1.3 the provisions of clause 4 hereof shall be implemented.

## 6 The ROT Stock

6.1 The Purchaser shall automatically acquire from the Vendor such right, title and interest as the Vendor may have in any asset forming part of the ROT Stock but the Parties recognise that the ROT Stock may not be the property of the Vendor being subject to third party claims including (but not limited to) reservation of title claims and liens. This Agreement has been entered into and the price for the Stock agreed on the specific basis that the Purchaser shall accept full responsibility in respect of all and any third party claims and that the Purchaser bears the full risk of them. The Purchaser agrees that it shall have no right to rescind avoid or vary this Agreement or to claim damages or a reduction in the consideration paid or payable under the terms of this Agreement if it transpires that the Purchaser shall have acquired no title to all or any of the ROT Stock.

6.2 Insofar as reasonably practicable, the Purchaser shall separate the ROT Stock from the Stock immediately following the Transfer Date and in any event shall keep full details of any of the ROT Stock which is sold, used for manufacturing or otherwise dealt with.

6.3 The Purchaser undertakes that it shall immediately on receiving written demand notify the Vendor and the Receivers in writing and will indemnify them against all and any Liabilities in respect of the ROT Stock whether or not arising before the Transfer Date.

6.4 If third party claims are made against the Vendor or the Receivers in respect of the ROT Stock the Vendor or the Receivers shall immediately notify the Purchaser.

6.5 Subject to the consent of the Receivers (which consent shall not be unreasonably withheld or delayed) and the Purchaser indemnifying the Vendor and the Receivers (by deposit of funds if so required by the Receivers) against all Liabilities immediately as they arise on a full indemnity basis the Purchaser shall be entitled to resist and/or settle any claim in respect of the ROT Stock in the name of the Vendor and to have the conduct both of such resistance and of any negotiation relating to it.

6.6 The Receivers shall provide the Purchaser (at the Purchaser's expense on a full indemnity basis) with such assistance as it may reasonably require in connection with those claims referred to in clause 6.5 above.

## 7 The Intellectual Property

7.1 The Purchaser acknowledges that the Intellectual Property may be subject to restrictions, limitations or deficiencies and that it may not be sufficiently transferable to the Purchaser to enable the Business to be carried on efficiently or at all. The Purchaser undertakes to make its own enquiries into all such matters and agrees that it shall have no right to rescind, avoid or vary this Agreement or to claim damages or a reduction in the consideration paid or payable under the terms of this Agreement if it transpires that the Purchaser shall not have acquired title to all or any of the Intellectual Property.

7.2 The Purchaser undertakes with the Vendor and the Receivers not to use the Intellectual Property without first obtaining any necessary consents and to indemnify the Vendor and the Receivers on a full indemnity basis immediately upon written demand against all and any Liabilities arising directly or indirectly because of the transfer of the Intellectual Property to the Purchaser or its purported sale under the terms of this Agreement or the use of it by the Purchaser or by any transferee or licensee from the Purchaser.

## 8 The Contracts

8.1 The Purchaser acknowledges that the Vendor may not be entitled to assign, and shall not be entitled to novate the Contracts and to that extent does not purport to do so.

8.2 The Vendor shall, for a period of two weeks from the Transfer Date, use reasonable efforts to co-operate with the Purchaser in trying to persuade the other parties to any Contract to have it assigned or novated to the Purchaser, although it is agreed and understood that the Vendor shall have little or no influence with such other parties and shall be under no obligation to make any payments directly or indirectly to such other parties to persuade them to do so.

8.3 The Purchaser undertakes to observe, fulfil, perform and discharge the outstanding obligations and liabilities of the Vendor and the Receivers under the Contracts so that if and to the extent that it is not possible or reasonably practicable for any of the Contracts to be novated or assigned to the Purchaser the Purchaser covenants with and undertakes to the Vendor and the Receivers that the Purchaser shall complete the Contract as agent for the Vendor.

8.4 The Purchaser accepts the risk that some or all of the Contracts may prior to the Transfer Date have been breached or terminated and that the contracting party may refuse to continue with the performance of its contractual obligations on the same terms and conditions at all or unless the Purchaser is willing to remedy such breach and that further a contracting party may exercise or purport to exercise rights of set off or counterclaim against the Purchaser.

8.5 Without limitation to the above, the Purchaser shall indemnify the Vendor and the Receivers on a full indemnity basis from and against all and any Liabilities arising in respect of all and any Contracts whether they have arisen prior to or on or after the Transfer Date and whether or not arising out of the Purchaser's acts or omissions.

8.6 If the Receivers have ordered any goods or services prior to the Transfer Date and those goods have not been delivered or services not performed prior to the Transfer Date the Purchaser shall pay for them together with any applicable VAT within two Business Days of delivery of an invoice in respect of them by the Receivers.

8.7 Notwithstanding any provision contained in this Agreement to the contrary it is agreed that all Debts arising in respect of goods and services under the

Contracts rendered prior to the Transfer Date shall be for the benefit of and belong to the Vendor.

## 9 Disclaimer

9.1 All representations, warranties or conditions express or implied, statutory or otherwise in respect of the Transferred Assets or any of the rights titles and interests agreed to be sold are expressly excluded (including, without limitation, warranties and conditions as to existence, quiet possession, title, merchantable quality, fitness for purpose and description).

9.2 The parties agree that the provisions of this Agreement are fair and reasonable and accord with normal practice in all the circumstances of a sale by a company in receivership in the light of the following matters:

9.2.1 full opportunity for inspection investigation and analysis of the Transferred Assets has been afforded to the Purchaser and its representatives and agents;

9.2.2 the Purchaser is fully aware that it must rely on its own inspection investigation and analysis or that of its professional advisers and that defects may not be apparent from such investigation and analysis;

9.2.3 the Purchaser is satisfied that it has made or has had made on its behalf all appropriate inspections, investigations and analyses as at the date hereof in view of the terms of this Agreement; and

9.2.4 the intervention of insolvency, the Receivers' limited knowledge of the Business and the constraints on selling necessarily imposed on the Vendor in such circumstances.

9.3 The Purchaser takes the Transferred Assets in their present state and condition subject to all faults.

9.4 The Purchaser is satisfied:

9.4.1 as to the condition and situation of the Transferred Assets;

9.4.2 as to the fitness and suitability of the Transferred Assets for such purpose as the Purchaser intends;

9.4.3 that no reliance is placed or has been placed on any information, warranty, statement or silence on the part of the Vendor or of the directors of the Vendor or of the Receivers or any of their partners, solicitors, valuers, auctioneers, employees or agents or all or any of them; and

9.4.4 that there is the possibility that the Purchaser may not acquire title to all or any of the Transferred Assets together with the fact that the Purchaser would have no remedy under this Agreement should that happen, and this is reflected in the price payable hereunder.

## 10 The Commercial Records

10.1 The Vendor shall allow the Commercial Records to remain in the possession of the Purchaser until at least six months from the Completion Date (or until the appointment of a liquidator of the Vendor, if earlier).

10.2 The Purchaser agrees to keep the Commercial Records safely on behalf of the Vendor and agrees not to remove or permit the removal of them from the United Kingdom.

10.3 The Purchaser may make copies of the Commercial Records at its own expense.

10.4 The Purchaser will allow the Vendor and/or the Receivers their representatives and agents, reasonable facilities without charge to inspect and copy any of the Commercial Records and shall return them to the Vendor forthwith on demand after the end of six months or after the appointment of any liquidator of the Vendor.

## 11 Debts

All sums paid to the Purchaser by debtors of the Vendor in or towards discharge of the Debts shall belong to the Vendor and the Purchaser will account to the Vendor or the Receivers, while they are joint receivers of the Vendor without set off, on a weekly basis. In the event that the Vendor or the Receivers receive any monies which are properly, payable to the Purchaser, they will forward such monies to the Purchaser on a weekly basis.

## 12 Third Party Assets

12.1 The Purchaser agrees:

12.1.1 not to hold itself out as owner of any of the Third Party Assets;

12.1.2 not to sell, offer for sale, assign or charge any of the Third Party Assets.

12.2 The Purchaser will keep the Third Party Assets:

12.2.1 in its possession;

12.2.2 at its expense; and

12.2.3 in as good repair as they were in at the Completion Date.

12.3 The Purchaser will deliver the Third Party Assets to the Receivers on request and will indemnify and keep indemnified the Receivers and the Vendor against all claims, demands and costs arising directly or indirectly from the giving of possession of the Third Party Assets to the Purchaser or from the breach by the Purchaser of its obligations under this clause.

## 13 Employees

13.1 In respect that the Purchaser is a wholly owned subsidiary of the Vendor the Transfer Regulations provide that on the transfer of the Business to a wholly owned subsidiary such as the Purchaser, that the novation of the employment liabilities under Regulation 5 of the Transfer Regulations is deemed not to have been effected until immediately before:

13.1.1 the Purchaser ceases (otherwise than by reason of its being wound up) to be a wholly owned subsidiary of the Vendor; or

13.1.2 the Business acquired in terms of this Agreement by the Purchaser is transferred by the Purchaser to another person.

13.2 Until such time as the transfer in accordance with clause 13.1 hereof takes place the Vendor and the Purchaser between themselves, albeit that the Employees will remain employed by the Vendor, agree that they will treat the Employees as if they were deemed to be employed by the Purchaser and the Purchaser acknowledges and accepts that:

13.2.1 notwithstanding that the Vendor before the Transfer Date may have issued notices of dismissal by reasons of redundancy to all or some of the Employees it is possible that the Employees so notified or some of them may have a claim against the Purchaser;

13.2.2 any of the Employees employed at the Transfer Date who may be subsequently engaged by the Purchaser may have retained their continuity of employment and their rights and benefits under the Employment Contract; and

13.2.3 any of the Employees not subsequently so engaged or who are so engaged on different terms of employment may have claims against the Purchaser;

but in any event the Purchaser agrees that it shall have no claim or rights to compensation whatsoever against the Vendor or the Receivers.

13.3 The Purchaser shall indemnify the Vendor against the cost of all wages, national insurance, PAYE and pension contributions, holiday pay, employers' liability and third party insurance premiums and against all claims, demands and liabilities (including all employers' liabilities for personal injury or otherwise) in respect of the Employees accruing from and including the Transfer Date and which would otherwise fall to be paid out of funds available in the receivership of the Vendor. Payment of the aforesaid items shall:

13.3.1 in the case of items ascertainable in advance be made not less than three days before the Vendor is liable to make such payments; and

13.3.2 in the case of all other items be made forthwith upon any amount being agreed or determined.

The Vendor shall apply all such payments made by the Purchaser in terms of this clause 13.3 in paying such wages, national insurance, PAYE and pension contributions and others promptly when due.

13.4 Neither the Vendor nor the Receivers shall incur any liability to the Purchaser in respect of any failure of the Employees or any negligence on the part of the Employees or in respect of any matter arising out of this clause, provided always that the Vendor and the Receivers shall maintain and pay all premiums relating to current employees' liability insurances.

13.5 The Purchaser will indemnify and keep the Vendor and the receivers indemnified on a full indemnity basis from and against all liabilities in respect of the Employees.

## 14 Value Added Tax

It is the intention of the parties hereto that the provisions of section 49 of the Value Added Tax Act 1994/Value Added Tax Regulations 1995 (SI 1995/2518)/ Value Added Tax (Special Provisions) Order 1995 (SI 1995/1268) shall apply to the transfer of the Business hereunder and accordingly:

14.1 each of the parties hereto shall on the Completion Date give notice of such transfer to the appropriate office of HM Customs and Excise in accordance with such regulations and requirements as may be applicable;

14.2 the Vendor shall on completion deliver to the Purchaser all such records as are referred to in the said section 49 unless the Commissioners of HM Customs and Excise, at the request of the Vendor, otherwise direct; and

14.3 the Purchaser warrants to the Vendor that it is duly and properly registered for VAT.

## 15 Passing of Risk

The Transferred Assets will be at the risk of the Purchaser from the Transfer Date and title thereto shall pass to the Purchaser when the aggregate consideration for the Business to be paid at the Completion Date has been paid in full.

## 16 The Premises

The sale and purchase of the Premises shall be subject to the terms and conditions set out in Schedule 5.

## 17 Set-Off

Without prejudice to any other provisions contained in this Agreement the Purchaser shall not be entitled to set-off any-claims it may have against the Vendor or the Receivers or any of them or exercise any liens whatsoever against or make any deduction on its own account from any moneys cheques bankers' draft or other negotiable instruments payable to the Vendor or the Receivers pursuant to this Agreement but such moneys cheques bankers' drafts or other negotiable instruments shall be paid in full forthwith upon the same being due in accordance with the terms of this Agreement.

## 18 Exclusion of Receivers' liability

For the avoidance of doubt, it is hereby declared that in the negotiation, execution and implementation of this Agreement, the Receivers were, are and will be acting only as agents for the Vendor and it is hereby acknowledged by the Purchaser that the Receivers shall not be personally liable on this Agreement or under any deed or other document executed in consequence of it or under any associated or collateral agreement or arrangement and if any personal liability of the Receivers which would in terms of the Act arise, it is hereby expressly excluded.

## 19 Change of Name

19.1 The Receivers shall use its reasonable endeavours to procure that, in so far as it is competent and legal for them to do so, the name of the Vendor is, at the expense of the Purchaser, changed as soon as practicable after the Completion Date and in any event not later than 28 days after the Completion Date to a name which does not include the name [ ] and shall not impede or prevent the Purchaser incorporating a company or companies bearing such names or changing the names of existing companies to a name including the word [ ].

19.2 Compliance with section 216 of the Act shall be a matter for the Purchaser and any person to whom those provisions apply and neither the Vendor nor the Receivers shall have any responsibility in that connection and the Purchaser hereby agrees to indemnify and keep indemnified the Vendor and the Receivers in respect of all matters arising out of such compliance.

## 20 Apportionments

20.1 Expenses of the Business (including salaries, wages and other emoluments of employees, rent, rates, vehicle licence payments, the costs of telephone and other services and all other normal expenses incidental to the running of the Business) shall to the extent that they relate to any period prior to the Completion Date, be the liability of the Vendor and the Receivers.

20.2 Expenses of the Business incurred prior to the Completion Date shall, to the extent that they relate to any period after the Completion Date, be payable by the Purchaser and where such expenses are or have been paid by the Vendor or the Receivers they shall be reimbursed to the Vendor and the Receivers by the Purchaser within seven days of being requested in writing by the Vendor and the Receivers.

## 21 General

21.1 This Agreement, supersedes all prior agreements between the parties in relation to its subject matter (all of which prior agreements are hereby terminated) and contains the entire agreement between the parties.

21.2 This Agreement shall be construed without reference to its clause headings.

21.3 The parties shall use their best endeavours to keep the terms of this Agreement confidential and no announcement regarding this transaction or the terms of it shall be made whether to the public, trade or otherwise except with the prior consent of the other party (such consent not to be unreasonably withheld) or in accordance with the Receivers' obligations to complete and file statutory returns or implement their statutory obligations.

21.4 The Purchaser will permit the Receivers, their staff, representatives and agents such facilities as they may reasonably require to enable the Receivers, to complete their duties as receivers in relation to the Vendor.

21.5 Time shall be of the essence of this Agreement.

21.6 This Agreement shall, so far as it remains to be performed, continue in full force and effect notwithstanding completion.

21.7 The Purchaser shall pay all stamp duty land tax arising on this Agreement and all agreements or other documents entered into to give effect to it.

## 22 Notices

22.1 Any notice or document required or permitted to be given under this Agreement may be given personally or by sending it by registered post to the registered office of the party to which the notice is to be given or to such other address as shall have been last notified to the other party for the purpose.

22.2 Any notice or document given by post shall be deemed to have been given 48 hours after it was, registered and posted and in proving that any notice or document was so given it shall be necessary only to prove that it was properly addressed, registered and posted.

## 23 Expenses

The Vendor, the Receivers and the Purchaser shall each be responsible for their respective legal and other expenses incidental to the preparation and execution and carrying into effect of this Agreement.

## 24 Exclusion of Third Party Rights

This Agreement does not create any right enforceable by a person not party to it.

## 25 Proper Law

This Agreement and all documents drafted and executed in pursuance this Agreement shall in all respects be interpreted in accordance with the law of Scotland and the parties hereto agree to submit to the exclusive jurisdiction of the Scottish courts.

IN WITNESS WHEREOF these presents consisting of this and the preceding pages, together with the five Schedules annexed hereto are subscribed as follows:

SIGNED for and on behalf of )

[ ] in receivership )

by [ ] as one of the Receivers in his )

capacity as their agent and without personal )

liability thereof all at [ ] )

on the [ ] )

in the presence of:- )

Witness

Address

Occupation

SIGNED for and on behalf of )

[ ] )

at [ ] on the [ )

] in the presence of:- )

Witness

Address

Occupation

This is the SCHEDULE 1 referred to in the Hive Down Agreement amongst [ ], [ ] and [ ] dated [ ].

### Leased Office Furniture and Equipment

All of that Office Furniture and Equipment which is situate at the Premises and which is used in connection with the Business and which is held by the Vendor subject to a lease or leases [or any third party rights].

This is the SCHEDULE 2 referred to in the Hive Down Agreement amongst [ ], [ ] and [ ] dated [ ].

## Part 1 – Fixed Equipment

## Part 2 – Loose Equipment

This is the SCHEDULE 3 referred to in the Hive Down Agreement amongst [ ], [ ] and [ ] dated [ ].

**The Employees**

This is the SCHEDULE 4 referred to in the Hive Down Agreement amongst [ ], [ ] and [ ] dated [ ].

### The Excluded Assets

1 all cash in hand or with bankers of the Vendor, all cheques, bills or other securities, the benefit of all deposits paid to suppliers or any other third parties and deposits or prepayments by third parties to the Vendor;
2 the Debts;
3 the benefit of all policies of assurance, insurance and indemnity and of all guarantees given to the Vendor;
4 the Commercial Records;
5 the statutory books of the Vendor;
6 the Excluded Records.

This is the SCHEDULE 5 referred to in the Hive Down Agreement amongst [ ], [ ] and [ ] dated [ ].

### The Premises

### Description of Property

1. Vacant possession of the Premises will be given to the Purchaser on the Completion Date [subject to the leases/rights of occupancy specified in Part [ ] of this Schedule.]
2. The minerals are included in the sale only in so far as the Vendor has right thereto.
3. The Purchaser shall be deemed to have satisfied itself as to the nature and extent of the title to the Premises tendered by the Vendor.
4. At the Completion Date the Vendor and the Receivers will grant and deliver to the Purchaser (subject to the terms of paragraph 3 hereof) validly executed Dispositions of the Premises, and will deliver or exhibit a valid marketable title to the Premises and will deliver or exhibit either (a) Searches in the Property Register for a period of twenty years and in the Personal Register for the prescriptive period showing no incumbrances or diligences which would preclude the Receiver from granting a good title; or (b) if at the Completion Date the provisions of section 2(1) or 3(3) of the Land Registration (Scotland) Act 1979 (which together with all amendments thereof and statutory instruments and rules issued thereunder are hereinafter referred to as 'the LR(S) Act') apply to the transfer of the Vendor's interest in the Premises, the Vendor and the Receivers will provide a Form 10 Report

brought down to a date as near as practicable to the Completion Date and showing no entries adverse to the Vendor's and the Receivers' interest (the cost (if any) of said Report being the responsibility of the Purchaser) and, in addition, the Vendor and the Receivers will furnish to the Purchaser such documents and evidence, including a plan as the Keeper may require to enable the Keeper to issue a Land Certificate in name of the Purchaser as the registered proprietor of the Premises and containing no exclusion of indemnity in terms of section 12(2) of the LR(S) Act.

The Land Certificate or Certificates to be issued to the Purchaser will disclose no entry, deed or diligence prejudicial to the Purchaser's interest other than such as are created by or against the Purchaser. Notwithstanding delivery of the said Dispositions this paragraph will remain in full force and effect and may be founded upon.

On Completion Date letters of obligation will be granted by the Vendor's solicitors and the Receivers' solicitors in usual terms (it being understood that any inhibitions or other diligences disclosed in the Personal Searches against the Vendor in respect of the period after the date of appointment of the Receivers shall not be discharged). No Companies Charges Register Search will be produced by the Vendor nor will any obligation whatsoever be given by the Vendor in respect of the Companies Charges Register.

5. In so far as the Receivers will be a party to any Dispositions of the Premises, warrandice from fact and deed only will be given by them and the Vendor will grant warrandice excluding said leases and rights of occupancy.

APPENDIX 10

# Agreement for the sale of the business

AGREEMENT **dated** **200**

AMONGST

(1) [ ] **LIMITED** (registered number [ ]) incorporated under the Companies Acts and having its registered office at [ ] (**the 'Vendor'**);

(2) [ ] **LIMITED** (registered number [ ]) incorporated under the Companies Acts and having its registered office at [ ] (**the 'Purchaser'**)

(3) [ ] both of [ ] (**the 'Receivers'**);

WHEREAS

(A) The Vendor carries on the business of [ ] and certain other activities ancillary thereto.

(B) The Receivers were appointed joint receivers of the Vendor on [ ] pursuant to powers contained in a Bond and Floating Charge dated [ ] and registered with the Registrar of Companies on [ ] given by the Vendor in favour of [ ].

(C) The Vendor has agreed to sell and the Purchaser has agreed to buy as a going concern such right, title and interest as the Vendor may have in the Business (as hereinafter defined) on the terms and conditions set out in this Agreement.

(D) The Receivers are party to this Agreement merely for the purpose of receiving the benefit of the waivers and exclusions of liabilities and indemnities in their favour in this Agreement.

IT IS AGREED **as follows:**

## 1 Definitions

1.1 In this Agreement the following expressions shall (unless the context otherwise requires) have the following meanings respectively:-

'Act' the Insolvency Act 1986;

| | |
|---|---|
| 'Assets' | the Transferred Assets and the Leased Office Furniture. and Equipment but not the Excluded Assets; |
| 'Business' | the business of [ ] carried on from the Premises by the Vendor; |
| 'Commercial Records' | all manuals, personnel records, books of account, sales, purchase and stock records, other records, written information, data and similar items used in and/or relating to the Business; |
| 'Completion Date' | [ ]; |
| 'Contracts' | means the contracts, orders and engagements of the Business (other than the Employment Contracts) entered into or made by the Vendor and/or the Receivers in the course of the Business insofar as they have not been fully performed by the Transfer Date; |
| 'Debts' | all book and other debts and other forms of monetary indebtedness of third parties due or owing to the Vendor at the close of business on the Transfer Date together with the benefit of all rights and securities (if any) of the Vendor in relation to such unpaid amounts; |
| 'Employees' | the employees of the Vendor who become employees of the Purchaser upon the transfer of the Business to the Purchaser including those listed in Schedule 3; |
| 'Employment Contracts' | any contract or arrangement with respect to the employment of the Employees entered into between the Vendor and the Employees whether in writing or otherwise; |
| 'Equipment' | the Fixed Equipment and the Loose Equipment; |
| 'Excluded Assets' | those assets owned by the Vendor listed in Schedule 4; |
| 'Excluded Records' | all documents relating to or created by the Receivers; |
| 'Fixed Equipment' | all plant, machinery, jigs, moulds, fixtures, fittings (not being landlord's fixtures), furniture, equipment and tools of the Vendor physically attached to the Premises at the Transfer Date including without prejudice to the generality of the foregoing those listed in Part 1 of Schedule 2; |
| 'General Assets' | all intangible assets and moveable assets (not being Debts or bank accounts) relating to the Business including rights of confidence, and |

| | |
|---|---|
| | the benefit of Employees' restrictive covenants; |
| 'Goodwill' | the goodwill of the Vendor in relation to the Business, including the benefit of the Vendor's trade connection with its customers and suppliers and the right to carry on the Business in succession to the Vendor from the Premises but provided always that (save as herein provided) nothing in this Agreement shall impose any obligation upon the Vendor or the Receivers to change the name of the Vendor; |
| 'Intellectual Property' | all business names, customer information, patterns, drawings, product names, intellectual property and design rights including (without limitation) trade marks or trade names (whether registered or not) all patents, patent applications, registered designs, copyright, letters patent, service marks, inventions, trade secrets, confidential information and know-how (together with the benefit but subject to the burden of any licences, consents or permissions relating to them) of or used by the Vendor in the Business as at the Transfer Date but only insofar as they can lawfully be assigned without infringing the rights of any third party or breaching any obligations to any third party or breaching any statutory obligation; |
| 'Leased Office Furniture and Equipment' | the office furniture and. equipment leased or hired to the Vendor or on hire purchase to the Vendor, used in the Business and listed in Schedule 1; |
| 'Liabilities' | all and any actions, proceedings, claims, demands, costs, expenses, penalties and liabilities whatsoever brought against or incurred directly or indirectly by the Vendor and the Receivers or any of them; |
| 'Loose Equipment' | all loose plant, machinery, jigs, moulds, equipment, tools, furniture, trade utensils and other moveables owned and used by the Vendor in connection with the Business as at the Transfer Date whether or not located at the Premises and being part of the items listed in Part 2 Schedule 2; |
| 'Premises' | the property specified in Schedule 5; |
| 'Receivers' | [ ]; |

| | |
|---|---|
| Solicitors' | |
| 'ROT Stock' | those items of the Stock (if any) in the possession of the Vendor on the Transfer Date which are subject to third party claims including without prejudice to the generality of the foregoing liens and such items which have been supplied to the Vendor pursuant to contracts in respect of which the supplier has claimed reservation of title in those items; |
| 'Purchaser's Solicitors' | ; |
| 'Stock' | all stock in trade and raw materials (other than any items which have been invoiced but not delivered to customers and the ROT Stock) of the Vendor which are situated on the Premises at the Transfer Date; |
| 'Third Party Assets' | assets in the possession of the Vendor immediately prior to the Transfer Date, but to which the Vendor has no entitlement, as against any third party, to transfer under this Agreement; |
| 'Transfer Date' | [ ] hours on [ ]; |
| 'Transferred Assets' | the Stock, the Goodwill, the Equipment, the Premises, the General Assets, the Work in Progress and the Intellectual Property but excluding the Excluded Assets; |
| 'Transfer Regulations' | the Transfer of Undertaking (Protection of Employment) Regulations 1981; |
| 'VAT' | Value Added Tax; |
| 'VATA' | Value Added Tax Act 1994; and |
| 'Work in Progress' | the benefit of the Contracts and all partly completed goods or services allocated by the Vendor or the Receivers to the Contracts. |

1.2 Each reference to a statute or provision of a statute shall be construed as a reference to that statute or provision as amended, extended or re-enacted by any other statute or provision of statute.

1.3 The headings in this Agreement are for convenience only and shall not affect its interpretation.

## 2 Sale of Business

2.1 The Vendor acting by the Receivers shall sell and the Purchaser shall purchase the Transferred Assets as at and from the Transfer Date.

2.2 The Transferred Assets will be sold by the Vendor subject to any subsisting reservation of title claims, charges, liens, encumbrances or other third party rights whatsoever.

2.3 Failure by the Vendor to pass any title, right or interest to or in any of the Transferred Assets shall not be a ground enabling the Purchaser to rescind or treat the Vendor as in breach of this Agreement or to claim a reduction of the purchase price.

## 3 Consideration

3.1 The aggregate consideration for the sale and purchase pursuant to clause 2 shall be the sum of [£ ] together with any VAT thereon (if any) which shall be for the account of the Purchaser and such consideration shall be apportioned between the Transferred Assets as follows:

| | | £ |
|---|---|---|
| i) | Goodwill | |
| ii) | Premises | |
| iii) | Equipment | |
| iv) | Work in Progress | |
| v) | Intellectual Property | |
| vi) | Stock | |
| vii) | General Assets | |
| | TOTAL | |

3.2 In ascertaining the value of Stock, the Vendor, the Receiver and the Purchaser shall procure that a physical stock-taking is carried out as at the Transfer Date and the value thereof agreed or determined in accordance with clause 3.4 as soon as practicable thereafter.

3.3 The aggregate consideration specified in clause 3.1 shall be increased or decreased (as the case may be) by the amount by which the value of Stock forming part of the Business as at the Transfer Date exceeds or is less than [ ] as the case may be and the amount of such increase or decrease shall be refunded by the Purchaser to the Vendor or by the Vendor to the Purchaser (as the case may be) within seven days of being agreed or determined in accordance with clause 3.4. The valuation of the Stock shall be ascertained on the basis of lower of cost or net realisable value as at the Transfer Date, using the same principles and methods consistent with those employed over the last three accounting periods by the Vendor in the valuation for the purposes of year end stock valuation excluding for such purposes slow moving or obsolete or damaged stock.

3.4 In the event of the stocktaking and/or the valuation referred to in clause 3.2 not being agreed within 14 days of the Transfer Date the stocktaking and/or valuation shall be referred to a valuer, acting as an expert and not as an arbiter appointed by agreement between the parties or failing agreement as nominated on the application of any party thereto by the President for the time being of the Institute of Chartered Accountants of Scotland whose decisions shall be final and binding on the parties.

## 4 Completion

4.1 Completion will take place on the Completion Date at the offices of the Receivers' Solicitors or wherever they shall direct.

4.2 At completion the Purchaser will pay to the Receivers' Solicitors on behalf of the Vendor and the Receivers (and as the Purchaser is hereby expressly authorised by the Vendor and the Receivers to pay) by direct bank transfer or otherwise as the Receivers shall direct an amount equal to [ ] to the Receivers' Solicitors bank account [ ] as agents for the Vendor and the Receivers whose receipt shall be a sufficient discharge to the Purchaser and such amount shall represent the aggregate of the consideration specified in clause 3.

4.3 In consideration of and subject to the Purchaser discharging its obligations pursuant to clause 4.2, the Vendor shall:

4.3.1 allow the Purchaser to take possession of such of the Transferred Assets as are transferable by delivery;

4.3.2 hold all other Transferred Assets on trust for the Purchaser absolutely pending assignation;

4.3.3 deliver to the Purchaser a VAT invoice for any element of the consideration upon which VAT is payable;

4.3.4 deliver to the Purchaser duly executed dispositions of the Premises.

4.4 Following completion of this Agreement the Vendor and/or the Receivers (but only so long as they retain their office in relation to the Vendor and provided that all and any personal liability of the Receivers is expressly excluded) shall at the Purchaser's expense and on a full indemnity basis:

4.4.1 execute and deliver such (if any) documents (in such form as the Receivers' Solicitors shall approve); and

4.4.2 do such further acts,

as shall be reasonably necessary to vest in the Purchaser such right, title and interest as the Vendor may have to the Transferred Assets transferred to the Purchaser in accordance with the terms of this Agreement.

## 5 The ROT Stock

5.1 The Purchaser shall automatically acquire from the Vendor such right, title and interest as the Vendor may have in any asset forming part of the ROT Stock but the Parties recognise that the ROT Stock may not be the property of the Vendor being subject to third party claims including (but not limited to) reservation of title claims and liens. This Agreement has been entered into and the price for the Stock agreed on the specific basis that the Purchaser shall accept full responsibility in respect of all and any third party claims and that the Purchaser bears the full risk of them. The Purchaser agrees that it shall have no right to rescind avoid or vary this Agreement or to claim damages or a reduction in the consideration paid or payable under the terms of this Agreement if it transpires that the Purchaser shall have acquired no title to all or any of the ROT Stock.

5.2 Insofar as reasonably practicable, the Purchaser shall separate the ROT Stock from the Stock immediately following the Transfer Date and in any event shall keep full details of any of the ROT Stock which is sold, used for manufacturing or otherwise dealt with.

5.3 The Purchaser undertakes that it shall immediately on receiving written demand notify the Vendor and the Receivers in writing and will indemnify them against all and any Liabilities in respect of the ROT Stock whether or not arising before the Transfer Date.

5.4 If third party claims are made against the Vendor or the Receivers in respect of the ROT Stock the Vendor or the Receivers shall immediately notify the Purchaser.

5.5 Subject to the consent of the Receivers (which consent shall not be unreasonably withheld or delayed) and the Purchaser indemnifying the Vendor and the Receivers (by deposit of funds if so required by the Receivers) against all Liabilities immediately as they arise on a full indemnity basis the Purchaser shall be entitled to resist and/or settle any claim in respect of the ROT Stock in the name of the Vendor and to have the conduct both of such resistance and of any negotiation relating to it.

5.6 The Receivers shall provide the Purchaser (at the Purchaser's expense on a full indemnity basis) with such assistance as it may reasonably require in connection with those claims referred to in clause 5.5 above.

## 6 The Intellectual Property

6.1 The Purchaser acknowledges that the Intellectual Property may be subject to restrictions, limitations or deficiencies and that it may not be sufficiently transferable to the Purchaser to enable the Business to be carried on efficiently or at all. The Purchaser undertakes to make its own enquiries into all such matters and agrees that it shall have no right to rescind, avoid or vary this Agreement or to claim damages or a reduction in the consideration paid or payable under the terms of this Agreement if it transpires that the Purchaser shall not have acquired title to all or any of the Intellectual Property.

6.2 The Purchaser undertakes with the Vendor and the Receivers not to use the Intellectual Property without first obtaining any necessary consents and to indemnify the Vendor and the Receivers on a full indemnity basis immediately upon written demand against all and any Liabilities arising directly or indirectly because of the transfer of the Intellectual Property to the Purchaser or its purported sale under the terms of this Agreement or the use of it by the Purchaser or by any transferee or licensee from the Purchaser.

## 7 The Contracts

7.1 The Purchaser acknowledges that the Vendor may not be entitled to assign, and shall not be entitled to novate the Contracts and to that extent does not purport to do so.

7.2 The Vendor shall, for a period of two weeks from the Transfer Date, use reasonable efforts to co-operate with the Purchaser in trying to persuade the other parties to any Contract to have it assigned or novated to the

Purchaser, although it is agreed and understood that the Vendor shall have little or no influence with such other parties and shall be under no obligation to make any payments directly or indirectly to such other parties to persuade them to do so.

7.3 The Purchaser undertakes to observe, fulfil, perform and discharge the outstanding obligations and liabilities of the Vendor and the Receivers under the Contracts so that if and to the extent that it is not possible or reasonably practicable for any of the Contracts to be novated or assigned to the Purchaser the Purchaser covenants with and undertakes to the Vendor and the Receivers that the Purchaser shall complete the Contract as agent for the Vendor.

7.4 The Purchaser accepts the risk that some or all of the Contracts may prior to the Transfer Date have been breached or terminated and that the contracting party may refuse to continue with the performance of its contractual obligations on the same terms and conditions at all or unless the Purchaser is willing to remedy such breach and that further a contracting party may exercise or purport to exercise rights of set off or counterclaim against the Purchaser.cu:

7.5 Without limitation to the above, the Purchaser shall indemnify the Vendor and the Receivers on a full indemnity basis from and against all and any Liabilities arising in respect of all and any Contracts whether they have arisen prior to or on or after the Transfer Date and whether or not arising out of the Purchaser's acts or omissions.

7.6 If the Vendor or the Receivers have ordered any goods or services prior to the Transfer Date and those goods have not been delivered or services not performed prior to the Transfer Date the Purchaser shall pay for them together with any applicable VAT within two Business Days of delivery of an invoice in respect of them by the Receivers.

7.7 Notwithstanding any provision contained in this Agreement to the contrary it is agreed that all Debts arising in respect of goods and services under the Contracts rendered prior to the Transfer Date shall be for the benefit of and belong to the Vendor.

## 8 Disclaimer

8.1 All representations, warranties or conditions express or implied, statutory or otherwise in respect of the Transferred Assets or any of the rights titles and interests agreed to be sold are expressly excluded (including, without limitation, warranties and conditions as to existence, quiet possession, title, merchantable quality, fitness for purpose and description).

8.2 The parties agree that the provisions of this Agreement are fair and reasonable and accord with normal practice in all the circumstances of a sale by a company in receivership in the light of the following matters:

8.2.1 full opportunity for inspection investigation and analysis of the Transferred Assets has been afforded to the Purchaser and its representatives and agents;

8.2.2 the Purchaser is fully aware that it must rely on its own inspection investigation and analysis or that of its professional advisers and that defects may not be apparent from such investigation and analysis;

8.2.3 the Purchaser is satisfied that it has made or has had made on its behalf all appropriate inspections, investigations and analyses as at the date hereof in view of the terms of this Agreement; and

8.2.4 the intervention of insolvency, the Receivers' limited knowledge of the Business and the constraints on selling necessarily imposed on the Vendor in such circumstances.

8.3 The Purchaser takes the Transferred Assets in their present state and condition subject to all faults.

8.4 The Purchaser is satisfied:

8.4.1 as to the condition and situation of the Transferred Assets;

8.4.2 as to the fitness and suitability of the Transferred Assets for such purpose as the Purchaser intends;

8.4.3 that no reliance is placed or has been placed on any information, warranty, statement or silence on the part of the Vendors or of the directors of the Vendors or of the Receivers or any of their partners, solicitors, valuers, auctioneers, employees or agents or all or any of them; and

8.4.4 that there is the possibility that the Purchaser may not acquire title to all or any of the Transferred Assets as the Vendor may only pass such title as it may have together with the fact that the Purchaser would have no remedy under this Agreement should that happen, and this is reflected in the price payable hereunder.

## 9 The Commercial Records

9.1 The Vendor shall allow the Commercial Records to remain in the possession of the Purchaser until at least six months from the Completion Date (or until the appointment of a liquidator of the Vendor, if earlier).

9.2 The Purchaser agrees to keep the Commercial Records safely on behalf of the Vendor and agrees not to remove or permit the removal of them from the United Kingdom.

9.3 The Purchaser may make copies of the Commercial Records at its own expense.

9.4 The Purchaser will allow the Vendor and/or the Receivers their representatives and agents, reasonable facilities without charge to inspect and copy any of the Commercial Records and shall return them to the Vendor forthwith on demand after the end of six months or after the appointment of any liquidator of the Vendor.

## 10 Debts

All sums paid to the Purchaser by debtors of the Vendor in or towards discharge of the Debts shall belong to the Vendor and the Purchaser will account to the Vendor or the Receivers, while they are joint receivers of the Vendor without set off, on a weekly basis. In the event that the Vendor or the Receivers receive any monies which are properly, payable to the Purchaser, they will forward such monies to the Purchaser on a weekly basis.

## 11 Third Party Assets

11.1 The Purchaser agrees:
- 11.1.1 not to hold itself out as owner of any of the Third Party Assets;
- 11.1.2 not to sell, offer for sale, assign or charge any of the Third Party Assets.

11.2 The Purchaser will keep the Third Party Assets:
- 11.2.1 in its possession;
- 11.2.2 at its expense; and
- 11.2.3 in as good repair as they were in at the Completion Date.

11.3 The Purchaser will deliver the Third Party Assets to the Receivers on request and will indemnify and keep indemnified the Receivers and the Vendor against all claims, demands and costs arising directly or indirectly from the giving of possession of the Third Party Assets to the Purchaser or from the breach by the Purchaser of its obligations under this clause.

## 12 Employees

12.1 The Purchaser acknowledges and accepts that:
- 12.1.1 as a consequence of the Transfer Regulations and notwithstanding that the Vendor before the Transfer Date may have issued notices of dismissal by reason of redundancy to all or some of the Employees it is possible that the Employees so notified or some of them may have a claim against the Purchaser;
- 12.1.2 any of the Employees employed at the Transfer Date who may be subsequently engaged by the Purchaser may have retained their continuity of employment and their rights and benefits under the Employment Contracts; and
- 12.1.3 any of the Employees not subsequently so engaged or who are so engaged on different terms of employment may have claims against the Purchaser;

but in any event the Purchaser agrees that it shall have no claims or rights to compensation whatsoever against the Vendor or the Receivers.

12.2 The Purchaser will indemnify and keep the Vendor and the Receivers indemnified on a full indemnity basis from and against all Liabilities in respect of the Employees.

## 13 Value Added Tax

It is the intention of the parties hereto that the provisions of section 49 of the Value Added Tax Act 1994/Value Added Tax Regulations 1995 (SI 1995/2518)/ Value Added Tax (Special Provisions) Order 1995 (SI 1995/1268) shall apply to the transfer of the Business hereunder and accordingly:

13.1 each of the parties hereto shall on the Completion Date give notice of such transfer to the appropriate office of HM Customs and Excise in accordance with such regulations and requirements as may be applicable;

13.2 the Vendor shall on completion deliver to the Purchaser all such records as are referred to in the said section 49 unless the Commissioners of HM Customs and Excise, at the request of the Vendor, otherwise direct; and

13.3 the Purchaser warrants to the Vendor that it is duly and properly registered for VAT.

## 14 Passing of Risk

The Transferred Assets will be at the risk of the Purchaser from the Transfer Date and such title as the Vendor may have thereto shall pass to the Purchaser when the aggregate consideration for the Business to be paid at the Completion Date has been paid in full.

## 15 The Premises

The sale and purchase of the Premises shall be subject to the terms and conditions set out in Schedule 5.

## 16 Interest

If completion is delayed beyond the Completion Date for any reason not attributable to default or delay of the Vendor or the Receivers, interest shall be payable (as well before as after judgment) to the Vendor in respect of the consideration due under clause 3 of this Agreement at the rate of 3 per cent over [ ] base rate current from time to time, such interest to be calculated on a daily basis and to be compounded at monthly rests.

## 17 Set-Off

Without prejudice to any other provisions contained in this Agreement the Purchaser shall not be entitled to set-off any claims it may have against the Vendor or the Receivers or any of them or exercise any liens whatsoever against or make any deduction on its own account from any moneys cheques bankers' draft or other negotiable instruments payable to the Vendor or the Receivers pursuant to this Agreement but such moneys cheques bankers' drafts or other negotiable instruments shall be paid in full forthwith upon the same being due in accordance with the terms of this Agreement.

## 18 Exclusion of Receivers' liability

For the avoidance of doubt, it is hereby declared that in the negotiation, execution and implementation of this Agreement, the Receivers were, are and will be acting only as agents for the Vendor and it is hereby acknowledged by the

Purchaser that the Receivers shall not be personally liable on this Agreement or under any deed or other document executed in consequence of it or under any associated or collateral agreement or arrangement and if any personal liability of the Receivers which would in terms of the Act arise, it is hereby expressly excluded. The Purchaser acknowledges that the Receivers are party to this Agreement merely for the purpose of receiving the benefit of the waivers and exclusions of liabilities and indemnities in their favour in this Agreement.

## 19 Change of Name

19.1 The Receivers shall use their reasonable endeavours to procure that, in so far as it is competent and legal for them to do so, the name of the Vendor is, at the expense of the Purchaser, changed as soon as practicable after the Completion Date and in any event not later than 28 days after the Completion Date to a name which does not include the name [ ] and shall not impede or prevent the Purchaser incorporating a company or companies bearing such names or changing the names of existing companies to a name including the word [ ].

19.2 Compliance with section 216 of the Act shall be a matter for the Purchaser and any person to whom those provisions apply and neither the Vendor nor the Receivers shall have any responsibility in that connection and the Purchaser hereby agrees to indemnify and keep indemnified the Vendor and the Receivers in respect of all matters arising out of such compliance.

## 20 Apportionments

20.1 Expenses of the Business (including salaries, wages and other emoluments of employees, rent, rates, vehicle licence payments, the costs of telephone and other services and all other normal expenses incidental to the running of the Business) shall to the extent that they relate to any period prior to the Completion Date, be the liability of the Vendor and the Receivers.

20.2 Expenses of the Business incurred prior to the Completion Date shall, to the extent that they relate to any period after the Completion Date, be payable by the Purchaser and where such expenses are or have been paid by the Vendor or the Receivers they shall be reimbursed to the Vendor and the Receivers by the Purchaser within seven days of being requested in writing by the Vendor and the Receivers.

## 21 General

21.1 This Agreement, supersedes all prior agreements between the parties in relation to its subject matter (all of which prior agreements are hereby terminated) and contains the entire agreement between the parties.

21.2 This Agreement shall be construed without reference to its clause headings.

21.3 The parties shall use their best endeavours to keep the terms of this Agreement confidential and no announcement regarding this transaction or the terms of it shall be made whether to the public, trade or otherwise except with the prior consent of the other party (such consent not to be unreasonably withheld) or in accordance with the Receivers' obligations to complete and file statutory returns or implement their statutory obligations.

21.4 The Purchaser will permit the Receivers, their staff representatives and agents such facilities as they may reasonably require to enable the Receivers, to complete their duties as receivers in relation to the Vendor.

21.5 Time shall be of the essence of this Agreement.

21.6 This Agreement shall, so far as it remains to be performed, continue in full force and effect notwithstanding completion.

21.7 The Purchaser shall pay all stamp duty land tax arising on this Agreement and all agreements or other documents entered into to give effect to it.

## 22 Notices

22.1 Any notice or document required or permitted to be given under this Agreement may be given personally or by sending it by registered post to the registered office of the party to which the notice is to be given or to such other address as shall have been last notified to the other party for the purpose.

22.2 Any notice or document given by post shall be deemed to have been given 48 hours after it was, registered and posted and in proving that any notice or document was so given it shall be necessary only to prove that it was properly addressed, registered and posted.

## 23 Expenses

The Vendor, the Receivers and the Purchaser shall each be responsible for their respective legal and other expenses incidental to the preparation and execution and carrying into effect of this Agreement.

## 24 Exclusion of Third Party Rights

This Agreement does not create any right enforceable by a person not party to it.

## 25 Proper Law

This Agreement and all documents drafted and executed in pursuance of this Agreement shall in all respects be interpreted in accordance with the law of Scotland and the parties hereto agree to submit to the exclusive jurisdiction of the Scottish courts.

IN WITNESS WHEREOF these presents consisting of this and the preceding pages, together with the five Schedules annexed hereto are subscribed as follows:

SIGNED for and on behalf of )

[ ] in receivership )

by [ ] as [one of the Receivers] in his )

capacity as their agent and without personal )

liability thereof all at [ ] )

on the [ ] )

in the presence of:- )

Witness

Address

Occupation

SIGNED for and on behalf of )

[ ] )

at [ ] on the [ )

] in the presence of:- )

Witness

Address

Occupation

This is the SCHEDULE 1 referred to in the Asset Sale Agreement amongst [ ], [ ] and [ ] dated [ ]

**Leased Office Furniture and Equipment**

All of that Office Furniture and Equipment which is situate at the Premises and which is used in connection with the Business and which is held by the Vendor subject to a lease or leases [or any third party rights].

This is the SCHEDULE 2 referred to in the Asset Sale Agreement amongst [ ], [ ] and [ ] dated [ ]

**Part 1 – Fixed Equipment**

**Part 2 – Loose Equipment**

This is the SCHEDULE 3 referred to in the Asset Sale Agreement amongst [ ], [ ] and [ ] dated [ ]

## The Employees

This is the SCHEDULE 4 referred to in the Asset Sale Agreement amongst [ ], [ ] and [ ] dated [ ]

### The Excluded Assets

1 all cash in hand or with bankers of the Vendor, all cheques, bills or other securities, the benefit of all deposits paid to suppliers or any other third parties and deposits or prepayments by third parties to the Vendor;
2 the Debts;
3 the benefit of all policies of assurance, insurance and indemnity and of all guarantees given to the Vendor;
4 the Commercial Records;
5 the statutory books of the Vendor;
6 the Excluded Records.

This is the SCHEDULE 5 referred to in the Asset Sale Agreement amongst [ ], [ ] and [ ] dated [ ]

## The Premises

## Description of Property

1. Vacant possession of the Premises will be given to the Purchaser on the Completion Date [subject to the leases/rights of occupancy specified in Part [ ] of this Schedule.]
2. The minerals are included in the sale only in so far as the Vendor has right thereto.
3. The Purchaser shall be deemed to have satisfied itself as to the nature and extent of the title to the Premises tendered by the Vendor.
4. At the Completion Date the Vendor acting through the Receivers will grant and deliver to the Purchaser (subject to the terms of paragraph 3 hereof) validly executed Disposition of the Premises, and will deliver or exhibit a valid marketable title to the Premises and will deliver or exhibit either (a) Searches in the Property Register for a period of twenty years and in the Personal Register for the prescriptive period showing no incumbrances or diligences which would preclude the Receiver from granting a good title; or (b) if at the Completion Date the provisions of section 2(1) or 3(3) of the Land Registration (Scotland) Act 1979 (which together with all amendments thereof and statutory instruments and rules issued thereunder are hereinafter referred to as 'the LR(S) Act') apply to the transfer of the Vendor's interest in the Premises, the Vendor and the Receiver will provide a Form 10 Report brought down to a date as near as practicable to the Completion Date and showing no entries adverse to the Vendor's and the Receivers' interest (the cost (if any) of said Report being the responsibility of the Purchaser) and, in addition, the Vendor and the Receiver will furnish to the Purchaser such documents and evidence, including a plan as the Keeper may require to enable the Keeper to issue a Land Certificate in name of the Purchaser as the registered proprietor of the Premises and containing no exclusion of indemnity in terms of section 12(2) of the LR(S) Act.
   The Land Certificate or Certificates to be issued to the Purchaser will disclose no entry, deed or diligence prejudicial to the Purchaser's interest other than such as are created by or against the Purchaser. Notwithstanding delivery of the said Disposition this paragraph will remain in full force and effect and may be founded upon.
   On Completion Date letters of obligation will be granted by the Vendor's solicitors and the Receivers' solicitors in usual terms (it being understood

that any inhibitions or other diligences disclosed in the Personal Searches against the Vendor in respect of the period after the date of appointment of the Receivers shall not be discharged). No Companies Charges Register Search will be produced by the Vendor nor will any obligation whatsoever be given by the Vendor in respect of the Companies Charges Register.

5. In so far as the Receiver will be a party to any Dispositions of the Premises, warrandice from fact and deed only will be given by them and the Vendor will grant warrandice excluding said leases and rights of occupancy.

[Signed by the parties to the Agreement]

APPENDIX 11

# Form of letter for collection of book debts

*On letterhead of the Purchaser to be typed in duplicate*

The Receiver,
Galaxy Products Limited,
10 Heavenly Mansions,
Pitlochry

[Date]

Dear Sir,

We refer to the Agreement ('the Agreement') among Galaxy Products Limited ('Galaxy'), you acting as receiver of Galaxy and us executed or about to be executed by Galaxy, you and us.

Definitions used in the Agreement shall bear the same meanings for the purposes of this letter.

We confirm that an arrangement has been agreed between us whereby we will in consideration of the goodwill of the Business, collect all book debts due to you as at the [Transfer Date] ('the Book Debts') in terms of the List of Debtors ('the List of Debtors') annexed and signed as relative hereto. The terms of the arrangement may be summarised as follows:

(1) We hereby undertake to collect the Book Debts specified in the List of Debtors on your behalf.

(2) Payment of all amounts collected by us shall be made to you within ten days of our receipt of the same and a breakdown of such amounts shall be made by the Purchaser showing the invoices to which such amounts relate.

(3) Subject to paragraph (4) hereof, you hereby reserve the right to recover the Book Debts in any manner you, at your sole discretion, consider appropriate, including without prejudice to the said generality, litigation, sequestration or liquidation.

(4) If we have not collected all or any of the Book Debts within 90 days of the date hereof, you shall be entitled to collect the same in such manner as you, at your sole discretion, may consider appropriate.
(5) We shall not be entitled to issue credit notes or in any other way absolve any debtor from full payment of his debt or grant any indulgence in respect thereof.
(6) We shall maintain separate records for each of the Book Debts which are recovered and make these available to you or your agents at any reasonable time or times.
(7) You shall be responsible for the maintenance of your sales ledgers.
(8) Title to and beneficial ownership of the Book Debts shall at all times remain vested in Galaxy and you respectively.
(9) We shall maintain a separate bank account for the collection of the Book Debts and obtain for you a letter from our bank confirming that they have no rights in terms of any floating charge that they hold in respect of such sums collected.

Yours faithfully,

On Duplicate

[Date]

I acknowledge to have received from you a letter dated [ ] of which the foregoing is a duplicate and as agent of Galaxy Products Limited and, without in any way accepting personal liability therefor, I confirm my agreement of its terms and conditions.

Receiver

Appendix 12

# Form of letter of indemnity to receiver in the case of early delivery of the business

To:

The Receiver,
Galaxy Products Limited,
10 Heavenly Mansions,
Pitlochry

[Date]

Dear Sirs,

We refer to the negotiations which are presently being conducted between us relating to the sale of the business of Galaxy Products Limited.

In view of the fact that we anticipate being able to conclude a formal agreement with you very shortly and in consideration of a continuance of such business in the ordinary course, we wish to confirm the following arrangements with you. All obligations and indemnities granted by us shall take effect and continue in full force and effect as from the opening of business on [ ] and shall so continue until the earlier of completion of such sale or the recall in writing by us to you of the terms of this letter ('the period of obligation and indemnity'). Without prejudice thereto, we shall in the event of such recall, honour all obligations and indemnities granted by us arising in respect of the period of obligation and indemnity. During the period of obligation and indemnity, we:

(1) shall, after due and proper consultation with you, order in our name all such raw materials and other supplies as may be reasonably required for the proper continuance of such business and we shall be responsible for payment for all such raw materials and other supplies.
(2) hereby undertake in conjunction with you to use all such raw materials and other supplies in a proper and timeous manner so as to ensure an orderly and efficient continuance of such business and fulfilment of all current contracts to your customers.

(3) hereby undertake to make proper insurance arrangements on a fully comprehensive basis against all normal commercial business risks including without prejudice thereto suitable provisions for the acts or omissions of any of our employees or agents.
(4) shall be responsible for the payment of all salaries and other overheads relating to such business but, as agreed with you, we shall be entitled to retain all profit during the period of obligation and indemnity.
(5) acknowledge and confirm that, notwithstanding the arrangements specified in this letter, title to and the beneficial ownership of such business shall always remain with Galaxy Products Limited.
(6) shall not intimate the existence of this agreement to anyone without your prior written approval and shall keep the terms hereof confidential.

We hereby indemnify you and we shall keep you indemnified against all liability howsoever arising in respect of any of the matters specified in this letter and in this connection, an indemnity against any such liability shall be deemed to include an indemnity against all demands, claims, costs, charges and expenses made, suffered or incurred by reason of or in connection with any such liability.

]Yours faithfully,

[Probative Execution by the Purchaser]

Appendix 13

# Share purchase agreement

AGREEMENT

BETWEEN

GALAXY PRODUCTS LIMITED (1)

(IN RECEIVERSHIP)

ROCOCO COCOA CO LIMITED (2)

AGREEMENT

Amongst

(1) GALAXY PRODUCTS LIMITED incorporated under the Companies Acts (Company Number [ ]) and having its registered office at 10 Heavenly Mansions, Pitlochry ("the Vendor") acting by its receiver, FREDERICK GALILEO, Chartered Accountant, Saturn House, Pitlochry ("the Receiver")

(2) ROCOCO COCOA CO LIMITED incorporated under the Companies Acts (Company Number [ ]) and having its registered office at Baroque House, Louis XC Avenue, Edinburgh ("the Purchaser")

and

(3) FREDERICK GALILEO, Chartered Accountant, Saturn House, Pitlochry ("the Receiver")

## 1. Introduction

(1) In terms of an agreement dated [ ] between the Vendor and the Company (as hereinafter defined) ("the Hive-Down Agreement") the

business and undertaking of the Vendor relating to the manufacture, distribution and sale of space invaders and associated products carried on by the Vendor at Pitlochry was transferred to the Company (as hereinafter defined), the consideration herefor being satisfied by way of an inter-company loan due by the Company (as hereinafter defined) to the Vendor.

(2) The Company (as hereinafter defined) which before the purchase of such business had never traded was incorporated on [ ] under the Companies Acts as a company limited by share and has a nominal capital of £100 divided into 100 shares of £1 each two of which have been issued and are in the beneficial ownership of the Vendor.

(3) The Vendor has agreed to sell and the Purchaser has agreed to purchase the whole of the issued share capital of the Company (as hereinafter defined) on the terms and conditions set out in this Agreement.

(4) The Receiver is party to this Agreement merely for the purpose of receiving the benefit of the waivers and exclusions of liabilities and indemnities in his favour in this Agreement.

## 2. Interpretation

(1) In this Agreement unless the context otherwise requires:
"the Company" means Orinoco Cocoa Co Limited registered in Scotland [Company Number ];
"Completion Date" means [ ]; and
"Shares" means the two issued shares of £1 each in the Company.

(2) The headings in this Agreement are inserted for convenience only and shall not affect its interpretation.

## 3. Sale of shares

The Vendor acting by the Receiver as the beneficial owner shall sell to the Purchaser and the Purchaser shall purchase from the Vendor as from the Completion Date the Shares being the whole of the issued share capital of the Company free from all options, liens, charges and encumbrance and with all rights now or hereafter becoming attached thereto.

## 4. Consideration

The consideration for the sale of the Shares shall be the sum of TWO POUNDS (£2).

## 5. Completion

(1) On the Completion Date the Vendor shall:

(1) deliver to the Purchaser one duly executed copy of the Hive-Down Agreement;

(2) deliver to the Purchaser duly executed transfers of the Shares in favour of the Purchaser and/or its nominee(s) together with relative share certificates;

(3) deliver to the Purchaser the books of the Company duly written up;

(4) deliver the title deeds, leases, other documents of title, licences and registrations relating to the assets and business of the Company;

(5) procure that a meeting of the directors of the Company shall be held and that at such meeting:

  (a) such transfers shall, subject to being duly stamped, be approved and registered by the directors;

  (b) such persons as shall be nominated by notice in writing given by the Purchaser to the directors of the Company shall be appointed as directors and the secretary respectively of the Company; and

  (c) all the directors of the Company (other than those appointed pursuant to the provisions of clause 5(5)(b)) and the secretary of the Company shall resign office as directors and the secretary respectively of the Company and from any other office or employment which they have respectively with the Company and that with immediate effect and without payment of compensation for loss of office or any other payment whatsoever and will deliver letters of resignation to that effect; and

(6) deliver to the Purchaser a duly executed discharge of the floating charge by the Company in favour of the Vendor.

(2) On the Completion Date, the Purchaser shall pay to Messrs [ ] Solicitors, [ ] on behalf of the Vendor and the Receiver (and as the Purchaser is hereby expressly authorised by the Vendor and the Receiver to pay) by banker's draft drawn on Banco Albinoni plc [Address] to the said Messrs [ ] an amount equal to [ ] representing the aggregate consideration of the Shares (£2) and full settlement of the inter-company loan referred to in clause 1(1).

## 6. Announcements

Neither the Vendor nor the Receiver nor the Purchaser shall make or authorise any announcement or public disclosures concerning the subject matter of this Agreement, either to the press or to shareholders or otherwise, except on terms and in manner mutually agreed between them.

## 7. Exclusion of Receiver's liability

In the negotiation, execution and implementation of this Agreement, the Receiver was, is and will be acting only as agent for the Vendor and the Receiver shall not be personally liable on this Agreement or under any deed or other document executed in consequence of it or under any associated or collateral agreement or arrangement.

## 8. Notices

(1) Any notice hereunder may be served by hand or by first class pre-paid post through the recorded delivery system addressed to the party to be served at such party's address as hereinbefore appearing.

(2) Any notice served by post shall be deemed to have been served twenty-four hours after the same is put into the post.

(3) Any notice requiring to be served on the Vendor and the Receiver shall be sufficiently served by being served on the Receiver.

## 9. Expenses

The Vendor and the Purchaser shall each be responsible for their respective expenses incidental to the preparation and execution and carrying into effect of this Agreement.

## 10. General

In so far as not implemented on the Completion Date this Agreement shall remain in full force and effect and the undertakings and warranties provided for herein shall be enforceable at the instance of the Vendor, the Receiver and the Purchaser and their respective assignees.

## 11. Prior agreements

This Agreement supersedes all previous agreements between the parties in relation to the matters herein specified and represents the entire understanding of the parties in relation thereto.

## 12. Proper law

This Agreement and all documents drafted and executed in pursuance of this Agreement shall in all respects b0e interpreted in accordance with the law of Scotland and the parties hereto agree to submit to the exclusive jurisdiction of the Scottish Courts.

SIGNED for and on behalf of GALAXY PRODUCTS LIMITED at

on 20 BY FREDERICK GALILEO as Receiver

thereof before the undernoted witness:

Witness

Address

Occupation

SIGNED for and on behalf of ROCOCO COCOA CO LIMITED at

on 20 by:

Director

Director/Secretary

# Exceptions to Restrictions on Appointment of Receivers

Section 72A of the IA 1986 was inserted by S250 of EA 2002, (as amended by the Insolvency Act 1986 (Amendment) (Administrative Receivership and Urban Regeneration etc.) Order 2003 (SI 2003/1832) and the Insolvency Act 1986 (Amendment) (Administrative Receivership and Capital Market Arrangements) Order 2003 (S1 2003/1468)). It prohibits the appointment of a receiver by the holder of a qualifying floating charge in respect of a floating charge created on or after 15th September 2003. It is impossible to contract out of these provisions. There are exceptions to this specified in Sections 72B and 72GA and in terms of section 72H(2) the Secretary of State may by order, create additional exceptions to 72A (1) or (2) or amend any of sections 72B to 72G.

## 72B First exception: capital market

(1) Section 72A does not prevent the appointment of an administrative receiver in pursuance of an agreement which is or forms part of a capital market arrangement if –

(a) a party incurs or, when the agreement was entered into was expected to incur, a debt of at least £50 million under the arrangement, and
(b) the arrangement involves the issue of a capital market investment.

(2) In subsection (1) –

'capital market arrangement' means an arrangement of a kind described in paragraph 1 of Schedule 2A, and
'capital market investment' means an investment of a kind descried in paragraph 2 or 3 of that Schedule

*NOTES*

Commencement: 15 September 2003

## 72C Second exception: public-private partnership

(1) Section 72A does not prevent the appointment of an administrative receiver of a project company of a project which –

(a) is a public-private partnership project, and
(b) includes step-in rights.

(2) In this section 'public-private partnership project' means a project –

(a) the resources for which are provided partly by one or more public bodies and partly by one or more private persons, or
(b) which is designed wholly or mainly for the purpose of assisting a public body to discharge a function.

(3) In this section –
'step-in rights' has the meaning given by paragraph 6 of Schedule 2A and 'project company' has the meaning given by paragraph 7 of that Schedule.

*NOTES*

Commencement: 15 September 2003

## 72D Third exception: utilities

(1) Section 72A does not prevent the appointment of an administrative receiver of a project company of a project which –
(a) is a utility project, and
(b) includes step-in rights

(2) In this section –
(a) 'utility project' means a project designed wholly or mainly for the purpose of a regulated business,
(b) 'regulated business' means a business of a kind listed in paragraph 10 of Schedule 2A,
(c) 'step-in rights' has the meaning given by paragraph 6 of that Schedule, and
(d) 'project company' has the meaning given by paragraph 7 of that Schedule.

*NOTES*

Commencement: 15 September 2003

## 72DA Exception in respect of urban regeneration projects

(1) Section72A does not prevent the appointment of an administrative receiver of a project company of a project which –
(a) is designed wholly or mainly to develop land which at the commencement of the project is wholly or partly in a designated disadvantaged area outside Northern Ireland, and
(b) includes step-in rights.

(2) In subsection (1) 'develop' means to carry out –
(a) building operations,
(b) any operation for the removal of substances or waste from land and the levelling of the surface of the land, or
(c) engineering operations in connection with the activities mentioned in paragraph (a) or (b).

(3) In this section –
'building' includes any structure or erection, and any part of a building as so defined but does not include plant and machinery comprised in a building.
'building operations' includes –
(a) demolition of buildings,
(b) filling in of trenches,

(c) rebuilding,
(d) structural alterations of, or additions to, buildings and
(e) other operations normally undertaken by a person carrying on business as a builder,

'designated disadvantaged area' means an area designated as a disadvantaged area under section 92 of the Finance Act 2001,
'engineering operations' includes the formation and laying out of means of access to highways,
'project company' has the meaning given by paragraph 7 of Schedule 2A,
'step-in rights' has the meaning given by paragraph 6 of that Schedule,
'substance' means any natural or artificial substance whether in solid or liquid form or in the form of a gas or vapour, and
'waste' includes any waste materials, spoil, refuse or other matter deposited on land.

*NOTES*

Commencement: 15 September 2003

## 72E Fourth exception: project finance

(1) Section 72A does not prevent the appointment of an administrative receiver of a project company of a project which –
(a) is a financed project, and
(b) includes step-in rights

(2) In this section –
(a) a project is 'financed' if under an agreement relating to the project a project company incurs, or when the agreement is entered into is expected to incur, a debt of at least £50 million for the purposes of carrying out the project,
(b) 'project company' has the meaning given by paragraph 7 of Schedule 2A, and
(c) 'step-in rights' has the meaning given by paragraph 6 of that Schedule.

*NOTES*

Commencement: 15 September 2003
See *Feetum v Levy* ((2005) Times, 24 February) where the exception was held not to apply and administrative receivers could not be appointed. The case confirms that, since the 'City exceptions' to the 2002 Act were introduced, it would be clear that they would be construed strictly.

## 72F Fifth exception: financial market

Section 72A does not prevent the appointment of an administrative receiver of a company by virtue of –
(a) a market charge with the meaning of section 173 of the Companies Act 1989 (c. 40),
(b) a system-charge within the meaning of the Financial Markets and Insolvency Regulations 1996 (SI 1996/1469),
(c) a collateral security charge within the meaning of the Financial Markets and Insolvency (Settlement Finality) Regulations 1999 (SI 1999/2979).

## 72G Sixth exception: registered social landlord

Section 72A does not prevent the appointment of an administrative receiver of a company which is registered as a social landlord under Part I of the Housing Act 1996 (c. 52) or under Part 3 of the Housing (Scotland) Act 2001 (asp 10).

*NOTES*

Commencement: 15 September 2003

## 72GA Exception in relation to protected railway companies etc.

Section 72A does not prevent the appointment of an administrative receiver of –

(a) a company holding an appointment under Chapter 1 of Part II of the Water Industry Act 1991,
(b) a protected railway company within the meaning of section 59 of the Railways Act 1993 (including that section as it has effect by virtue of section 19 of the Channel Tunnel Rail Link Act 1996),or
(c) a licence company within the meaning of section 26 of the Transport Act 2000.

*NOTES*

Commencement: 15 September 2003

APPENDIX 15

# Statement of Insolvency Practice 1 (Scotland) **A Receiver's Responsibility for the Company's Records (Scotland)**

## 1. Introduction

1.1 This statement of insolvency practice is one of a series issued by the Council of the Society with a view to harmonising the approach of members to questions of insolvency practice. It should be read in conjunction with the Explanatory Foreword to the Statements of Insolvency Practice and Insolvency Technical Reminders issued in June 1996. The statement has been prepared for the sole use of members in dealing with receiverships in Scotland. Members are reminded that SPI Statements of Insolvency Practice are for the purpose of guidance only and may not be relied upon as definitive statements. No liability attaches to the Council or anyone involved in the preparation or publication of Statements of Insolvency Practice. This statement applies to Scotland only.

1.2 This statement has been prepared to summarise what is considered to be the best practice in circumstances where receivers are approached by liquidators or directors seeking access to or custody of a company's books and records. The best practice is considered below both with regard to company records maintained prior to the appointment of a receiver and with regard to those records prepared after the receiver's appointment.

## 2. Company records maintained prior to appointment of a receiver

2.1 The records which a company maintains prior to the appointment of a receiver may be classified under two main headings.

2.2 The first comprises the non-accounting records which the directors are required to maintain by the Companies Act 1985 (as amended) (the statutory records). These consist of various registers (eg of members) and minute books (eg of directors' meetings).

2.3 The second category of records maintained by a company prior to the appointment of a receiver includes accounting records required by statute and all other non-statutory records of the company (statutory accounting and other non-statutory records). Taking each in turn:-

## 3. Statutory records

3.1 The company's statutory records should be kept at its registered office or other permitted place (see paragraph 3.6 below) having regard to the provisions of the Companies Act 1985, sections 288, 353, 383 and 407 (registers of directors, members, minute books and charges).

3.2 Directors' powers to cause entries to be made in these statutory records do not cease on the appointment of a receiver. Indeed, the directors' statutory duties to maintain them are unaffected by his appointment.

3.3 A receiver would have the power to inspect the statutory records as part of his right to take possession of, collect and get in the property of the company (cf. Schedule 2, paragraph 1 to the Insolvency Act 1986). He is not, however, placed under an obligation to maintain those records after his appointment and should not normally do so.

3.4 The abolition by section 130 of the Companies Act 1989 of the requirement for a company formed under the Companies Acts to have a common seal means that in many cases the company in receivership will have no common seal. Provided that an appropriately worded attestation clause is used, deeds can be executed without the use of the common seal. Given that the common seal may still be used for the execution of deeds by the company, however, it is considered best practice for the receiver to take possession of it.

3.5 On appointment, a receiver has two possible options:-

(i) To leave the statutory records in the custody of the directors so that they are in a position to continue to carry out their statutory duties to maintain them.

(ii) To take possession of the statutory records for safe keeping. In such circumstances, the receiver should remind the directors of their statutory responsibilities to maintain the records and allow them free access for this purpose. It would also be advisable for the receiver to prepare a detailed receipt for all the records taken into his possession. This should be signed by a director or other responsible official of the company in receivership.

3.6 The receiver may change the company's registered office to that of his own firm, in which case, the statutory records should also be transferred to the new registered office and the procedure outlined in paragraph 3.5 (ii) above followed.

3.7 Any statutory records (and if applicable any seals) taken into a receiver's possession (see paragraphs 3.3 and 3.4) should be returned to the directors (or liquidator) on the receiver's ceasing to act.

## 4. Statutory accounting and non-statutory records

4.1 All such records as are necessary for the purposes of a receivership should be taken into the receiver's possession and/or control and any which he will definitely not require may be left with the directors. If the receiver encounters difficulty in obtaining possession of the records, the provisions of Sections 234 – 236 of the Insolvency Act 1986 may be of assistance. These are the provisions allowing a receiver to apply to the court for an order for property in the control of any party to be handed to him, placing officers and others under a statutory obligation to co-operate with the receiver and allowing him to apply to the court for an order summoning officers of the company in receivership and others before it for questioning.

4.2 A receiver is under no statutory duty to bring these records up to date to the date of his appointment although for practical purposes (such as to give prospective purchasers some indication of the financial state of the business) it may be necessary for him to do so.

4.3 If a receiver does not take possession of all the records it would be advisable for him to make a list of all those not taken into his custody with a note of their whereabouts.

4.4 When making sales of certain assets (eg book debts or plant and machinery) it may be necessary for the receiver to hand over to the purchaser company records (eg debtors' ledger or plant registers) relating to those assets. In such circumstances, the receiver should ensure that the relevant asset sale agreement specifies the need for these records to be made available to the company on request. Although this will invariably be a matter of negotiation between the receiver and his purchaser, it would be preferable for him to retain the originals of such records. He may make copies available to the purchaser or allow the purchaser to retain them for a short time for the purpose of making copies. Once again, appropriate provision should be made in the asset sale agreement as to the particular circumstances and as to whom is to bear the costs.

4.5 If a receiver transfers the business of the company to a third party as a going concern, section 49 and paragraph 6 of Schedule 11 to the Value Added Tax Act 1994 place the obligation of preserving any records relating to the business upon the transferee. This applies unless the Commissioners of Customs & Excise, at the request of the transferor, otherwise direct.

4.6 This is a wide-ranging obligation. It applies regardless of whether the VAT registration is itself transferred or whether the transfer is treated as supply of neither goods nor services.

4.7 The categories of records covered by Schedule 11 paragraph 6 are wide-ranging. They include orders and delivery notes, purchase and sale records, annual accounts, VAT accounts and credit and debit notes.

## 5. Entitlement of liquidator to records

5.1 The case of *Engel* v *South Metropolitan Brewing & Bottling Company* ([1892] 1 Ch 442) is authority under English law to the effect that a liquidator becomes entitled to possession of all books and records relating to the 'management and business' of the company which are not necessary to support the title of the chargeholder as against a court-appointed receiver. The court held that a court-appointed receiver can be compelled to deliver such documents to the liquidator against the liquidator's undertaking to produce them to the receiver on request. While there is no equivalent authority with respect to a receiver appointed by the holder of a floating charge, general practice supports the proposition that delivery up of records in return for an undertaking and subsequent production on request should occur (Lightman & Moss, *Law of Receivers of Companies, 2nd Edition* paragraph 11 – 17).

## 6. Post appointment records

### *6.1 Statutory Accounting Records*

**Relating to the period prior to the appointment of a liquidator**

6.1.1 The receiver should establish appropriate accounting records as from the date of his appointment. The English case of *Smiths Limited v Middleton* ([1979] 3 A11 ER 842) shows that he has a duty to render full and proper records to the company in order that the company (and its directors) may comply with the duties imposed by sections 221, 226, 227 and 241 Companies Act 1985 (preparation and approval of accounts).

6.1.2 A receiver is also under obligation to make returns of his receipts and payments pursuant to Rule 3.9 of the Insolvency (Scotland) Rules 1986. The statutory requirements and the best practice to be followed in the preparation of insolvency practice entitled 'Preparation of Insolvency Office Holders' Receipts and Payments Accounts', to which members are referred to further information.

6.1.3 When a liquidator is appointed, the *Engel* case would seem to apply so that the liquidator becomes entitled to possession of records (see paragraph 5.1 above).

6.1.4 Receivers have no statutory authority to destroy such records and on ceasing to act must hand these over to the company's directors or, if it is in liquidation, to the liquidator.

**Relating to the period after the appointment of a liquidator**

6.1.5 The receiver's obligation to make returns of receipts and payments and to maintain accounting records (paragraph 6.1.2 above) remains in force after the appointment of a liquidator.

6.1.6 Section 69 Insolvency Act 1986 allows any member, creditor, the Registrar of Companies or the liquidator to enforce these duties.

## 7. Other records

7.1 The remaining records, books and papers relating to a receivership may be subdivided between 'company records', 'chargeholder's records' and 'receiver's personal records'

### *7.2 Company Records*

7.2.1 Company records will include as a minimum all those records which exist as a result of carrying on the company's business and dealing with the assets. These records fall in the same category as the non-statutory records mentioned in paragraphs 4.1 to 5.2 above. They should be treated in the same way, being returned to the company's directors or if it is in liquidation, to its liquidator when the receiver ceases to act.

7.2.2 In the English case of *Gomba Holdings UK Limited v Minories Finance Limited* ([1989] 5BCC 27) consideration was given to precisely which records fall within the definition of 'company records'. It was held that an administrative receiver acts in several capacities during the course of a receivership. In addition to being agent of the company, he owes fiduciary obligations to his appointor and to the company. It is only documents generated or received pursuant to his duty to manage the company's business or dispose of its assets which belong to the company.

### *7.3 Chargeholder's Records*

7.3.1 As explained above, in the *Gomba* case quoted in paragraph 7.2.2. above it was held that documents containing advice and information to the appointor and 'notes, calculations and memoranda' prepared to enable the receiver to discharge his professional duty to his appointor or to the company belong either to the appointor (if he wishes to claim them) or to the receiver. They do not belong to the company.

### *7.4 Receiver's Personal Records*

A receiver's personal records are those prepared by him for the purpose of better enabling him to discharge his professional duties. They will include, for instance, his statutory record which he is required to maintain by Regulation 17 of the Insolvency Practitioners' Regulations 1990 ('the Regulations'). The record must take the form set out in Schedule 3 to the Regulations.

## 8 Best practice

8.1 It is considered best practice that all records mentioned above, with the exception of the chargeholder's records (paragraph 7.3. above) and a receiver's personal records (paragraph 7.4. above) should be made available on request to the company acting by its directors or, if it is in liquidation, its liquidator, unless the receiver is of the opinion that disclosure at that time would be contrary to the interests of the appointor, for instance because of current negotiations for the sale of assets (*Gomba Holdings UK Limited v Homan*, [1986] 3 All ER 94). Subject to the interests of the chargeholder, it appears from this case that directors are entitled to such information as they need to enable them to exercise their residual powers and to perform their residual statutory duties considered above.

8.2 Disclosure of the receiver's personal records is a matter for his discretion, although in any legal action brought against him productions may be ordered by the Court.

8.3 Where there is no liquidator and the directors cannot be traced (or the receiver has reason to suppose that they are not reliable) he will need to consider whether he feels it necessary to present a petition for the company to be wound up using his powers under Schedule 2 to the Insolvency Act 1986. Whether or not a liquidator is appointed, the receiver has no statutory power to destroy a company's records even after the expiry of the statutory period for which the company would need to retain them (usually six years). Thus, if he does so without the authority of the company or the liquidator, he does so at his peril. Note also that the record a receiver is required to keep by the Regulations must be preserved for a period of ten years from the later of the date upon which the receiver ceases to hold office or any security or caution maintained in respect of the company ceases to have effect (Regulation 20).

Issued June 1998

# Society of Practitioners of Insolvency Technical Release 5
# Non-preferential claims by employees dismissed without proper notice by insolvent employers

## Introduction

1. This Technical Release has been prepared for the use of insolvency practitioners (IPs) in dealing with the treatment of employees' non-preferential claims in insolvencies in England and Wales. The purpose of this Release is to harmonise members' practice and try to ensure that it is acceptable to the Redundancy Payments Service (RPS) of the Department of Trade and Industry in processing claims under the Employment Rights Act 1996 (ERA). It has been approved in draft form by the RPS but no liability attaches to the RPS in respect of such approval nor is the RPS in any way bound by any statement contained in this Technical Release.

## Payment in Lieu of Notice – Basis of Calculation

2. Payments in lieu of notice are a liability of the employer and depend on the terms of the relevant contract of employment, subject to the minimum periods of notice laid down by s86 ERA. The amount of the claim, calculated as below, is payable by the RPS out of the National Insurance Fund in the case of an insolvent employer under s184(1)(b) ERA, only insofar as it relates to the minimum statutory period of notice (but not any additional contractual period) up to the current statutory weekly maximum and subject to the definition of 'a week's pay'. Payment by the RPS does not prejudice the right of an employee to seek recovery of any other debts, or debts in excess of the statutory limits, from the insolvent employer in the usual way. Nor does payment by the RPS imply that the IP is bound to admit a claim, whether by the employee or by the RPS in subrogation, which the IP does not agree is legally valid.
3. The basis on which the RPS' liability under s184(1)(b) ERA has been interpreted by the courts is that the amount payable should be computed on a similar basis to damages for wrongful dismissal at common law. The essential principle is that the employee's income (as limited by the definition

of a week's pay in s221 ERA (formerly Sch 14 Employment Protection (Consolidation) Act 1978 (EPCA)) should be restored during the notice period to that which would have been received if proper notice had been given, but that the employee should take reasonable steps to mitigate the damage suffered by the employer's failure to give proper notice.

4. The guidance below gives, in the light of existing case law, the approach approved by the RPS's and SPI's legal advisers. The case law is, however, not definitive in all respects and, if on particular points an IP proposes an alternative approach which does not conflict with established precedent, and provides a sensible and equitable assessment, it is likely to be accepted by the RPS.
5. The starting point for the calculation is a (gross) week's pay as defined in s221 ERA. The case of *Secretary of State v Haynes* [1980] ICR 371 is authority that only the loss of remuneration payable under ss86-91 and 220-9 ERA (formerly Sch 3 and 14 EPCA) is to be taken into account by the RPS in calculating the putative 'damages'. Thus fringe benefits, even where they are a contractual entitlement, are disregarded by the RPS except where, like luncheon vouchers, they are sufficiently close to pay to form part of a week's pay. Any benefit in kind (eg free accommodation) is also disregarded (*S & U Stores Limited v Wilkes* [1974] ITR 425). The Haynes case is also regarded by the RPS as authority for excluding payments such as holiday credits, and by analogy employers' pension contributions, which do not form part of the remuneration payable to the employee in respect of the week or weeks in question.
6. In effect, it was held by the Employment Appeal Tribunal (EAT) in the Haynes case that the RPS's liability under ERA s184(1)(b) is somewhat narrower than the employer's common law liability, in that the RPS is concerned only with 'remuneration'. Thus, in that case, the purchase of holiday stamps was not regarded as pay in respect of the week in which they would have been purchased, partly because the employee would have lost his rights entirely if he had not taken the holiday by a certain date. In the Wilkes case, it was held that an additional weekly sum of expenses which was a genuine pre-estimate of anticipated expenditure by the employee was not 'remuneration', although any profit element would have been. It is accepted that use of a company car could not be classified as 'remuneration', but it does not necessarily follow that the employer's pension contributions can similarly be excluded and it is submitted that the Haynes case is not authority for excluding them. Thus, there are certain items, such as the value of use of a company car, which the employee could possibly claim against the employer (non-preferential) but not against the RPS.

## Irrelevant Factors

7. The following factors should be disregarded in assessing the employee's claim:

## (a) Redundancy Pay

The decision in *Basnett v J & A Jackson Limited* [1976] ICR 63 provides that redundancy pay is not a mitigating factor in assessing the amount of a claim for damages or pay in lieu of notice, on the basis that the redundancy entitlements are not founded on or connected with a breach of contract. This view has been adopted by the RPS and is thought to be the correct approach despite an earlier contrary decision in *Stocks v Magna Merchants Limited* [1973] 2 All ER 329 and the acceptance of the decision in that case in *Aspden v Webbs Poultry and Meat Group (Holdings) Limited* [1996] IRLR 521. In *Wilson v National Coal Board*, New Law Journal 4/12/80 p1146, a personal injuries case, the House of Lords confirmed the general principle here expressed, although they decided in that particular case, on its special facts, that redundancy pay should be deducted. (Gross damages were assessed on the basis that the employee would have continued in employment for the rest of his working life but for the injury, so it would be unreasonable not to make the deduction in such a case).

## (b) Discretionary Social Security Benefits

See para 11(c) below regarding non-discretionary benefits.

## (c) National Insurance Contributions (NIC)

Despite the first instance decision in *Cooper v Firth Brown Limited* [1963] 2 All ER 31 (a personal injuries case), it is considered that NIC of the employee should not be deducted from any payment of salary in lieu of notice. There are two reasons for this. First, the individual may lose the benefits which he would otherwise have obtained from these NIC and would thus be penalised twice if he lost the amount of the NIC themselves as well as the benefits. Secondly, if the individual is employed for at least one day during the week of his notice period, his NIC for that week will have already been paid.

## (d) Retirement Pension

It is clear from the Court of Appeal decision in *Hopkins v Norcros Plc* [1994] ICR 11 that a pension payable under an employer's scheme should be treated as purchased by the employee's past work and is not deductible. As regards state pensions, the Pensioners' Earnings Rule was abolished in the 1989 Finance Act. It is no longer appropriate to deduct retirement pension monies from payment in lieu of notice claims. However, see para 9(b) below regarding possible additional claims for loss of pension benefit.

### (e) Protective Awards (possibly)

Previous practice was to deduct from pay in lieu of notice the amount of any protective award insofar as it related to the same period. Indeed s190(3) Trade Union and Labour Relations (Consolidation) Act 1992 (TULCRA) specifically provided for mutual deduction between the two amounts and the practice was upheld by the Court of Appeal in *Potter v Secretary of State for Employment* [1997] IRLR 21 (subject to appeal to the House of Lords). However, it was held in *EC Commission v UK* [1994] IRLR 412 that this power of deduction was not compatible with EC law in that its effect was that UK law provided no sufficient deterrent to encourage employers to comply with the consultation requirements of s188 TULCRA and s190(3) was accordingly repealed as from 30 August 1993. Therefore, it is now the RPS's practice not to reduce pay in lieu of notice by reference to a protective award or vice versa, where the first dismissal covered by the award was after 28 November 1993.

The textbooks seem to have assumed that the right of deduction has been effectively removed but it is submitted that this is highly doubtful. A protective award is an award ordering the employer to pay 'remuneration' for the protected period, that is, a period commencing on the date when the first relevant dismissal takes effect (or of the award, if earlier). Pay in lieu of notice relates to remuneration over, in many cases, precisely the same period. The repeal, without more, of an express provision for mutual deduction does not take away a right of deduction which may well be implicit by reference to s190 as it now remains. There is also an argument that the rule against double proof would prevent a liquidator from admitting proofs under both heads, though this is likely to apply only if, notwithstanding the view of the RPS, the employer itself remains entitled to apply the deduction.

In view of the risk of duplicated claims, IPs should be more inclined than in the past to defend protective award cases and may refer to the RPS in cases of doubt.

### (f) Other Benefits

Any benefits payable to an employee which arise from a private contract, as opposed to the State scheme, should not be set off in mitigation. Examples of these might include, as well as an occupational pension (see para 7(d) above), unemployment pay from a welfare scheme administered by a trade union.

## Additional Claims

8. The following factors may be required to be taken into account so as, where appropriate, to increase a person's claim:

### *(a) Fringe Benefits*

Fringe benefits, such as a company car and car fuel, medical insurance subscriptions or rent-free accommodation, are likely to give rise to an additional claim where these are a contractual entitlement. A claim from an employee may well arise even though the RPS cannot consider fringe benefits under the ERA.

The value of a company car was considered in *Shove v Downs Surgical Plc* [1984] ICR 532, where the loss of use of a 4,200 cc Daimler over two and a half years, including petrol for 5,000 miles pa private motoring, was assessed at £10,000. On the other hand, in *Clark v BET plc*, [1997] IRLR 348, Timothy Walker J assessed entitlement to a chauffeur-driven car for business and private use including all running expenses, which was in fact used privately only for visits to the opera, theatre and dinner, and in essence placed at nil for tax purposes, apart from travel to and from work, at £2,000 pa.

The Inland Revenue for the 1994/95 tax year revised the basis on which the taxable benefit of a car is taxed. These rules were introduced to reflect more accurately the true value of a company car and the taxable benefit charge also provides a useful indicator of the value of the benefit. The Automobile Association also produces annual tables giving up-to-date information on the costs of running cars of various sizes and these are a more accurate, if more favourable to the employee, method of assessing the value of a company car to an employee.

### *(b) Lost Pension Scheme Benefits*

The employer's likely contributions to a pension scheme in respect of the employee and/or any additional benefits expected to accrue to the employee during the contractual period of notice are likely to be claimed. Of course, the contributions will not necessarily fairly reflect the benefit and in many cases an actuarial calculation will be required. It is normally only in cases of fixed-term contracts where the pension scheme is determinable within the contract period that pension entitlements may to some extent be excluded from the calculations: see *Beach v Reid Corrugated Cases Limited* [1956] 1 WLR 807.

## Mitigation

9. The principle of mitigation applies to payments in lieu of notice since the claim of an employee dismissed with no, or short, notice is in essence one for damages for breach of contract and an insolvent employer must apply all possible reductions. Mitigation is particularly difficult to apply since it may be notional as well as actual (what would the employee have earned if he had made the effort to find a job?). To facilitate accurate calculation of mitigation, the amount of the payment cannot normally be calculated until after the notice period has expired.

10. Mitigation does not apply where the contract itself provides for pay in lieu as an alternative to notice since there is then no breach of contract and the pay in lieu is a contractual entitlement: see *Abrahams v Performing Rights Society* [1995] IRLR 486. This is most likely to arise in the contracts of senior executives.
11 The different elements that may come into the calculation of mitigation are discussed separately as follows:

### (a) Remuneration

Any income earned or received by the employee during the notice period, which would not have been earned or received if the contract of employment had not been terminated, should be deducted from the payment in lieu of notice. The authority for this is *Secretary of State for Employment v Wilson* [1978] ICR 200.

### (b) Notional Earnings

A deduction for notional earnings because of the employee's failure to mitigate his loss may be made in those relatively rare circumstances where the notice period is substantial and/or it is sufficiently clear that the employee had the opportunity to obtain other income in the notice period and unreasonably failed to take that opportunity. It is reasonable, where notice of less than, say, three months is involved, not to pursue the question of notional, as opposed to actual, mitigation in respect of alternative earnings very far. The objective must be to produce a figure which is not over-generous but which genuinely compensates the employee for his loss over the notice period and therefore should not lead to litigation. The EAT confirmed in the case of *Secretary of State v Jobling* [1980] ICR 380 that the duty to mitigate does not drive an employee to unreasonable lengths, even though in that particular case they did decide that deduction for notional earnings should be made, because Mr Jobling deliberately chose not to draw a salary that was readily available.

### (c) Non-discretionary Benefits

Any social security benefits or allowances which are not discretionary received by the employee during the period of notice, such as sickness pay, invalidity pay and maternity allowance should be deducted. The House of Lords in the case of *Westwood v Secretary of State for Employment* [1985] ICR 209 held, following *Parsons v BNM Laboratories Limited* [1964] 1 QB 95, that unemployment benefit (now replaced by Jobseeker's Allowance (JSA)) should mitigate the claim. Further authority in support of this is *Lincoln v Hayman* [1982] 2 All ER 819, where the Court of Appeal held that supplementary benefit as well as unemployment benefit should be deducted from special damages in a personal injury case.

The question of mitigation of notional JSA in cases where the employee has failed to claim JSA does not arise (except in rare cases where it is income-based) because no JSA is paid where pay in lieu is due, whether or not it has been received, pursuant to The Jobseeker's Allowance Regulations 1996 (SI 1996 No 207) reg 105(6).

## *(d) Unfair Dismissal*

Any compensation for unfair dismissal awarded by an industrial tribunal should be deducted only to the extent that it represents loss of earnings in the notice period. It was held in *Berry v Aynsley Trust Limited* [1976] BLT No. 394 New Law Journal 27/10/77 p1052 and more recently in *Aspden v Webbs Poultry & Meat Group (Holdings) Limited* [1996] IRLR 521 that a deduction should be made in respect of a tribunal award of compensation for unfair dismissal. However, it is submitted that the basic award should not be taken into account and any compensatory award should only be taken into account to the extent that it reflects loss of earnings in the notice period, if it can be apportioned in this way. The Court of Appeal held in *O'Laiore v Jackel International Limited* (No 2) [1991] ICR 718 that a Tribunal's maximum award (then £8,000) was not deductible because it could not be allocated specifically to the notice period so the employer could not establish double recovery for the same loss. It may be worth noting, however, that the basic award should be taken into account in the rare case where it is payable on the particular dismissal but would not have been if full notice had been given at the time of the short notice, eg, if the employee would have reached 65 in the meantime: see *Shove v Downs Surgical Plc* (para 89(a) above).

## *(e) Protective Awards (possibly)*

See para 7(e) above.

## *(f) Tax*

(i) Amounts below £30,000. The full amount of tax which would have been payable by the employee if the amount in question had been paid as salary may be deducted from the amount due by the company and retained by the employer. In certain cases, it may seem that the cost of calculating the deduction would not be justified in view of the small amount of assets available in the liquidation. However, the RPS insist on a basic rate notional deduction being made on the notice payment which they pay under the ERA.

(ii) Amounts exceeding £30,000. The correct principle is, it is submitted, to start by estimating the net amount which would have been received by the employee after the deduction of tax from his gross income (ie his actual loss) and then to take into account his liability to tax on the damages, so that the net amount payable to him should, as far as possible, equal the net loss suffered.

The tax position is considered more fully in the Appendix.

Issued August 1999

## Appendix
## Tax on Pay in Lieu of Notice

1. The following paragraphs set out, at the time of issue, what is understood to be the tax position on payments in lieu of notice. IPs should note that this is an area where there has been considerable professional comment and discussion. They are therefore advised to obtain their own detailed guidance.
2. In *British Transport Commission v Gourley* [1956] AC 185, the House of Lords decided that damages awarded in a personal injuries action for loss of earnings should be reduced by such amount as the plaintiff would have paid in tax had he in fact received those damages in the form of taxable income. If this reduction were not made, then clearly the plaintiff would be over-compensated for his loss, to the extent that the damages themselves were not subject to tax. This principle has been extended to damages awarded for wrongful dismissal by the EAT case of *Secretary of State for Employment v Cooper and Vinning* [1987] ICR 766 and must, it is submitted, also apply to payments in lieu of notice as these are similarly compensatory in nature. However, it should be noted that pay in lieu of notice is itself taxable where the employer is entitled to make such a payment under the contract instead of giving the full period of notice (see para 11 above).
3. The Inland Revenue has recommended that notional tax be assessed at the basic rate rather than using the individual's last known code number, since most employees should recover the tax allowances lost during the notice period, either as a direct refund or in subsequent employment.
4. Sometimes an employee (usually one who has remained unemployed) feels that he has still, at the end of the tax year(s) to which his notice payment relates, had too much notional tax deducted, because he has not used up his personal allowance from his total taxable income for the whole tax year(s). In these circumstances an employee may apply for a refund direct to the RPS and should request form RP13.
5. Where a notice period includes the date of a change in Basic Rate Income Tax, the balance remaining after any mitigation should be divided by the number of days (including Saturdays, Sundays and/or any other day on which the employee did not normally work) and then multiplied by the number of days before and after the date of change to give two sums on which the appropriate percentages can be calculated. It is also acceptable for the two tax calculations to be rounded down to the nearest pound.
6. In the case of payments in lieu of notice, the position is complicated by the fact that payments will be taxable to the extent that they exceed £30,000

(unless they are wholly taxable because there is a contractual entitlement to make a cash payment in lieu of notice (see App para 2 above)). The Income and Corporation Taxes Act 1988 ss 148 and 188 provide that any payment made in consideration of, or in connection with, the termination of the holding of an office or employment is (except as provided in Section 188) taxable on such portion (if any) as exceeds £30,000. There have been a number of interpretations as to how the Gourley principle should be applied in the light of the predecessors of Sections 148 and 188 but the correct method of calculating damages exceeding £30,000 would appear to be that adopted in *Shove v Downs Surgical Plc* (see para 9(a) above). This approach involves taking into account the tax to be paid on the payment so that the net amount received by an employee reflects the actual (net) loss suffered by him.

For Example

Entitlement to one year's notice or damages in lieu. Annual Salary £60,000 plus benefits. 1997/98 tax bands.

| | £ | £ | |
|---|---|---|---|
| Gross salary | 60,000 | 60,000 | |
| Benefits in kind (life assurance, medical cover, car etc) (a) (say) | 10,000 | 10,000 | |
| | 70,000 | 70,000 | |
| Personal allowance | 4,045 | (4,045) | |
| Taxable amount | 65,955 | | |
| 20% on | £4,100 | 820 | |
| 23% on | £22,000 | 5,060 | |
| 40% on | £39,855 | 15,942 | (21,822) |
| | 65,955 | | |
| Tax Relief for married couples (allowance) (say) | | 275 | |
| Net loss – 12 months' salary after tax (70,000-21,547) | 48,453 | | |
| Less net mitigation (b) say | (5,000) | (5,000) | |
| Total net damages (c) | 43,453 | | |
| To receive a net receipt of £43,453: | | | |
| Total net damage | 43,453 | | |
| Tax free slice | (30,000)<br>13,453 | 30,000 | |
| Gross up £13,453 x 100/77(d) | 17,471 | | |
| Amount to be awarded | 47,471 | | |

Notes to example

(a) The value of any benefits in kind provided (eg the provision of cars and health cover) will need to be ascertained. Strictly speaking the value of benefits in kind should be added to the gross salary to determine total remuneration.

(b) It will be noted that mitigation has been taken into account after the tax calculation. This was the method adopted in the Shove case. The RPS take the view that notional tax should be assessed after mitigation in order to ensure that an individual does not suffer financial loss from the failure to be given notice, even though an assessment before mitigation might in particular cases give more precise results. However, it is submitted that the employee is not adversely affected provided that the mitigation figure is itself a net one. Nevertheless, when calculating an ERA s184(1)(b) payment, IPs need to understand the RPS's method of making a notional deduction for tax after all other mitigating items which have been dealt with gross. It remains the responsibility of the IP to agree such claims submitted by the RPS.

(c) No amount has been deducted from the net damages for accelerated receipt.

(d) Grossing up is at the standard rate because the total income (including the excess over £30,000) is taken to be less than (£26,100 + £4045 =) £30,145 and in any event the employer is not concerned with higher rate tax where a form P45 has already been issued.

7. The fact that the payment will not in any event be paid in full because the employer is insolvent, and thus that the tax payable on the full sum will be reduced or not payable at all, should not be used so as further to reduce the claim.

8. In arriving at the reduction to be made under the Gourley principle, the Courts would, when assessing a damages claim with the benefit of hindsight, work on the basis of the ex-employee's actual liability to Income Tax during the year in question. Any deductions made by the employer in respect of payments in lieu of notice must of necessity be based on an estimated Income Tax liability and the most obvious and practical solution is to base the deduction upon the basic rate as that will in most cases be the employee's marginal rate of tax and it is the marginal rate which is appropriate. It may well be that the employee can show just cause why the notional deduction should be reduced because of an actual or expected change in circumstances but the obligation must rest on him to do so.

9. Where amounts over £30,000 are paid and a form P45 has already been issued, basic rate Income Tax must be deducted by the employer in respect of the excess over £30,000 and paid over to the Revenue. If form P45 has not yet been issued, the PAYE code should be applied and tax charged using the appropriate tax table rates. The employee will receive a tax credit in respect of this deduction to set against his liability to Income Tax.

# Society of Practitioners of Insolvency
# Technical Release 6
# Treatment of Directors' Claims as 'Employees' in Insolvencies

## Introduction

1. This Technical Release gives guidance to members on the approach to be adopted when dealing with the assessment of claims from directors as 'employees' of insolvent companies in a manner acceptable to the Redundancy Payments Service (RPS) of the Department of Trade and Industry. It has been approved in draft form by the RPS but no liability attaches to the RPS in respect of such approval nor is the RPS in any way bound by any statement contained in this Technical Release. Members are reminded that Technical Releases are for purposes of guidance only and may not be relied on as definitive statements. Members are also referred to the Technical Release entitled 'Non-Preferential Claims of Employees Dismissed Without Proper Notice by Insolvent Employers'.

## What Constitutes an 'Employee'?

2. The Employment Rights Act 1996 (ERA) provides for payment from the National Insurance Fund of some arrears of wages, holiday pay, pay in lieu and redundancy pay owed to the employees of insolvent companies.
3. Section 230(1) of the ERA defines an 'employee' as 'an individual who has entered into or works under (or, where the employment has ceased, worked under) a contract of employment'.
4. Section 230(2) of the ERA defines 'contract of employment' as a 'contract of service or apprenticeship, whether express or implied, and (if it is express) whether oral or in writing'.

## The Position of Directors

5. In law, a company director is an office-holder. However, a director can also be an employee and this matter has to be considered on the basis of the evidence concerning the director's relationship with the company. It is essentially a matter of fact in each individual case.

6. The Employment Appeal Tribunal (EAT) in the case of *Eaton v Robert Eaton Limited* [1988] IRLR 83, gave guidance on the factors to be considered as follows:
   (a) Did the director have a descriptive title (eg managing director or technical director)?
   (b) Was there an express contract of employment? If not, was there a board minute or memorandum in writing constituting an agreement to employ the director as an employee as required by section 318 of the Companies Act 1985?
   (c) Was remuneration paid by way of salary or director's fees?
   (d) Was remuneration fixed in advance or paid on an 'ad hoc' basis?
   (e) Was remuneration by way of entitlement or, in effect, gratuitous?
   (f) Did the director merely act in a directorial capacity or was he/she under the control of the board of directors in respect of the management of his/her work?
7. Another factor to be considered is whether the director paid Schedule E (PAYE) Income Tax and Class 1 National Insurance Contributions (NIC). As the working conditions of office-holders are more related to those of 'employed earners' than those of 'self employed earners', they are treated for NIC and Tax purposes as 'employed earners'. However, payment of Tax and NIC as an 'employed earner' does not of itself confer employee status for the purposes of employment legislation: see *Wilson v Trenton Service Station Limited* EAT/100/87 23 June 1987. Indeed, this factor was considered to be 'neutral' in *Fleming v Secretary of State for Trade and Industry (SSTI)* [1997] IRLR 682, though it was taken into account in *SSTI v Bottrill* (below). Equally, deductions at the 'self-employed' rate do not necessarily preclude entitlement under the redundancy and insolvency provisions.
8. Where a director has forgone or postponed payment of 'salary' for a period, that may be evidence that his relationship with the company is not one of employment, since it is normally a fundamental term of a contract of employment that, in return for services, an employee will receive remuneration. The fact that a director is an investor in the company, guaranteeing a loan to it will also point against his being an employee: see *McQuisten v Secretary of State for Employment (SSE)* EAT/1298/95 11 June 1996.
9. In *Buchan v SSE* and *Ivey v SSE* [1997] IRLR 80, the EAT suggested the following questions:
   (a) Is the director under the control of another?
   (b) Is the director an integral part of another's organisation?
   (c) Is the director in effect in business on his own account?
   (d) What is the economic reality of the relationship between the director and the 'employer'?
   (e) Is there mutuality of obligation between them?
   (f) What is their respective bargaining power?

   The decision-making body has to consider the relevance of all the factors, decide what weight to give to each of them, evaluate them and balance one against the other in order to arrive at a conclusion.

## Directors with Controlling Shareholdings

10. Particular difficulties may arise in relation to a director who holds 50% or more of the voting shares in a company. In *Buchan v SSE* above, the EAT went on to hold that: , :

> 'If the claimant is able, by reason of a beneficial interest in the shares of the company, to prevent his dismissal from his position in the company, he is outside the class of persons intended to be protected by the provisions of the [ERA] and is not an employee within the meaning of that Act.'

The EAT concluded in that case that a director owning 50% or more of the issued shares of the company could virtually never be its employee for the purposes of the ERA.

11. On the other hand, in *SSTI v Bottrill* [1998] IRLR 120, the EAT found that the reasoning behind the above rule laid down by *Buchan v SSE* was unsound. The position was rather that:

> 'The shareholding of a person in the company by which he alleges he was employed is a factor to be taken into account, because it might tend to establish either that the company was a mere simulacrum or that the contract under scrutiny was a sham.'

12. In the *Bottrill* case, a managing director who was also, temporarily, 100% shareholder was nevertheless held to be an employee on the facts as a whole. There was one other director and two other employees. The intention was that 80% of the shares should go to the US supplier, which in any event had 'real control'. Facts indicating employment were:
(a) he paid tax and NIC on that basis;
(b) he had no other employment;
(c) his contract of employment was signed and dated and indicated that he was an employee;
(d) he was entitled to holidays and sick pay;
(e) he worked every day from 8.30 am to 5.30 pm;
(f) he was paid by salary and not director's fees.
Against that were:
(g) his theoretical control over the company;
(h) the fact that he has taken only 8 out of 16 days' holiday in the last year;
(i) he had not received pay for the last month (because the cheque book was not available).

The *Bottrill* case subsequently went to the Court of Appeal ([1999] IRLR 326). The Court of Appeal upheld the decision of the EAT and stated that:

> ' ... whether or not an employer/employee relationship exists can only be decided by having regard to all the relevant facts. If an individual has a controlling shareholding that is certainly a fact which is likely to be significant in all situations and in some cases it may prove to be decisive. However, it is only one of the factors which are

relevant and certainly it is not to be taken as determinative without considering all the relevant circumstances.'

Counsel for the SSTI requested further guidance on the subject generally and the Court of Appeal responded as follows:

'We are anxious not to lay down rigid guidelines for the factual enquiry which the tribunal of fact must undertake in the particular circumstances of each case, but we hope that the following comments may be of assistance.

'The first question which the tribunal is likely to wish to consider is whether there is or has been a genuine contract between the company and the shareholder. In this context how and for what reasons the contract came into existence (for example, whether the contract was made at a time when insolvency loomed) and what each party actually did pursuant to the contract are likely to be relevant considerations.

'If the tribunal concludes that the contract is not a sham, it is likely to wish to consider next whether the contract, which may well have been labelled a contract of employment, actually gave rise to an employer/employee relationship. In this context, of the various factors usually regarded as relevant (see, for example, Chitty on Contracts 27th ed. (1994) para. 37 – 008), the degree of control exercised by the company over the shareholder employee is always important. This is not the same question as that relating to whether there is a controlling shareholding. The tribunal may think it appropriate to consider whether there are directors other than or in addition to the shareholder employee and whether the constitution of the company gives that shareholder rights such that he is in reality answerable only to himself and incapable of being dismissed. If he is a director, it may be relevant to consider whether he is able under the Articles of Association to vote on matters in which he is personally interested, such as the termination of his contract of employment. Again, the actual conduct of the parties pursuant to the terms of the contract is likely to be relevant. It is for the tribunal as an industrial jury to take all relevant factors into account in reaching its conclusion, giving such weight to them as it considers appropriate.'

15. Thus, no single factor is likely to be conclusive and the RPS looks at all the factors to establish whether the director was an employee for the purposes of the ERA, as will an Employment Tribunal if necessary, and as too must the insolvency practitioner. The ERA provides for a right to refer to an Employment Tribunal in the event of disagreement with a decision made by the RPS or the insolvency practitioner. It is very difficult to appeal successfully against a decision of an Employment Tribunal on this question because appeals are permitted only on matters of law and the decision on this point is usually treated as one of fact.

## Dividends

16. The principles are equally applicable to admitting a claim for dividend purposes. The effect of such claims, or the entitlement to claim, will affect not only the direct claim by the director, but also those by banks or other creditors making subrogated claims.
17. In marginal cases, IPs are requested to liaise and consult with the RPS as suggested in their booklet *Guidance for Employers' Representatives*.
18. The IP has no authority to accept or reject claims on behalf of the RPS; nor is the RPS's view in a particular case binding on the IP.

Issued August 1999

# Statement of Insolvency Practice 13 (Scotland)
# Acquisition of Assets of Insolvent Companies by Directors

## 1. Introduction

1.1. This statement of insolvency practice is one of a series issued by the Council of the Society with a view to harmonising the approach of members to questions of insolvency practice. It should be read in conjunction with the Explanatory Foreword to the Statements of Insolvency Practice and Insolvency Technical Reminders issued in June 1996. Members are reminded that SPI Statements of Insolvency Practice are for the purpose of guidance only and may not be relied upon as definitive statements. No liability attaches to the Council or anyone involved in the preparation of publication of Statements of Insolvency Practice. This statement applies to Scotland only.

1.2. The purpose of this statement of insolvency practice is to:

- ensure that members are familiar with the legal obligations of directors in relation to the acquisition of assets of companies by them or persons connected with the company (as defined by section 249 of the Insolvency Act 1986) (together in this statement referred to as "directors") and the statutory provisions relating to such acquisitions;
- ensure that members are aware of their legal obligations as insolvency office holders in relation to the disposal of assets to directors and of relevant statutory provisions;
- set out best practice with regard to the disposal of assets to, and their acquisition by, directors;
- set out best practice with regard to the disclosure of such transactions.

This statement has been produced in recognition of the fact that the acquisition of assets of insolvent and prospectively insolvent businesses by directors may give rise to concerns that assets may have been disposed of at less than market value and that those who have been prejudiced by the insolvency of the disposing company may be exposed to further risk through continued trading by those who have or may have had responsibility for the insolvency of the disposing company. It recognises that connected party transactions may be in the best interests of creditors but requires such transactions to be conducted with the greatest degree of propriety and with disclosure to those interested as soon as reasonably practicable.

## 2. Scope

The statement covers the following:

- legal obligations of directors and related statutory provisions; :
- obligations of members acting as:
  - professional adviser to the directors as the people responsible for the conduct of the company's affairs;
  - insolvency practitioner assisting the directors in the convening of meetings of members and creditors in connection with the winding up of the company as a creditors' voluntary liquidation;
- obligations of members acting as:
  - nominee in relation to a proposed company voluntary arrangement;
  - office holder -

    as supervisor of such arrangement if approved by members and creditors;
    as administrator;
    as receiver or administrative receiver;
    as provisional liquidator;
    as liquidator in a winding up by the court or in a creditors' voluntary liquidation.

In this statement the word 'director' includes directors by whatever name called and shadow directors, and the word 'assets' includes all tangible and intangible assets including the goodwill and the right to use any trading name of the company.

## 3. The legal obligations of directors and statutory provisions

The following are the principal legal obligations and some of the statutory provisions of particular relevance to directors of a company which is or is prospectively insolvent.

The overriding obligation of directors of a company is to act in the best interests of the company, its creditors and its members. Failure to do so exposes directors to claims for misfeasance or breach of duty.

At any time when the directors knew or ought to have known that insolvent liquidation is unavoidable they have an obligation to take such action as is appropriate to protect the interests of creditors. Failure to do so renders them liable to claims under section 214 of the Insolvency Act 1986.

Transactions at an undervalue and preferences as defined in the Insolvency Act 1986 may be set aside at the instance of a liquidator or administrator.

The acquisition of assets of a company by directors or parties connected with them may require approval by the members of the company by resolution (Companies Act 1985 section 320). It is the duty of directors to ensure that when it is required, such approval is obtained before any relevant transaction is undertaken. Any transaction requiring approval but undertaken without it will be voidable at the instance of the company unless the conditions set out in subsection 322 (2) of the Companies Act 1985 apply, and may give rise to claims against directors on any gains made by them.

The use by any person connected with a company which has gone into insolvent liquidation of the name of that company or of a similar name is only permissible if the provisions of section 216 of the Insolvency Act 1986 are complied with or the circumstance specified in rules 4.80 to 4.82 of the Insolvency (Scotland) Rules 1986 apply. Failure to comply renders the persons concerned liable to prosecution and personal liability for the debts of the company under section 217.

## 4. The obligations of members acting in an advisory capacity

### *4.1. Members acting as Professional Advisers to Directors*

4.1.1. Members acting in an advisory capacity in relation to the affairs of companies in financial difficulties must at all time have regard to the general professional conduct guidance of the body by whom they are authorised to act as a permit holder. Subject to this overriding obligation, an advising member should:

- agree and record the identity of the instructing client. This is particularly important where advice is given in relation to insolvent companies and members should ensure that it is clear whether the instructing party is the company, its board of directors or one or more of its directors individually;
- act in the interests of his client with objectivity, integrity and independence;
- ensure that his client is made aware of the matters set out in paragraph 3 above;
- keep under consideration whether his client has any conflicts of interest or duty and bring any such conflicts to the attention of his client. Where a client persists in disregarding material conflicts of interest or duty, the member should cease to act unless the client agrees to limit the client's

retainer to one such duty or interest and to take advice on the other elsewhere;
- not accept instructions to assist a client in conduct which will undermine public confidence in the proper administration of insolvency procedures.

4.1.2. Members should bear in mind that, when asked to advise in relation to the planning or execution of a transaction, they may incur civil or criminal liability through participation, even in an advisory capacity, and will in any event be acting improperly if they assist directors in any conduct which amounts to misfeasance. A member should cease to act if his advice to an officer that a proposed act or omission would amount to misfeasance is disregarded. However, this does not prejudice any duty of a member to give confidential advice in the interests of a client in relation to events which occurred before the member was instructed.

4.1.3. Members acting in an advisory capacity which may lead to their assisting the directors in relation to the creditors' voluntary liquidation of the company should bear in mind the requirements for disclosure at the section 98 meeting of transactions between the company and its directors (and connected parties) in the period of one year prior to the winding up and the names of those who advised the directors (as such) in relation to such transactions as set out in Statement of Insolvency Practice 8 (SCOT).

## 4.2. Members acting in relation to Section 98 Meetings

4.2.1. Where a member is assisting the directors in relation to the convening of meetings of members and creditors for the purposes of a creditors' voluntary liquidation, he should ensure that his advice to directors as such in the period prior to the commencement of the winding up is given on the same basis as set out in paragraph 4.1 above. There can be circumstances when it is in the best interest of creditors for a connected party transaction to be undertaken with complete propriety but it is essential that such a transaction is not undertaken without a thorough appraisal of its propriety and the benefits expected to accrue to creditors from it.

4.2.2. In paragraph 4.1.3 reference has been made to the disclosure requirements in Statement of Insolvency Practice 8 (SCOT). It is the duty of the advising member to inform the directors of the need for full disclosure of connected party transactions.

4.2.3. Members should consider, if any connected party transactions are undertaken at any time when they are acting as advisers to the directors, whether it is appropriate for them to seek appointment as liquidator, bearing in mind the obligations of liquidators to investigate antecedent transactions.

## 5. Members acting as office holders

5.1. The obligations on both directors and office holders in relation to the maximisation of realisations of assets or the optimisation of the position of members and creditors of the company do not in any way preclude disposals by way of connected party transactions. Members should ensure that such transactions are conducted with due regard to their own and the directors' obligations.

5.2. There are no requirements of Scots law which require assets to be disposed of by any particular method. There is an overriding duty to obtain the best price for assets whether sales are effected by private treaty sale, by sale by tender or at auction. While it is recognised that circumstances may arise when full exposure to the market of the availability of assets for purchase is not practicable, members are reminded that they should normally, unless sale by auction is the chosen means of disposal, take steps to advertise assets for sale or circularise (for example, by use of mailing lists) known prospective interested parties.

5.3. It is the member's duty to ensure that all transactions between the company (of which he is acting as office holder) and the directors and connected parties are conducted on a fully arm's length basis and, as regards the value of any assets which are the subject of any such transaction, on the basis of a professional appraisal of the value of those assets. When such appraisal is not conducted by an independent valuer the office holder should ensure that he has conducted all due enquiries as to the value of the assets and retains appropriate documentation in his papers. Where assets are sold without professional valuation, the office holder should consider seeking the views of the committee, if there is one. It is his duty to ensure that the value of the assets is maximised but this does not require him to obtain the maximum value for each individual asset if disposal of a parcel of assets or the assets as a whole will, in aggregate, maximise total realisations. Since the allocation of the consideration between the constituent assets affects interests of creditors, it should be made on a basis which can be justified objectively.

5.4. Where a member is acting as provisional liquidator and it is proposed that assets of the company should be acquired by directors, the sanction of the court should be obtained.

5.5. Where a member is acting as nominee or supervisor in relation to a voluntary arrangement, he should ensure that any connected party transactions are in the best interests of the company, its members and creditors, and are only undertaken in accordance with the terms of the arrangement as approved by the members and creditors. When a connected party transaction is proposed as part of an arrangement or has taken place in the year prior to the date of his appointment as nominee he should ensure that it is included in the proposals on a full disclosure basis.

## 6. Disclosure of connected party transactions

6.1. The requirement for disclosure of connected party transactions in the reports to meetings of members and creditors in creditors' voluntary winding up proceedings has been referred to above.

6.2. Where, prior to the section 98 meetings, directors have indicated that they may wish to make an offer to the liquidator (when appointed) for assets of the company, this should normally be disclosed at the meeting and the advising members should advise the creditors that if they form a liquidation committee the liquidator will, unless there are overriding commercial reasons why this should not be done, advise the committee of any offers for assets made by the directors and they will have the opportunity to comment on such offers. While the sanction of the committee is not required for a connected party transaction and full responsibility for it will rest with the liquidator, discussion of the proposed transaction with the committee should assist the liquidator in dispelling any concerns which creditors may have about it. In both voluntary and compulsory liquidations, the liquidator has a statutory obligation to give notice to the committee where he disposes of any property of the company to a person who is connected with the company. If it is not appropriate for there to be prior discussion with the committee the liquidator should report to the committee that he has contracted a disposal by way of connected party transaction as soon as reasonably practicable.

6.3. The liquidator should report any connected party transaction to members and creditors when he first reports to them after the transaction has taken place.

6.4. In administration order proceedings a member who is preparing an independent report (as provided for in Rule 2.1 of the Insolvency (Scotland) Rules 1986) should consider whether that report should contain details of any transactions between the company and its directors or other connected parties: any which might bear upon the court's consideration as to whether it is appropriate that an administration order be made should be included. In administration the administrator should include in his proposals under section 23 et seq. of the Insolvency Act 1986 reference to any connected party transaction undertaken in the period of two years prior to the making of the administration order and in the period since the making of that order, or proposed to be undertaken. If a creditors' committee is appointed, the members of the committee should be advised of any such transaction undertaken after the meeting of creditors to consider the proposals.

6.5. In receivership, the receiver should include in his report to the creditors at the Section 67 meeting, information regarding any connected party transaction if this has taken place prior to the meeting and, if it takes place after that meeting, report it to any creditors committee appointed at that meeting.

6.6. Any disclosure made in accordance with the requirements set out in paragraphs 6.1 to 6.5 above should provide creditors with sufficient information to have a full appreciation of the nature of the transaction, and should normally include the following information:

- The date of the transaction
- Details of the asset involved and the nature of the transaction
- The consideration for the transaction and when it was paid
- The name of the counterparty
- The nature of the counterparty's connected party relationship with the vendor
- If the transaction took place before the appointment of the member as office holder, the name of any adviser to the vendor
- Whether the purchaser and (if the transaction took place before the appointment of the member as office holder) the vendor were independently advised
- Where the transaction took place before the commencement of liquidation or administration, the scope of the office holder's investigation and the conclusion reached
- Where the disclosure is to a liquidation committee and the committee has not been consulted prior to contract, the reason why such consultation did not take place
- Where, in a liquidation, the disclosure is to creditors, whether the liquidation committee (if there is one) has consulted and the outcome of such consultation.

Issued September 1998

# Statement of Insolvency Practice 7 (Scotland) **Preparation of Insolvency Office Holders' Receipts and Payments Accounts (Scotland)**

## 1. Introduction

...

1.2 The purpose of this statement of insolvency practice is to:

- set out best practice with regard to the presentation of accounts prescribed in the insolvency legislation;
- set out best practice with regard to the presentation of financial information to creditors and other interested parties in a manner which is useful to the reader.

1.3 Insolvency practitioners are reminded that they are responsible for the submission of returns using the prescribed forms (or in similar format approved by the agency to which the returns are required to be submitted) within the times specified in the legislation. They should not await reminders or default notices.

## 2. Statutory returns and other receipts and payments accounts

### *2.1 Statutory Returns required*

The statutory requirements for the filing of returns of receipts and payments are laid down in the Insolvency Act 1986, the Bankruptcy (Scotland) Act 1985 (as amended) and rules and regulations made thereunder, and reference should be made to the relevant provisions for full details of those requirements. The following is a summary of the types of return required:

- Abstracts of receipts and payments are required in statutory format in:
    - Administrations

Receiverships
Liquidations

...

### *2.2 Other Receipts and Payments Accounts*

Reports to members, creditors, committees and other interested parties should include in the body of the report or by way of annexure to that report details of receipts and payments. This will normally be in the form of a summary account.

...

## 4. Abstracts: presentation

Where abstracts are required they should be prepared as far as possible on the basis of the guidance set out in sections 6 to 10 of this statement.

Practitioners are reminded that in voluntary arrangements abstracts should only include monies coming into the hands of the supervisor and the payments made out of those monies.

## 5. Other receipts and payments accounts: presentation

Information regarding receipts and payments in reports to members, creditors, committees and other interested parties will normally be in the form of a summary account which should be prepared adopting the principles set out below and in sections 6 to 10 of this statement.

Information provided should follow any legal requirements contained in the Insolvency Act 1986 and related subordinate legislation. Subject to such requirements the information provided should be in a form which enables the reader to understand the financial outcome to the date of the account and relate it to information provided at the inception of the proceedings.

Receipts and payment accounts should, as far as possible, show categories of items using the same headings as the Statements of Affairs with the 'estimated to realise' figures on the Statement of Affairs shown so that these latter figures can be compared with actual realisations to date. Where this is not appropriate (due, for example, to there having been material changes in the composition of the assets between the date to which the Statement of Affairs figures were made up and the date of the insolvency) other categories may be used. In some cases it may also be necessary, in order to facilitate comparison between estimated and actual realisations, to reclassify or analyse Statement of Affairs figures. n:

Receipts and payments accounts should reflect all transactions to date on a cumulative basis as well as the figures since any previous accounts (if any) were provided.

In the case of reports to secured creditors the account may be in a specific format agreed with the chargeholder but should so far as possible adopt the provisions of this statement.

Where separate bank accounts have been opened for specific purposes, the combined transactions relative to such accounts should be incorporated in the receipts and payments account. There is no need to report that separate accounts have been operated, or transfers made between them.

Information which is to be provided in accordance with this Statement may be provided in a separate document issued with the receipts and payments account or by way of note.

When presenting information for the benefit of creditors, IP's should modify, as appropriate, the information contained within the statutory accounts to make it more meaningful.

## 6. Detailed presentational matters for statutory accounts

In the preparation of abstracts and other receipts and payments accounts referred to in sections 4 and 5 above respectively, the following principles should be followed:

### *6.1 Assets*

Asset realisations accounted for by persons acting on behalf of the office holder should be shown gross (ie before the deduction of costs of realisation). The costs of realisation should be shown separately as payments.

When assets subject to charges are sold by the office holder (or on his instructions) the gross realisations should be shown as receipts and related costs and the amounts accounted for to the chargeholder shown as payments. In the interests of clarity, and particularly where there are several assets charged to the same creditor, items relating to charged assets should be shown separately from other items.

When assets subject to charges are sold by the chargeholder or other person with a legal right to do so, or on any such person's instructions, the net amount, if any, received should be shown in the account with the gross realisation(s), costs of realisation and the amount retained shown separately either by way of narration or in a note to the account. When assets are realised in these circumstances and no monies are received by the office holder the gross realisations and related costs should be shown either in the narrative column or by way of a note and a 'nil' realisation included in the account.

### *6.2 Liabilities*

Payments to creditors should be stated by category distinguishing payments recognising effective diligence, in settlement of reservation of title claims, to secured creditors, to preferential creditors, to floating charge creditors and to unsecured creditors. The dates of payments to creditors ranking in the insolvency and the amount (pence in the £) should be stated.

### *6.3 Trading under office holder's control*

Amounts received and paid in the course of trading should be distinguished from the other realisations of assets and the related costs. The preparation of a separate trading receipts and payments account should be considered where this will assist the reader in understanding the financial implications of the office holder's actions. Care should be taken to ensure that when assets in existence at the commencement of the office holder's duties (for example stock and work-in-progress) are used in trading this is made clear by way of note.

Similarly where such classes of assets are sold at or after the cessation of trading and are shown in the main body of the account and the proceeds include amounts arising from assets created in the course of trading this fact should also be stated by way of note. When a separate trading receipts and payments account is prepared the balance of that account should be shown as a single item in the main receipts and payments account.

Note should be taken of the fact that a trading account on a cash basis without regard to debts not collected and liabilities not settled will not provide a full account of trading and this should be made clear by way of note to the account.

The guidance in this section does not apply when the office holder is not responsible for trading but only receives the surplus on trading or part of that surplus (for example, in the case of a voluntary arrangement where the company carries on the business under the terms of the arrangement).

### *6.4 Hive-downs*

The proceeds received from the sale of shares in, or from loans to, a hive-down company as consideration for the sale of the business or assets to it, should be shown in the office holder's account classified according to the categories of assets transferred and apportioned as provided for in the hive-down agreement.

Payments made directly by a hive-down company for such assets should be similarly treated.

A trading account for a hive-down company should be prepared adopting the same principles as set out above for a trading account when no hive-down is undertaken and this should be annexed to the main account.

If separate fees have been charged to the insolvent estate for the management of the hive-down company these should be separately disclosed. If such fees have been charged to the hive-down company they should be shown by way of note to the office holder's account and also disclosed in any accounts of the hive-down company which are prepared.

### *6.5 Value Added Tax (VAT)*

Where a company or individual is or was registered for VAT and receipts and payments included VAT which is to be accounted for or reclaimed by the office holder as arising after the commencement of the insolvency proceedings the receipts and payments should be shown net of VAT with the amount due to/from HM Customs & Excise at the date of the account included in the account separately.

If the insolvent entity has not been registered for VAT, payments should be shown inclusive of VAT and the fact that VAT is not recoverable stated by way of note.

### *6.6 Third Party Funds*

Any amounts received which are not part of the estate should be shown as receipts with the subsequent payments to the true owner shown as a deduction from the receipts with any agreed fee charged to the person entitled to the monies also being disclosed.

## 7. Professional fees

7.1 All sums paid to the practitioner and his firm should be clearly identified as such. The practitioner's fees should be stated separately with subheadings (where applicable) for remuneration, out of pocket expenses, other disbursements, management fees (including those related to the management of hive-down companies) and fees for preparing statutory accounts and taxation matters, etc. Sums paid to any sub-contractor for work which would normally be carried out by office holders themselves should be identified as such and shown separately.

7.2 Payments to outside parties in which the office holder or his firm or any associate of his (as defined in the Insolvency Act section 435) has an interest should be treated as payments to the office holder or his firm and disclosed separately.

7.3 Where charges are made to recover the cost of facilities provided by the office holder's firm (or any associate of his) the amounts should be separately stated.

7.4 Where the office holder's fees and disbursements have (in whole or in part) been paid otherwise than from the realisation of the assets (for example by directors of a company or a creditor) details of the amounts received by the office holder, the source of those funds and the nature of the payments (for example remuneration) should be given by way of a note.

7.5 The cost of professional and other advisers' services to the office holder should be shown using appropriate categories (for example, legal fees and valuation fees).

## 8. Employment Rights Act funds

Amounts received and disbursed under the Employment Rights Act (under arrangements, now superseded for new cases, which involved the office holder as Employer's Representative making payments on behalf of the Secretary of State) do not form part of the insolvent's estate. They should be dealt with through a separate bank account. The receipts and payments should not be recorded in the office holder's account except where loans to employees have been made under the Loan Scheme.

The employees' representative's fees do not form part of the remuneration from the estate and do not need to be disclosed in the receipts and payments account.

## 9. Statement of funds held

If the composition of the balances held is not disclosed on the face of the account, an analysis should be shown separately.

Where any monies are held which do not form part of the estate and are due to be paid to third parties, the amount so held should be stated.

The operation of the Cheques Act 1992 may necessitate clearance of payment instruments otherwise than through accounts designated for the purpose of the insolvent estate (for example the office holder's firm's client account). Any amounts so held should be shown separately.

## 10. General

The requirement to show how any amount in an account (or by way of a note to that account or in any report to which the account is annexed) has been arrived at does not necessitate the repetition of that information in subsequent accounts issued to the same recipient(s) where that amount is shown either separately or as part of a cumulative total.

Issued August 1999

# Statement of Insolvency Practice 9 (Scotland)
# **Remuneration of Insolvency Office Holders**

## 1 Introduction

1.1 This Statement of Insolvency Practice (SIP) is one of a series issued to licensed insolvency practitioners with a view to maintaining standards by setting out required practice and harmonising practitioners' approach to particular aspects of insolvency.

SIP 9 is issued under procedures agreed between the insolvency regulatory authorities acting through the Joint Insolvency Committee (JIC). It was commissioned by the JIC, produced by the Association of Business Recovery Professionals, and has been approved by the JIC and adopted by each of the regulatory authorities listed below:

Recognised Professional Bodies:
- The Association of Chartered Certified Accountants
- The Insolvency Practitioners' Association
- The Institute of Chartered Accountants in England and Wales
- The Institute of Chartered Accountants in Ireland
- The Institute of Chartered Accountants of Scotland
- The Law Society
- The Law Society of Scotland

Competent Authority:
- The Insolvency Service (for the Secretary of State for Trade and Industry)

The purpose of SIPs is to set out basic principles and essential procedures with which insolvency practitioners are required to comply. Departure from the standard(s) set out in the SIP(s) is a matter that may be considered by a practitioner's regulatory authority for the purposes of possible disciplinary or regulatory action.

SIPs should not be relied upon as definitive statements of the law. No liability attaches to any body or person involved in the preparation or promulgation of SIPs.

1.2 The purpose of this statement of insolvency practice is to:

- ensure that members are familiar with the statutory provisions relating to office holders' remuneration;
- set out required practice with regard to the observance of the statutory provisions;
- set out required practice with regard to the provision of information to those responsible for the approval of fees to enable them to exercise their rights under the insolvency legislation;
- set out required practice with regard to the disclosure and drawing of disbursements.

The statement has been produced in recognition of the principle that those with a direct financial interest in the level of office holders' fees should feel confident that the rules relating to the charging of remuneration have been properly complied with, and that those charged with responsibility for approval of fees have access to sufficient information about the basis of fees to be able to make an informed judgement about the level of remuneration in any particular case. The statement applies to Scotland only.

1.3 Members should be aware that the drawing of remuneration otherwise than in accordance with the relevant statutory provisions will render them in breach of the law.

1.4 The statement is divided into the following sections:

- The statutory provisions
- Provision of information when seeking fee approval
- Provision of information after fee approval
- Asset realisations
- Expenses and disbursements
- Payment in full
- Closure of cases

## 2 The statutory provisions

2.1 The statutory provisions relating to the remuneration of office holders are set out in the Insolvency (Scotland) Rules 1986 ('the Rules') (as amended) and the Bankruptcy (Scotland) Act 1985 (as amended) ('the Bankruptcy Act'). The relevant provisions are set out in full in appendix A. The main provisions relating to the most common types of insolvency appointment are summarised in the following paragraphs.

...

## 2.6 Receiverships

2.6.1 The remuneration of a receiver appointed over property under powers contained in a floating charge will be a matter for agreement between the receiver and the holder of the floating charge under which he is appointed.

2.6.2 In terms of Section 58 (2) of the Insolvency Act 1986, where the remuneration to be paid to the receiver has not been determined by agreement between the receiver and the holder of the floating charge by virtue of which he was appointed, or where it has been so determined but is disputed by any of the following:

a) the receiver;
b) the holder of any floating charge or fixed security over all or any part of the property of the company;
c) the company;
d) the liquidator of the company;

it may be fixed instead by the Auditor of the Court of Session on application made to him by any of the aforementioned parties.

…

## 3 The provision of information when seeking approval of remuneration

…

3.4 Where remuneration is sought during the course of an assignment an up to date receipts and payments account should always be available. Where the remuneration is based on time costs the office holder should be prepared to disclose the time spent and the charge-out value in the particular case, together with such additional information as may reasonably be required having regard to the size and complexity of the case. The additional information should comprise a sufficient explanation of what the office holder has achieved and how it was achieved to enable the value of the exercise to be assessed (whilst recognising that the office holder must fulfil certain statutory obligations that might be seen to bring no added value for creditors) and to establish that the time has been properly spent on the case. That assessment will need to be made having regard to the time spent and the rates at which that time was charged, bearing in mind the complexity, responsibility, value and nature of assets with which he has had to deal. Appendix C sets out a suggested format, with explanatory notes, for producing the information required to enable this assessment to be carried out. It provides for a degree of analysis of time by activity and grade of staff and sets out suggested categories for the purpose of this analysis. Whilst the approach embodied in Appendix C is potentially applicable to all types and sizes of case, the degree of analysis and form of presentation should be proportionate to the size and complexity of the case, and not all categories of activity will always be relevant.

3.5 The case records required to be maintained and retained under the Insolvency Regulations 1994 should include sufficient information to show full details of the time spent on the case by the office holder and his staff in cases where remuneration is on a time cost basis.

3.6 Where the remuneration is charged on a percentage basis the office holder should provide details of any work which has been or is intended to be sub-contracted out which would normally be carried out by office holders themselves.

3.7 A receiver appointed in relation to a company should on request provide the information detailed in paragraphs 3.4 to 3.6 to the company's liquidator.

...

Effective Date: 1 July 2004

## Appendix A

The following is the full text of the rules relating to the remuneration of office holders in the various types of proceedings covered by this statement of insolvency practice.

...

### *A.7 Receiverships*

**Section 58 Remuneration of Receiver**

**58(1) [Agreement with floating charge holder]** The remuneration to be paid to a receiver is to be determined by agreement between the receiver and the holder of the floating charge by virtue of which he was appointed.

**58(2) [Where not determined under (1)]** Where the remuneration to be paid to the receiver has not been determined under subsection (1), or where it has been so determined but is disputed by any of the persons mentioned in paragraphs (a) to (d) below, it may be fixed instead by the Auditor of the Court of Session on application made to him by:

(a) the receiver

(b) the holder of any floating charge or fixed security over all or any part of the property of the company;

(c) the company; or
(d) the liquidator of the company.

**58(3) [Remuneration in excess to that fixed]** Where the receiver has been paid or has retained for his remuneration for any period before the remuneration has been fixed by the Auditor of the Court of Session under subsection (2) any amount in excess of the remuneration so fixed for that period, the receiver or his personal representatives shall account for the excess.

…

# Statement of Insolvency Practice 15 (Scotland)

# Reporting and providing information on their functions to committees (and commissioners in sequestrations) in formal insolvencies

...

## 2 Scope

This Statement concerns:

- Written reporting by insolvency office holders to committees in Corporate Insolvencies or to Commissioners in Sequestrations, both where there are statutory requirements to do so and in other cases.
- The provision of information to members of committees or commissioners about the rights, duties and functions of the committee or commissioners.

The Statement does not apply to members' voluntary liquidations.

The Statement applies to Scotland only. References to rules are to the Insolvency Rules (Scotland) 1986 and the Insolvency (Scotland) Amendment Rules 2003, and references to regulations are to the Insolvency Regulations 1994 and Bankruptcy (Scotland) Act 1985.

...

## 5 Receiverships

In receiverships the following requirements apply:

- The receivers must send an account of his receipts and payments to each member of the committee (rule 3.9).
- If the receiver intends to resign he must give the committee at least seven days' notice of his intention to do so, in terms of The Receivers (Scotland) Regulations 1986.
- When a receiver vacates office he must within 14 days forthwith give notice to the members of the committee (rule 3.11).

Apart from these there are no statutory requirements for written reports. However, members should ensure that any arrangements made for reporting to a committee in such cases are properly documented and adhered to.

...

## 7. Provision of Information to Members of Committees and Commissioners on their Rights, Duties and Functions

The Association of Business Recovery Professionals has produced a series of guides for members of committees and Commissioners for use in formal insolvency proceedings. The texts of the guides are appended to this Statement. In all cases where there are Commissioners or a committee is established the insolvency office holder should ensure that the guide appropriate to the type of procedure concerned, or the equivalent information in some other suitable format, is made available to the Commissioners or members of the committee, either at the meeting at which the Commissioners are elected or the committee is established or as soon as practicable thereafter.

Effective date: 1 July 2004

## Annexe B
## Guidance for Members of Creditors' Committees in Receivership

### *Contents*


General 1
Membership 2
General 2.1
Representatives 2.2
Resignation and Termination of Membership 2.3
Vacancies 2.4
Establishment of committee 3
Formalities of Establishment 3.1
Formal Defects 3.2
Proceedings 4
Chairman 4.1
Quorum 4.2
Meetings 4.3
General 4.3.1
First Meeting 4.3.2
Subsequent Meetings 4.3.3
Notice of Venue 4.4
Information from Receiver 4.5

| | |
|---|---|
| Voting Rights and Resolutions | 4.6 |
| Records of Meetings | 4.7 |
| Postal Resolutions | 4.8 |
| Review of Receiver's Security or Caution | 5 |
| Information to be provided to the Committee | 6 |
| Receiver's Receipts and Payments Account | 6.1 |
| Resignation of Receiver | 6.2 |
| Death of Receiver | 6.3 |
| Vacation of Office | 6.4 |
| Confidentiality of Documents | 7 |
| Expenses of committee members | 8 |
| Committee members' dealing with the company | 9 |
| Receivers' security or caution | Appendix |


# 1. General

1.1 Receivership is a remedy available to a creditor holding security created before 15 September 2003, which includes a floating charge, over all (or substantially all) the assets of a company. A receiver is appointed by the holder of the security but normally acts as agent of the company over whose assets he is appointed. The primary duty of a receiver is to his appointor. Whilst he also owes certain duties to the company and is required to provide information to the unsecured creditors, neither the creditors nor any committee appointed by them have any authority *to* sanction any of his actions.

1.2 The receiver must (unless the court directs otherwise) convene a meeting of the unsecured creditors within three months of his appointment and lay before it a report on matters relating to the receivership. The meeting convened to receive the report may also establish a creditors' committee. The function of the committee is to represent to the receiver the views of the unsecured creditors, and to act in relation to him in such manner as may be agreed from time to time. The committee may also require the receiver to attend before it at any reasonable time and furnish it with such information relating to the carrying out by n-:him of his functions as it may reasonably require..

1.3 The margin references are to the Insolvency Act 1986, the Insolvency (Scotland) Rules 1986 (both as amended) and the Receivers (Scotland) Regulations 1986.

# 2. Membership

## 2.1 General

2.1.1 The committee must consist of at least three, and not more than five, creditors. Any creditor of the company who has lodged a claim is eligible to be a member of the committee, so long as his claim has not been rejected for the purpose of his entitlement to vote.

2.1.2 It is the creditors themselves who are the members of the committee, not the individuals who represent them. Thus a company or partnership which is a creditor may be a member of the committee but can only act through a representative appointed in accordance with paragraphs 2.2.1 to 2.2.3 below.

## *2.2 Representatives*

2.2.1 A member of the committee may, in relation to the business of the committee, be represented by another person duly authorised by him for that purpose. Such representative must hold a mandate entitling him so to act (either generally or specially) signed by or on behalf of the committee member, and for this purpose any proxy or any authorisation under section 375 of the Companies Act 1985 in relation to any meeting of creditors of the company shall, unless it contains a statement to the contrary, be treated as a letter of authority to act generally signed by or on behalf of the committee member. The chairman at any meeting of the committee may call on a person claiming to act as a committee member's representative to produce his mandate, and may exclude him if it appears that his mandate is deficient

2.2.2 No member may be represented by –

* a body corporate,
* a partnership,
* an undischarged bankrupt, or
* a disqualified director.

2.2.3 No person may act as representative of more than one committee member, or as both a member and a representative of another member, on the same committee.

2.2.4 Where the representative of a committee member signs any document on the member's behalf, the fact that he so signs must be stated below his signature.

## *2.3 Resignation and Termination of membership*

2.3.1 A member of the committee may resign by notice in writing delivered to the receiver. A person's membership of the committee is automatically terminated if

(a) his. estate is sequestrated or he becomes bankrupt or grants a trust deed for the benefit of or makes a composition with his creditors, or
(b) at three consecutive meetings of the committee he is neither present nor represented (unless at the third of those meetings it is resolved that this rule is not to be applied in his case), or

(c) he ceases to be, or is found never to have, been, a creditor, or
(d) he becomes disqualified to act as a, director.

2.3.2 A member of the committee may be removed by resolution, at a meeting of creditors.

### *2.4 Vacancies*

2.4.1 If there is a vacancy in the membership of the committee it need not be filled if the receiver and a majority of the remaining committee members so agree, provided the number of members does not fall below three. The receiver may appoint any creditor qualified to be a member of the committee to fill the vacancy, provided a majority of the other members of the committee agree and the creditor consents to act.

2.4.2 Alternatively, a meeting of creditors may resolve that a creditor be appointed (with his consent) to fill the vacancy. 14 days notice must have been given of the resolution to make such an appointment (whether or not of a person named in the notice). Where the vacancy is filled by an appointment made by a creditors meeting at which the receiver is not present, the chairman of the meeting shall report to the receiver the appointment which has been made.

## 3. Establishment of Committee

### *3.1 Formalities of Establishment*

3.1.1 The committee does not come into being, and accordingly cannot act, until the receiver has issued a certificate of its due constitution.

3.1.2 The receiver will not issue the certificate until at least three of the persons who are to be members of the committee have agreed to act but he shall issue it forthwith thereafter. Such agreement may be given by the creditor's' proxy-holder or representative under section 375 of the Companies Act 1985 present at the meeting establishing the committee, unless the proxy or authorisation specifically preludes such agreement being given.

3.1.3 If the chairman of the meeting which resolves to establish the committee is not the receiver, he shall forthwith give notice of the resolution to the receiver and inform him of the names and addresses of the committee members.

### *3.2 Formal Defects*

The acts of the committee are valid notwithstanding any defect in the appointment, election or qualifications of any committee member or the representative of any committee member, or in the formalities of its establishment.

## 4. Proceedings

### *4.1 Chairman*

Subject to paragraph 4.5.3 below, the chairman at any meeting of the committee will be the receiver, or a person nominated by him in writing to act. A person so nominated must be either:
(a) one who is qualified to act as an insolvency practitioner in relation to the company, or
(b) an employee of the receiver or his firm who is experienced in insolvency matters.

### *4.2 Quorum*

A meeting of the committee is duty constituted if due notice of it has been given to all members and at least two members are present or represented.

### *4.3 Meetings*

#### 4.3.1 General

The committee will meet where and when determined by the receiver, subject as follows:

#### 4.3.2 First meeting

The receiver must call the first meeting of the committee within three months of its establishment.

#### 4.3.3 Subsequent meetings

Subsequent meetings of the committee must be called by the receiver
(a) if so requested by a member of the committee or his representative the meeting must then be held within 21 days of the request being received by the receiver, and
(b) for a specified date, if the committee has previously resolved that a meeting be held on that date.

### *4.4 Notice of venue*

The receiver must give 7 days' written notice of the time and place of any meeting to every member of the committee (or his representative designated for that purpose), unless this requirement has been waived by or on behalf of any member. Such waiver may be signified either at or before the meeting.

### *4.5 Information from Receiver*

4.5.1 Where the committee resolves to require the attendance of the receiver under section 68(2) of the Insolvency Act 1986, he must be given at least 7 days' notice. The notice to him must be in writing, signed by a majority of the current members of the committee or their representatives.

4.5.2 The meeting at which the receiver's attendance is requited must be fixed by the committee for a business day, and held at such time and place as the receiver determines.

4.5.3 Where the receiver so attends, the members of the committee may elect any one of their number to be chairman of the meeting in place of the receiver or his nominee.

### *4.6 Voting Rights and Resolutions*

At any meeting of the committee each member (whether present himself or by his representative) has one vote, and a resolution is passed when a majority of the members present or represented have voted in favour of it.

### *4.7 Records of Meetings*

Every resolution passed must be recorded in writing, either separately or as part of the minutes of the meeting. The record must be signed by the and kept as part of the sederunt book.

### *4.8 Postal Resolutions*

4.8.1 It is possible for resolutions to be passed by post. The receiver must send to every member (or his representative designated for the purpose) a copy of the proposed resolution on which a decision is sought, which must be set out in such a way that agreement with, or dissent from, each separate resolution may be indicated by the recipient on the copy so sent.

4.8.2 However, any member of the committee may, within 7 business days from the date of the receiver sending out a resolution, require the receiver to summon a meeting of the committee to consider the matters raised by the resolution. In the absence of such a request, the resolution is deemed to have been passed by the committee if and when the receiver is notified in writing by a majority of the members that they concur with it.

4.8.3 A copy of every resolution so passed, and a note that the concurrence of the committee was obtained, must be kept in the sederunt book.

## 5. Review of Receiver's Security or Caution

The receiver is required to have in place security or caution for the proper performance of his functions (see Appendix). It is the duty of the committee to review from time to time the adequacy of the receiver's security or caution.

## 6. Information to be provided to the Committee

### *6.1 Receiver's Receipts and Payments Account*

The receiver must send to each member of the committee an account of his-receipts and payments:

* within 2 months after the end of 12 months from the date of his appointment, and of every subsequent period of 12 months, and
* within 2 months after he ceases to act as receiver.

### *6.2 Resignation of Receiver*

If the receiver intends to resign he must give the committee at least seven days' notice of his intention to do so.

### *6.3 Death of Receiver*

If the receiver dies, the holder of the floating charge by which he was appointed must, as soon as he becomes aware of the death, give notice of it to the members of the committee.

### *6.4 Vacation of Office*

When the receiver vacates office he must give notice to the members of the committee within 14 days of having done so.

## 7. Confidentiality of Documents

7.1 Where the receiver considers that any document forming part of the record of the receivership-
(a) should be treated as confidential, or
(b) is of such a nature that its disclosure would be calculated to be injurious to the interests of the creditors,

he may decline to allow it to be inspected by a person (including a member of the committee) who would otherwise be entitled to inspect it.

7.2 A person refused inspection may apply to the court for the refusal to be overruled.

## 8. Expenses of Committee Members

8.1 Any reasonable travelling expenses directly incurred by committee members or their representatives either attending meetings of the committee or otherwise on the committee's business will be paid by the receiver as an expense of the receivership.

8.2 However, such expenses will not be paid in respect of any meeting of the committee held within three months of a previous meeting, unless the meeting in question is summoned at the instance of the receiver.

## 9. Committee Members' dealing with the Company

9.1 Membership of the committee does not prevent a person from dealing with the company while the receiver is acting, provided that any transactions in the course of such dealings are entered into on normal commercial terms.

9.2 The court may, on the application of any interested party, set aside any transaction which appears to it to be contrary to the above requirement, and may give directions for compensating the company for any loss incurred in consequence.

9.3 Circumstances may occasionally arise where a legal action or dealing involving a member of the committee or a person connected with him make it inappropriate for him to attend discussions on the subject in the committee . In such circumstances the member may be asked not to attend a meeting or part of a meeting at which the matter is discussed.

## Appendix
## Receiver's Security or Caution

The receiver is required to have in place security or caution for the proper performance of his functions. The security or caution takes the form of a bond under which –

(a) a cautioner undertakes to be jointly and severally liable with the receiver for the proper performance of the duties and obligations laid on him under the insolvency legislation;
(b) the liability of the cautioner and the receiver is in both a general penalty sum and a specific penalty sum in respect of the individual case, and is limited to a sum equivalent to the losses caused by any fraud or dishonesty of the receiver, whether acting alone or in collusion with one or more persons, or the fraud or dishonesty of any person or persons committed with the connivance of the receiver;
(c) a bordereau (schedule of risk) is submitted to the cautioner containing an entry completed by the receiver evidencing the acceptance by the cautioner of liability in respect of the receiver acting in the case in the amount of the specific penalty sum; and
(d) any claims under the bond are made firstly in respect of the specific penalty sum.

The general penalty sum must be £250,000 and the specific penalty sum not less than the estimated value of that part of the company's assets which, at the date of the receiver's appointment, would appear to be available for the unsecured creditors (in respect of both preferential and non-preferential claims) were the company to go into liquidation on that date. The minimum specific penalty sum is £5,000 and the maximum £5,000,000. If, at any time, the receiver forms the opinion that the value of the assets is higher than the penalty sum under the current specific penalty he must obtain a further specific penalty to bring the penalty sum equal to that value (subject to the maximum limit of £5,000,000).

APPENDIX 16

# Unlimited guarantee

UNLIMITED GUARANTEE

by

GALAXY PRODUCTS LIMITED AND OTHERS

in favour of

BANCO ALBINONI plc

To: BANCO ALBINONI plc

WE, GALAXY PRODUCTS LIMITED, incorporated under the Companies Acts and having our registered office at 10 Heavenly Mansions, Pitlochry, ROCOCO COCOA CO LIMITED and ROCOCO COCOA CO (SCOTLAND) LIMITED, both incorporated under the Companies Acts and having our registered offices at Baroque House, Louis XV Avenue, Edinburgh, ORINOCO COCOA CO LIMITED and ORINOCO COCOA CO (SCOTLAND) LIMITED, both incorporated under the Companies Acts and having our registered offices at 20 Neo-Classical Lane, Edinburgh all jointly and severally hereby guarantee you payment on demand of all sums for which we or any one or more of us ('the Companies') are now or may become liable to you in any manner of way whatsoever with interest thereon at such rate as may be charged by you to the Companies at the time from the date of your last annual balance preceding application by you to us for payment: AND WE FURTHER DECLARE that you shall be entitled to make calls on us from time to time at your discretion for such sums as you may fix, to account of our liabilities hereunder: AND ALSO that without prejudice to your rights under this guarantee and at your discretion, you may grant to the Companies or to any persons liable with or for them, any time or other indulgence, and may compound with them, accede to trust deeds and draw dividends, all without notice to us: AND WE ALSO DECLARE that this guarantee shall be a security to you to the above extent for any balance which may remain due to you after applying any dividends, compositions or payments which you may receive from the Companies or from any person liable with or for them and that we shall not be entitled to require any assignation of the debts hereby guaranteed or any part thereof or to rank *in competition with you* (the addition of these words covers the impact of the 'prescribed part' which the holder of a floating charge gives up following the introduction of the Enterprise Act 2002 and avoids any situation arising where a holder of the floating charge cannot claim and under the terms of the guarantee precludes a guarantor from claiming) on the estates of the Companies in respect of any payments made by us hereunder, or to have the benefit of any securities or any claims against third parties held by you until the whole sums due to you by the Companies have been paid in full: AND DECLARING that our liability hereunder shall not depend upon, or be affected by the powers of the Companies or their directors or other agents in regard to borrowing as contained in their respective Memoranda and Articles of Association or otherwise, or the validity or invalidity of any security given by the Companies, but the obligation hereby undertaken shall be binding upon us: AND DECLARING ALSO that this guarantee is a continuing obligation and shall remain in force until recalled by us or our respective successors in writing and is without prejudice to any further or other guarantees granted or to be granted by us or any of us to you on behalf of the Companies.

SIGNED for and on behalf of

GALAXY PRODUCTS LIMITED at

on 20

and subscribed for it and on its behalf by:

Director

Director/Secretary

SIGNED for and on behalf of

ROCOCO COCOA CO LIMITED at

on

20 and subscribed

for it and on its behalf by:

Director

Director/Secretary

SIGNED for and on behalf of

ROCOCO COCOA CO (SCOTLAND)

LIMITED at

on 20

and subscribed for it and on its behalf by:

Director

Director/Secretary

SIGNED for and on behalf of

ORINOCO COCOA CO LIMITED at

on 20

and subscribed for it and on its behalf by:

Director

Director/Secretary

SIGNED for and on behalf of

ORINOCO COCOA CO (SCOTLAND)

LIMITED at

on 20

and subscribed for it and on its behalf by:

Director

Director/Secretary

# Letter of set-off

LETTER OF SET-OFF

by

GALAXY PRODUCTS LIMITED AND OTHERS

in favour of

BANCO ALBINONI plc

]To: BANCO ALBINONI plc

WE, GALAXY PRODUCTS LIMITED, incorporated under the Companies Acts and having our registered office at 10 Heavenly Mansions, Pitlochry, ROCOCO COCOA CO LIMITED and ROCOCO COCOA CO (SCOTLAND) LIMITED, both incorporated under the Companies Acts and having our registered offices at Baroque House, Louis XV Avenue, Edinburgh, ORINOCO COCOA CO LIMITED and ORINOCO COCOA CO (SCOTLAND) LIMITED, both incorporated under the Companies Acts and having our registered offices at 20 Neo-Classical Lane, Edinburgh do hereby request and authorise you to hold all sums standing or that may stand to the credit of any of the current accounts in our names in your books in security and for payment of any advances made or to be made by you to any one or more of us and of all interest and charges accrued and to accrue thereon and of any other obligations for which any one or more of us now or may hereafter become liable to you in any way whatever. Declaring that you shall have full power at any time and in your discretion, without notice to us or any of us to apply all sums standing or that may stand to the credit of any of such accounts, or any part thereof, in payment or in reduction of such advances and obligations and interest and charges thereon: And we also declare that all sums standing or that may hereafter stand to the credit of any of such accounts shall be held by you in addition and without prejudice to any other security which you now or may hereafter hold for such advances and obligations and interest and charges thereon and that we shall not be entitled to rank *in competition with you* (for an explanation for these additional words see the note in Appendix 16) on the estates of any of the other companies executing these presents in respect of any sums applied by you until the whole sums due to you by any one or more of us shall have been paid in full.

SIGNED for and on behalf of

GALAXY PRODUCTS LIMITED at

on 20

and subscribed for it and on its behalf by:

Director

Director/Secretary

SIGNED for and on behalf of

ROCOCO COCOA CO LIMITED at

on 20

and subscribed for it and on its behalf by:

Director

Director/Secretary

SIGNED for and on behalf of

ROCOCO COCOA CO (SCOTLAND) LIMITED at

on 20

and subscribed for it and on its behalf by:

Director

Director/Secretary

SIGNED for and on behalf of

ORINOCO COCOA CO LIMITED at

on 20

and subscribed for it and on its behalf by:

Director

Director/Secretary

SIGNED for and on behalf of

ORINOCO COCOA CO (SCOTLAND)

LIMITED at

on 20

and subscribed for it and on its behalf by:

Director

Director/Secretary

# Assignation

ASSIGNATION

by

BANCO ALBINONI plc

in favour of

ROCOCO COCOA CO LIMITED

WE, BANCO ALBINONI plc, having our registered office at Corelli Square, Edinburgh considering that by unlimited guarantee dated [ ] and executed by ROCOCO COCOA CO LIMITED, having its registered office at Baroque House, Louis XV Avenue, Edinburgh ('Rococo') Rococo guaranteed payment to us of all sums due or to become due on an account kept in our books *inter alia* in name of GALAXY PRODUCTS LIMITED ('Galaxy') having its registered office at 10 Heavenly Mansions, Pitlochry and that whenever required by us; Further Considering that Rococo has in full and final implement of such unlimited guarantee made payment to us of the sum of [ ] due by Galaxy on its account with us and has required us to grant these presents; Therefore we hereby assign to Rococo and its assignees whomsoever (1) the said sum of [ ] of principal and interest respectively and the liability of Galaxy therefor with all our right, title and interest in and to the premises; and (2) the Bond and Floating Charge granted by Galaxy dated [ ] and our right, title and interest, present and future therein to the extent of [Ratio of Debt Paid / Aggregate Amount paid by Guarantors] thereof; And that to the effect of enabling Rococo and its foresaids to operate any claim of relief they may have against Galaxy; And we warrant the foregoing assignation from our own facts and deeds only; And we have herewith delivered up to Rococo such unlimited guarantee.

SIGNED for and on behalf of

BANCO ALBINONI plc at

on 20

and subscribed for it and on its behalf by:

Director

# Index


**Abstract of receipts and payments 10.33**
**Accession**
- retention of title, and 5.41, 5.42

**Agency of receiver 3.54-3.62**
- contract of employment, and 3.55
- personal liability, and 3.54-3.62
- suspension of powers, and 3.57
- termination on winding up 3.58-3.62
  - Cork Committee 3.60
  - English law 3.59

**Agreement for sale of business**
- form, App.10

**Appointment of receiver 1.01-1.69.** *see also* **Insolvency practitioner**
- acceptance 1.40
  - docquet 1.40
- Accountant in Bankruptcy, notification to 1.41
- attachment to property covered by floating charge 1.42
- breach of floating charge 1.27-1.31
- checking validity 1.56-1.60
  - defect in procedural steps 1.60
  - documents to be examined 1.56-1.59
- circumstances justifying 1.27-1.32
- clause purporting to convert floating charge into fixed charge, and 2.35
- consignation of funds in court, and 2.36
- continuing professional relationship 1.07, 1.08, 1.09
- Cork Report on 1.03
- court, by 1.22
  - circumstances justifying 1.32
  - mode of 1.61
- deed of appointment, App.4
- directors, and. *see* Directors
- effect 2.01-2.43
- effect of other floating charges 2.31, 2.32
- effective date 1.38
- execution of instrument of appointment 1.34-1.37
  - payment on demand, and 1.35-1.37

**Appointment of receiver**—*contd*
- extent of security 2.33-2.36
- failure to register floating charge 1.43, 1.44
  - rectification of register 1.45-1.49
- fixed charge, effect of 2.30
- form of wording 1.24-1.26
- holder of floating charge, by 1.01, 1.20, 1.21
- investigation of assets 2.53
- letter of request, App.3
- mode of 1.33
- notification to Registrar 1.38. *see also* Notification of appointment
- personal nature of 1.02
- precedence 1.63-1.65
- receipt of instrument of appointment 1.39
- Registrar of Companies, notification to 1.41
- restrictions on
  - exceptions to, App.14
- vacation. *see* Vacation of appointment of receiver

**Arrestment**
- distributions, and 9.08, 9.09

**Arrestors**
- ranking of securities and guarantees, and 8.17

**Assignation**
- form, App.18

***Assignatus utitur jure auctoris***
- set-off, and 4.75

**Attachment of floating charge 2.01-2.20**
- book debts 2.10
- corporeal moveable property 2.09
- diligence, and, 2.16-2.20. *see also* Diligence
- effect 2.03
- fixed security, conversion into 2.11-2.14
  - book debts, and 2.12
  - *jus crediti*, and 2.13
- heritable property 2.07, 2.08
- incorporeal moveable property 2.10

**Attachment of floating charge**—*contd*
property and undertaking of company 2.04-2.06
ranking of holder 2.37-2.43
Burnett's Trustee v Grainger sale of property, and 2.40
extortionate credit transactions 2.39
fraudulent trading, and 2.38
gratuitous alienation, and 2.37
proceeds of misfeasance action 2.41
trust assets 2.42
unfair preference, and 2.37
wrongful trading, and 2.38
security for principal and interest 2.15
specific property and assets, effect on 2.07-2.14
**Avoidance of floating charges 8.45-8.48**
company deemed unable to pay debts 8.47, 8.48
exclusion of avoidance provisions 8.50-8.53
existing overdraft, where 8.57
gratuitous alienation 8.58
new bank, and 8.54
unfair preference 8.58

**Bills of lading 4.33-4.37**
endorsed with instruction to deliver to order of sellers' agent's bank 4.37
endorsement in favour of company in receivership 4.36
nature of 4.34
**Book debts**
attachment of floating charge, and 2.10
fixed charge by English registered company over 8.18-8.20
letter for collection
form, App.11
sale of receivership assets, and 7.18, 7.19
**Building contracts 4.05-4.07**
deed of novation 4.07
express exclusion of receiver's personal liability 4.06
standard form 4.05
***Burnett's Trustee v Grainger* sale of property**
ranking of floating charge holder, and 2.40

**Caveat**
against interim interdict, App.8
against liquidation, App.8
form, App.8
**Committee of creditors 10.34-10.39**
dealings with company 10.38
exclusions 10.37
functions 10.34, 10.36
furnishing of information to 10.35
modifications 10.37
proceedings 10.34
**Commixtion**
retention of title, and 5.43-5.47
**Company records**
responsibility of receiver for, App.15
**Confusion**
retention of title, and 5.43-5.47
**Continuing professional relationship**
meaning 1.07, 1.08, 1.09
**Contracts 4.01-4.10**
building. *see* Building contracts
continuing essential contracts 4.08-4.10
commercial realities, and 4.09
monopoly suppliers 4.10
events of default 4.02
exclusion of personal liability of receiver 4.04
general position 4.01-4.04
receiver as agent, and 4.03
**Copyright 4.59, 4.60**
drawings, on 4.59, 4.60
engineering certifications, on 4.59, 4.60
**Corporeal moveable property**
attachment of floating charge, and 2.09
**Course of dealing**
retention of title, and. *see* Retention of title
**Creditor, letter to**
form, App.6
**Crown**
set-off 4.87-4.89
**Crystallisation of floating charge.** ***see*** **Attachment of floating charge**
**Custodian of goods, receiver as 4.28-4.32**
contract of storage 4.29-4.32
exclusion of liability for damage 4.30
goods belonging to third parties 4.28-4.32

**Data protection 4.90**
**Debtor, letter to**
form, App.5
**Deed of appointment**
form, App.4
**Deed of novation**
building contract, and 4.07
**Diligence**
effect of attachment of floating charge 2.16-2.20
inhibition, and 2.17, 2.18
inhibition registered before appointment of receiver 2.17
poinding, and 2.16
sequestration for rent 2.19
**Directors 6.04, 6.05**
acquisition of assets of insolvent companies by, App.15
borrowing limits exceeded 8.21
claims as 'employees', App.15
effect of receivership on 6.04, 6.05
meeting
extract minute, App.2
powers
dealing with property subject to charge 2.22

**Directors**—*contd*
powers—*contd*
effect of appointment of receiver 2.21-2.27
institution of proceedings 2.23
preventing sale of property 2.25
protection of assets 2.26
sisting of receiver 2.24
remuneration
effect of appointment of receiver 2.29
responsibilities
effect of appointment of receiver 2.28
**Distributions 9.01-9.36.** ***see also* Payments**
arrestment, and 9.08, 9.09
expenses of receiver 9.11-9.13
liability of receiver 9.11-9.13
order of priority 9.01, 9.02
priority of debts, 9.14-9.26. *see also* Priority of debts
provisions of section 60, 9.01-9.10
reasonable expenses of realisation 9.05
remuneration of receiver 9.11-9.13
right to combine accounts 9.27-9.34
payments by way of commission 9.33
separate wages account 9.32
rights of persons who have 'effectually executed diligence' 9.08
**Duties of receiver 3.43-3.53**
company, to 3.44-3.48
agency 3.47
negligence, and 3.46
creditor other than holder of floating charge, to 3.51
debenture holder, to 3.45
employees, to 3.52
guarantor, to 3.49, 3.50
pension schemes, in relation to 3.53
statutory framework 3.43

**Employees 6.06-6.34**
dismissed without proper notice by insolvent employers
non-preferential claims, App.15
entitlements under employment protection legislation 6.14
guarantee payment 6.20
maternity pay 6.18
notice 6.16
occupational pension schemes 6.27
preference for wages 6.10-6.13
protective award 6.17
redundancy payments 6.15
rights on receivership 6.10-6.34
sale of business, and, 6.28-6.34. *see also* Sale of business
sale of receivership assets, and 7.42, 7.43
suspension on medical grounds 6.21
**Employees**—*contd*
termination of contract of employment 6.06-6.09
time off to act as pension trustee 6.24, 6.25
time off to look for employment or arrange training 6.23
time off for trade union or employee representative activities 6.22
treatment of claims on receivership 6.26
treatment of directors' claims as, App.15
unfair dismissal, 6.19. *see also* Unfair dismissal
**English registered company**
fixed charge over book debts 8.18-8.20
**Extortionate credit transaction**
ranking of floating charge holder, and 2.39

**Fair and reasonable landlord test 4.25, 4.26**
assignation, and 4.26
key considerations 4.25
**Fixed charge**
effect 2.30
**Fixed security**
meaning 2.11, 2.14
**Floating charge**
appointment of receiver by holder. *see* Appointment of receiver
assignation, validity of 1.66
attachment. *see* Attachment of floating charge
attachment to property covered by 1.42
avoidance 1.50-1.55. *see also* Avoidance of floating charges
competition between receiver and liquidator 1.67-1.69
crystallisation. *see* Attachment of floating charge
failure to register 1.43, 1.44
form, App.1
ranking 2.43
rectification of register 1.45-1.49
effect 1.46
interaction of two standard securities 1.47
**Fraudulent trading**
ranking of floating charge holder, and 2.38

**Goodwill**
sale of receivership assets, and 7.21
**Gratuitous alienation**
ranking of floating charge holder, and 2.37
**Guarantee payment.** ***see* Employees**

**Heritable property**
attachment of floating charge, and 2.07, 2.08

**Hire-purchase contracts 4.42-4.44**
settlement 4.44
**Hive down agreement 7.37-7.38**
form, App.9
nature of, 7.37A
reasons for 7.38
**Hypothec 4.61-4.63.** ***see also*** **Liens**
sequestration for rent, and 4.61-4.63

**Incorporeal moveable property**
attachment of floating charge, and 2.10
**Indemnity, letter of**
early delivery of business
form, App.12
**Information where receiver appointed**
enforcement provisions 10.40
forms 10.50
provisions of Rules of general application 10.47-10.49
**Inhibitions**
ranking of securities and guarantees, and 8.14-8.16
**Insolvency office holders**
provision of information, App.15
receipts and payments accounts, App.15
remuneration, App.15
reporting, App.15
**Insolvency practitioner.** ***see also*** **Appointment of receiver**
authorisation of members of recognised professional bodies 1.10-1.16
authorised 1.04
application for 1.13
grant 1.14-1.16
recognised bodies 1.12
reference to Insolvency Practitioners Tribunal 1.17-1.19
refusal 1.14-1.16
withdrawal 1.14-1.16
qualification 1.04-1.06
**Intellectual property 4.38-4.41**
nature of contract 4.41
provision for re-transfer 4.39
**Interest**
ranking of securities and guarantees, and 8.05-8.07
**Interim interdict**
caveat against, App.8
**Invoices**
notification of appointment on 10.13, 10.14

**Landlord**
company in receivership as 4.12-4.14
**Landlord, letter to**
form, App.7
**Leases**
company in receivership as landlord 4.12-4.14
company in receivership as tenant 4.15-4.27

**Leases**—*contd*
company in receivership as tenant—*contd*
'all the circumstances of the case' 4.24
arrangements in relation to rent 4.17
background 4.18
conventional irritancy cannot be purged 4.19
entitlement to irritate lease 4.16
fair and reasonable landlord test, 4.25, 4.26. *see also* Fair and reasonable landlord test
personal liability of receiver, and 4.21
reform, proposals for 4.27
statutory restrictions on exercise of right to irritancy 4.22-4.24
wording qualifying irritancy rights 4.20
pre-receivership contracts, and 3.69
right to receive rent 4.13, 4.14
**Leasing contracts 4.42-4.44**
settlement 4.44
**Legal problems arising on receivership 4.01-4.90**
**Letter for collection of book debts**
form, App.11
**Letter of indemnity**
early delivery of business
form, App.12
**Letter of request to appoint receiver, App.3**
**Letter of set-off**
form, App.17
**Letter to creditor**
form, App.6
**Letter to debtor**
form, App.5
**Letter to landlord**
form, App.7
**Letters of obligation 7.47-7.56**
change of name 7.60-7.61
Companies Charges Register 7.49, 7.54-7.56
our client's title 7.50
personal obligation 7.48
Personal Register 7.49, 7.52, 7.53
Property Register, 7.49, 7.51A
wording 7.47
**Letters of set-off 8.22-8.39**
***Lex situs***
retention of title, and 5.35-5.39
**Liability of receiver 3.54-3.62.** ***see also*** **Agency of receiver**
appointment invalid, where 3.71-3.73
challenge to validity of floating charge 3.73
indemnity 3.72
personal liability 3.71
**Licences 4.11**
**Liens 4.48-4.58**

**Liens**—*contd*
enforcement
denial of possession of documents, and 4.52, 4.53
general 4.49-4.54
maritime, 4.55-4.58. *see also* Maritime liens
position where person claiming factored own debts 4.51
solicitor
documents, over 4.54
special 4.49-4.54
**Liquidation**
caveat against, App.8
**Liquidator**
competition with receiver 1.67-1.69

**Management buy-outs 7.39**
**Maritime liens 4.55-4.58**
possessory 4.58
scope 4.56
statutory 4.57
**Maternity pay. *see* Employees**
**Misfeasance action**
proceeds of
ranking of floating charge holder, and 2.41

**Name of company**
change of 7.60-7.61
**Notification of appointment 10.01-10.08**
advertisement 10.06, 10.12
appointment by court, where 10.08, 10.09
form 10.02
invoices, on 10.13, 10.14

**Occupational pension schemes. *see* Employees**
**Officers of company 6.01-6.05. *see also* Directors**
effect of receivership on 6.01-6.05
**Option in loan documentation to heritable creditor 8.10-8.12**
**Ownership of documents created by receivers 4.71, 4.72**
documents belonging to company 4.71, 4.72

**Payments 9.01-9.36. *see also* Distributions**
order of priority 9.01, 9.02
provisions of section 60, 9.01-9.10
reasonable expenses of realisation 9.05
**Pensions**
sale of receivership assets, and 7.57-7.59
**Permits 4.111**
**Powers of receiver 3.01-3.42**
advisers, appointment 3.09, 3.10
agents, appointment 3.18
arbitration 3.13
arrangements 3.23

**Powers of receiver**—*contd*
borrowing 3.08
carrying on of business 3.21
change of registered office 3.27
charge, contained in 3.01
company seal, use of 3.15
compromises 3.23
disposal of interest in property 3.36-3.39
employees, in relation to 3.18
establishment of subsidiaries 3.25
execution of deeds 3.16
exercise outwith jurisdiction 3.41, 3.42
incidental payments 3.20
incidental powers 3.32
insurances 3.14
leases 3.22
legal proceedings 3.12
negotiable instruments 3.20
persons dealing with receiver 3.40
powers subject to rights of certain persons 3.33-3.35
pre-receivership contracts. *see* Pre-receivership contracts
ranking in debtors' estates 3.26
sale of property 3.07
seeking directions 3.11
solicitor, appointment 3.09, 3.10
statutory 3.02-3.32
suspension, effect 3.70
taking possession of property 3.03-3.06
delivery by liquidator 3.06
importance of 3.03
powers of court 3.04
supply of information 3.05
tenancies 3.22
uncalled capital 3.24
winding-up petitions 3.28-3.31
circumstances justifying 3.28-3.31
work on property 3.19
**Pre-receivership contracts 3.63-3.69**
carrying on business, and 3.67
failure to implement 3.68
leases 3.69
specific implement 3.64-3.66
voidable 3.63
**Preferential creditors 9.15-9.36**
contributions to occupational pension schemes 9.17
remuneration of employees 9.14-9.36
amounts payable 9.18
'gross' 9.35, 9.36
money advanced for purpose of remuneration or accrued holiday remuneration 9.20-9.26
'net' 9.35, 9.36
orders 9.19
payments by way of commission 9.33
**Priority of debts 9.14-9.26**
preferential creditors, 9.15-9.36. *see also* Preferential creditors

**Protective award.** *see* **Employees**

**Ranking of securities and guarantees 8.01-8.58**
- additional interest 8.05-8.07
- arrestors 8.17
- avoidance of certain floating charges, 8.45-8.58. *see also* Avoidance of floating charges
- directors' borrowing limits exceeded 8.21
- fixed charge by English registered company over book debts 8.18-8.20
- general position 8.01, 8.02
- guarantors, general duty to 8.13
- inhibitors 8.14-8.16
- interest 8.05-8.07
- letters of set-off 8.22-8.39
  - suggested approach 8.23-8.39
- option in loan documentation to heritable creditor 8.10-8.12
- proper division of guarantee liability 8.40-8.44
- ranking agreements 8.03
- running account 8.04
- unlimited guarantees 8.22-8.39
  - suggested approach 8.23-8.39
- wages preference 8.08, 8.09

**Receiver**
- competition with liquidator 1.67-1.69

**Redundancy payments.** *see* **Employees**

**Registration of appointment 10.01-10.08**
- non-registration 10.11
- receiver should seek confirmation 10.10

**Rent**
- right to receive 4.13, 4.14
- sequestration for
  - hypothec, and 4.61-4.63

**Report by receiver 10.23-10.32**
- assessment of sum available for other creditors 10.26
- copy to liquidator 10.29
- dispensing with requirement to lay before meeting of unsecured creditors 10.28
- exclusions 10.31
- matters excluded 10.30
- matters to be dealt with 10.25
- penalty 10.32
- persons to whom sent 10.24
- publication of notice 10.27
- time for 10.23

**Reports on conduct of directors of insolvent companies 10.41-10.46**
- duty to provide 10.41
- manner of 10.42-10.46

**Retention of title 5.01-5.47**
- accession, and 5.41, 5.42
- commixtion, and 5.43-5.47
- confusion, and 5.43-5.47
- course of dealing 5.09-5.16
  - incorporation, arguing against 5.16

**Retention of title**—*contd*
- course of dealing—*contd*
  - previous transactions 5.11, 5.12
  - reasonableness test 5.14, 5.15
  - standard form contract 5.14
  - verbal contract 5.10
- English law 5.04
- incorporation in contract 5.07, 5.08
- inmixed goods 5.40
- meaning 5.03
- practical application 5.05, 5.06
- resolution of dispute 5.17-5.18
  - negotiation 5.18
  - standard form of letter 5.17
- *Romalpa* clauses 5.01
- *specificatio*, and 5.31
- specification, and 5.41, 5.42
- stocktaking, and 5.05, 5.06
- trusts over funds 5.19-5.40
  - beneficial interest, and 5.24-5.26
  - existence of trust fund 5.23
  - *lex situs* 5.28-5.30, 5.35-5.39
  - mercantile agent, and 5.34
  - principles 5.19
  - reality of transaction 5.22
  - specification 5.27, 5.28-5.30
  - subrogation, and 5.32
- validity of conditions 5.19-5.40
  - division of long clause 5.20
  - principles 5.19

***Romalpa* clauses.** *see* **Retention of title**

**Sale of business 6.28-6.34**
- transfer of undertakings 6.28-6.34
  - defence 6.29
  - dismissal, and 6.30, 6.31
  - liabilities that transfer or do not transfer on relevant transfer 6.33, 6.34
  - obligations to inform representatives of employees 6.32

**Sale of receivership assets 7.01-7.61**
- assignation of rights and obligations under contracts 7.11, 7.12
  - supplies on or about transfer date 7.13, 7.14
  - third parties, and 7.12
- book debts 7.18, 7.19
- books and records of company 7.15
- courses open to receiver 7.02
- duties of receiver, and 7.04
- early transfer of business 7.22
- employees 7.42, 7.43
- evaluation of business, and 7.01
- finalising documentation 7.41
- finished goods, status of 7.10
- form of agreements 7.05-7.09
  - definition 7.05, 7.06
  - stocktaking 7.07-7.09
- form of 7.23
- goodwill 7.21
- hive down agreement. *see* Hive down agreement

**Sale of receivership assets**—*contd*
information brochure 7.03
disclaimer 7.03
letters of obligation, 7.47-7.56. *see also* Letters of obligation
liabilities prior to transfer date 7.20
management buy-outs 7.39
mechanics of 7.23
missives 7.24
patents 7.16
pension matters 7.57-7.59
power of execution by receiver after appointment of liquidator 7.46
premises 7.17
preparation of financial package 7.40
property matters 7.44, 7.45
receiver, liability of 7.26
section 61 petition 7.34-7.36
stamp duty 7.33
terms 7.27-7.31
consideration 7.29
exclusion of warranty 7.30
good title 7.31
interpretation 7.28
recital, 7.27A
trade marks 7.16
VAT 7.32
vendor, designation of 7.25, 7.26
**Section 61 petition**
sale of receivership assets, and 7.34-7.36
**Sequestration for rent**
appointment of receiver, and 2.19
hypothec, and 4.61-4.63
**Set-off, 4.73-4.89**
assignation of debt, and 4.80, 4.81
*assignatus utitur jure auctoris*, and 4.75
case law 4.74
claim arising post appointment of liquidator 4.85
Crown 4.87-4.89
elements 4.73
fixed security, and 4.82-4.84
insolvency law, and 4.78
letter
form, App.17
no concursus debiti et crediti, where 4.76, 4.77, 4.79
uncertainties as to 4.86
**Share purchase agreement**
form, App.13
***Specificatio***
retention of title, and 5.31
**Specification**
retention of title, and 5.41, 5.42
**Stamp duty**
sale of receivership assets, and 7.33
**Statements of Insolvency Practice (Scotland), App.15**
**Statement to be made by officers to receiver 10.15-10.22**
contents 10.18
persons specified 10.17
release from requirement to submit 10.21
Sederunt Book 10.19

**Tenant**
company in receivership as. *see* Leases
**Third parties, rights against insurers 4.45-4.47**
Act of 1930, 4.45-4.47
**Transfer of undertakings.** *see* **Sale of business**
**Trust assets**
ranking of floating charge holder, and 2.42

**Unfair dismissal 6.19**
basic award 6.19
compensatory award 6.19
enhancement of compensation on failure to obey tribunal order to reinstate or re-engage 6.19
**Unfair prejudice**
**Unlimited guarantee 8.22-8.39**
form, App.16

**Vacation of appointment of receiver 11.01-11.12**
circumstances 11.01
indemnity 11.04, 11.05
notification 11.06-11.08
ownership of documents 11.09
re-floating of charge, effect 11.10-11.12
joint receivers 11.11
single receiver 11.10
removal from office 11.03
remuneration 11.04, 11.05
resignation 11.02
**VAT**
sale of receivership assets, and 7.32

**Wages**
ranking of securities and guarantees, and 8.08, 8.09
**Winding-up petition**
threatened 4.64-4.70
appointment of liquidator 4.64-4.66
bad debt relief, and 4.68
caveats 4.69
members' voluntary liquidation 4.67
prevention of liquidator's appointment 4.70
value added tax 4.68
**Wrongful trading**
ranking of floating charge holder, and 2.38

